Autodesk Maya 2015
Basics Guide

Kelly L. Murdock

SDC
Publications

SDC Publications
P.O. Box 1334
Mission, KS 66222
913-262-2664
www.SDCpublications.com
Publisher: Stephen Schroff

Copyright 2014 Kelly L. Murdock

All rights reserved. This document may not be copied, photocopied, reproduced, transmitted, or translated in any form or for any purpose without the express written consent of the publisher, SDC Publications.

It is a violation of United States copyright laws to make copies in any form or media of the contents of this book for commercial or educational proposes without written permission.

Examination Copies
Books received as examination copies are for review purposes only and may not be made available for student use. Resale of examination copies is prohibited.

Electronic Files
Any electronic files associated with this book are licensed to the original user only. These files may not be transferred to any other party.

Trademarks
Maya is a registered trademark of Autodesk, Inc. All other trademarks are property of their respective owners.

The author and publisher of this book have used their best efforts in preparing this book. These efforts include the development, research and testing of the material presented. The author and publisher shall not be liable in any event for incidental or consequential damages with, or arising out of, the furnishing, performance, or use of the material.

ISBN-13: 978-1-58503-917-3
ISBN-10: 978-1-58503-917-9

Printed and bound in the United States of America.

Credits

Acquisitions Editor
Stephen Schroff

Project Editor
Karla Werner

Website/Cover Design
Zach Werner

Copy Editor
Rachel Schroff

Dedication

I started college thinking that it would be a breeze cause I'd prepared myself diligently and even paid my fees.

My first class was huge with 500 students or more, and I quickly realized that this class would be a chore.

I studied math, science and history and took classes by the score, and found myself yearning for the easy classes from days of yore.

I did alright and worked really hard and even got some good grades, and prepared myself for the time when I would enter the trades.

But, the more I learned, the more I viewed the stuff I didn't know, and regardless of how much I studied, new knowledge continues to flow.

At the end of my college days, I think I was much smarter cause I learned how to learn and how to be a self-starter.

I discovered with the depth of the things that there are to learn, that I really know nothing and for lifelong learning I should yearn.

Dedicated to all the college students out there that are struggling to learn enough to get by.

Acknowledgments

I would like to acknowledge several individuals who have been such a huge help on this project. First of all, Stephen Schroff, who has been great as my point contact.

I'd also like to thank my editors, Karla Werner and Rachel Schroff. I'd also like to thank all the people at SDC Publications who work behind the scenes to create such great titles.

Thanks to all the wonderful people at Autodesk who have really stepped up their efforts to support me in this project. And thanks to the great development team at Alias for creating such a great software package.

I'd always be remiss if I didn't thank my family, without whose support I'd never get to the end of a book. To Angela, for driving me harder than I drive myself. To Thomas, for his help in clearing out the basement so we could do the needed improvements, and to Eric, for being a constant reminder of all the activities that I've forgotten while I'm writing.

About the Author

Kelly L. Murdock has a background in engineering, specializing in computer graphics. This experience has led him to many interesting experiences, including using high-end CAD workstations for product design and analysis, working on several large-scale visualization projects, creating 3D models for several blockbuster movies, working as a freelance 3D artist and designer, 3D programming, and a chance to write several high-profile computer graphics books.

Kelly's book credits include fourteen editions of the *3ds max Bible, Lightwave 3D 8 Revealed, Maya 6 Revealed, Poser 6 Revealed,* two editions of the *Illustrator Bible* and co-author on five edtions of the *Adobe Creative Suite Bible, Adobe Atmosphere Bible, gmax Bible, 3d Graphics and VRML 2.0, Master Visually HTML and XHTML,* and *JavaScript Visual Blueprints.*

In his spare time, Kelly enjoys playing basketball and collecting video games.

Table of Contents at a Glance

Introduction

Writing computer books is always a journey. As an experienced 3ds max author, I was anxious to try out Maya and was pleasantly surprised with a number of features that are really awesome. Maya is a different paradigm with an amazing amount of power. In writing this book, I approached the software as a beginner, and was careful to explain points that are potential stumbling blocks.

Writing this book was actually like writing two books at once. The unique format is split into concepts and objectives. The concept sections explain the features and what must be done to complete a task and the objective sections show you with an example what must be done to complete a task.

As you read through this title, be aware that Maya is a very complex piece of software and this book didn't have the space to cover every aspect of the software, so instead I focused on the main features and topics. The coverage is enough to get you up and running, but you'll want to do some exploring along the way to flesh out you skill with the software.

Kelly L. Murdock

Table of Contents

Chapter 1
Learning the Maya Interface

IN THIS CHAPTER

1.1 Work with menus.

1.2 Use the Status Line buttons.

1.3 Access the Shelf.

1.4 Explore the Channel Box and Layer Editor.

1.5 Identify the animation controls, the Command Line, and the Help Line.

1.6 Use the Toolbox and Quick Layout buttons.

1.7 Discover the Secret menus.

Maya is a program, created by Autodesk, used to model, animate, and render 3D scenes. 3D scenes created with Maya have appeared in movies, television, advertisements, games, product visualizations, and on the Web. With Maya, you can create and animate your own 3D scenes and render them as still images or as animation sequences.

Several versions of Maya exist and the difference between them lies in the features that are included in each. The commercial version of Maya includes everything you need to create and render 3D scenes and animations. An advanced version of Maya also includes the Fluid Effects, Cloth, and Hair and Fur features. A freely available version of Maya called the Personal Learning Edition is also available. The Personal Learning Edition is identical to Maya Complete, except that all renderings include a watermark making it a great place to start if you want to learn Maya.

At first glance, the Maya interface can be a little daunting, with buttons, controls, and parameters everywhere, but if you look closer you'll realize that all of the controls are grouped into logical sets. Becoming familiar with these various sets of controls makes the interface much easier to work with.

Along the top edge of the interface are the menus and a toolbar of buttons called the **Status Line**. The menus will change depending on the mode that you're working in. Below the Status Line is a tabbed row of buttons. This row of buttons is called the **Shelf**, and it offers a convenient way to group sets of commands together. To the right of the interface is a panel of parameters called the **Channel Box**. These parameters, known as attributes, will change as different objects are selected. Under the Channel Box is the **Layer Editor**.

Along the bottom of the interface are the Time Slider, the Range Slider, and the animation controls, which are used to specify and move between the different frames of an animation sequence; also at the bottom are the **Command Line**, for entering textual commands, and the **Help Line**. Finally, the horizontal column of buttons to the left of the interface is known as the **Toolbox** and the **Quick Layout buttons**. These buttons are used to select and transform scene objects and to change the interface layout.

A key concept that you need to understand as you begin to work with the interface is that there are several ways to access the same command. For example, you can create a sphere using the Create, Polygon Primitives, Sphere menu command or by using the Polygon Sphere button in the Polygons shelf. This design is intentional, allowing beginners an intuitive method for accessing a command and giving advanced users an access method that lets them work quicker as they learn the shortcuts.

One of the quickest ways to access advanced-user commands is with the Secret menus. These context-specific pop-up menus appear when you right-click in the interface. Another quick way to access commands is with keyboard shortcuts, known as **hotkeys**.

Maya gives users the option to customize the interface. Using the customization features, you can create a custom set of command icons, define keyboard shortcuts, and even alter menus. Many of the customization options are included in the Window, Settings/Preferences menu.

Lesson 1.1: Work with Menus

The main menu commands are the first place you should look for commands when you're new to Maya. The commands are listed as text, making them easier to find until you learn what the various buttons do. Each menu can include several submenus. Submenus are identified by a small, right-pointing arrow at the right end of the menu.

Changing Menu Sets

The menus are dynamic and change depending on the **menu set** that is selected. You can change between the menu sets using the drop-down list that is to the very left of the Status Line, as shown in Figure 1-1. The options include Animation, Polygons, Surfaces, Dynamics, Rendering, and nDynamics.

Tip

> Each of the menu sets has an associated hotkey. These hotkeys are F2 for Animation, F3 for Polygons, F4 for Surfaces, F5 for Dynamics, and F6 for Rendering.

The first six menu commands, File, Edit, Modify, Create, Display, and Window, are available in all menu sets.

Figure 1-1
Menu set selection list

Viewing Keyboard Hotkeys

Several menu commands have a keyboard hotkey listed to the right of the menu, as shown in Figure 1-2. Pressing these hotkeys on the keyboard executes the command. Hotkeys provide a quick and easy way to execute a command, and learning to use them will make you much more efficient. You can customize hotkeys using the Hotkey Editor, which you open with the Window, Settings/Preferences, Hotkeys menu command.

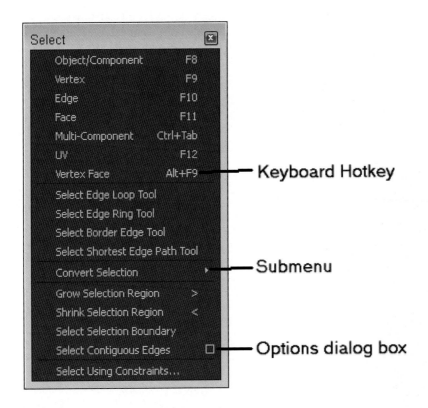

Figure 1-2
Hotkeys and option dialog boxes are displayed in the menus

Accessing Option Dialog Boxes

Several menus also include a small box icon to the right of the menu, also shown in Figure 1-2. These box icons will open an Options dialog box for the selected command. These Options dialog boxes, such as the Group Options dialog box shown in Figure 1-3, include parameters that you can change. They also include Apply buttons that let you apply the command with the given parameters without closing the dialog box. The **option dialog box** values are persistent. Any values that are changed will maintain their setting the next time the command is used. You can reset an options dialog box to its default values using the Edit, Reset Settings menu command in the dialog box menu.

Figure 1-3
Settings dialog box for Create, Polygon Primitives, Sphere

Using Tear-Off Menus

At the very top of most menus is a double line called the **tear-off menu**. Clicking on this line makes the menu a tear-off menu and displays it as a separate panel, like the one shown in Figure 1-4, that you can move about by dragging on its title bar. Tear-off menus are convenient because they make the menu commands accessible with one click, but you need the space to leave the tear-off menu open without covering something else.

Note

In an effort to make the tear-off menu smaller, the keyboard hotkeys aren't displayed on a tear-off menu.

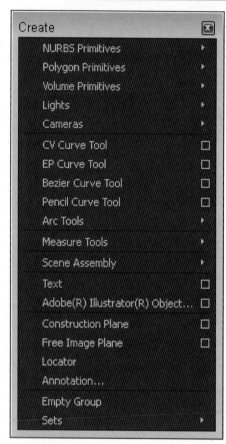

Figure 1-4
Tear-off menu

Understanding Tools versus Actions

If you peruse the menus, you'll see many commands that end in the word *Tool*. Tools, when selected, are active until another tool is selected, but actions are only executed once. The last tool used is displayed at the bottom of the **Toolbox** for easy re-selection. Double-clicking a tool's button will open the Tool Settings interface on the right side of the interface, as shown for the Move tool in Figure 1-5. You can also open the Tool Settings using the Show/Hide Tool Settings button at the right end of the Status Line. Tool settings are also persistent and can be reset using the Reset Tool button at the top of the Tool Settings interface.

Show/Hide Tool Settings

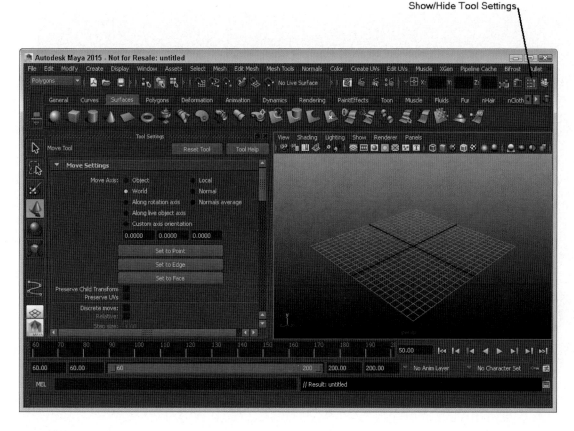

Figure 1-5
Tool Settings

Lesson 1.1-Tutorial 1: Use a Menu Command to Create a Polygon Sphere

1. Click on the Create menu, and then select the Polygon Primitives submenu and click on the Options icon to the right of the Sphere menu to open the options dialog box, as shown in Figure 1-3.

2. In the Polygon Sphere Options dialog box, click the Apply button.

    A single sphere objects will appear at the origin in the Workspace.

3. Click the Close button to exit the dialog box.

4. Click on the Create menu, and then select the Polygon Primitives submenu and click on the Cone menu command. A cone object is added to the scene overlapping the sphere.

5. Press the 5 key to see the objects as shaded objects. The objects resemble a simple crystal ball, as shown in Figure 1-6.

6. Select File, Save Scene As and save the file as **Crystal ball.mb**.

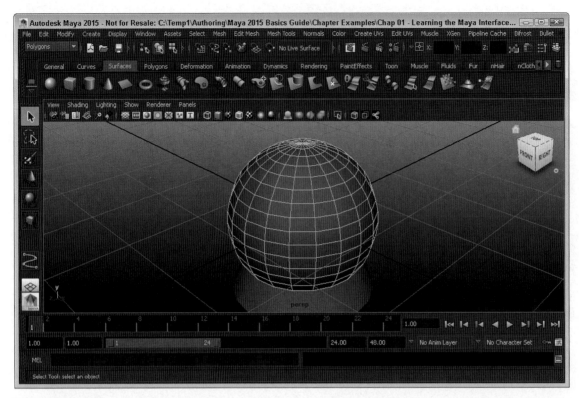

Figure 1-6
A simple crystal ball created with sphere and cone objects

Lesson 1.2: Use the Status Line Buttons

Directly below the menus are a long row of buttons that are collectively known as the Status Line. These buttons are constant and cannot be changed, but you can hide them. The buttons are divided into groups that are separated by a dividing bar. These button groups include, from left to right, the Menu Set menu, File buttons, the Selection Mode menu, Selection Mode buttons, Selection Mask buttons, Snapping buttons, History buttons, Rendering buttons, the Select field, and the Show/Hide Editors buttons, as shown in Figure 1-7. Most of these button groups are presented and discussed in the lesson that corresponds to their features.

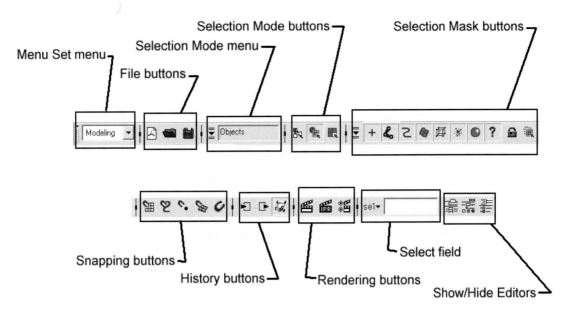

Figure 1-7
Status Line groups

Using Pop-up Help

When you first begin to use the Status Line buttons, it can be tricky to know which button does what, but you can view the button's title as a **Pop-up Help** by holding the mouse cursor over the top of the button, as shown in Figure 1-8. Pop-up Help is available for all buttons in the entire interface.

Note

If Pop-up Help starts to get annoying, you can disable it or set its Display Time using the Help panel in the Preferences dialog box opened with the Window, Settings/Preferences, Preferences menu command.

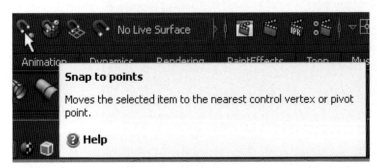

Figure 1-8
Pop-up Help

Watching for Cursor Clues

Another helpful visual clue is that the cursor changes when it is over any interface button that has an available right-click pop-up menu. This new cursor displays a small menu icon under the cursor arrow, like the one shown in Figure 1-9. When this icon appears, you can right-click to access an additional menu of options. The cursor also changes when certain tools are used.

Figure 1-9
Cursor indicating a right-click pop-up menu

Expanding and Collapsing Icon Button Groups

Each button group in the Status Line is divided by a vertical line with a small rectangle through its center. This divider is called the Show/Hide Bar, and if you click on it, and then all buttons included in that section will be hidden. Click again to make the buttons reappear. Figure 1-10 shows several collapsed and expanded button sets.

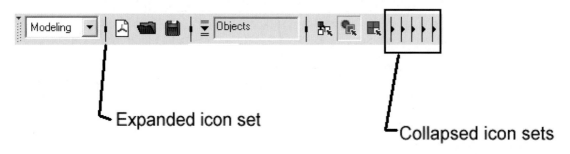

Figure 1-10
Expanded and collapsed button sets

Opening and Saving a Scene

To the right of the Menu Set selection list is a set of buttons that you can use to create a new scene, open an existing scene, or save the current scene. Both the Open and Save buttons will open a file dialog box, as shown in Figure 1-11, in which you can select the directory and file name. When saved, the file name will appear on the title bar.

Figure 1-11
File dialog box for Windows

Opening Editors

At the right side of the Status Line are four Sidebar buttons, shown in Figure 1-12, that don't belong to a button group and that are always visible. These Sidebar buttons are used to show and hide one of the sidebar panels that appear to the right of the view panel including the Attribute Editor, Tool Settings, and Channel Box/Layer Editor. The Attribute Editor lists all the attributes for the selected object, the Tool Settings will list all the configurable settings for the selected tool and the Channel Box is a subset of attributes that can be animated, known as being *keyable* and the Layer Editor lets you divide the scene objects into layers.

Note

In the Interface panel of the Preferences dialog box, you can select to have each of the editors open as a separate window instead of the main window.

Figure 1-12
Sidebar buttons

Showing and Hiding Interface Elements

You can also hide any interface element by clicking on the dotted double line at the top (or to the left) of the interface element, as shown for the Status Line in Figure 1-13. Right-clicking and holding down the mouse button on the Show/Hide bar presents a pop-up menu of all interface elements. You can make hidden interface elements visible again using the Display, UI Elements menu. You can use the Display, UI Elements, Hide UI Elements menu command to hide all UI elements at once.

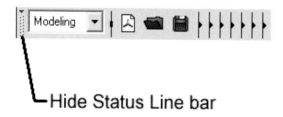

Figure 1-13
Hide interface element bar

Lesson 1.2-Tutorial 1: Open a File

1. Move the mouse over the Status Line buttons at the left end until the Pop-up Help reads *Open a scene*.

2. Click on this button.

    A file dialog box appears, similar to the one shown in Figure 1-11.

3. Locate the directory where the Skateboard.mb file is located.

4. Click on the Skateboard.mb file name and click the Open button.

   The saved file is then loaded into Maya, as shown in Figure 1-14.

Note

Before Maya opens a file, it gives you a chance to save the current file.

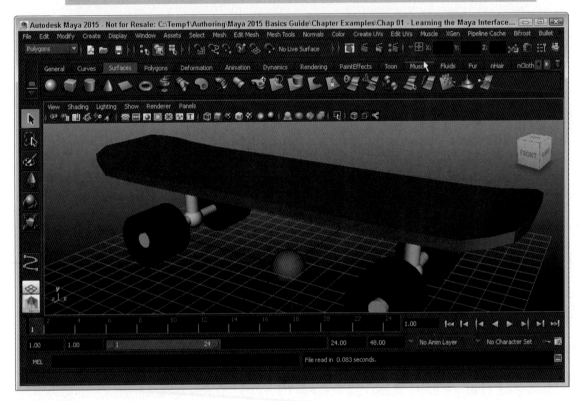

Figure 1-14
Opened skateboard file

Lesson 1.2-Tutorial 2: Save a File

1. Click on the Create menu, and then select the Polygon Primitives submenu and click on the Sphere menu to add a sphere to the skateboard scene.

2. Move the mouse over the Status Line buttons at the left end until the Pop-up Help reads *Save the current scene.*

3. Click on this button.

   This file is automatically saved replacing the existing file. When saved, the file name appears in the title bar.

Note

You can save the scenes with a new file name using the File, Save As menu command.

Lesson 1.2-Tutorial 3: Maximize the Workspace Interface

1. Click on the dotted double line on the left end of the Status Line.

   The Status Line becomes hidden.

2. Click on the other dashed double lines for the Shelf, the Channel Box, and the Toolbox.

3. Click on the dashed double lines for the controls at the bottom of the interface.

   All interface elements will now be hidden, maximizing the Workspace, as shown in Figure 1-15.

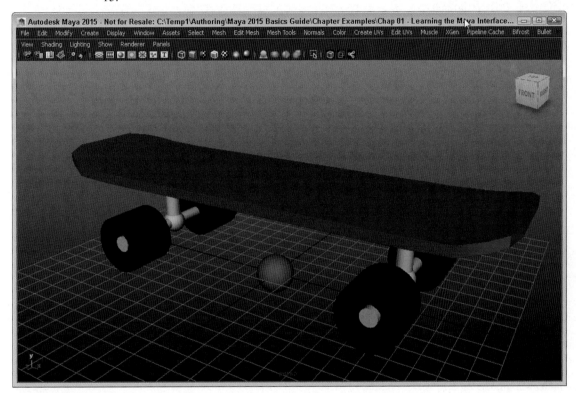

Figure 1-15
A maximized Workspace interface

4. Select the Display, UI Elements, Status Line menu command.

   The Status Line interface element reappears.

5. Use the Display, UI Elements, Show UI Elements menu to make the rest of the interface elements reappear.

Lesson 1.3: Access the Shelf

The Shelf is like a toolbar on steroids. It includes several tabbed panels of buttons. To select a different set of buttons, just click on one of the tabs and the buttons in its set will appear. Figure 1-16 shows the buttons for the Polygons tab.

Figure 1-16
The Shelf

Using the Shelf Menu

At the left end of the Shelf are two menu icons. The top one looks like a mini-tab and you can use it to select a Shelf tab from a menu. The bottom menu icon is an arrow. You can use it to hide all of the Shelf tabs, open the Shelf Editor, create and delete shelves, Load a custom shelf, and save all shelves. You can save some interface space by hiding the Shelf tabs. To do this, select Shelf Tabs menu command from the Shelf menu to toggle the option off.

Creating and Deleting Shelves

The Shelf menu can also be used to create and delete shelves. The New Shelf menu command will open a simple dialog box, as shown in Figure 1-17, in which you can name the new shelf. The new empty shelf will then appear at the right end of the tabs. Selecting the Delete Shelf menu command will delete the currently selected shelf.

Figure 1-17
Create New Shelf dialog box

Adding Icons and Menu Commands to a Shelf

You can add buttons from any shelf to another shelf by selecting the button and dragging it with the middle mouse button onto the tab of the shelf that you wish to add it to. Menu commands can also be added to the current shelf by clicking on the menu command with the Ctrl/Command and Shift keys held down. You can delete shelf icons by dragging them with the middle mouse button to the Delete Shelf icon (which looks like a small trash can) on the right end of the tabs.

Note

Maya uses all three mouse buttons. If you are using a two-button mouse with a scroll wheel, the scroll wheel acts as the middle mouse button. If your two-button mouse doesn't have a scroll wheel, you can use the Ctrl/Command (command) key and the left mouse button as the middle mouse button. For a Macintosh one-button mouse, the command key and the mouse button act as the middle mouse button and the Option key and the mouse button act as the right mouse button.

Adding Layouts and Scripts to a Shelf

You can add custom layouts to a shelf. Just pick the shelf you want to hold the custom layout and then choose Panels, Panel Editor from the Panel menu. In the Layouts tab, shown in Figure 1-18, select the custom layout that you want to add to the current shelf and click the Add To Shelf button. You can drag scripts from the Script Editor with the middle mouse button and drop them into a shelf. Scripts appear on the Shelf as a button labeled 'MEL', which stands for Maya Expression Language, Maya's scripting language.

Figure 1-18
Panel Editor

Using the Shelf Editor

The Shelves menu includes an option that will open the Shelf Editor dialog box. Using this editor, shown in Figure 1-19, you can reorder and rename the tabs and shelves, edit the icons within each shelf, and change the settings for the shelves.

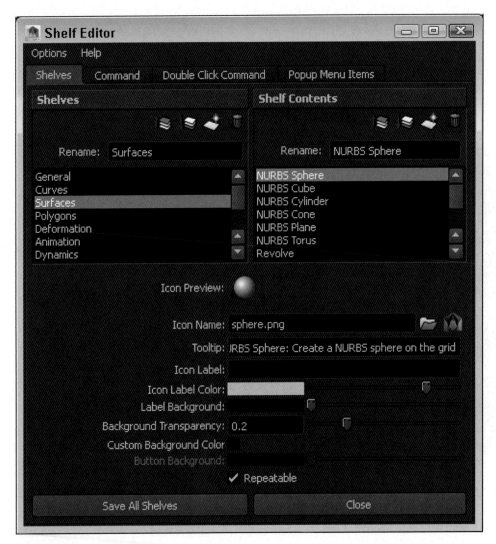

Figure 1-19
Shelf Editor

Lesson 1.3-Tutorial 1: Create a New Shelf

1. Click on the Shelf menu and select New Shelf.

    The Create New Shelf dialog box appears.

2. Type the name **MyShelf** for the new shelf and click OK.

    A new tab with the typed name appears at the right end of the Shelf.

Lesson 1.3-Tutorial 2: Populate a New Shelf

1. Select the MyShelf tab to make it active.

2. Hold down the Shift and Ctrl/Command keys and select Create, NURBS Primitives, Sphere.

    A sphere icon is added to the new shelf.

3. Repeat Step 2 with other primitive objects found in the Create menu.

    Each of the selected menu commands appears on the new shelf, as shown in Figure 1-20.

4. Select the Panel, Panel Editor panel menu command.

The Panel Editor dialog box appears.

5.   Select the Layout tab and choose the Four View option. Then click the Add to Shelf button and then the Close button.

When the Four View option is selected, the view window changes to show four separate views. After clicking the Add to Shelf button, a new icon appears in the current shelf.

6.   Locate the Move tool in the Toolbox and drag the icon with the middle mouse button to the new shelf.

Dragging an icon with the middle mouse button adds the icon to the current shelf. Figure 1-20 shows the new shelf.

7.   Select Save All Shelves from the Shelf menu.

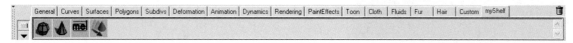

Figure 1-20
A custom shelf of menu commands

Lesson 1.4: Explore the Channel Box and Layer Editor

When an object is selected, its keyable attributes (or channels) appear within the Channel Box, shown in Figure 1-21, to the right of the interface. Each attribute has a value associated with it. These values are often numbers, but they can be a state like on or off, or a color. You can change these values by selecting the channel's value, entering a different value, and pressing the Enter key.

Tip

Use the two double-arrow buttons underneath the Layer Editor to widen or shrink the Channel Box and the Layer Editor.

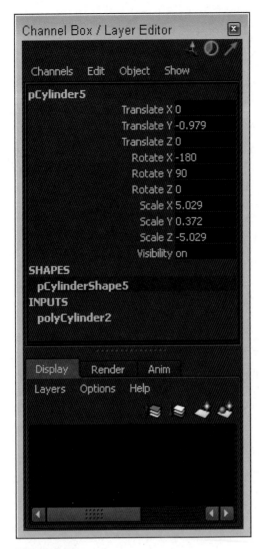

Figure 1-21
The Channel Box

Selecting Attributes

You can select a single attribute by clicking on its title. When selected, the attribute title will be highlighted. Holding down the Ctrl/Command key while clicking on several attributes will allow you to select multiple attributes at once; you can also drag the mouse over several attributes to select them.

Using Channel Sliders

You can interactively change attribute values by selecting an attribute in the Channel Box and then dragging with the middle mouse button in the view panel. Using the buttons at the top of the Channel Box, shown in Figure 1-22, you can change the channel slider settings to Slow, Medium, or Fast. The higher the setting, the faster the attribute will change as you drag. You can also select a linear or hyperbolic slider setting. The Linear setting will cause attribute values to change linearly as you drag with the mouse, but the Hyperbolic setting will cause the value to change more and more rapidly the longer you drag the mouse.

Tip

You can also enter += and a number to add that amount to the current value. For example, typing **+=2** in an

16

> attribute field for a Radius value of 5.0 changes it to 7.0. You can also use -=, *= and /= to subtract, multiply and divide relative values.

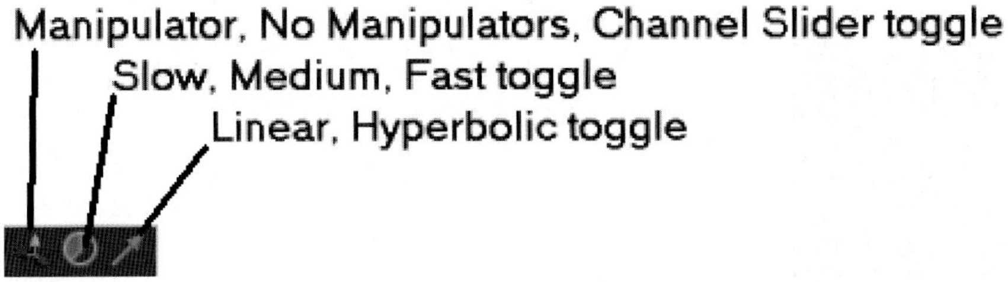

Manipulator, No Manipulators, Channel Slider toggle
Slow, Medium, Fast toggle
Linear, Hyperbolic toggle

Figure 1-22
Channel Box settings

Locking Attributes

Locked attributes cannot be changed. You can lock an attribute by selecting it and choosing the Lock Selected menu command from the Channels menu. Locked attributes will be appear "grayed out," as shown in Figure 1-23. Unlock any locked attributes using the Channels, Unlock Selected menu command.

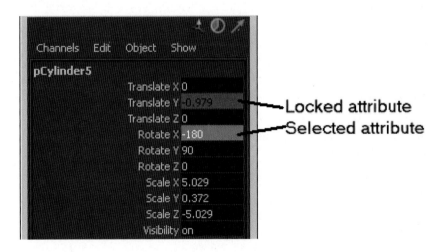

Figure 1-23
Locked attributes in the Channel Box

Adding and Deleting Layers

The Layer Editor, shown in Figure 1-24, divides the scene elements up into layers, making them easy to show and hide. Clicking the Create a New Layer button in the Layer Editor creates a new layer. You can give each layer a name, display type, and color. Delete layers using the Layers menu. Deleting a layer does not delete its objects. At the top of the Layer Editor are options for creating Display and Render layers. Render layers are discussed in Chapter 14.

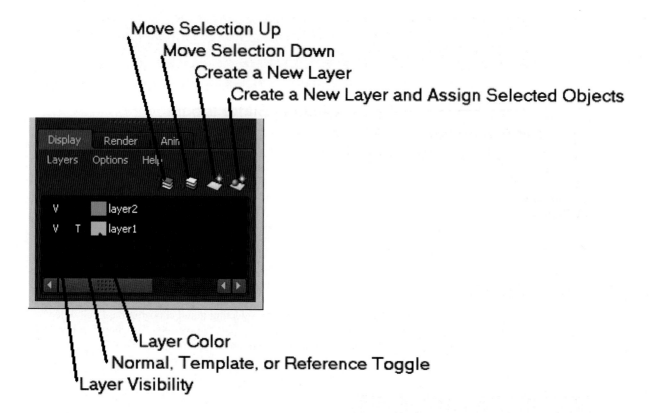

Figure 1-24
Layer Editor

Adding Objects to a Layer

You can add selected objects to a layer by right clicking on that layer and selecting Add Selected Objects from the pop-up menu. You can also use the Layers menu to select all objects in a layer and to remove objects from a layer. Objects assume the layer color when unselected.

Hiding All Layer Objects

You can hide Layer objects by clicking the first column in the Layer Editor. This column sets the visibility for the layer objects and is a simple toggle button that you can turn on or off. The letter *V* appears when the layer objects are visible and the column is empty when the layer objects are hidden.

Freezing All Layer Objects

The second column can be set to Normal, Template or Reference. The letter *T* appears in this column when the layer is a template. Template layers cannot be selected or moved while they are templates. References are proxy objects that stand in for complex objects. The third column is the layer color. Double-clicking on this column (or on the layer name) opens the Edit Layer dialog box, shown in Figure 1-25, where you can select a new color, change the layer's attributes, or change the layer's name.

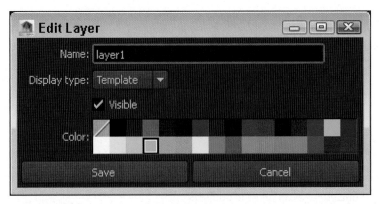

Figure 1-25
Edit Layer dialog box

Lesson 1.4-Tutorial 1: Change Channel Box Attributes

1. Select File, Open Scene. Locate and open the Rocket.mb file.

    This file includes a simple rocket centered about the grid origin. All attributes for the rocket object are displayed in the Channel Box.

2. Enter a 5 in the Translate X attribute and press the Enter key.

    The rocket object is moved five units along the X-axis.

3. Click on the Translate Y attribute in the Channel Box and drag upward in the Workspace with the middle mouse button.

    The rocket object is moved along the Y-axis a distance equal to the amount that the mouse was dragged and the attribute value is changed, as shown in Figure 1-26.

4. Select File, Save Scene As and save the file as **Translated rocket.mb**.

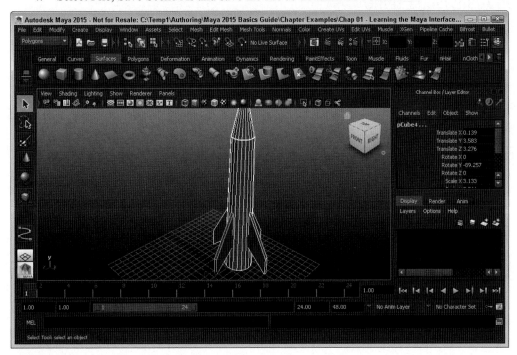

Figure 1-26
Translated rocket

Lesson 1.4-Tutorial 2: Create and Rename a New Layer

1. Click the Create a new layer button in the Layer Editor.

   A new layer appears in the Layer Editor.

2. Double-click on the layer to open the Edit Layer dialog box.

3. Type in a name for the new layer and click the Save button.

Lesson 1.4-Tutorial 3: Add Objects to a New Layer

1. Select Create, Polygon Primitives, Sphere to create a sphere object.

2. Select the Edit, Select All menu command to select all of the objects.

3. In the Layer Editor, right click on the new layer and select Add Selected Objects from the pop-up menu.

   All objects are added to the new layer.

4. In the Layer Editor, click on the first column in which the V is displayed.

   All objects on the layer are hidden.

Lesson 1.5: Identify the Animation Controls, the Command Line, and the Help Line

At the bottom of the interface are several interface controls that are used to move through the various animation frames. Below these is a Command Line where you can type in commands to be executed. At the very bottom of the interface is a Help Line where context-specific information is displayed.

Selecting an Animation Frame

All current animation frames are displayed on the Time Slider at the bottom of the interface, as shown in Figure 1-27. You move between the different frames by dragging the black time marker or by entering the frame number in the field to the right of the Time Slider.

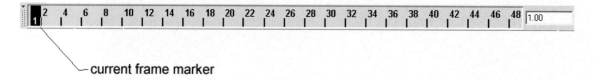

current frame marker

Figure 1-27
Time Slider

Setting an Animation Range

Below the Time Slider is the Range Slider, as shown in Figure 1-28. Using this slider, you can focus on a specific range of animation frames. The Time Slider changes as the Range Slider is moved.

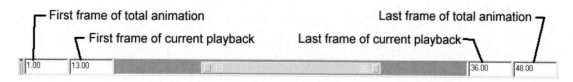

Figure 1-28
Range Slider

Playing an Animation

To the right of the animation frame value are several controls for playing, rewinding, and moving through the animation frames, as shown in Figure 1-29. Using these buttons, you can jump to the animation start (or end), step back (or forward) one frame, step back (or forward) one key, or play the animation forward (or backward).

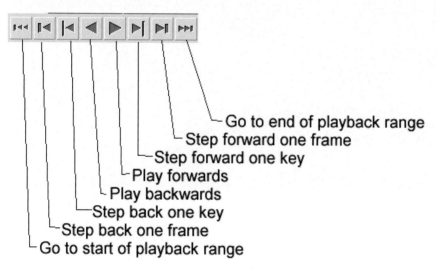

Figure 1-29
Animation controls

Accessing the Animation Preferences

Beneath the Go to End button is a button, shown in Figure 1-30, that will open the Preferences dialog box, as shown in Figure 1-31. This dialog box includes all of the preferences for Maya, but when it is opened using this button the Timeline category is selected, allowing you to change the animation preferences.

Figure 1-30
Animation Preferences button

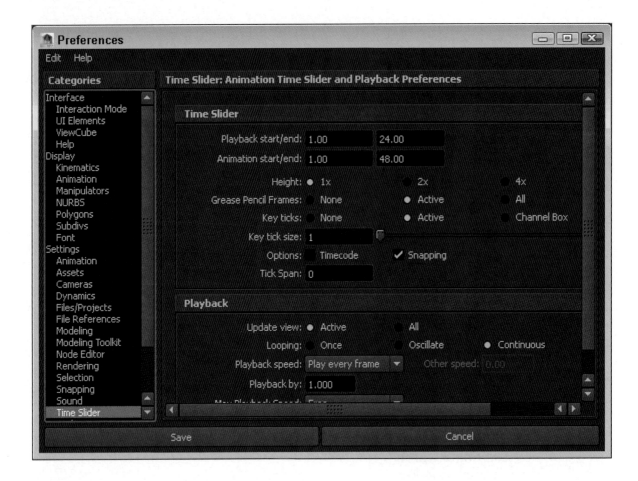

Figure 1-31
Preferences dialog box

Using the Command Line

In the Command Line, you can enter textual commands to be executed. All commands should end with a semicolon. The results of these commands are displayed in the dark-colored Results line to the right of the Command Line. To the right of the Results line is the Show Script Editor button, shown in Figure 1-32, that opens the Script Editor, where you can enter more detailed scripts. More on the Script Editor is covered in Chapter 15, "Using MEL Scripting."

Tip

All commands that are entered into the Command Line are saved in a buffer. Using the Up and Down Arrow keys, you can scroll back and forth through the existing commands. Pressing the Enter key executes the listed command.

Figure 1-32
Script Editor button

Viewing the Help Line

At the very bottom of the interface is the Help Line, as shown in Figure 1-33. Within this line, Maya lists instructions that it expects to happen next based on the selected tool or mode. If you're stuck on what to do next, take a look at the Help Line.

HelpLine: Displays short help tips for tools and selections

Figure 1-33
Help Line

Lesson 1.5-Tutorial 1: Play an Animation

1. Select File, Open Scene and open the Billiard balls.mb file.

   This file includes a simple animated scene.

2. Click on the time marker in the Time Slider and drag it to the left.

   The objects in the scene will move as the frames are increased. A frame of the animation sequence is shown in Figure 1-34.

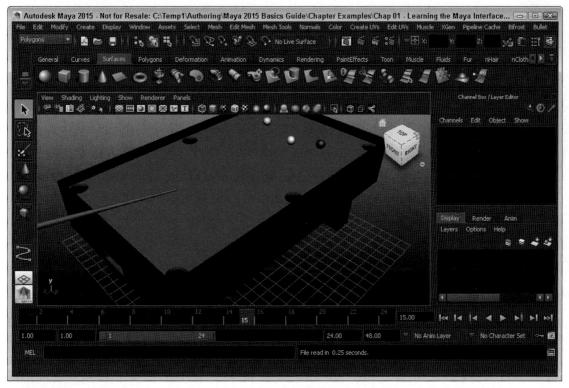

Figure 1-34
Animated billiard table

3. Click the Play Forwards button

   The entire animation sequence will play over and over.

4. Click the Stop button to pause the animation.

Lesson 1.5-Tutorial 2: Enter a Command

1. Select Create, Polygon Primitives, Sphere to create a sphere object.

2. Click on the view panel away from the sphere to deselect it.

3. In the Command Line, type, **select pSphere1;** and press the Enter key.

    The sphere object is selected.

4. In the Command Line, type, **move -z 10;**.

    The sphere is moved ten units along the z-axis.

5. Select File, Save Scene As and save the file as **Command line sphere.mb**.

Lesson 1.6: Use the Toolbox and Quick Layout Buttons

On the left side of the interface is a column of buttons collectively known as the Toolbox, as shown in Figure 1-35. Below the Toolbox are several layout buttons known collectively as the Quick Layout buttons.

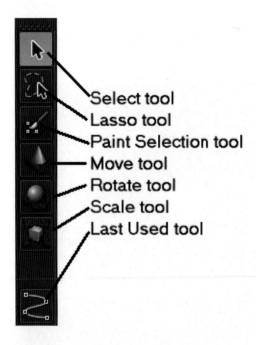

Figure 1-35
Toolbox

Selecting Objects

The first two buttons in the Toolbox are used to select objects in the scene. These are the Select Objects tool and the Lasso tool. The Select Object tool lets you select objects by clicking on objects or by dragging a rectangular border. The Lasso tool lets you drag a freehand outline over the object you want to select.

Holding down the Shift key while clicking on objects with the Select Objects tool will add objects to the selection set. All selected objects will appear white except for the last object selected, which will appear light green. This light green object is known as the *key object*.

Using the Transform Tools

The Toolbox also includes the Move, Rotate, and Scale tools. When any of these tools are selected, a manipulator will appear at the center (pivot point) of the selected object. With these tools, you can transform the selected object. Manipulator lets you transform the tool along a single axis or within a single plane, as shown for the Move tool in Figure 1-36. You can also click on the transform values displayed near the manipulator and enter new values using the keyboard.

Tip

> Once a transform handle on one of the transform tools is selected, it turns yellow. You can then drag the selected handle using the middle mouse button.

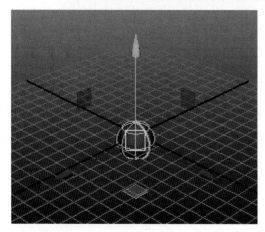

Figure 1-36
Universal Manipulator tool

Understanding Manipulators

Each of the transform manipulators has a color-coded components that will let you constrain a transform to a single axis—red is for the X-axis, green is for the Y-axis, and blue is for the Z-axis, as shown in Figure 1-37. The selected manipulator axis will turn yellow and dragging will transform the object along the selected axis.

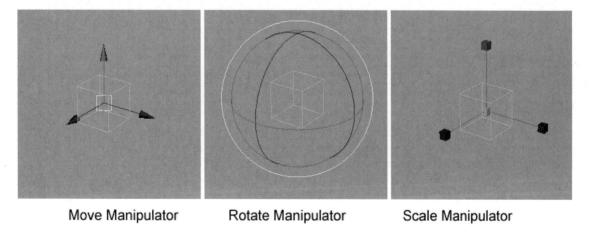

Move Manipulator   Rotate Manipulator   Scale Manipulator

Figure 1-37
Transform Manipulators

There are many other manipulators besides the transform manipulators. For example, when a spot light object is selected, you can enable a manipulator that lets you alter its light properties such as its falloff cone, direction and intensity by dragging in the view. Object manipulators are made active by clicking on the Show Manipulator button in the Toolbox.

Beneath the Show Manipulator Tool button in the Toolbox is another button that holds the last tool that was used. Remember that any menu item or button that includes the word *Tool* in its name will remain active until another tool is selected and will appear at the bottom of the Toolbox.

Note

The last slot in the Toolbox is reserved for tools selected from the menus. The Toolbox tools will not occupy this slot.

Switching Layouts

Beneath the Toolbox are several buttons, as shown in Figure 1-38, that allow you to quickly change the layout of the Maya interface. The default layout options include Single Perspective View, Four View, Perspective/Outliner, Perspective/Graph Editor, Hypershade/Perspective, and Perspective/Hypergraph/Graph. The arrow button underneath these layout buttons presents a pop-up menu of additional layout options.

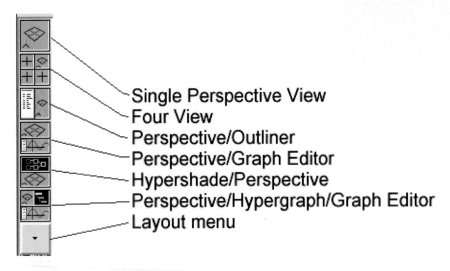

Figure 1-38
Quick Layout buttons

Customizing Layouts

You can change the layout that each button opens by right-clicking on the layout buttons and selecting the layout from the pop-up menu. If you right-click on the Model View button at the bottom of the Quick Layout buttons, you can select the number of panes that are displayed. If multiple panes are selected, the Model View button will be divided into the number of panes that you selected. Clicking on the Model View button will let you change the view that is displayed in the view that is clicked on.

Resizing and Editing View Panels

When multiple view panels are visible, you can resize the individual panels by dragging the dividers between the panels. Only one view panel can be active at a time.

Tip

Using the Spacebar, you can toggle between making the active view panel fill the entire Workspace and returning to the previous layout. For example, if the Four View layout is selected and the Top view panel is

> the active view panel, pressing the Spacebar maximizes
> the Top view panel.

You can use the Panels menu command on the Panel menu to change the view for any panel. You can find the Panels menu at the top of each view panel. The Panels, Saved Layouts, Edit Layouts menu command to open the Panels dialog box, shown in Figure 1-39. With this dialog box you can create a new panel and edit custom layouts.

Figure 1-39
Panels dialog box

Lesson 1.6-Tutorial 1: Select an Object

1. Open the Five spheres.mb file.

    This file includes five sphere objects.

2. Click on the Select tool and click on the center sphere.

    The sphere in the scene turns light green and its attributes appear in the Channel Box.

3. Hold down the Shift key and click on the other spheres in the scene.

    All spheres in the scene are selected and the last sphere clicked on will be light green, as shown in Figure 1-40.

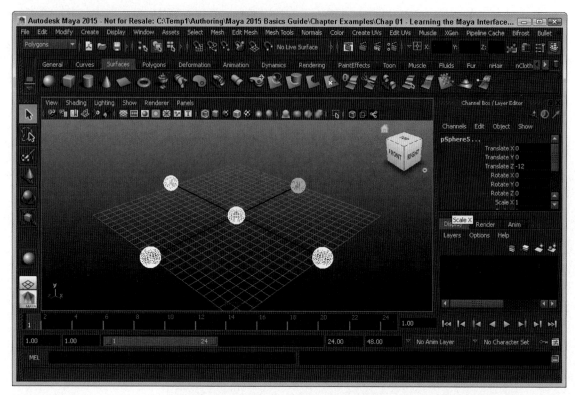

Figure 1-40
Selected objects

Lesson 1.6-Tutorial 2: Transform an Object

1. Open the Five spheres.mb file again.

2. Click on the Select tool and click on the center sphere.

3. Click the Move tool in the Toolbox and drag the green (Y-axis) upward.

4. The sphere moves upward in the scene.

5. Click the Scale tool in the Toolbox and drag the red (X-axis) to the right.

6. The sphere is elongated along the X-axis, as shown in Figure 1-41.

7. Select File, Save Scene As and save the file as **Elongated sphere.mb**.

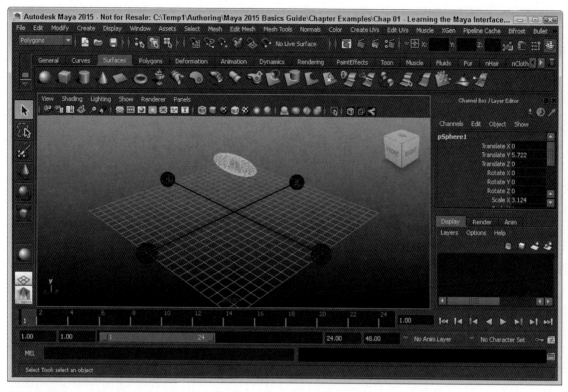

Figure 1-41
Transformed objects

Lesson 1.6-Tutorial 3: Change the Interface Layout

1. Click on the Show/Hide Channel Box button at the right end of the Status Line.

2. Click on the Four Views button in the Quick Layout buttons.

   The layout is changed to show four views, as shown in Figure 1-42.

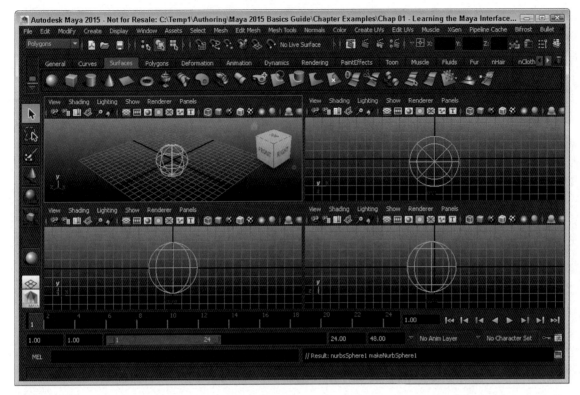

Figure 1-42
Four views

Lesson 1.7: Discover the Secret Menus

Once you get used to the menu commands, you can learn to work faster using the hidden menus. These menus will pop-up different commands when you right-click on objects in the scene.

Accessing the Marking Menus

For quick access to many common commands, you can open a **marking menu** by right-clicking in the view panel and holding the mouse button down until the menu appears. You can then move the cursor between the different menu options and release the mouse button to select the desired menu command. Figure 1-43 shows the marking menu for a polygon sphere object.

Tip

You can access a marking menu of selection options by holding down the q key while clicking in the view panel. You can access other custom marking menus in a similar manner such as Move Tool options (w), Rotate Tool options (e), Scale Tool options (r), Polygon Brush options (o), Select All menu (a), and Menu Sets (h).

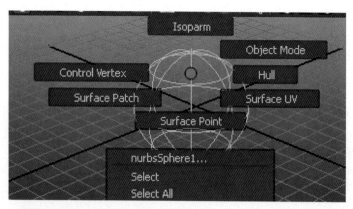

Figure 1-43
Marking menu

Customizing Marking Menus

You can alter the contents of a marking menu, assign a hotkey to a marking menu, or add a marking menu to the **Hotbox** using the Marking Menu Settings dialog box, shown in Figure 1-44. You access this dialog box using the Window, Settings/Preferences, Marking Menus menu command.

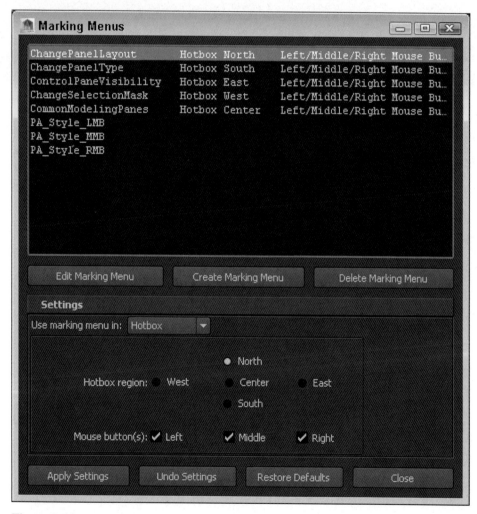

Figure 1-44
Marking Menus Settings dialog box

Using the Hotbox

The Hotbox, shown in Figure 1-45, is a complete set of customizable menus that you can access by pressing and holding the Spacebar. Using the Hotbox Controls option in the Hotbox, you can select which menu commands appear in the Hotbox.

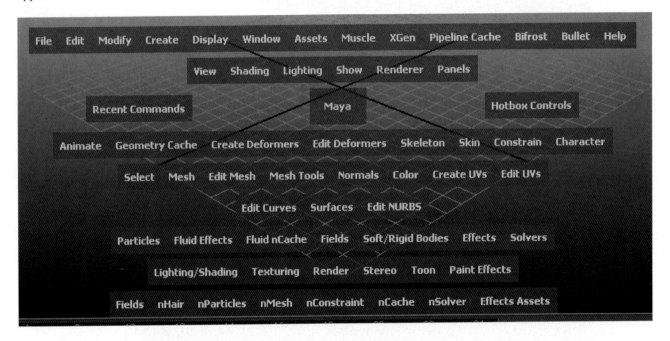

Figure 1-45
Hotbox

Customizing the Hotbox

If you select the Hotbox Controls option from the Hotbox, you can select which menu sets to include in the Hotbox. You can also select to Show or Hide all menus.

Lesson 1.7-Tutorial 1: Access a Marking Menu

1. Select Create, Polygon Primitives, Sphere to create a sphere object.

2. Click on the view panel away from the sphere to deselect it.

3. Right-click on the sphere and choose Select from the pop-up marking menu.

    The sphere object is selected.

Lesson 1.7-Tutorial 2: Use the Hotbox

1. Move the cursor to the center of the view panel and press and hold the Spacebar.

    The Hotbox appears centered around where the cursor is located, as shown in Figure 1-46.

2. Drag the cursor to the Create button and select the Polygon Primitives, Sphere command.

    The sphere object appears in the view panel.

3. Release the Spacebar.

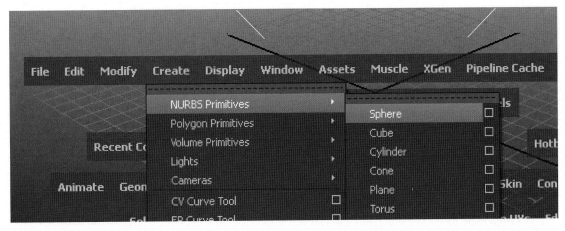

Figure 1-46
The Hotbox

Chapter Summary

This chapter takes you through a tour of the Maya interface, covering the basic interface elements, including the menus, the Status Line buttons, the Shelf, the Channel Box, the Layer Editor, the Animation Controls, the Command Line, the Help Line, the Toolbox, and the Quick Layout buttons. This chapter also explains how to work with these various interface elements and presents the marking menus and the Hotbox as other ways to work with the interface.

What You Have Learned

In this chapter, you learned

* How to switch between the different menu sets.

* How to use keyboard hotkeys.

* How to access option dialog boxes from menus.

* How to tear off menus.

* The difference between tools and actions.

* How to use pop-up help to identify buttons.

* How to identify a change in the cursor denoting right-click menus.

* How to expand and contract button sets.

* How to open and save scene files.

* How to show and hide the different interface elements.

* How to use the Shelf.

* How to add and delete items from a Shelf.

* How to use parameters in the Channel Box.

* How to use the Layer Editor.

* How to work with the animation controls.

* How to use the Command and Help Lines.

* How to select and transform objects using the Toolbox tools.

* How to add soft modifications to objects with the Soft Modification tool.

* How to switch between the different layouts.

* How to use and customize the marking menus and the Hotbox.

Key Terms From This Chapter

* **Menu set.** A dynamic set of menu options selected from a drop-down list at the top left of the interface.

* **Hotkey.** A keyboard shortcut that executes a command when pressed.

* **Option dialog box.** A dialog box with additional options opened using the icon found to the right of specific menu options.

* **Tear-off menu.** A panel of menu options that is removed to float freely from the interface.

* **Status Line.** A set of toolbar icons located at the top of the interface.

* **Pop-up help.** A small text title that appears when the cursor is held over the top of an icon.

* **Shelf.** A customizable set of buttons organized into separate groups.

* **Channel Box.** A panel of editable parameters that relate to the current selection.

* **Layer.** A selection of objects grouped together into a set that can be easily selected.

* **Animation controls.** A set of buttons used to control animation frames.

* **Command Line.** A text field where you can enter text commands.

* **Help Line.** A text field that presents the next action that is expected.

* **Toolbox.** A set of selection and transformation icons located to the left of the interface.

* **Quick Layout buttons.** A set of buttons for changing the interface layout.

* **Universal Manipulator.** A manipulator that moves, rotates, and scale objects all at once.

* **Soft Modification tool.** A tool used to edit local surface areas of the current object.

* **Marking menu.** A dynamic set of menus accessible by right-clicking on an object.

* **Hotbox.** A comprehensive set of menu options accessible by pressing the Spacebar.

Chapter 2

Controlling the View Panel

IN THIS CHAPTER

2.1 Change the view.

2.2 Change display options.

The **View panel** is where you'll do most of your work. It is the large central panel in the middle of the interface that shows the scene objects. Each View panel also includes a menu of options, called the Panel menu, that you can use to control what is displayed.

The objects displayed in the view panel are determined by a hidden camera that is pointing at the scene. You can change the view that is shown in the view panel by moving, zooming, and rotating this hidden camera. Do so by using the Camera tools that are found in the View panel menu or by holding down the Alt/Option key and dragging and using various mouse button combinations to rotate, zoom, and pan the view.

In addition to changing the view, you can also select to view the scene objects using different **wireframe** resolutions or as a shaded, or textured view. Each option shows the scene objects in more or less quality. By changing the quality of the object being displayed, you can control how quickly the entire scene is updated. For some complex scenes, you may want to set a low quality setting so you can work on the timing of an animation or you may want to set the quality high to see how the texture wraps around an object.

The view panel menu also includes commands that let you frame a selected object, move between the various views, and show or hide specific object types. Various other interfaces, such as the **Outliner**, **Hypergraph,** and Visor are useful interfaces for working with objects. You can display these interfaces also within a view panel.

Lesson 2.1: Change the View

The first thing to learn when dealing with view panels is how to change the view. Changing the view panels lets you see the specific area that you want to work on. All the view panel controls have easy-to-use hotkeys associated with them for quick access.

Using the Tumble, Track, Dolly, and Camera Tools

You can accomplish most view changes using the Alt/Option key and the mouse buttons. To **tumble** (or rotate) the camera, hold down the Alt/Option key while dragging with the left mouse button. To **track** (or pan) the camera, hold down the Alt/Option key and drag with the middle mouse button. To **dolly** (or zoom) in and out of the scene, hold down the Alt/Option key and drag with the right mouse button.

Tip

For each of these modes, the mouse cursor changes to match the various modes, as shown in Figure 2-1.

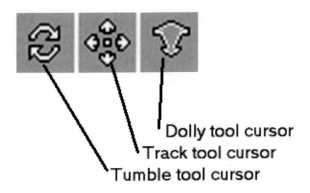

Dolly tool cursor
Track tool cursor
Tumble tool cursor

Figure 2-1
Tumble, track, and dolly cursors

You can also zoom in on a specific area by dragging over the rectangular area that you want to zoom in on with the Ctrl/Command and Alt/Option keys held down. If you drag from left to right, you'll zoom in; dragging from right to left causes the view to zoom out.

You can also change the view using one of the additional other camera tools. These tools are accessed from the View, Camera Tools panel menu. The Camera Tools panel menu include the Tumble, Track, Dolly and Zoom tools that are the same as those accessed with the Alt/Option key held down, but it also includes some additional tools, including the Roll, Azimuth Elevation, Yaw-Pitch, and Fly tools. The Roll tool spins the scene about its center point. The Azimuth Elevation tool raises or lowers the camera relative to the ground plane. The Yaw Pitch tool rotates the entire scene about the camera instead of rotating the camera about the scene like the Rotate tool. The Fly tool lets the entire scene rotate freely about the camera and uses the Ctrl/Command key to move towards and away from objects.

Tip

If you ever get lost when manipulating a camera, you can always return to the default view using the View, Default Home panel menu command.

Framing an Object

If you want to focus the view on a selected object or objects, use the View, Frame panel menu command (or by press the f hotkey). This command zooms and pans the view automatically so the selected object or objects fill the view panel, as shown in Figure 2-2. You can also focus on all the objects in the scene whether they are selected or not with the View, Frame All panel menu command (or by pressing the a hotkey).

Tip

These commands are also found in the Window menu. The hotkey to frame all objects in all views is Shift+A and the hotkey to frame the selected object in all views in Shift+F.

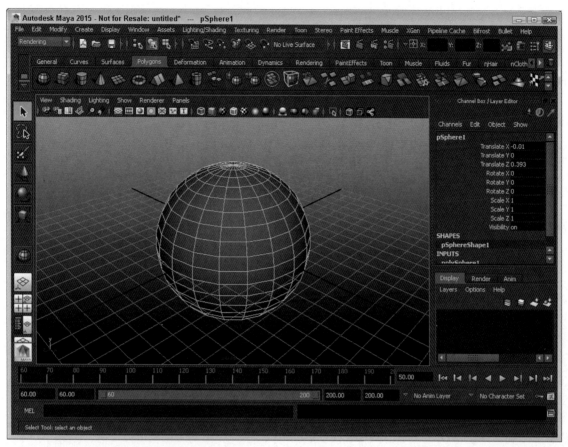

Figure 2-2
Framed object

Using the ViewCube

In the upper-right corner of the default Perspective view panel is a handy little tool known as the **ViewCube**, shown in Figure 2-3. Clicking on any of the ViewCube faces changes the view for the panel. The options allow you to quickly change between the Top, Bottom, Left, Right, Front and Back views. You can also click on the ViewCube corners to view the scene from a perspective view and clicking on the Home icon in the upper left, changes the view to the default perspective angle.

Figure 2-3
ViewCube

Moving Through Views

You can return to the previous view using the View, Previous panel menu command and the View, Next panel menu command moves back to the original view. The hotkeys for these panel menu commands are the [and] keys. You can also bookmark a view using the View, Bookmarks, Edit Bookmarks panel menu command. This opens the Bookmark Editor dialog box, in which you can create, delete and manage your bookmarks. All new bookmarks that you create show up in the View @@> Bookmarks panel menu. The View, Predefined Bookmarks panel menu also includes several default bookmarks that you may select including Perspective, Front, Top, and so on.

Tearing Off Panels

If you prefer to work with windowed views that are separate from the interface, you can tear off the panel with the Panels, Tear Off panel menu command. You can also tear off just a copy while leaving the original view panel part of the interface with the Panels, Tear Off Copy panel menu command. Figure 2-4 shows a panel that has been torn-off. You can resize any tear-off panel by dragging on its borders or corners.

Note

When a panel is torn away from the main interface, the Panels panel menu is replaced with a Help menu option.

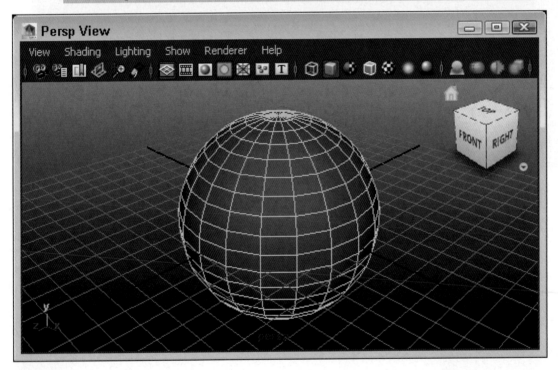

Figure 2-4
A tear-off view panel

Using Heads-Up Displays

The Display, Heads Up Display menu includes several options that you can select that overlays information over the active panel. These options include Object Details, Poly Count, Animation Details, Frame Rate, Camera Names, View Axis, and Origin Axis. This information is displayed above the existing view, as shown in Figure 2-5.

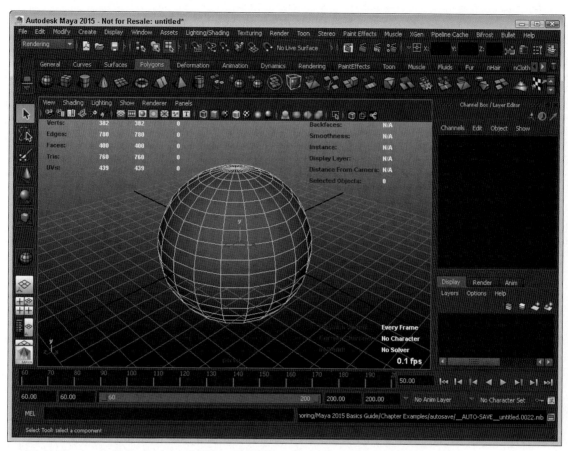

Figure 2-5
The Heads-Up Display with Poly Count and Object Details options

Opening Other Interfaces Within a Panel

The view panels aren't just used to display scene objects, they may also be used to hold any of Maya's other interfaces or editors including a Render View. Selecting an item from the Panels, Panel panel menu opens the selected interface within the active panel. The list of interfaces that may be opened include the Outliner, Graph Editor, Dope Sheet, Trax Editor, Hypergraph, Render View, and so on. Figure 2-6 shows four view panels with the Outliner, Hypergraph, Render View and Perspective views open.

Figure 2-6
View panels displaying the Outliner, the Hypergraph, and the Render View interfaces

Lesson 2.1-Tutorial 1: Change the Object's View

1. Select the File, Open Scene menu command and select the Shark.mb file to open.

   A side view of the shark object is displayed in a single view perspective view panel.

2. Hold down the Alt/Option key and drag in the View panel with the left mouse button. Rotate the shark so that its mouth is visible.

   The shark is rotated about the center of the View panel, as shown in Figure 2-7.

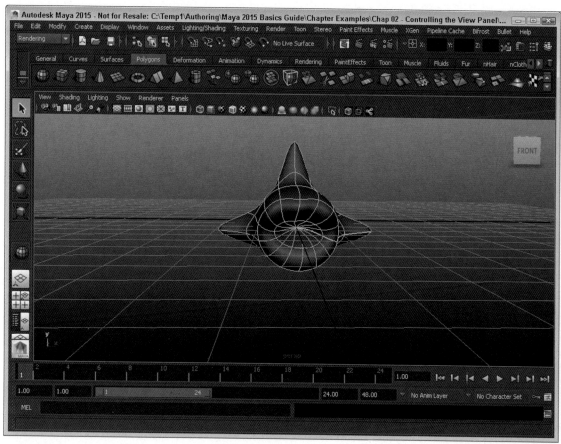

Figure 2-7
Rotated view of the shark

3. Hold down the Alt/Option key and drag with the middle mouse button.

   The camera moves in the direction of the mouse, thereby panning the view.

4. Hold down the Alt/Option key and drag with the right mouse button.

   The camera zooms in on the shark, as shown in Figure 2-8.

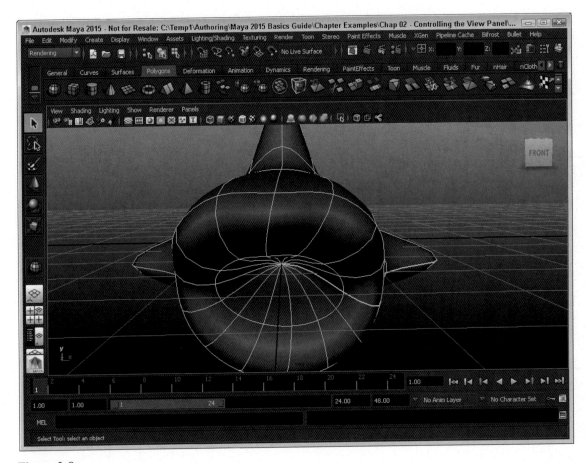

Figure 2-8
Zoomed view of the shark

5. After looking at the shark's mouth up close, press the *f* key to frame the shark.

    The camera zooms out until the entire shark is visible in the view panel.

6. Press the [and] keys to move back and forth through the views.

7. Select the Display, Heads Up Display, Object Details menu command.

    Various details about the object are displayed in the upper-right corner of the view panel, as shown in Figure 2-9.

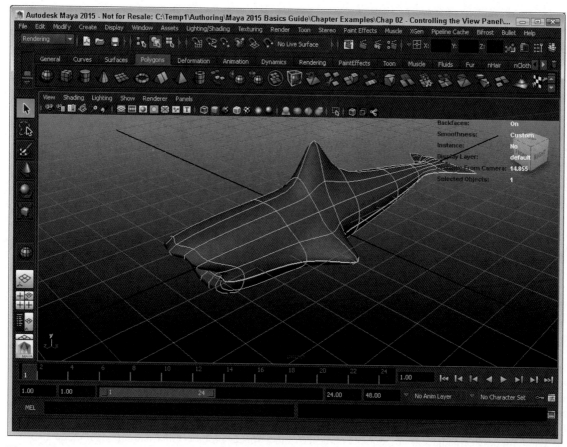

Figure 2-9
Shark with Object Details

Lesson 2.2: Change Display Options

Complex objects can take a long time to update in the View panels. You can increase the speed at which objects are updated by having the view panels display the objects at a lower **resolution** or you can view the affect of lighting and texture maps applied to the objects using other display modes.

Changing Resolution

Objects in the scene can be viewed at different-quality settings. Low-quality settings show complex scenes in near real-time, whereas high quality complex scenes may take a while to be viewed.

To view NURBS objects using the Rough setting, press the 1 key. The 2 key gives you a medium representation of the objects, and the 3 key displays the objects using a fine quality setting. Figure 2-10 shows these three levels of resolution.

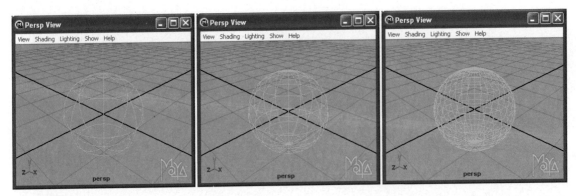

Figure 2-10
Rough, Medium, and Fine NURBS spheres

Note

The wireframe resolution settings only have an impact on NURBS objects. Polygon objects are unaffected by these settings.

Changing Shading

Using the options found in the **Shading** panel menu (and several hotkeys), you can change the type of shading that displays the scene objects. The Shading, Wireframe panel menu command (or the 4 key) displays all objects in the scene using a wireframe display method. The Wireframe option only shows the object edges. The Shading, Smooth Shade All panel menu command (or the 5 key) shows all objects using a smooth shaded view. The Shading, Flat Shade All panel menu command shows all objects using a flat shaded view. Flat shading doesn't smooth between adjacent polygons making the object appear blocky. The Shading panel menu also includes options to view all objects as Bounding Box and as Points. Figure 2-11 shows a simple sphere as a wireframe, with smooth shading and with flat shading.

Figure 2-11
Wireframe, Smooth Shading and Flat Shading

For the smooth and flat shading options, the Shading panel menu also includes commands to apply the smooth or flat shading to only the selected items.

The Shading panel menu includes three additional shading options. The Wireframe on Shaded option displays wireframe edges along with shading, the X-Ray option makes all objects semi-transparent and the Transparency Sorting option causes objects to be displayed depending on their transparency values.

Displaying Textures

The Shading, Hardware Texturing panel menu command (or the 6 key) displays the objects using a shaded view with textures. Figure 2-12 shows a NURBS sphere displayed with and without textures.

Note

If the scene objects don't have a texture applied, then smooth shaded objects will look the same as texture shaded. Applying textures to objects is covered in Chapter 8.

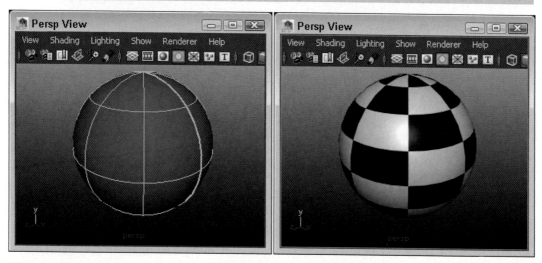

Figure 2-12
Textured and non-textured views

Enabling Backface Culling and Improving Wireframes

The Shading, **Backface Culling** panel menu command toggles the display to show only those faces that are facing the viewing camera. All the faces on the backside of the objects are obscured. Figure 2-13 shows a semi-transparent sphere with and without the Backface Culling options enabled.

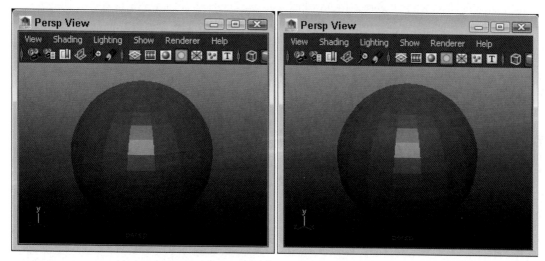

Figure 2-13
Backface culling enabled and disabled

The Shading, Smooth Wireframe panel menu command toggles the anti-aliasing of wireframe edges making them much smoother and less jaggy.

Isolating Objects

To change the view so only the selected objects are displayed and framed, choose the Show, Isolate Select, View Selected panel menu command. This command is a toggle option that hides all objects except for those that are selected. Choosing the option again makes all objects reappear. When in isolation mode, the word, "Isolate" appears in front of the view title at the bottom of the view panel. The Show, Isolate Select panel menu also includes options to Auto Load New Objects, Add and Remove Selected Objects, which let you change which objects are isolated.

Hiding and Showing Objects

As your scene increases in the number of objects, it can become difficult to find specific objects. To help focus on a specific object and to prevent other objects from being accidentally moved, you can use the toggle menus in the Show panel menu to hide and show All objects, no objects or specific object types.

For a more permanent method of hiding objects, you can hide selected objects using the Display, Hide, Hide Selected (Ctrl/Command+h) menu command. In the Display, Hide menu, there are also commands to Hide Unselected Objects (Alt/Option+h) , Hide All, and hide only specific geometry types. The Display, Show menu includes similar commands for making objects visible again.

Tip

> A more effective way to hide objects is to group scene objects by layers and use the Layer Editor controls to hide all the objects on a specific layer.

Changing Object Name and Color

To help identify objects, you can name the selected object by clicking on the object name that appears in the top of the Channel Box for the selected object and typing a new name. This name identifies the object in the external interfaces such as the Outliner and the Hypergraph.

You can also change the object's wireframe color using the Display, Wireframe Color menu command. This opens a simple dialog box, shown in Figure 2-14, in which you can choose from a palette of colors. Double-clicking on any of the colors opens a Color Selector in which you can customize the color.

Figure 2-14
Changing wireframe color

Lesson 2.2-Tutorial 1: Change the Object's Resolution

1. Select the File, Open Scene menu command and select the Shark.mb file to open.

    A side view of the shark object is displayed in a single view perspective view panel.

2. Press the 1 key on the keyboard.

    The shark is displayed using the lowest resolution setting, as shown in Figure 2-15.

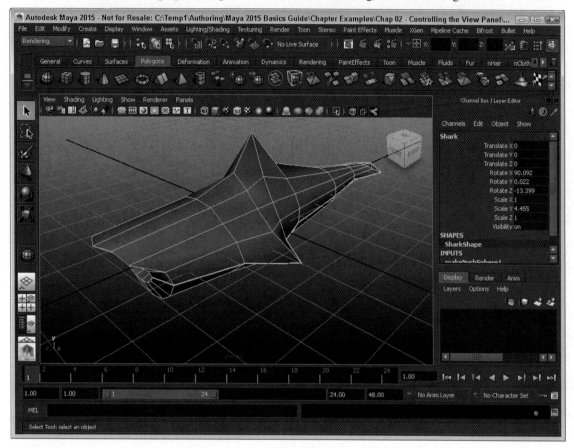

Figure 2-15
Shark at the lowest resolution setting

3. Press the 2 key on the keyboard, followed by the 3 key.

    The shark is displayed at the medium and then the high-resolution setting.

4. Press the 4 key to see the shark in wireframe mode, as shown in Figure 2-16, and on the 5 key to see the shark smooth shaded.

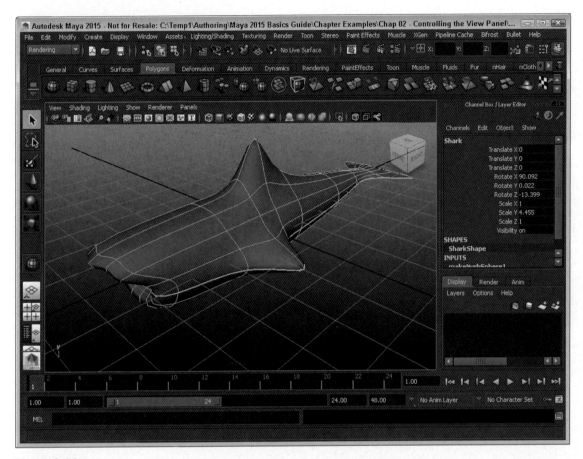

Figure 2-16
The wireframe shark

Lesson 2.2-Tutorial 2: Change the Object's Name and Color

1. Select the File, Open Scene menu command and select the Shark.mb file to open.

2. Click on the object's name in the Channel Box and type the name **Great White Shark**.

    The transform and shape nodes for the shark object are changed.

3. Select the Display, Wireframe Color menu command. In the dialog box that opens, double-click on the light blue color. In the Color Chooser that opens, select a bright cyan color and click the Accept button. Then click the Apply button in the Wireframe Color dialog box.

4. Click away from the shark and press the 4 key to see the new color in wireframe view.

    The wireframe shark is now displayed using the new wireframe color.

5. Select File, Save Scene As and name the new scene **Great White Shark**.

Chapter Summary

This chapter covers the view panel and explains how to use the view panel to change the scene view and also how to alter the scene display options. These options give you the chance to switch between different resolutions and views (wireframe, shaded, and textured views).

What You Have Learned

In this chapter, you learned

*   How to change the view using the various camera tools.

*   How to frame an object within the view panel.

*   How to use the ViewCube.

*   How to move through the various views.

*   How to tear off the current view panel.

*   How to use the heads-up display.

*   How to open an interface within a view panel.

*   How to isolate, hide, and show objects.

*   How to change an object's name and wireframe color.

Key Terms From This Chapter

*   **View panel.** The central scene window where objects are displayed.

*   **Tumble.** The act of rotating a camera to change the view's orientation.

*   **Track.** The act of panning the camera to change the view's focal point.

*   **Dolly.** The act of zooming the camera to change the view's focus width.

*   **Framing.** The process of zooming and panning the camera to focus on the selected object.

*   **ViewCube.** A manipulator icon in the upper-right corner of the view panel for quickly changing the current view.

*   **Heads-Up Display.** A menu command for adding informative text to the view panel.

*   **Resolution.** A measure of the detail (or number of elements) used to display scene objects.

*   **Shading.** A display method used to show scene objects as solid objects.

*   **Wireframe.** A display method that shows scene objects using contour lines.

*   **Textures.** Bitmaps images that are wrapped about a scene object.

*   **Backface Culling.** A display option that makes object elements located on the backside invisible.

Chapter 3
Working with Objects

IN THIS CHAPTER

3.1 Select objects and components.

3.2 Transform, group, and parent objects.

3.3 Snap and align objects.

3.4 Understand nodes and attributes.

Next, you'll need to learn to work with objects. Working with objects includes selecting, transforming, and applying commands to selected objects.

Before an object can be transformed or edited, it needs to be selected. Selecting objects is as easy as clicking on the object or dragging over it with the Select Tool, but there are other ways to select objects such as clicking on their name in the Outliner or selecting its node in the Hypergraph.

Each object is made up of components that can be selected and transformed to change the object at a detailed level. Understanding how to work with these components is the key to editing objects. Maya includes a component mode to display and select components, as well as, a mode for working with objects.

Objects and components are transformed using the tools found in the Toolbox. These tools let you move, rotate, and scale the selected object or component about a defined pivot point. To facilitate the moving of multiple objects, you can combine multiple selected objects together into a group or as a hierarchy of objects using the Group and Parent commands.

The Snap and Align commands make it easy to position objects exactly where you want them. Maya includes options to snap to grid points, to curves or to points. You can even specify that an object is "live" which makes all new objects snap to its surface.

You can break the entire scene into nodes that make up the scene. Each node has attributes associated with it. You can view these nodes in the Hypergraph. As nodes are connected, their history is recorded. You can revisit this history to make changes to the scene. Understanding how to edit an object's attributes is the key to editing with precision.

Lesson 3.1: Select Objects and Components

There are several ways to select objects. The easiest is to click on an object with the Select tool (located in the Toolbox), shown in Figure 3-1. You can also select object by dragging rectangular outline over the objects that you want to select or to draw an outline around the object with the Lasso tool, shown in Figure 3-2. When dragging an outline or drawing with the Lasso tool, all objects that are at least partial contained within the outline are selected.

Tip

```
The hotkey for the Select Tool is the Q key.
```

Figure 3-1
The Select tool

Figure 3-2
The Lasso tool

Selecting Multiple Objects

Holding down the Shift key while clicking on objects allows you to select multiple objects. You can remove selected objects from the current selection set by holding down the Ctrl/Command key while clicking on the object to remove.

Understanding the Key Object

When multiple objects are selected, the last object selected is colored light green, as shown in Figure 3-3. This color indicates the **key object**. Several tools use the key object for certain operations. For example, when moving multiple objects, the key object's pivot point is used as the rotation center.

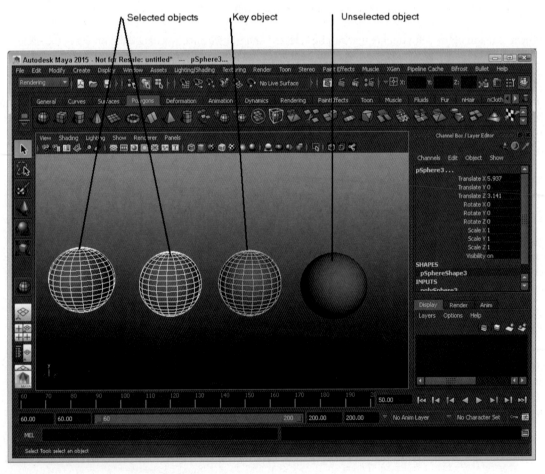

Figure 3-3
The key object

Using Selection Masks

If the scene is replete with many different types of objects, you can apply a **selection mask** to limit the types of objects that can be selected. The selection masks, shown in Figure 3-4, are located on the Status Line and consist of Handles, Joints, Curves, Surfaces, Deformations, Dynamics, Rendering, and Miscellaneous.

Note

A different set of selection masks are available for component mode, including Points, Parm Points, Lines, Faces, Hulls, Pivots, Handles, and Miscellaneous.

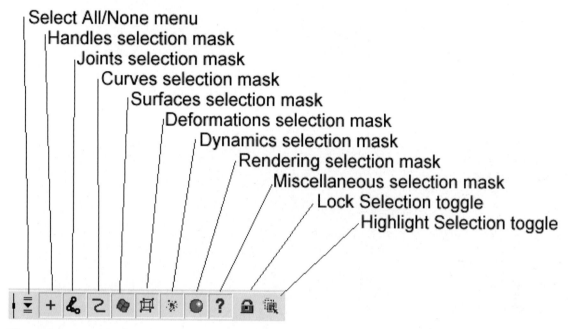

Figure 3-4
The selection masks

Selecting by Menu

The Edit menu includes several selection commands, including Select All, Select Hierarchy, Invert Selection, and Select All by Type.

Saving a Selection Set

A selection set is a grouping of objects that don't alter the hierarchy of the scene and are useful if you want to quickly select a number of objects and remember the selection. You can create a selection set using the Create, Sets, Set menu command. Sets appear in the Outliner for recall.

The Create, Sets, Quick Select Set menu command opens a simple dialog box where you can name the quick select set and these sets are less permanent than those sets listed in the Outliner and are recalled using the Edit, Quick Select Set menu.

Switching to Component Mode

If you click on the Select by Component Type button (see Figure 3-5) in the Status Line, the components for the selected object are displayed. Using the same methods discussed above allows you to select and work with components. The hotkey to toggle between Object and Component selection modes is F8.

Figure 3-5
The Select by Component Type button

Selecting Components

Objects are made of components such as vertices, edges, and faces. The type of components depends on the type of object. Maya lets you switch between object mode and component mode. While in component mode, you can select, edit, and transform components.

Tip

> The right-click marking menu lets you choose to display the various component types.

Components are selected just like selecting objects by dragging an outline over the components that you want to select with the Select Tool or the Lasso Tool. The selected components are colored yellow and the unselected components are colored magenta, as shown in Figure 3-6.

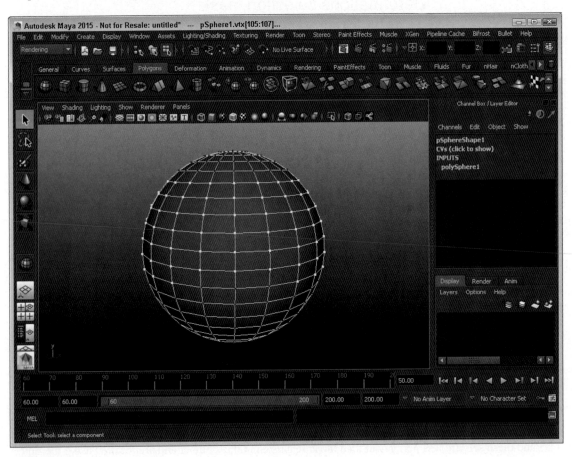

Figure 3-6
Selected components are yellow

The Edit, Paint Selection Tool changes the cursor to a paintbrush that lets you select components by painting over the object's surface.

Lesson 3.1-Tutorial 1: Select Multiple Objects

1. Select the File, Open Scene menu command and select the Box of donuts.mb file to open.

2. Click on the Select tool at the top of the Toolbox.

3. Hold down the Shift key and click on each of the donuts.

    The last donut selected is highlighted light green and all other donuts are white. The light green donut, shown in Figure 3-7, is the key object.

4. Select the Create, Sets, Quick Select Set menu command and name the quick set **Donuts** in the dialog box that appears.

    The selected donuts may now be recalled at any time using the Edit, Quick Select Sets, Donuts menu command.

5. Select the File, Save Scene As menu command and save the file as **Selected donuts**.

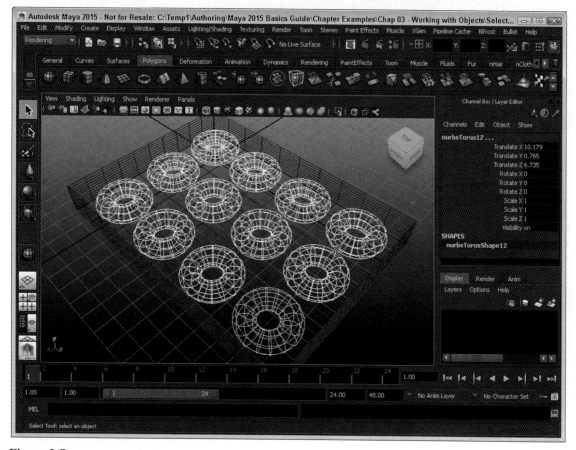

Figure 3-7
Selected objects

Lesson 3.1-Tutorial 2: Select Components

1. Select the File, Open Scene menu command and select the Box of donuts.mb file to open.

2. Click on the Lasso tool in the Toolbox and encircle portions of the middle two donuts.

3. Then hold down the Ctrl/Command key and encircle a portion of the underside of the box to deselect it.

4. Click on the Select by Component Type button in the Status Line (or press the F8 key).

5. Hold down the Shift key and encircle the center of both donuts.

6. Press the F key to focus in on the selected donuts.

The center Control Vertices (CV) points for the selected donuts are selected and are displayed in yellow, as shown in Figure 3-8.

7. Select the File, Save Scene As menu command and save the file as **Selected donut centers**.

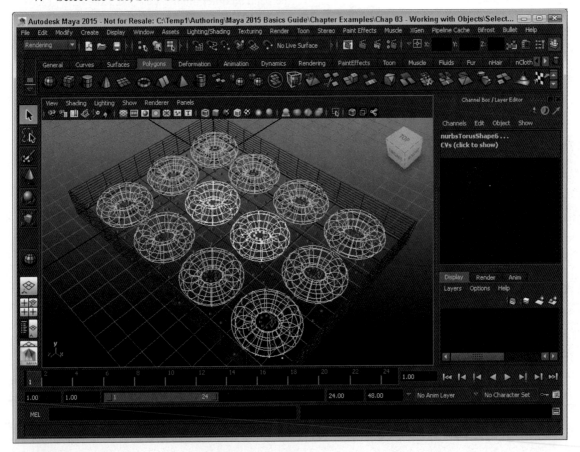

Figure 3-8
Component mode

Lesson 3.2: Transform, Group, and Parent Objects

Transforming involves positioning and orienting objects in the correct location for the scene. All transformations take place about the object's pivot point.

Understanding Pivot Points

Every object has a pivot point. The pivot point is the point about which the object is transformed. By default the pivot is usually positioned at the center of the object, as shown in Figure 3-9. You can reposition an object pivot point by pressing the Insert key to enter pivot point editing mode. You can then use the transformation tools to move and rotate the pivot point. Press the Insert key again to exit pivot point mode. You can move the pivot to the object's center using the Modify, Center Pivot menu command.

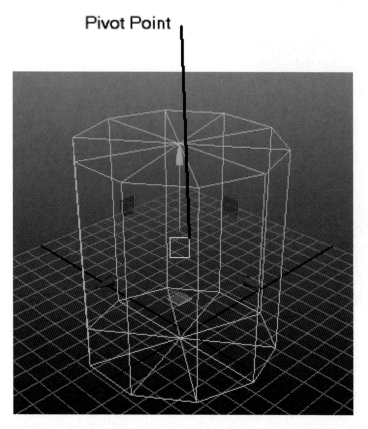

Figure 3-9
The pivot point

Transforming Objects Along an Axis

Objects can be transformed using the Move, Rotate, and Scale tools found in the Toolbox. Selecting any of these tools makes a manipulator appear at the pivot point for the selected object. You can constrain the transformation to a single axis by clicking on one of the axis manipulators. The selected constrained axis turns yellow. You can transform along the selected axis by dragging the selected manipulator (or by dragging in any direction in the View panel with the middle mouse button).

Tip

> You can also constrain a transform to a single axis by
> holding down the Shift key and dragging in the
> direction of the axis arrow.

Transforming Objects Within a Plane

You can transform objects within an orthographic view like the Top or Front view in two directions at once using the square handle located at the center of the manipulator. In a Perspective view, you can constrain the transform to a single plane by holding down the Ctrl/Command key while clicking on the axis arrow that points to the plane you want to constrain to. The square manipulator handle aligns to the plane that it is constrained to. Clicking on the square handle with the Ctrl/Command key held down toggles it back to the camera plane. Figure 3-10 shows an object constrained to move in the YZ-plane.

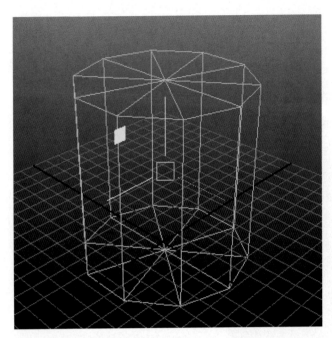

Figure 3-10
An object constrained to the YZ-plane.

Constrained Rotations

The Rotate tool also has a manipulator, but it looks and works a little differently than the Move tool. The Rotate manipulator, shown in Figure 3-11, includes three circular rings that surround the pivot point that allow you to rotate about each of the axes. There is also a yellow ring the surrounds the entire manipulator that lets you spin the object about its center. If multiple objects are selected, then the pivot point is at the center of the key object.

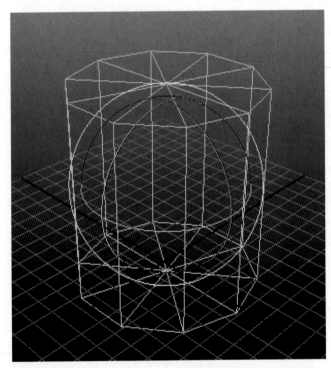

Figure 3-11
The Rotate manipulator

Grouping Objects Together

When multiple objects are selected together they are transformed together, but once another object is selected, the grouping is lost. To permanently create a group that can be reselected, use the Edit, Group (Ctrl/Command+g) menu command. This new group shows up as a selectable node in the Outliner, as shown in Figure 3-12. You can dissolve a group using the Edit, Ungroup menu command.

Figure 3-12
Groups displayed in the Outliner

Parenting Objects

Another way to combine objects is to parent one object to another. All child objects are transformed along with the parent object, but children objects can move independently of the parent. To create a parent-child link between two objects, select the child object and then select the parent object and use the Edit, Parent (hotkey: P) menu command. The key object (the last-selected object) is the parent object.

Lesson 3.2-Tutorial 1: Move Pivot Point

1. Select the File, Open Scene menu command and select the Earth and moon.mb file to open.

2. Click on the smaller sphere object to select it.

3. Click on the Rotate tool in the Toolbox and drag the green Y-axis manipulator handle to rotate the moon object about its center.

4. Click on the Move tool and press the Insert key on the keyboard to enable pivot point mode.

5. Drag the red X-axis manipulator handle to the center of the large sphere and press the Insert key again to exit pivot point mode.

6. Click on the Rotate tool again and drag the green Y-axis handle again.

This time, the moon rotates around the center Earth object, as shown in Figure 3-13.

7. Select the File, Save Scene As menu command and save the file as **Rotating moon.mb**.

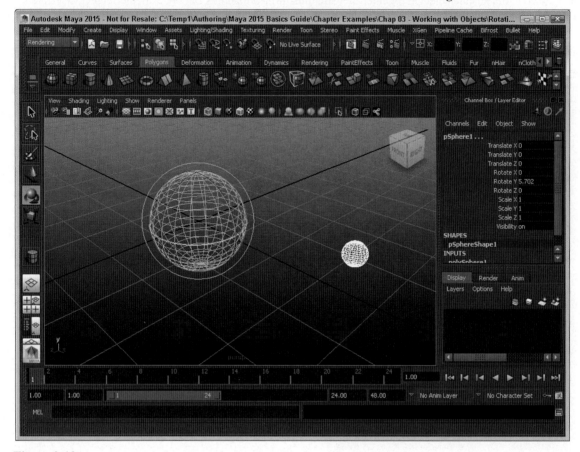

Figure 3-13
Moon rotates about the moved pivot point

Lesson 3.2-Tutorial 2: Transform Car Wheels

1. Select the File, Open Scene menu command and select the Car and wheels.mb file to open.

2. Drag over all the wheels in the Top view to select them all.

3. Click on the Rotate tool in the Toolbox and drag the red X-axis manipulator handle to rotate the wheels about their center 90 degrees so they are correctly positioned relative to the car body.

4. Click on the Move tool and select one of the wheels and drag its center manipulator in the Top view panel to align it to the car body. Repeat this step for the other wheels.

    With all the wheels correctly positioned, the car looks as shown in Figure 3-14.

5. Select the File, Save Scene As menu command and save the file as **Car with wheels.mb**.

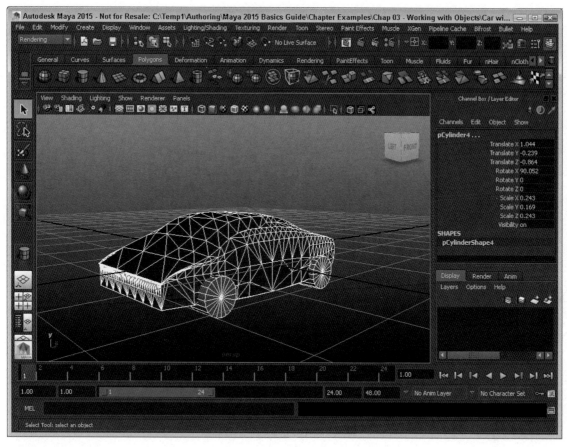

Figure 3-14
Car with transformed wheels

Lesson 3.2-Tutorial 3: Parent an Object

1. Select the File, Open Scene menu command and select the Hand and fingers.mb file to open.

2. With the Shift key held down, click on all the fingers and the thumb objects, and then on the hand object.

   With the hand selected last, it becomes the key object.

3. Select the Edit, Parent menu command.

   This command links all the objects together, with the hand object being the parent and fingers being its child, as shown in Figure 3-15.

4. Click on the Move tool and drag the hand object.

   When the parent object is selected and moved, its child objects are also selected and moves along with it.

5. Select the File, Save Scene As menu command and save the file as **Parented hand.mb**.

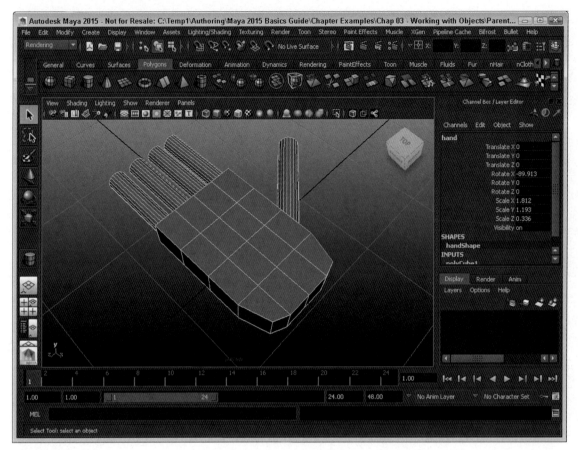

Figure 3-15
Parented objects

Lesson 3.3: Snap and Align Objects

Transforming objects leaves you to eyeball the precise location of the object, but you can precisely position objects using the Snap and Align features. You can tell when a snapping feature is enabled because the center of the manipulator is a circle instead of a square.

Using Grids

When Maya is first started, a default grid is visible in the view panel. The Display, Grid menu command toggles the default grid on an off. Select the Display, Grid, Options menu command opens a dialog box, shown in Figure 3-16, where you can specify the dimensions, color and display options of the default grid. The default grid is useful in snapping objects into place.

Figure 3-16
Grid Options dialog box

Duplicating with Transform

Another common way to precisely position several objects is with the Edit, Duplicate with Transform (Shift+D) menu command. If you create an object, you can use the Edit, Duplicate (Ctrl/Command+d) menu command to create a duplicate of the selected object. With this command, the duplicate object is positioned directly on top of the original object. But, if you create a duplicate object and transform it with the transform tools, the Duplicate with Transform menu command remembers the transform and duplicates the transform while creating the duplicate.

Snapping Objects

With the Move tool selected, you can snap the selected object to a specific grid point, to a curve, to surface points, or to a view plane using the Snap buttons located on the Status Line (see Figure 3-17). Just enable one or more of the snapping buttons and move the object, and it is automatically positioned so that its pivot point is in the same position as the object it is snapped to. You can also snap to a specific point by holding down the middle mouse button and moving the mouse over the snap point with the correct snap mode enabled.

Tip

```
Holding down the x hotkey, you can enable Grid
snapping, holding down the c hotkey, you can enable
Curve snapping and holding down the v hotkey enables
Point snapping.
```

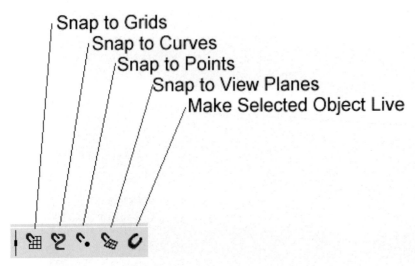

Figure 3-17
Snap buttons

Snapping to a Live Object

With the Modify, Make Live menu command, you can designate that objects that are created or moved are snapped to the surface of the Live object. The live object is displayed using a dark green color. This allows you to draw curves on the surface of the "live" object. Selecting the Modify, Make Not Live menu command changes an object back into a normal object

Aligning Objects

With two or more objects selected, you can use the Modify, Snap Align Objects menu command to align objects by point or object. The Options dialog box for the Align Objects menu command (see Figure 3-18) lets you align the objects by Min, Mid, Max, Dist, or Stack in each of the axes. The Align tool displays several alignment icons (see Figure 3-19) in the view panel. Choosing one of these icons aligns the selected objects. All selected objects are aligned with the key object.

Figure 3-18
Align Objects options

Alignment icons

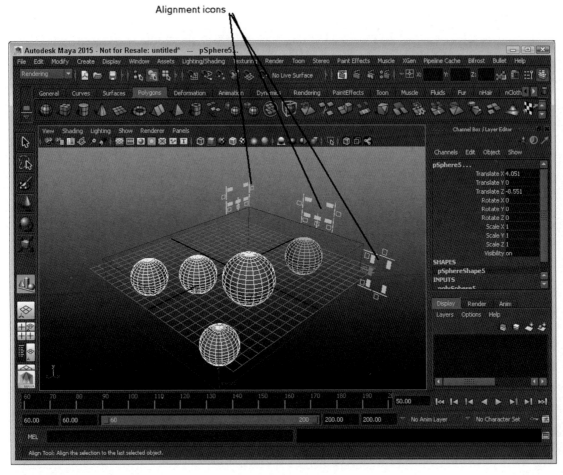

Figure 3-19
The Align tool

Aligning Points

Using component mode, you can select one, two or three points on each object that you want to align and use the Modify, Snap Align Objects, Point to Point or 2 Points to 2 Points or 3 Points to 3 Points menu commands to align objects using the selected points.

Caution

In order to use the point alignment options, the selected points must be roughly the same distance apart.

Snapping Surfaces Together

Another common way to align objects is with the Modify, Snap Align Objects, Snap Together tool. This tool lets you click and drag a cursor over the surface of the selected object. An arrow cursor points away from the surface. Clicking on a second object lets you drag over the surface to locate where the connection is made. A line connects the two surfaces at their designated connection points, as shown in Figure 3-20. Pressing the Enter key completes the snapping.

Snap Together tool arrow path

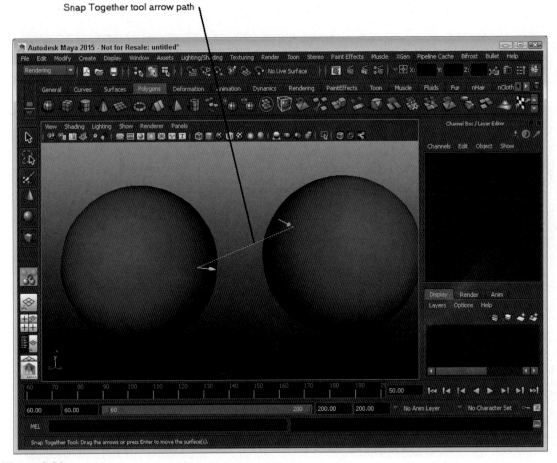

Figure 3-20
The line shows the points that are to be connected

Lesson 3.3-Tutorial 1: Snap Objects to Grid Points

1. Select the File, Open Scene menu command and select the Stairs.mb file to open.

2. Click on the single stair object to select it.

3. Click on the Snap to Grids button in the Status Line.

4. Select the Edit, Duplicate menu command (or press the Ctrl/Command+d hotkey) to create a duplicate stair object.

    The duplicate stair object is positioned in the same position as the original stair object.

5. Select the Move tool in the Toolbox and drag the duplicated stair object upward along the Y-axis in the Front view panel and to the right along the negative Z-axis in the Side view panel.

    With the Snap to Grids option enabled, moving the stair object snaps to the nearest grid point. This makes it easy to correctly and precisely align the stairs.

6. With the duplicate stair selected, choose the Edit, Duplicate with Transform menu command several times to create a set of stairs, as shown in Figure 3-21.

7. Select the File, Save Scene As menu command and save the file as **Snapped stairs**.

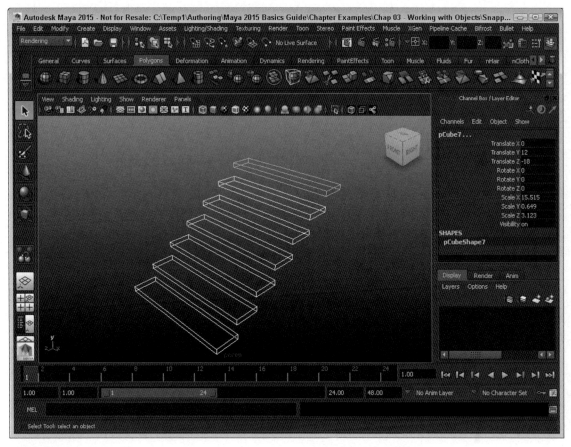

Figure 3-21
Snapped stairs

Lesson 3.3-Tutorial 2: Snap to a Curve

1. Select the File, Open Scene menu command and select the Heart necklace.mb file to open.

2. Click on the heart object to select it.

3. Click on the Snap to Curves button in the Status Line.

4. Select the Move tool in the Toolbox.

5. Click the curve with the middle mouse button and drag the heart object to its correct position on the necklace.

    With the Snap to Curve option enabled, clicking on the curve with the middle mouse button snaps the heart object to the curve, as shown in Figure 3-22.

6. Select the File, Save Scene As menu command and save the file as **Snapped heart necklace**.

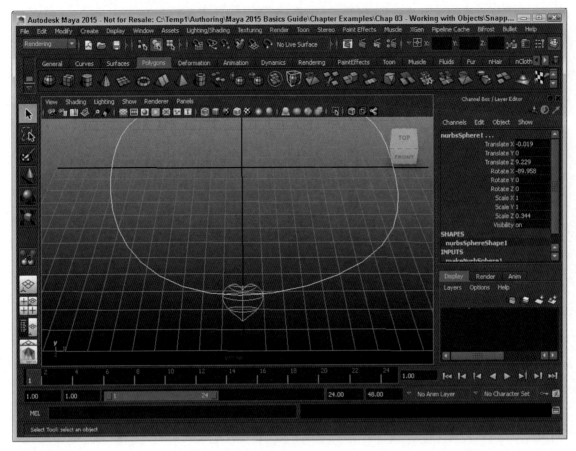

Figure 3-22
Heart snapped to a curve

Lesson 3.3-Tutorial 3: Snap to a Live Object

1. Select the File, Open Scene menu command and select the Simple cube.mb file to open.

2. Click on the cube object to select it.

3. Select the Modify, Make Live menu command.

    The cube object turns dark green to mark that is live.

4. Click on the sphere object to select it.

5. Select the Move tool in the Toolbox.

6. Drag the sphere to one of the cube corners.

    Because the cube is a live object, the sphere cannot be moved beyond the borders of the cube.

7. Select the Edit, Duplicate menu command and drag the duplicated sphere to another of the cube's corners. Repeat this until every corner has a sphere, as shown in Figure 3-23.

8. Click away from all objects to deselect all objects, and then choose the Modify, Make Not Live menu command to return the cube to its original state.

9. Select the File, Save Scene As menu command and save the file as **Cube with snapped spheres**.

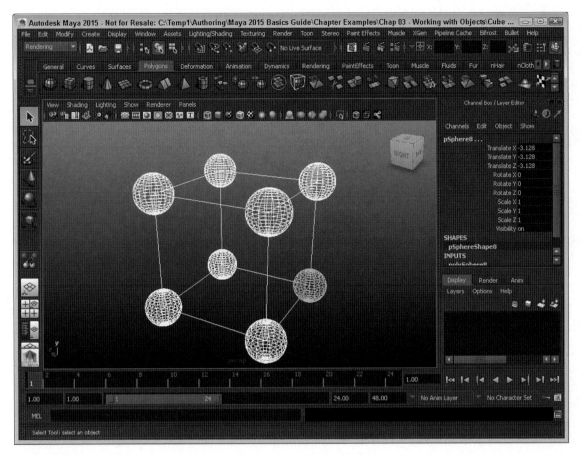

Figure 3-23
Spheres snapped to live cube object

Lesson 3.3-Tutorial 4: Align Letters

1. Select the File, Open Scene menu command and select the Misaligned letters.mb file to open.

2. Click on the letter M to select it.

3. Select the Modify, Snap Align Objects, Align Tool menu command to enable the Align tool.

4. Hold down the Shift key and click on the top of the other letters.

   With the Align Tool enabled and two or more objects selected, several light-blue alignment icons appear in the View panel.

5. Click on the Align Bottoms icon to align the letters.

6. Drag over the last two letters and click the Align Top icon to slide the letter y downward relative to the other letters (see Figure 3-24).

7. Select the File, Save Scene As menu command and save the file as **Aligned letters**.

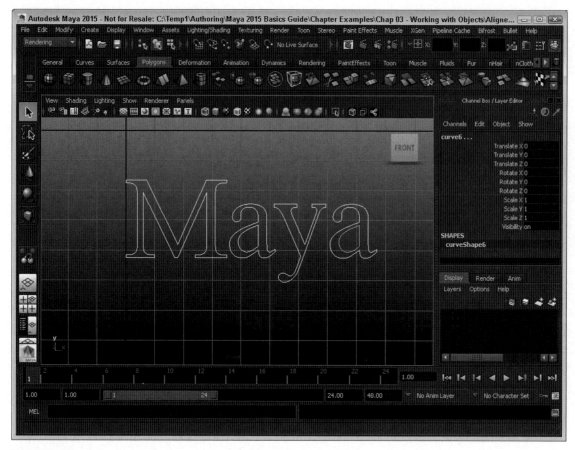

Figure 3-24
Aligned letters

Lesson 3.4: Understand Nodes and Attributes

In addition to a visual representation found in the View panel, each object is also a represented as a node. Nodes can be viewed using the Outliner and the Hypergraph. Each node holds *attributes*, which are the values that determine the properties of the node. For example, each object has a Transform node that holds information on the object's position. You can see the keyable attributes for the selected node in the Channel Box and all nodes in the Attribute Editor.

Understanding the Various Node Types

Maya includes several different node types. A Transform node holds the position, rotation, and scale information; a Shape node holds other type of geometry information; Rendering nodes include materials and textures that control how an object looks; and Light nodes hold information about the scene lights.

Working with Nodes

The child nodes for an object are visible in the Channel Box, where you can change their attributes (see Figure 3-25). In addition to the child nodes for an object, you can select to view all of the Input and Output nodes for a node using the buttons on the Status Line. You can also see all these related nodes as tabs in the Attribute Editor, shown in Figure 3-26. The Attribute Editor can be opened (replacing the Channel Box) using the Window, Attribute Editor menu command or by clicking on the Show Attribute Editor button on the Status Line.

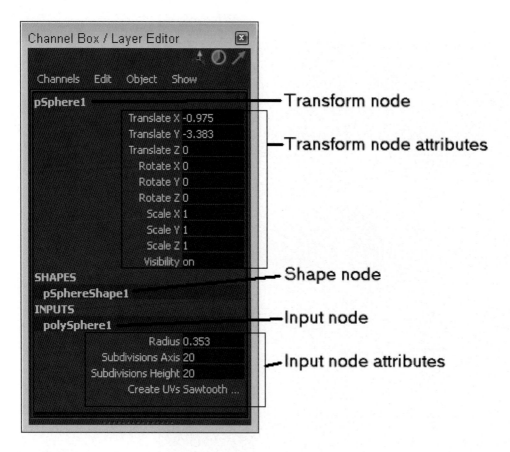

Figure 3-25
Channel Box nodes and attributes

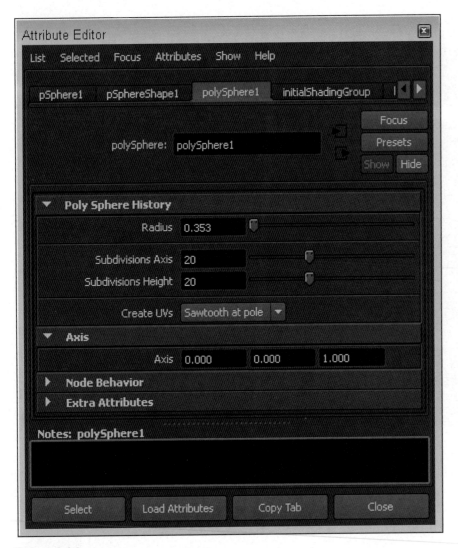

Figure 3-26
The Attribute Editor

Viewing Nodes as a Scene Hierarchy in the Outliner

To view all scene nodes as a hierarchical list, you can open the Outliner using the Window, Outliner menu command. The Outliner, shown in Figure 3-27, displays all child objects underneath their parents. It also includes hidden objects, such as the hidden view cameras and the default lights. The Outliner is also an easy place to select objects. Dragging and dropping nodes with the middle mouse button lets you re-order the hierarchy creating parent and children objects.

Figure 3-27
The Outliner

Viewing Dependency with Hypergraph

Another way to view nodes is with the Hypergraph also accessed from the Window menu. The Hypergraph can display nodes in two modes—as a Scene Hierarchy, shown in Figure 3-28, or as Input and Output Connections, shown in Figure 3-29. Both modes show the nodes as small boxes and the relationships between the different nodes are represented with interconnecting lines. The middle mouse button can also be used in the Hypergraph also to parent nodes to other nodes.

Tip

You can use the Alt/Option+middle mouse button and the Alt/Option+right mouse button to pan and zoom with the Hypergraph. The mouse scroll wheel can also zoom the Hypergraph. You can also use the *f* hotkey to frame the selected nodes.

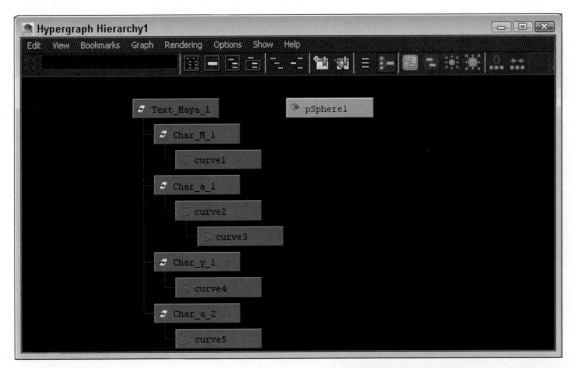

Figure 3-28
Hypergraph, Scene Hierarchy.

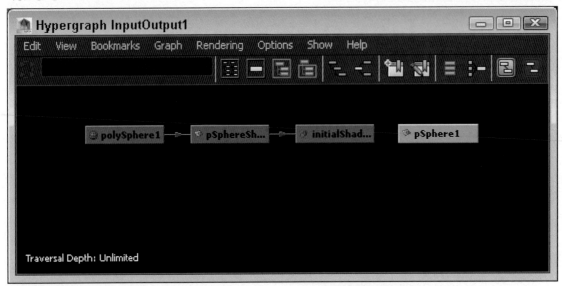

Figure 3-29
Hypergraph, Input and Output Connections

Editing Attributes

All the keyable attributes associated with an object can be viewed in the Channel Box, but this is just a subset of the total number of attributes. A complete set of attributes may be viewed in the Attribute Editor. Attributes that have a purple background are controlled by another attribute and cannot be changed. You can change multiple attribute values at the same time by holding down the Shift key and selecting them.

Using Undo, Redo, and Repeat

You can undo your mistakes using the Edit, Undo menu command (Ctrl/Command+z) and redo using the Edit, Redo menu command (Shift+z). You can also repeat the last command using the Edit, Repeat menu command (hotkey: g). The Edit, Recent Commands menu opens a dialog box (Figure 3-30) that lists the recently executed commands. Using this dialog box, you can selectively choose which actions to undo.

Figure 3-30
Recent Commands dialog box.

Deleting construction history

Every command in Maya is saved in a cache referred to as the construction history. As you work with objects, the history that is saved adds overhead to the object, which can slow down the system. You can simplify an object by deleting its construction history using the Edit, Delete by Type, History. This removes the dependency between curves and surfaces, but results in a simplified object.

Lesson 3.4-Tutorial 1: Explore Dependent Nodes

1. Select the File, Open Scene menu command and select the House shape.mb file to open.

2. Click on the house shape on the left to select it.

    The shape on the left is the curve used to create the extruded shape, which is shown on the right. The curve is light green and the dependent extrusion is light purple, as shown in Figure 3-31. In the Channel Box, three nodes are visible: the curve object's Transform node, called curve1; the Shape node, called curveShape1; and the Output node, called extrude1. The curve node feeds the extrude output node.

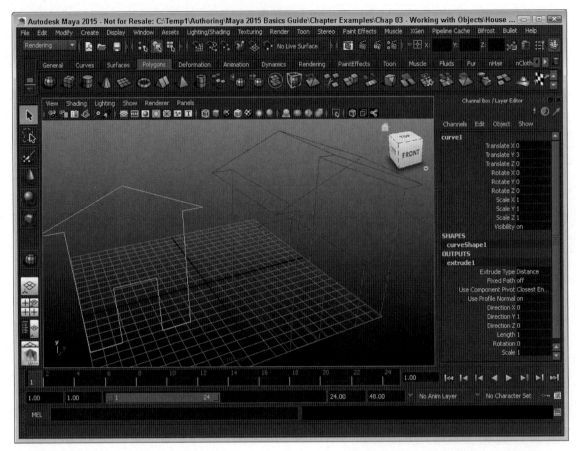

Figure 3-31
The extrusion is dependant on the shape.

3. Click on the output node labeled extrude1 in the Channel Box.

    The attributes for this node are displayed.

4. Click on the Select by Component Type button in the Status Line

    The CVs for the curve are displayed.

5. Select the Move tool in the Toolbox and drag to alter the shape's CVs.

    Changing the curve changes the extruded surface also, as shown in Figure 3-32.

6. Select the File, Save Scene As menu command and save the file as **Modified house shape**.

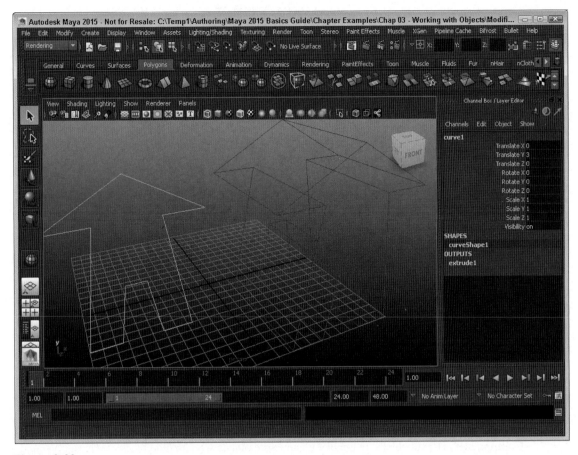

Figure 3-32
The modified house

Lesson 3.4-Tutorial 2: Delete Construction History

1. Select the File, Open Scene menu command and select the House shape.mb file to open.

2. Click on the house shape on the right in the Top view panel to select it.

3. Select the Edit, Delete by Type, History menu command.

    The extrusion surface is now independent on the curve on the left.

4. Select the File, Save Scene As menu command and save the file as **Independent house shape**.

Chapter Summary

This chapter covers how to select objects using the Select and Lasso tools. Once you select an object, you can transform and edit it using the other Toolbox tools. You can group several objects and parent them together to create complex objects that move together. The Snap and Align tools control how objects are moved and positioned relative to one another. Finally, the Attribute Editor along with the Outliner and the Hypergraph create and manipulate scene hierarchies.

What You Have Learned

In this chapter, you learned

*   How to select objects.

*   The importance of the key object.

* How to use selection masks and selection sets.

* How to select object components.

* How to use and move pivot points.

* How to transform objects along an axis or within a plane.

* How to group and parent objects together into hierarchies.

* How to duplicate with a transform.

* How to use grids and snap objects together.

* How to snap to a live object.

* How to align objects.

* The various node types.

* How to view nodes in the Attribute Editor, the Outliner, and the Hypergraph.

* How to edit attributes.

* How to undo, redo, and repeat commands.

Key Terms From This Chapter

* **Key object.** The last object that is selected. The key object is the base object for certain commands.

* **Selection mask.** A filter that limits the types of objects that can be selected.

* **Selection set.** A selection of objects that are named for quick recall.

* **Components.** The subobjects that make up an entire object. Can include faces, vertices, CVs, and so on.

* **Pivot point.** The point about which the object or objects are rotated.

* **Grouping.** The process of collecting multiple objects together into a named group.

* **Default grid.** An invisible array of points that mark the origin of the scene.

* **Snapping.** The process of automatically moving an object to precisely align with a specific component.

* **Aligning.** The process of moving objects so that certain components have the same position.

* **Node.** A selectable scene container that holds specific attributes.

* **Attributes.** Values that determine the properties of the node.

* **Outliner.** An interface that displays all scene objects as simple nodes.

* **Hypergraph.** An interface that shows all scene objects as nodes in a hierarchical display.

* **Construction history.** A list of commands executed to build a scene.

Chapter 4
Drawing and Editing Curves

IN THIS CHAPTER

4.1 Create curves

4.2 Edit curve details.

4.3 Modify curves,

4.4 Apply curve operators.

4.5 Create simple surfaces from curves.

4.6 Create text.

The first step when starting out modeling is to learn to work with curves. Curves aren't rendered, but they form the basis of all NURBS surfaces and learning to work with them gives you an advantage as you begin to model NURBS surfaces. Understanding how to create surfaces from curves is an essential part of NURBS modeling.

To understand curves in Maya, you need to understand the curve components. Each Maya curve consists of several control vertices (**CVs**) that define its curvature. The first CV is displayed as a small square and the second CV is a lowercase letter u. All other CVs are marked as dots. The order of the CVs is significant, as the curve is used to make a surface. You can see the CVs that make up a curve by selecting Component mode or by selecting Control Vertex from the right-click marking menu.

The control vertices are often easier to see if the curve's hulls are displayed. A **hull** is a line that connects two adjacent CVs. You can display all hulls for a curve using the marking menu.

Maya curves also include edit points. Edit points are positioned on the curve's path and are displayed as a small x. Each edit point is linked to a CV, and moving the edit point moves the CVs and vice versa. Moving CVs offers more control than moving edit points. You can view a curve's edit points using the marking menu.

Maya includes primitive 2D shapes like circle and square and tools for creating arcs, but most of the curves you create are freehand. Maya allows several different ways to create curves. The **CV Curve tool** creates a curve by positioning the CVs, the **EP Curve tool** creates curves when you click on the location of the edit points that lie on the curve's path, and the Pencil Curve tool lets you draw curves in the view panel.

Outlined text is another special class of curves that you can create and edit.

Once curves are created, you can edit the curves by selecting and moving the individual CVs and edit points. You can combine, align, close, reverse, and simplify curves using the menu commands found in the Edit Curves menu. Learning to use the Edit Curves commands is another vital step in preparing curves to be turned into surfaces.

You can use selected curves to create surfaces using a number of different techniques, including Revolve, Loft, Extrude, and Bevel.

Lesson 4.1: Create Curves

Maya includes several tools that may be used to create curves, and there are also some curve primitives available in the Create menu. Each of these tools work by placing points or vertices and having Maya compute the curve lines that are drawn between these points.

Creating Circles and Squares

At the bottom of the Create, NURBS Primitives menu are two menu commands that you can use to create a perfect circle and a square. These shapes are positioned at the center of the grid. Using the options dialog box (shown in Figure 4-1) for the circle primitive, you can set several options including the axis about which the shape is oriented, the Sweep Angle (for creating partial circles), the Radius, and the number of Sections that make up the shape for the circle. Options for the square primitive include the orientation axis, side lengths, and Spans per Side.

Note

Creating a NURBS square primitive results in four separate straight-line segments that you can select independently.

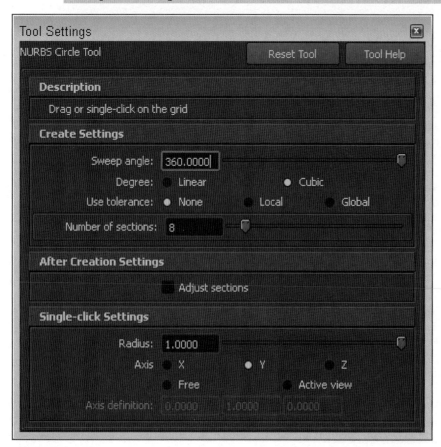

Figure 4-1
NURBS Circle Options

Creating Arcs

There are actually two methods for creating arcs found in the Create, Arc Tools menu. One method uses three points. The first and last point mark the endpoints of the arc and the middle point marks a point on the arc. The second method uses only two points. The first point marks one end of the arc and the second point can be dragged to set the curvature and the second endpoint. Once the arc points are positioned, you can move them by dragging the vertices. Clicking the two-point arc's circle manipulator changes the direction of the arc. Figure 4-2 shows both arc creation methods.

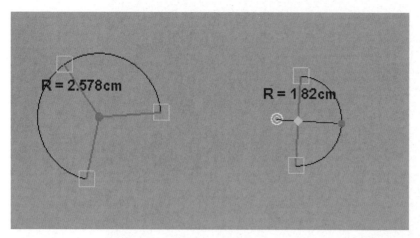

Figure 4-2
Three- and two-point circular arcs

Creating Smooth Curves

In Maya, you can create smooth curves by positioning the curve's control vertices (CVs) with the Create, CV Curve tool or by positioning the curve's edit points with the Create, EP Curve tool. The difference between these two tools is that the curve passes through all vertices of a curve created with the EP Curve tool and the curve only passes through the end vertices of a curve created with the CV Curve tool. After clicking to place the vertices, you can press the Enter key or click on the Select tool to end the curve. Figure 4-3 shows an example of each of these curves.

Tip

```
Pressing the Insert key while placing vertices allows
you to move the last placed vertex. Pressing the Insert
key again lets you continue adding vertices. Pressing
the Delete key deletes the last-created vertex.
```

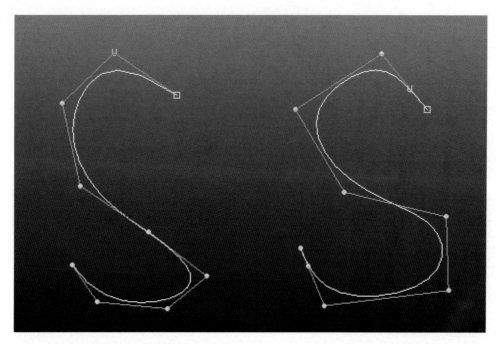

Control Vertex (CV) curve   **Edit Point (EP) curve**

Figure 4-3
CV and EP curves

Creating Straight Line Curves

In the Options dialog box for the CV and EP Curve tools, you can select the degree of the curve. Selecting the 1 Linear option causes all curve spans to be straight lines. Higher degree values requires more CVs before a span is created. Figure 4-4 shows the various **curve degrees**.

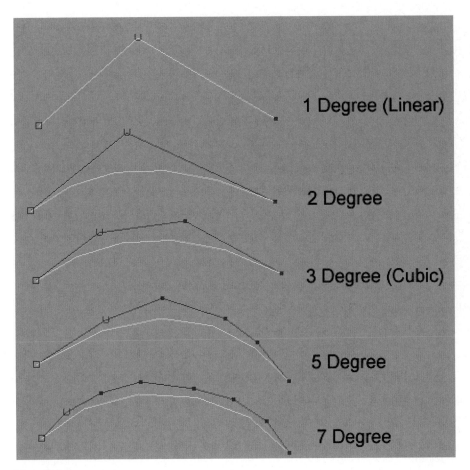

Figure 4-4
Curve degrees

Drawing Freehand Curves

You can draw freehand curves using the Pencil Curve tool, which is also found in the Create menu. This automatically creates a curve with as many vertices as it takes to represent the drawn curve. Clicking the Select by Component Type button on the Status Line shows all the vertices for the selected curve and using the right-click marking menu lets you display the Control Vertices or Edit Points that make up the curve.

Simplifying and Smoothing Curves

Freehand curves can result in a large number of vertices. You can reduce the total number of vertices used to represent a curve with the Edit Curves, Rebuild Curve menu command. The Rebuild Curve Options dialog box, shown in Figure 4-5, includes several options for defining what the reduced curve should look like. Selected curves can also be smoothed using the Edit Curves, Smooth Curve command. This provides a way to quickly improve the smoothness of a hand-drawn curve. The Smooth Curve Options dialog box includes a Smoothness value that determines how aggressively the curve is smoothed.

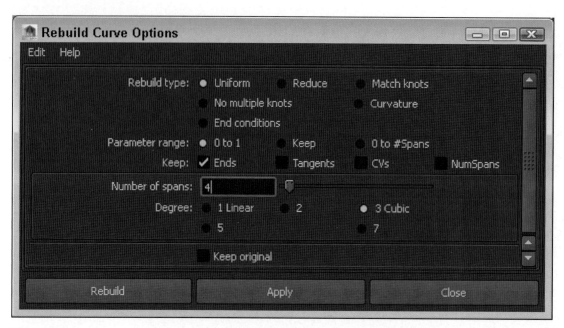

Figure 4-5
Rebuild Curve Options

Lesson 4.1-Tutorial 1: Create an Eye Using Arcs and Primitive Shapes

1. Click on the Create menu, and then select the NURBS Primitives submenu and click on the icon to the right of the Square menu to open the Options dialog box.

2. In the NURBS Square Options dialog box, select the Y Normal Axis, set the Length of Side 1 and 2 options to 1.0 and click the Create button.

   A simple square shape appears at the origin in the view panel.

3. With the square selected, click on the View, Frame Selected panel menu command or press the f key. Then click on the Model View button in the Quick Layout Buttons and select the Top View pop-up menu command.

4. In the Status Line, click on the Snap to Points button to enable point snapping.

5. Click on the Create, Arc Tools, Two Point Circular Arc menu command then click on two opposite corners of the square in the Top view panel and press the Enter key. Then select the Two Point Circular Arc tool again and click on the same two opposite corners of the square in the opposite order and press the Enter key again.

   Two circular arcs appear positioned between the opposite corners of the square.

6. Click on the Create menu, and then select the NURBS Primitives submenu and click on the icon to the right of the Circle menu to open the Options dialog box.

7. In the NURBS Circle Options dialog box, select the Y Normal Axis, set the Sweep Angle setting to 360 and the Radius value to 0.25, and then click the Create button.

   A circle appears in the center of the eye.

8. Select all edges of the square object and press the Delete key to delete the square shape. The eye shape is displayed, as seen in Figure 4-6.

9. Select File, Save Scene As and save the file as **Eye shape.mb**.

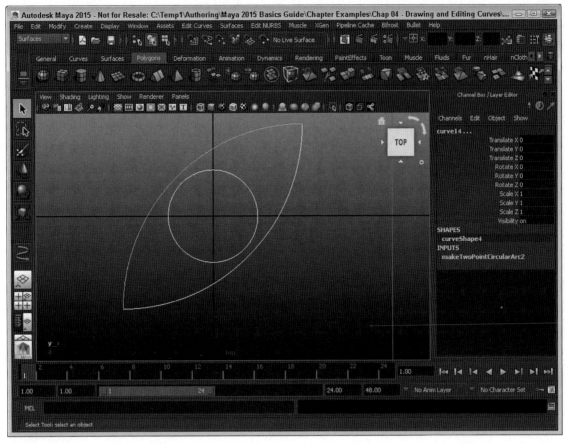

Figure 4-6
Eye shape

Lesson 4.1-Tutorial 2: Draw and Compare CV, EP, and Freehand Curves

1. Click on the Model View button at the bottom of the Quick Layout Buttons and select the Top View pop-up menu command.

    The view panel changes to show the Top view.

2. In the Status Line, click on the Snap to Grids button to enable grid snapping.

3. Select Create, CV Curve Tool and click on grid intersection points in a zig-zag pattern.

4. Select Create, EP Curve Tool and click on grid intersection points beneath the CV Curve in the same zig-zag pattern.

    Notice how the curve created with the CV Curve tool winds between the placed points and the second curve has the line run through the grid snap points.

5. Select Create, Pencil Curve Tool and draw the same zig-zag pattern beneath the other two curves.

    Notice how the Pencil Curve tool doesn't snap to the grid and is freehand. Figure 4-7 shows the resulting curves.

6. Select File, Save Scene As and save the file as **Wavy zig-zag lines.mb**.

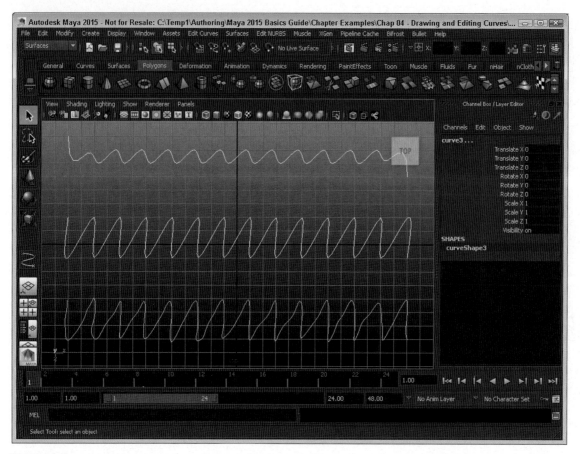

Figure 4-7
CV, EP and Freehand curves

Lesson 4.1-Tutorial 3: Simplify Freehand Curves

1. Click on the Model View button at the bottom of the Quick Layout Buttons and select the Top View pop-up menu command.

    The view panel changes to show the Top view.

2. Select Create, Pencil Curve Tool and draw a freehand spiral in the center of the Top panel.

3. Click on the Show or Hide the Attribute Editor button on the right end of the Status Line to display the Attribute Editor. Look at the number of spans for the freehand spiral.

    A single span is the distance between each edit point. It defines the complexity of the curve and is related to the number of CVs. Figure 4-8 shows the freehand spiral.

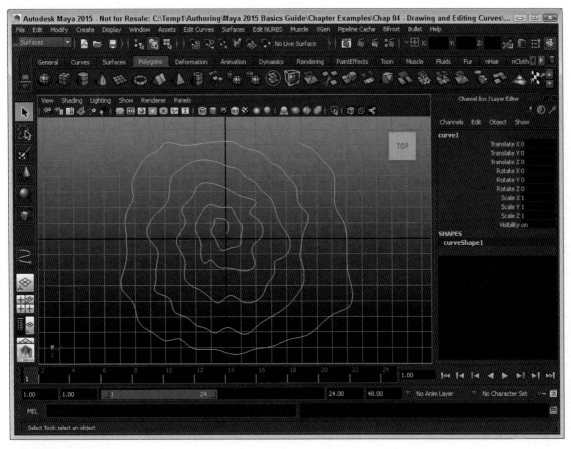

Figure 4-8
The freehand spiral

4. Open the options dialog box for Edit Curves, Rebuild Curve. Set the number of spans to half its original value and click the Apply button.

The curve is significantly reduced and simplified, as shown in Figure 4-9.

5. Continue to decrease the number of spans in the options dialog box by half and click the Apply button again until the curve is simplified as much as it can be without changing its shape.

Note

If you've reduced the curve too much, you can use the Edit, Undo menu command to return the curve to its previous state.

6. Select File, Save Scene As and save the file as **Rebuilt freehand spiral.mb**.

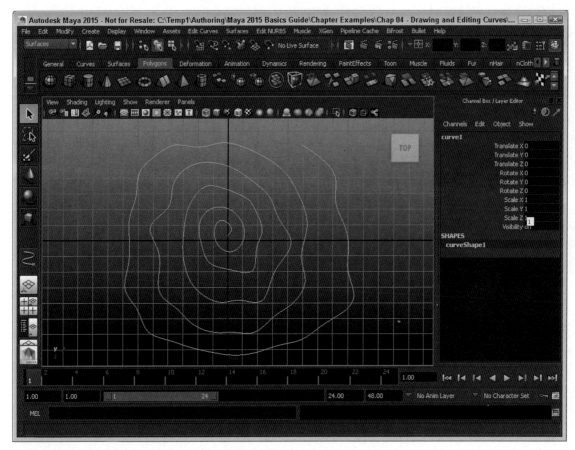

Figure 4-9
Rebuilt freehand spiral

Lesson 4.2: Edit Curve Details

There are two methods for editing curve details. One method is to use component mode and to move the CVs or edit points. This alters the curvature of the curve around the vertex. An easy way to select CVs or edit points is to right-click and select the component type that you want to move from the marking menu. Components can only be moved in Component mode, which is available on the Status Line.

Note

The Rotate and Scale tools can be used when multiple vertices are selected but they have no affect when a single vertex is selected.

Using the Curve Editing Tool

Another method for editing curves it to use the Curve Editing tool. This tool places a manipulator, shown in Figure 4-10, on the curve that lets you select any position on the curve and move it regardless of its vertices. When you first click on a curve with the Curve Editing tool, the Slide Along Curve manipulator is highlighted yellow. If you drag the Point Position handle along the curve, the entire curve moves. You can also click and drag the Point Position handle to alter the curve.

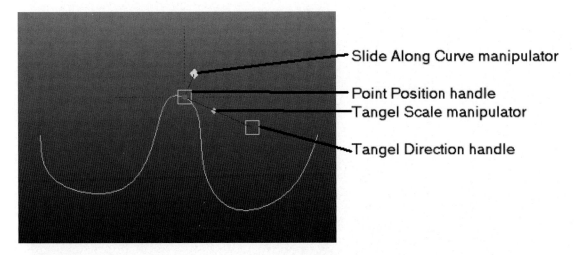

Figure 4-10
The Curve Editing manipulator

Altering Tangents

The Curve Editing tool also makes the point's Tangent Direction handle selectable. This tangent determines the direction that the curve flows into and out of the selected point. It is identified as a light blue square connected by a black line. Figure 4-11 shows the effect of dragging the Tangent Direction handle. Clicking on one of the dotted axes aligns the tangent with that axis. The Tangent Scale manipulator controls how sharp the curve is at that point.

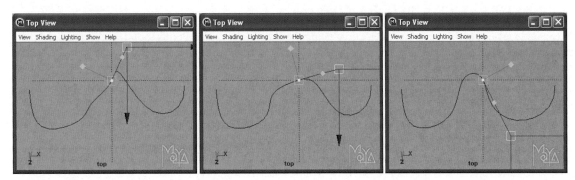

Figure 4-11
Changing tangent direction

Adding Sharp Points to a Curve

To add a sharp point to a curve, you'll have to several vertices on top of each other. Vertices may be stacked on an selected Edit Point using the Edit Curves, Insert Knot menu command. The Insert Knot Options dialog box lets you select to add another additional point on top of the selected Edit Point or in between the selected Edit Points. When two knots are added to the same point, the CV is placed on top of the Edit Point causing a sharp corner in the curve, as shown in Figure 4-12.

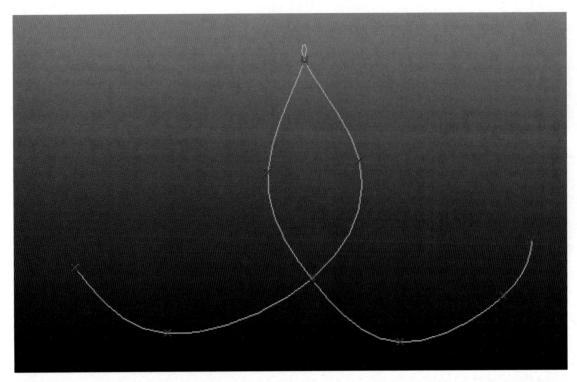

Figure 4-12
Duplicated Edit Points make sharp corners

Adding Points to the End of a Curve

You can add vertices to the end of an open curve using the Edit Curves, Add Points tool. If a curve is selected, clicking with the Add Points tool adds a new CV to the end of the curve. If an Edit Point is selected, clicking with the Add Points tool creates a new edit point.

Note

You can also add points to the end of a curve with the Edit Curves, Extend, Extend Curve menu command. The Options dialog box for Extend Curve allows you to extend the curve's start, end or both a specified distance or to a specific point's location.

Closing and Opening Curves

Closed curves are curves whose last vertex is attached to the first, making it a complete loop. A circle is a good example of a closed curve. Several 3D operations require that a curve be closed. You can automatically close an open curve using the Edit Curves, Open/Close Curves menu command. Closed curves can be made open by using the same command. Figure 4-13 shows the curve in the previous figure that has been closed with the Open/Close Curves menu command.

Note

With a closed curve, it can be difficult to select the beginning or ending CV point. The Edit Curves, Selection menu includes commands for selecting all CVs, First CV on Curve and Last CV on Curve.

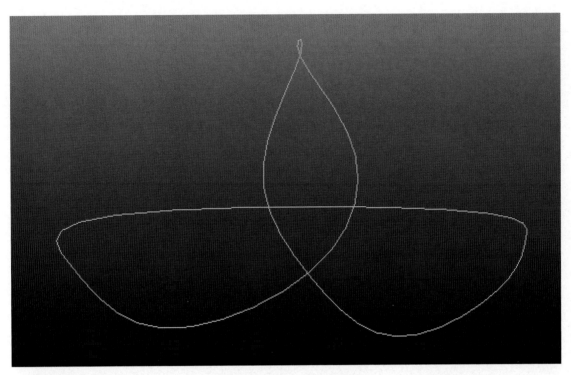

Figure 4-13
Closed curve

Lesson 4.2-Tutorial 1: Create and Edit a Star Shape

1. Click on the Model View button at the bottom of the Quick Layout Buttons and select the Top View pop-up menu command.

    The view panel changes to show the Top view.

2. Open the Options dialog box for the Create, EP Curve tool and select the 1 Linear Curve Degree option.

    The option creates straight lines.

3. In the Status Line, click on the Snap to Grids button to enable grid snapping.

4. Click in the Top panel to create 11 vertices for a star. Then press the Enter key to exit the EP Curve tool.

5. In the Status Line, click the Select by Component button and make sure the Points selection mask button is selected.

    The curve's CVs should be displayed, as shown in Figure 4-14.

6. Select the Move tool in the Toolbox and drag over the CV that you want to move and then drag it to its new location.

7. Select File, Save Scene As and save the file as **Star.mb**.

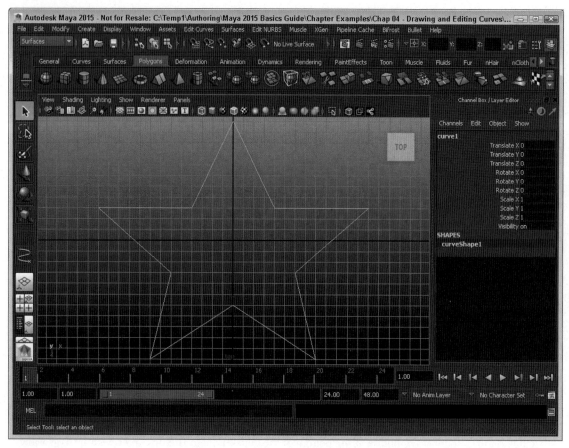

Figure 4-14
Star shape

Lesson 4.2-Tutorial 2: Use the Curve Editing Tool

1. Select the File, Open menu command and open the Tulip curve.mb file.

2. Select the Edit Curves, Curve Editing tool menu command and click on the upper-right corner of the curve.

   The Curve Editing manipulator appears, allowing you to drag the selected point to modify the curve.

3. Drag the upper-right portion of the curve outward to make it symmetrical with the left side of the curve.

4. Click with the Curve Editing tool on the center point, and then drag the highlighted yellow square with the middle mouse button to slide the manipulator to the very bottom of the center curve.

5. Click on the outer light blue square manipulator to select it and then click on the red horizontal axis to align the tangent with this axis.

   With the tangent manipulator aligned with an axis, the curve is symmetrical, as shown in Figure 4-15.

6. Select the Move tool in the Toolbox and drag over the CV that you want to move and then drag it to its new location.

7. Select File, Save Scene As and save the file as **New tulip curve.mb**.

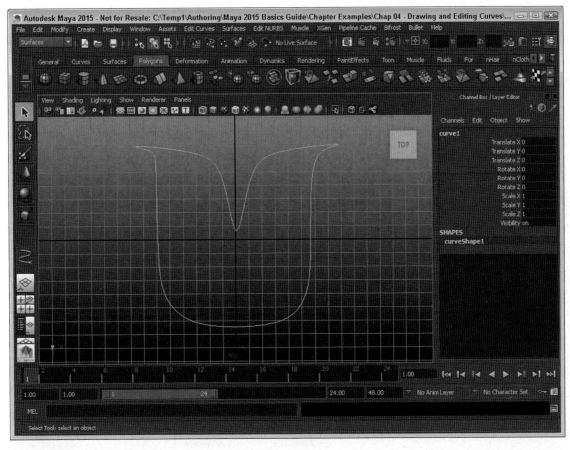

Figure 4-15
Tulip shape

Lesson 4.2-Tutorial 3: Create Sharp Points

1. Click on the Model View button at the bottom of the Quick Layout Buttons and select the Top View pop-up menu command.

    The view panel changes to show the Top view.

2. Click on the Snap to Grids button in the Status Line to enable grid snapping.

3. Select the Create, EP Curve tool and click five times to create a closed square, and then press the Enter key to exit the tool.

    The closed curve now looks like a rounded square with one sharp corner where the first and last point are located.

4. Click the Select by Component button on the Status Line to display the curve's CVs.

5. Right-click on the curve and select the Edit Points pop-up menu command to display the curve's Edit Points.

6. Hold down the Shift key and select the three rounded corner Edit Points and choose the Edit Curves, Insert Knot menu command. The select the same corner points again and apply the Edit Curves, Insert Knot menu command again.

    The second time a new knot is added to the Edit Point, the CV is added on top of the Edit Point.

7. Select all four corner Edit Points and CVs together and then click on the Scale tool button and drag from the center manipulator outward.

With the added knots, each corner becomes a sharp point, as shown in Figure 4-16.

8.   Select File, Save Scene As and save the file as **Sharp corner square.mb**.

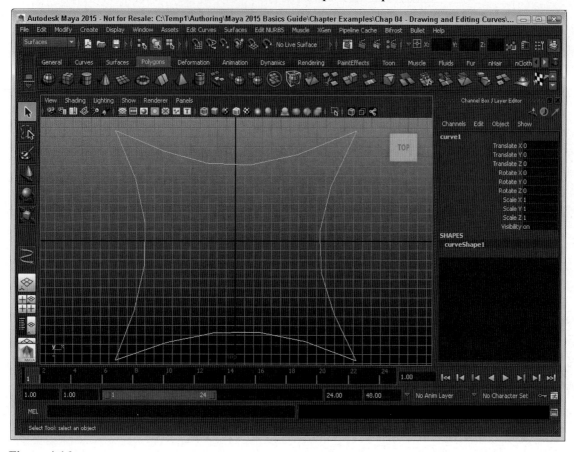

Figure 4-16
Sharp points from double knots

Lesson 4.2-Tutorial 4: Close a Curve

1.   Click on the Model View button at the bottom of the Quick Layout Buttons and select the Top View pop-up menu command.

     The view panel changes to show the Top view.

2.   Click on the Snap to Grids button in the Status Line to enable grid snapping.

3.   Select the Create, EP Curve tool and click in the view panel to create an open shape. Press the Enter key when done.

4.   With the curve selected, choose the Edit Curves, Open/Close Curves menu command.

     Another line segment is added to the curve that joins the first and last points while maintaining the curvature of the curve, as shown in Figure 4-17.

5.   Select File, Save Scene As and save the file as **Closed curve.mb**.

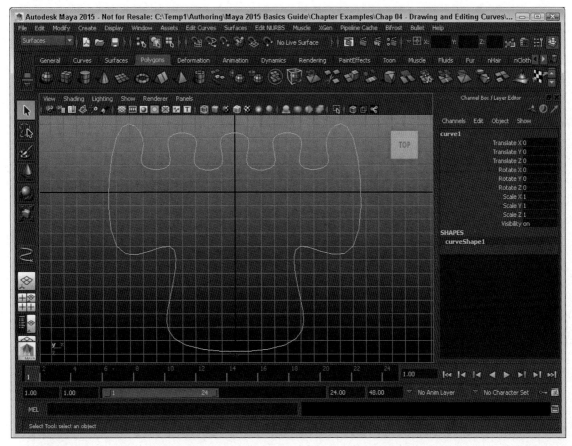

Figure 4-17
Closed curve

Lesson 4.3: Modify Curves

In addition to editing curves, the Edit Curves menu also includes a Modify Curves submenu that includes several preset commands for modifying curves in many unique ways such as Straighten, Smooth, Curl, Bend and Scale Curvature.

Locking Length

At any time during the curve modification process, you can select the Edit Curves, Modify Curves, Lock Length menu command. This command causes the length of the curve to be set and locked, so it won't change as modification commands are applied. There is also an Unlock Length command from removing the lock.

Straightening Curves

Curves drawn with the Pencil Curve tool aren't always the straightest curves, but you can straighten them easily with the Edit Curves, Modify Curves, Straighten menu command. The direction of the straightened curve follows the initial direction of the first point.

Smoothing Curves

The Edit Curves, Modify Curves, Smooth menu command gradually reduces the curvature of a curve by reducing it to a straight line. This is different than the Edit Curves, Smooth Curve menu command, which removes abrupt changes in the curve while maintaining its curvature. Figure 4-18 shows a freehand curve (on top) that has been smoothed once (middle curve) and twice (bottom curve).

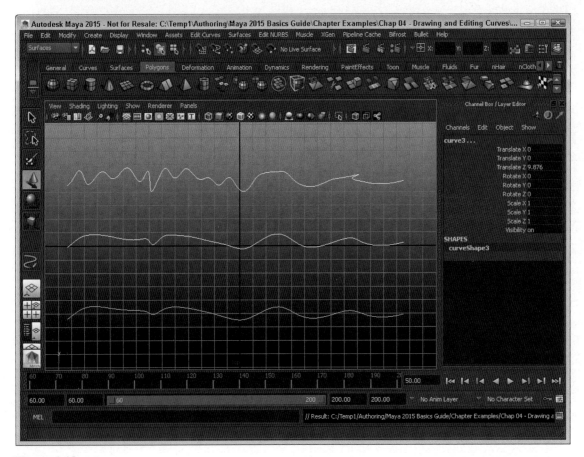

Figure 4-18
Smoothed curves

Curling and Bending Curves

The Edit Curves, Modify Curves, Curl menu command moves the CVs relative to one another to cause the curve to curl about itself creating several loops in the curve. The Edit Curves, Modify Curves, Bend menu command is similar to the Curl command, except all CVs move together to bend the entire curve together and the Curl command causes loops to appear in several places along the curve. Figure 4-19 shows the Curl (right) and Bend (left) commands multiple times to a curve.

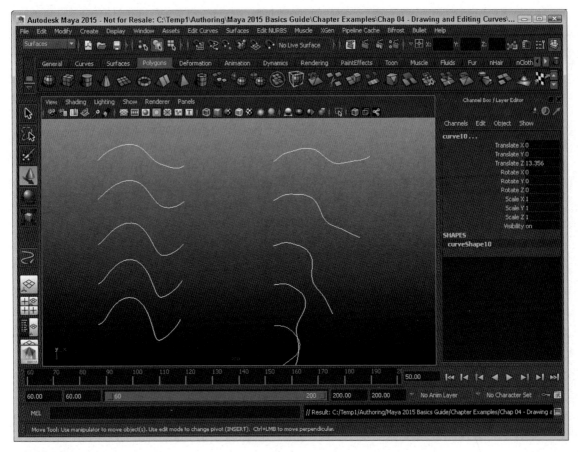

Figure 4-19
Curled and bend modified curves

Scaling Curvature

The Edit Curves, Modify Curves, Scale Curvature menu command modifies a curve by exaggerating the curve. If the curve includes lots of curves, this command scales the entire curve using the first curve it finds. A Scale Factor lower than 1.0 removes some of the curvature from the curve.

Lesson 4.3-Tutorial 1: Curl a Curve

1. Click on the Model View button at the bottom of the Quick Layout Buttons and select the Top View pop-up menu command.

    The view panel changes to show the Top view.

2. Select the Edit Curves, Pencil Curve tool menu command and draw a curve across the top of the view panel.

3. With the curve selected, choose the Edit, Duplicate menu command and drag the duplicate curve downward slightly.

4. With the duplicate curve selected, select the Edit, Duplicate with Transform menu command multiple times or press the Shift+D keyboard shortcut multiple times.

    By duplicating the curves multiple times, creates a multiple parallel aligned curves, as shown in Figure 4-20.

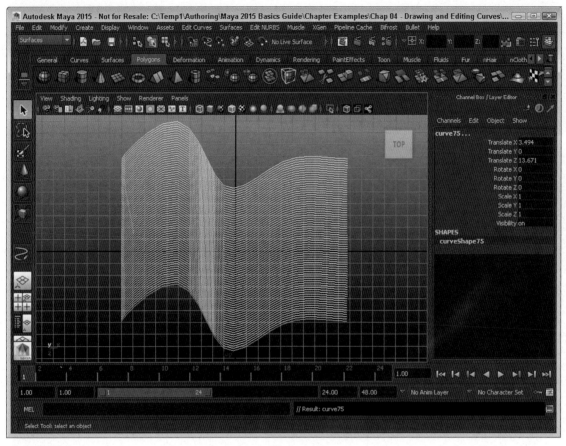

Figure 4-20
Parallel curves

5. Select the Edit, Select All menu command to select all the curves.

6. With all the curves selected, choose the Edit Curves, Modify Curves, Smooth menu command.

    The Smooth menu command removes the harshness that comes from drawing a freehand curve.

7. Select the Edit Curves, Modify Curves, Curl menu command multiple times.

    The Curl menu command adds some bumps to the parallel lines, as shown in Figure 4-21.

8. Select File, Save Scene As and save the file as **Curled curves.mb**.

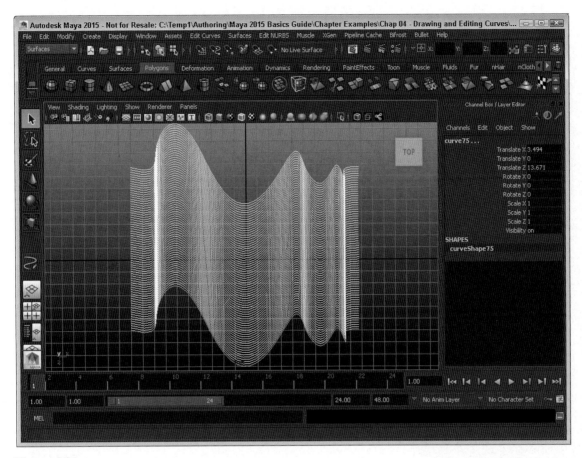

Figure 4-21
Curled curves

Lesson 4.4: Apply Curve Operators

In the Edit Curves menu, shown in Figure 4-22, you'll find several operations that can be used to edit curves in unique ways. Many of these operators require that more than one curve is selected. If you're having trouble with the curve operator, check out the Help Line for information on curve is expected to be selected.

Figure 4-22
The Edit Curves menu

Attaching Curves

If two curves are selected, you can connect the closest ends of each curve together using the Edit Curves, Attach Curves menu command. The Attach Curves Options dialog box, shown in Figure 4-23, includes options to connect or blend the two curves. The Connect option joins the curves with a minimal change in the curvature of the original curves and Blend smoothes the two curves together based on the Blend Bias value. If you keep the original curves, changes made to the original curves are also applied to the combined curve.

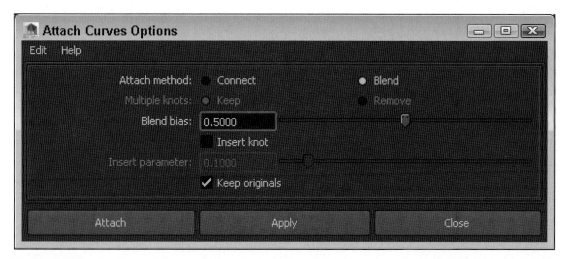

Figure 4-23
Attach Curves options

Aligning Curves

With two curves selected, you can align the curves. The Align Curves Options dialog box, shown in Figure 4-24, lets you choose to align a curve's position, tangent, or curvature. When the Position option is selected, you can select which curve to move—the first, second, or both (which moves both curves halfway). With the Tangent or Curvature options selected, you can select to modify the tangent of either curve or both.

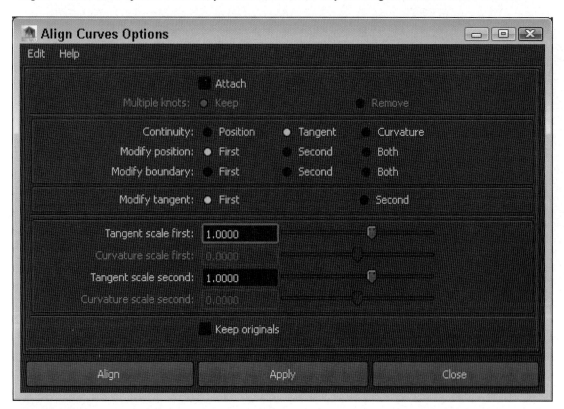

Figure 4-24
Align Curves Options

Detaching and Cutting Curves

You can split a curve into two separate curves by selecting an edit point and using the Edit Curves, Detach Curves menu command. If several edit points are selected, the curve is subdivided into a separate curve for each selected edit point. If two intersecting curves are selected, the Edit Curves, Cut Curves menu command can be used to cut the curves where they intersect. The Options dialog box includes an option to use only the last curve to cut the other curves. You can also select to keep the longest segment, all curve segments, or the segments with curve points.

Finding Curve Intersections

The Edit Curves, Intersect Curves menu command finds and marks the intersections between two curves. In the Intersect Curves Options dialog box, you can specify a tolerance that finds all curve intersections within the given Tolerance value.

Offsetting Curves

An **offset curve** is a curve that is created by moving all of the curve vertices perpendicular a given distance from their current positions. This can be done to a selected curve using the Edit Curves, Offset, Offset Curve menu command. Using the Offset Curve Options dialog box, shown in Figure 4-25, you can adjust the offset value. A Positive value offsets the curve on the right and a negative value offsets the curve on the left. The Loop Cutting and Cutting Radius options can be used to change tight details from becoming loops and sharp points.

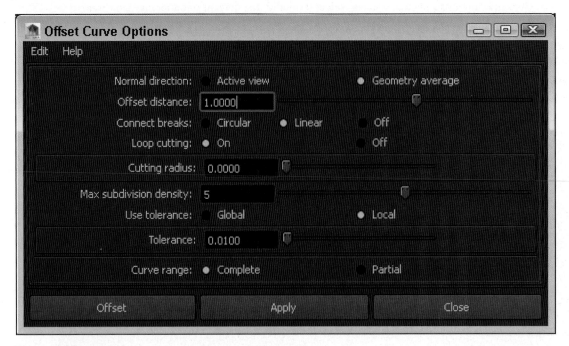

Figure 4-25
Offset Curve Options

Filleting Curves

A **fillet** rounds the intersection between two curves. For example, if two sides of square are selected, using the Edit Curves, Curve Fillet menu command creates a new curve that rounds the corner. In the Fillet Curve Options dialog box, shown in Figure 4-26, you can select to trim, join, and keep the original curve. The Radius value determines how much roundness to apply.

Figure 4-26
Fillet Curve options

Lesson 4.4-Tutorial 1: Connect Cursive Letters

1. Select the Create, Pencil Curve Tool menu command and draw a cursive letter in the Top view panel.

2. Draw another cursive letter that is separate from the first in the Top view panel.

3. Continue to draw individual cursive letters until all letters for the word are complete.

4. Select all letters and choose the Edit Curves, Smooth Curve menu command.

5. Select the first two letters and choose the Edit Curves, Attach Curves menu command.

    The curves that make up the two separate letters are combined into one.

6. Repeat Step 5 with the remaining letters. Figure 4-27 shows the results.

    The Attach Curves menu command combines all the separate curves into one, but in Figure 4-27, you can still see parts of the original curves.

7. Select File, Save Scene As and save the file as **Cursive word.mb**.

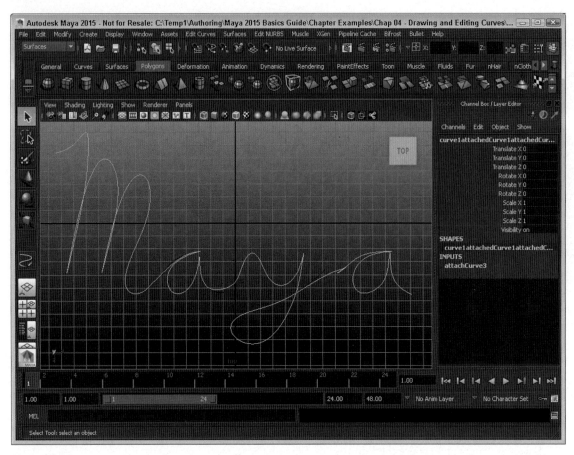

Figure 4-27
Attached cursive letters

Lesson 4.4-Tutorial 2: Align Flower Petals

1. Select the Create, Pencil Curve Tool menu command and draw several disconnected flower petals in the Top view panel.

2. Select all petals and choose the Edit Curves, Smooth Curve menu command.

3. Select a flower petal curve and with the Shift key held down, select the next adjacent flower petal curve.

4. Select the Edit Curves, Align Curves, Options dialog box menu command.

5. In the Align Curves Options dialog box, enable the Attach option and click the Apply button.

    The non-key selected flower petal curve is connected to the other.

6. Hold down the Shift key and select the next adjacent flower petal curve and press the Apply button again.

7. Repeat Step 5 until all of the flower petal curves are part of the same curve.

8. Select Edit Curves, Open/Close Curves to complete the curve.

    The petal curves are now combined and connected into a single curve, as shown in Figure 4-28.

9. Select File, Save Scene As and save the file as **Aligned flower petals.mb**.

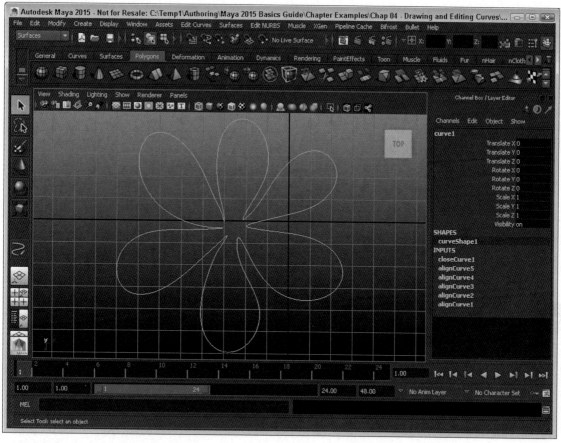

Figure 4-28
Aligned flower petal curves

Lesson 4.4-Tutorial 3: Offset Curves

1. Select the Create, Pencil Curve Tool menu command and draw a single line with several smooth bumps in the Top view panel.

2. With the curve selected, choose the Edit Curves, Offset, Offset Curve, Options menu command. Then click the Apply button.

   Another curve appears that is offset from the first.

3. In the Offset Curve Options dialog box, set the Offset Distance value to 0.5 and then click the Apply button again.

4. Repeat Step 3 with Offset Distance values of 0.25 and 0.12.

5. Select the original curve again and enter an Offset Distance value of –1 and click the Apply button.

6. Repeat Step 3 again with the Offset Distance values of –0.5, -0.25, and –0.12.

   The resulting offset curves looks like a river, as shown in Figure 4-29.

7. Select File, Save Scene As and save the file as **Offset river.mb**.

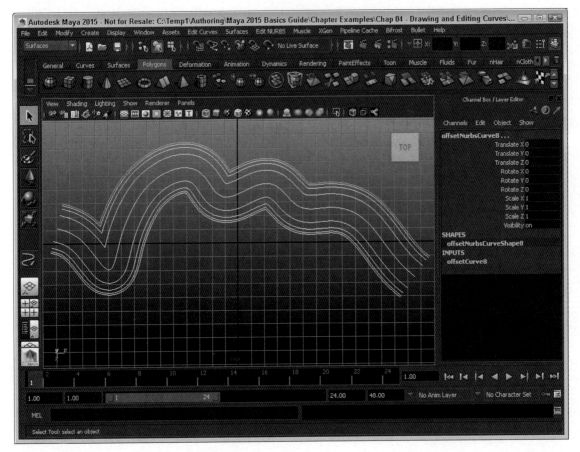

Figure 4-29
Offset river curves

Lesson 4.4-Tutorial 4: Fillet Curves

1.   Select the Create, NURBS Primitives, Square menu command to create a square in the Top view panel.

2.   Drag over one of the square corners to select two of its edges.

3.   Select the Edit Curves, Curve Fillet, Options menu command. Enable the Trim option, set the Radius value to 0.1, and click the Apply button.

   A fillet is applied to the two edges, rounding the corner of the square.

4.   Drag over another corner to select two more edges and click the Apply button again.

5.   Repeat Step 4 with the remaining two corners. Figure 4-30 shows the results.

6.   Select File, Save Scene As and save the file as **Rounded square.mb**.

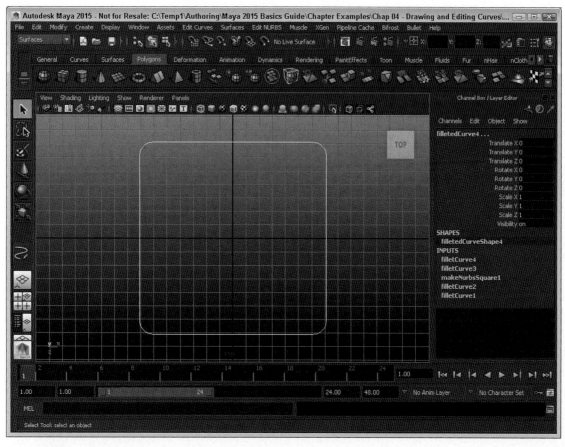

Figure 4-30
A rounded square

Lesson 4.5: Create Simple Surfaces from Curves

The Surfaces menu, shown in Figure 4-31, includes many options for turning a selected curve into a surface. For all surfaces, you can select in the Options dialog box what the geometry is output as. The options include NURBS, Polygons, Subdivision Surface, or Bezier curves.

Figure 4-31
The Surfaces menu

Revolving a Curve

A curve can be revolved around an axis to form a circularly symmetrical object using the Surfaces, Revolve menu command. The Revolve Options dialog box, shown in Figure 4-32, can be used to select which axis is used for the revolution. You can also specify a start and end sweep angle to revolve only partially. A revolved curve can be used to create a baseball bat, a wine glass, or any symmetrically round object.

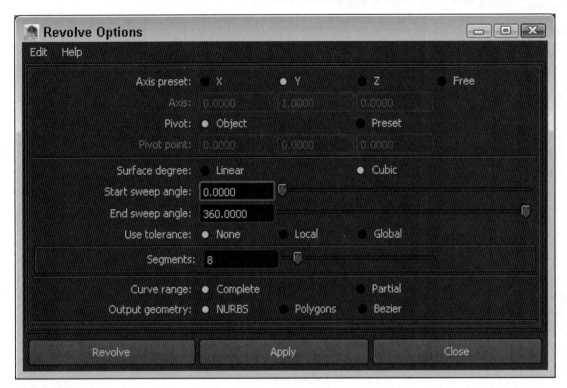

Figure 4-32
Revolve options

Lofting a Set of Curves

If the symmetrically round shape you're trying to create has differently shaped cross sections, you can create these using a **loft** operation. The Surfaces, Loft menu command only works if two or more curves are selected. Lines that combine the curves to create a surface are followed in the order they were created.

Caution

If the curve direction between different lofted cross sections is switched, the resulting lofted surface is twisted. You can fix this by enabling the Auto Reverse option in the Options dialog box or with the Edit Curves, Reverse Curve Direction menu command.

Creating Planar Curves

If you have several intersecting curves that form a closed area or a single closed curve, you can turn them into a planar surface with the Surfaces, Planar menu command.

Creating a Surface from Boundary Curves

Planar surfaces are created from curves that are co-planar, but curves that aren't in the same plane can also be used to create a surface using the Surfaces, Boundary menu command. The curves that define the surface boundary can be ordered automatically or as selected. If the Common End Points option is set to Required, the corner points between curves need to be positioned together, but if the Optional option is selected, the corner points don't need to match.

Extruding Curves

Extruded curves move a cross section curve perpendicular to the plane it resides in to create a surface. This movement can be in a specified direction a given amount, as shown in Figure 4-33. The extrusion could also be along a profile while maintaining the cross section's orientation (with the Flat option) or along a profile where the cross section is always perpendicular to the profile curve (with the Tube option). You can also specify rotation and scale values, which indicate the amount the cross section is rotated or scaled as it is extruded. To create an extrude, select the cross section curve first and then the path curve and then select Surfaces, Extrude.

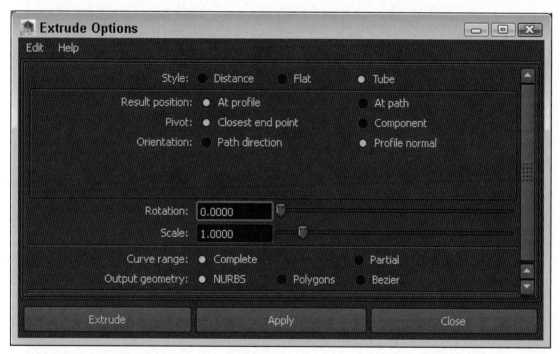

Figure 4-33
Extrude options

Using the Birail Tools

A *birail* sweeps a curve (rail1) along a profile to a second curve (rail2). The Surfaces, Birail menu includes three options: Birail 1 Tool, Birail 2 Tool, and Birail 3+ Tool. The difference between them is the number of profile curves that each tool can use. To create a birail surface, create two rail curves and at least one profile curve, select the profile curve and select the Birail tool. The Help Line instructs you to then choose the first rail curve followed by the second rail curve.

Caution

    The profile and rail curves must intersect at their
    corner points in order for the birail operation to
    work. Use the Snap Points feature in the Status Line to
    ensure that the points intersect.

Lesson 4.5-Tutorial 1: Revolve a Baseball Bat

1. Click on the Model View button at the bottom of the Toolbox and select Top View from the pop-up menu.

   The view panel changes to show the Top view.

2. Select Create, CV Curve Tool and click in the Top panel to create the profile of baseball bat that extends horizontally.

3. After initially placing the CVs for the curve, click on the Select by Component button (or press F8) in the Status Line and click the Move tool in the Toolbox and move the CVs to where you want them.

4. After moving the CVs, click the Select by Object button in the Status Line. Then, open the Options dialog box for the Surfaces, Revolve menu command, select the X Axis, and click the Apply button. The resulting bat is shown in Figure 4-34.

5. Select File, Save Scene As and save the file as **Revolved baseball bat.mb**.

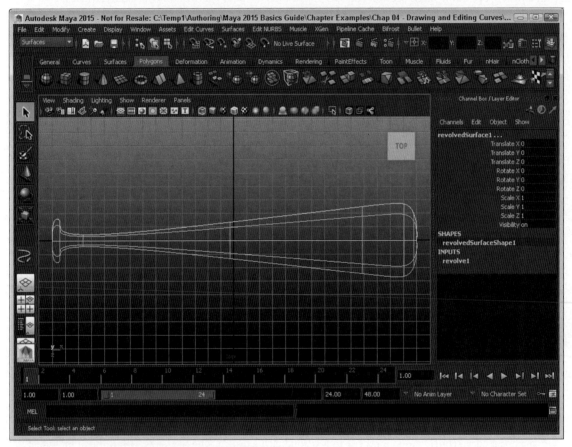

Figure 4-34
Revolved baseball bat

Lesson 4.5-Tutorial 2: Loft a Banana

1. Click on the Four View button from the Quick Layout buttons.

2. Select Create, NURBS Primitive, Circle menu command.

   A single circle appears in the view panel at the origin.

3. Select Edit, Duplicate to create a duplicate circle on top of the existing one.

4. Select the Move tool in the Toolbox and drag the duplicated circle in the Front panel upward and slightly to the left.

5. With the duplicated circle still selected, click on the Scale tool in the Toolbox and drag from the center of the circle outward until the circle is about four times the size of the original circle.

6. Select the original circle at the origin and select Edit, Duplicate to create another copy.

7. With the Move tool, drag this second duplicate circle upward twice as far as the first duplicated circle.

8. With the Shift key held down, click on the circles in order from the bottom to the top.

9. Select the Surfaces, Loft menu command.

   All three circles are joined into together into a surface, as shown in Figure 4-35.

10. Select File, Save Scene As and save the file as **Lofted banana.mb**.

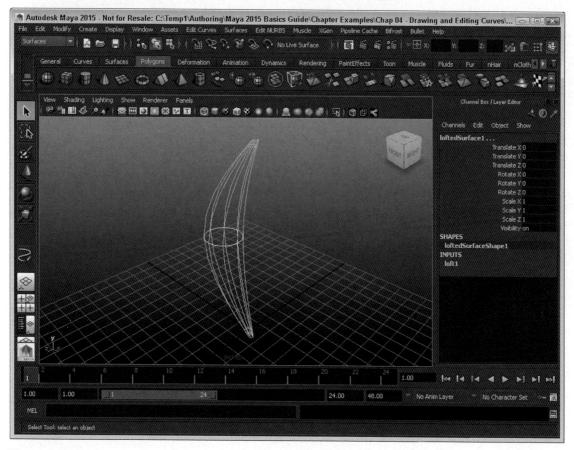

Figure 4-35
The lofted banana

Lesson 4.5-Tutorial 3: Create a Planar Surface

1. Click on the Model View button from the Quick Layout buttons and select the Top View from the pop-up menu.

2. Select the Create, EP Curve Tool menu command. Double-click on the tool in the Toolbox and in the Tool Settings panel that opens, set the Curve Degree to 1 Linear.

3. Enable the Snap to Grids button in the Status Line.

4. Click in the Top view panel to create the outline of a shirt and press the Enter key when finished.

5. With the shirt curve selected, choose the Surfaces, Planar menu command.

6. Press the 5 key to see the shaded surface.

   The shirt curve is filled in, becoming a surface, as shown in Figure 4-36.

7. Select File, Save Scene As and save the file as **Planar shirt.mb**.

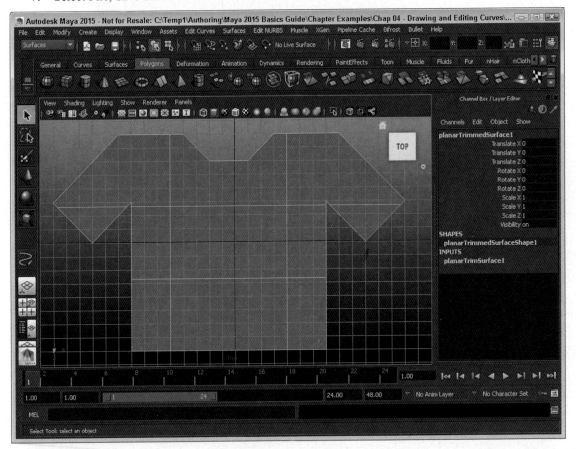

Figure 4-36
The planar shirt

Lesson 4.5-Tutorial 4: Extrude a Circle

1. Click on the Four View button from the Quick Layout buttons.

2. Select the Create, NURBS Primitive, Circle menu command.

3. Select the Scale tool and drag the center handle in the Top view panel to increase the circle's size to fill the view panel.

4. Select the Rotate tool in the Toolbox and drag the red X-axis manipulator to rotate the duplicated circle in the Top view panel 90 degrees.

5. Select Edit, Duplicate to create a duplicate circle on top of the existing one.

6. Select the Rotate tool from the Toolbox and drag the blue Z-axis manipulator to rotate the duplicated circle in the Side view panel 90 degrees.

7. Drag over both circles to select them both, and then choose Surfaces, Extrude, Options to open the Extrude Options dialog box.

8. Select the Tube, At Path, Component, and Profile Normal options and set the Scale value to 2.0., and then click the Extrude button.

9. Select the Perspective view panel and press the 5 key to see the shaded surface.

   The circle that is the key object is swept around the path of the other circle with the scale gradually increasing to double its size. Figure 4-37 shows the interesting resulting surface.

10. Select File, Save Scene As and save the file as **Extruded circle.mb**.

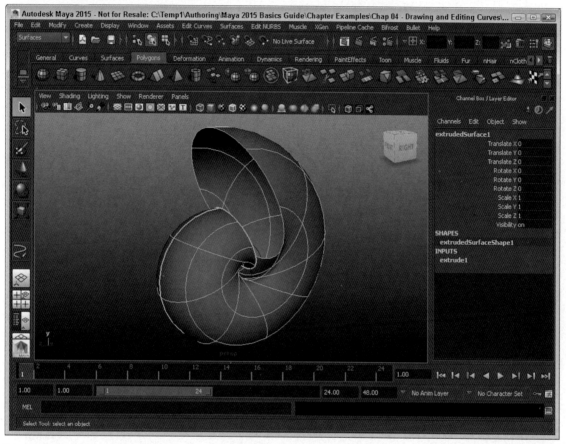

Figure 4-37
Extruded scaled circle

Lesson 4.5-Tutorial 5: Create a Birail Surface

1. Click on the Four View button from the Quick Layout buttons.

2. Select the Create, NURBS Primitive, Square menu command.

   A single square made from four straight-line curves appears in the Top view panel at the origin.

3. Select the Scale tool and drag on the center handle to increase the size of the square to fill the view panel.

4. Click on the Select by Component Type button in the Status Line (or press the F8 key).

5. Drag over the middle two CVs in the top and bottom lines.

6. Select the Move tool and drag the CVs upward in the Front view panel.

7. Drag over the middle two CVs in the left and right lines in the Top view panel.

8. Drag downward in the Front view panel.

The connected curves are displaced so that the adjacent lines curve away from each other.

9. Click away from all the curves to deselect them and click on the Select by Object Type button in the Status Line.

10. Select the Surfaces, Birail, Birail 2 Tool menu command.

The Help Line displays the order in which the curves need to be clicked.

11. Drag over the left and right lines of the square in the Top view. Then drag over the top and bottom lines in the Top view panel.

12. Press the 3 key to see the new NURBS surface at a higher resolution.

The resulting surface, shown in Figure 4-38, runs along the rails between the profile curves.

13. Select File, Save Scene As and save the file as **Birail surface.mb**.

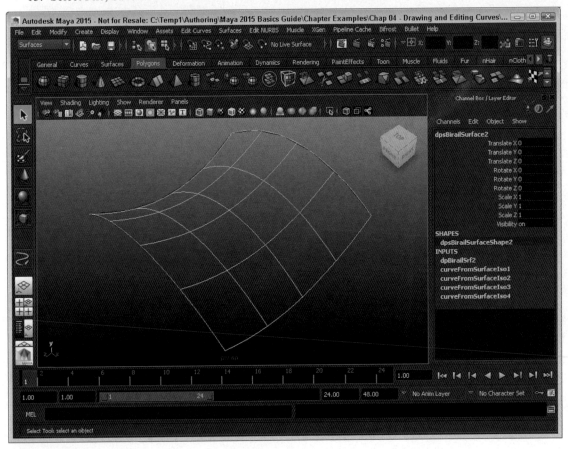

Figure 4-38
The birail surface

Lesson 4.6: Create Text

Simple text can be created as curves using the Create, Text menu command. The Text Curves Options dialog box, shown in Figure 4-39, includes a field in which you can enter some text. You can also select the font to use from a list of available system fonts. The Type options include Curves, Trim, and Poly. The Trim option creates a trimmed NURBS surface and the Poly option creates a polygon surface, both of which can be rendered. The text appears in the view panel starting at the grid's origin.

Figure 4-39
Text Curves Options

Creating a Beveled Surface

The Surfaces, Bevel menu command creates a **beveled** extruded surface from a selected curve. Using the Bevel Options dialog box, shown in Figure 4-40, you can select to bevel the top side, bottom side, or both. You can also specify the bevel width and depth and the extrude height. The bevel corners can be straight or circular arcs and the cap edge can be convex, concave, or straight. The Surfaces menu also includes a Bevel Plus command, which offers many more options, including the ability to add caps and to choose the bevel style.

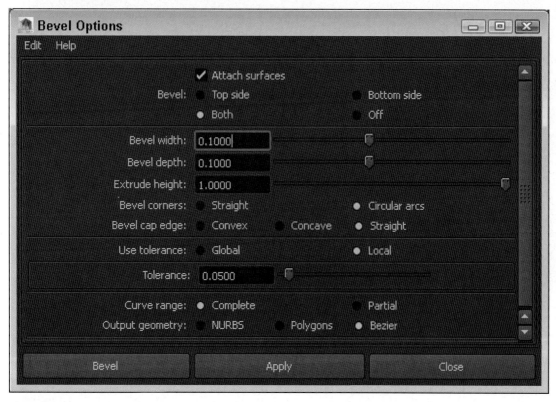

Figure 4-40
Bevel options

Lesson 4.6-Tutorial 1: Create and Bevel Text

1. Click on the Four View button from the Quick Layout buttons.

2. Open the Options dialog box for the Create, Text menu command. Type the text in the Text field and set the Type setting to Curves. Then click the Apply button.

   The entered text appears in the view panel as curves.

3. With the first letter selected, open the Options dialog box for the Surfaces, Bevel menu command. Select Both with an Bevel Width and Depth settings of 0.5 and an Extrude Height setting of 1.0, and then click the Apply button.

4. Select the second letter and click the Apply button again, and then repeat for all the remaining letters and the letter interiors.

   The text curves are extruded and beveled, as shown in Figure 4-41.

5. Select File, Save Scene As and save the file as **Beveled text.mb**.

Figure 4-41
Beveled text

Lesson 4.6-Tutorial 2: Create a Sign

1. Click on the Model View button and select Top View.

2. Select the Create, NURBS Primitives, Circle menu command. Select the Scale tool and drag on the center handle.

   A circle is created and increases in size.

3. Select the circle curve. Select the Edit Curves, Offset, Offset Curve menu command. Set the Distance value in the Channel Box for the Input node to 2.0.

   The circle is duplicated and offset.

4. Select the Create, EP Curve Tool menu command. Click outside the outer circle in the upper-right corner and again in the lower-left corner to create a curve that runs diagonally through the circles. Press the Enter key to complete the curve.

5. Select the Edit, Duplicate menu command. Select the Move tool and drag the center handle.

   The diagonal line is duplicated and offset.

6. Select two intersecting curves, the diagonal lines and the circles. Select the Edit Curves, Intersect Curves menu command. Select the curve you want to cut, the diagonal line. Hold down the Shift key and select the intersecting curve. Select the Edit Curves, Cut Curves menu command. Select the portion of the curve to delete and press the Delete key.

7. Select the inner portions of the sign and choose the Edit Curves, Attach Curves, Option menu command. In the Attach Curves Options dialog box, choose the Connect option and click the Apply button.

   The ends of both lines are trimmed.

8. Select the curve you want to extrude. Select the Surfaces, Extrude, Options menu command. Select the Distance option, choose the Specify option with the Y-axis and enter an Extrude Length value. Click the Extrude button.

   The selected curves are extruded.

9. Select the Create, Text, Options menu command. Enter the text you want to create. Select a font to use. Click the Create button.

   Text is added to the scene.

10. Select the curves to use for the planar surface. Select the Surfaces, Planar menu command.

    The resulting sign is shown in Figure 4-42.

11. Select File, Save Scene As and save the file as **No 2D sign.mb**.

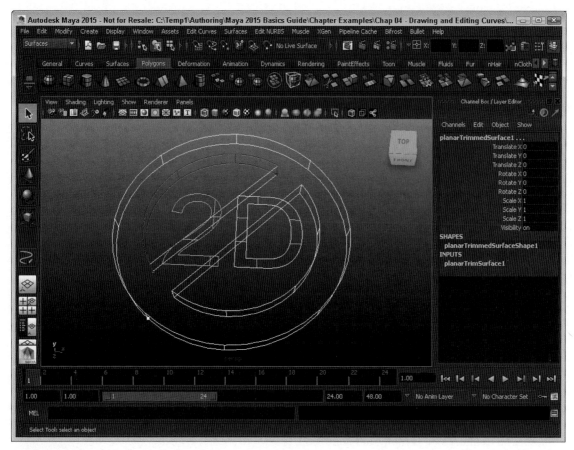

Figure 4-42
A simple sign created using curves and text

Chapter Summary

This chapter covers the details of creating and working with curves. 2D curves are an essential modeling construct and are often used to create more complex 3D surfaces. The Create menu includes several ways to draw curves including the CV, EP, Pencil and Arc tools. The Edit Curves menu includes many curve operations for changing the shape of the selected curve. You can also edit a curve by moving its components. The Surfaces menu includes commands for extruding, revolving, and other commands for creating 3D surfaces from a simple 2D curve. The Text operation is a unique curve operation that lets you create text using a specific font and characters.

What You Have Learned

In this chapter, you learned

* How to create primitive shapes such as circles and squares.

* How to create arcs, smooth curves, freehand curves, and straight lines.

* How to smooth curves.

* How to use the Curve Editing tool.

* How to change the curve shape by altering its tangents.

* How to add points to a curve.

* How to open and close curves.

* How to straighten, curve, smooth, and bend curves.

* How to attach, detach, align, and cut curves.

* How to find curve intersections.

* How to offset and filet a selected curve.

* How to create a 3D surface from a curve by revolving, lofting, and extruding curves.

* How to use the birail tools.

* How to create and bevel text.

Key Terms From This Chapter

* **CV.** Control Vertex. A curve component that defines the curvature of the curve.

* **Hull.** A set of straight lines that connects a curve's CV points.

* **CV curve.** A curve created by placing CV points.

* **EP curve.** A curve created by placing points that the curve passes through.

* **Curve degree.** The amount of curve applied to a line.

* **Linear curve.** A curve with a degree of 1, resulting in straight lines.

* **Curve Editing tool.** A tool used to edit the curvature of a curve using handles attached to the curve.

* **Tangent.** A handle that determines the direction and severity of the curvature of a curve.

* **Offset curve.** A duplicated curve that is moved parallel to the selected curve.

* **Filleting.** The process of smoothing a corner of a curve.

* **Revolving.** The process of creating a surface by rotating a curve about an axis.

* **Lofting.** The process of creating a surface by connecting several cross sections together.

* **Extruding.** The process of creating a surface by moving the curve perpendicular to itself.

* **Beveling.** The process of smoothing a surface by adding a face to the surface edges.

Chapter 5
Working with NURBS Surfaces

IN THIS CHAPTER

NURBS is an acronym for *Non-Uniform Rational B-Spline*. These splines are mathematically defined lines that you can manipulate to form unique shapes. A *NURBS surface* is a solid object created from NURBS curves. NURBS surfaces are useful for modeling organic objects like flowers and trees where the surfaces flow into one another.

NURBS surfaces, like NURBS curves, can be edited by moving their control vertices (CVs). You can also display hulls for the NURBS surfaces to see how the various CVs are connected. Using the right-click marking menu, you can select to see all the components that make up a NURBS surface.

Another common component for NURBS surfaces are **isoparametric curves** (isoparms, for short). *Isoparms* are representative lines that show the object surface. The direction of an isomparm is defined using the U and V coordinate system with U-direction isoparms running horizontally and V-direction isoparms running vertically.

At the Rough resolution (enabled by pressing the 1 key) the number of isoparms is greatly reduced, but at the Fine resolution (enabled by pressing the 3 key), many additional isoparms are shown. New isoparms can be created easily by dragging from an existing isoparm to mark the location of the new isoparm. Marked isoparms can be made permanent using the Edit NURBS, Insert Isoparms menu command.

The area between the Isoparms is called a *patch*. Each patch face has two sides. The side that is rendered is determined by the direction of a hidden vector that is called the *normal*. It extends perpendicular to the patch face.

NURBS surfaces can be created using the Create, NURBS Primitives menu or by using one of the Surfaces menu commands on a NURBS curve. Once the NURBS surface is created you can use the operations found in the Edit NURBS menu to work with it.

Some of the operations found in the Edit NURBS menu let you attach and detach, align, open and close, extend, offset and fillet surfaces. These operations all require that one or more surfaces are selected before they can be used. The Help Line explains exactly what must be selected to use an operation.

The Edit NURBS menu also includes several tools and commands that may be used to edit NURBS surfaces including the **Surface Editing tool**, the Sculpt Geometry tool, and the Break and Smooth Tangent commands. The Surface Editing tool lets you click on a surface location and move it with a manipulator or change its tangent. The Sculpt Geometry tool lets you push, pull, and smooth a surface using an interactively changeable brush. Breaking tangents lets you create hard edges on NURBS surfaces.

Trimming is the process of adding holes to NURBS surfaces. This is accomplished by marking the area to trim with a NURBS curve. These curves must be attached to the surface by projecting it onto the surface, marking an intersection between another surface or by drawing on a live object.

Booleans offer a way to combine, subtract, and extract an intersecting volume between two overlapping NURBS surfaces.

Stitching NURBS surfaces together attaches the surfaces so that moving one causes the other to move with it. Maya lets you stitch object by points, edges or using a Global Stitch command.

You can also convert between the various modeling types using the Modify, Convert menu. This menu allows you convert between NURBS, polygons, and subdivision surfaces.

Lesson 5.1: Learn the NURBS Primitives

The simplest NURBS surfaces are the primitive objects that can be created using the Create, NURBS Primitives menu. The NURBS primitives include the sphere, cube, cylinder, cone, plane, and torus (which is shaped like a doughnut), as shown in Figure 5-1. When selected, the primitive object appears at the grid's origin.

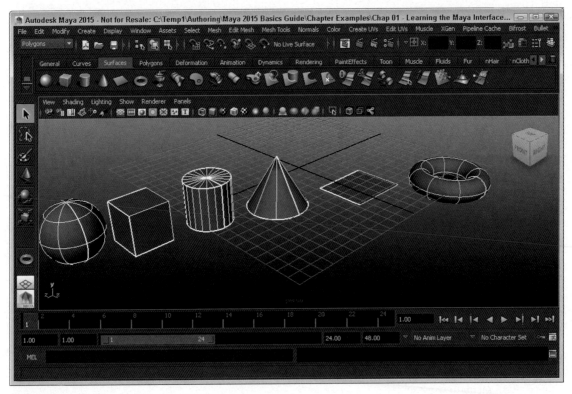

Figure 5-1
NURBS primitives

Creating Spheres and Cubes

For the NURBS sphere primitive, you can select the axis about which the sphere is oriented. You can also change the start and end sweep angle values to create a partial sphere, as shown in Figure 5-2 using the Sphere Options dialog box. The Radius value determines the size of the sphere and the number of sections and spans define the number of isoparms that are shown in the sphere. The cube NURBS primitive includes similar orientation axis. You can also specify the cube's width, length, and height values and the U and V Patches options set the number of isoparms.

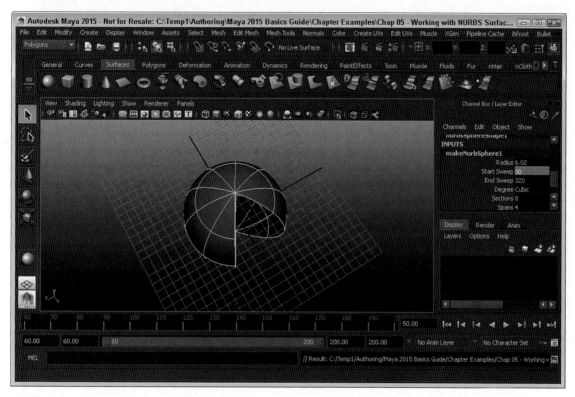

Figure 5-2
Partial Sweep NURBS primitives

Creating Cylinders and Cones

The cylinder and cone NURBS primitives include Start and End Sweep Angles settings for creating partial objects. You can also enter radius and height values and whether the object includes a cap on the top, bottom, or both. The number of sections and spans determines the number of patches that make up the object.

Creating a Plane and a Torus

For plane NURBS primitives, you can set the width and length values. For the torus NURBS primitive, you can set start and end sweep angle values, as well as radius and minor radius values.

Inserting Isoparms

The number of isoparms is initially set by the number of segments and spans, but you can add more patches to a NURBS primitive using the Edit NURBS, Insert Isoparms menu command. If you select Isoparm display mode from the marking menu, you can drag from an existing isoparm to the location where you want the new isoparm to be located. This location is marked with a yellow dashed line, shown in Figure 5-3. If you apply the Insert Isoparms menu command with the At Selection option enabled, a new isoparm is created. The Between Selections option lets you create new isoparms for the U or V direction for the entire object.

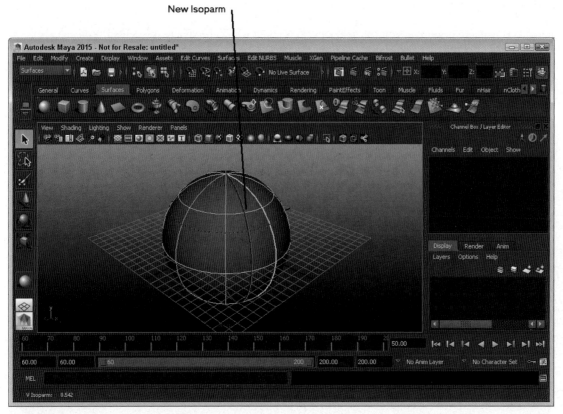

Figure 5-3
Inserted isoparm

Lesson 5.1-Tutorial 1: Create a Candle from Primitives

1. Click on the Four Views button in the Quick Layout Buttons.

2. Create a cylinder object using the Create, NURBS Primitives, Cylinder menu command.

3. Click on the Scale tool and drag the green Y-axis manipulator to increase the cylinder's height.

4. Create another cylinder object using the Create, NURBS Primitives, Cylinder menu command.

5. Drag the center handle in the Top view with the Scale tool to reduce the diameter of the cylinder, and then drag on the green Y-axis manipulator upward to lengthen the cylinder. Select the Move tool and drag the green Y-axis manipulator to move the small cylinder to the top of the larger cylinder.

    The larger cylinder is for the candle and the smaller cylinder is the wick.

6. Create another cylinder object using the Create, NURBS Primitives, Cylinder menu command.

7. Drag the center handle in the Top view with the Scale tool to increase the diameter of the cylinder, and then drag on the green Y-axis manipulator downward to reduce the cylinder's height. Select the Move tool and drag the green Y-axis manipulator to move the large flat cylinder to the base of the candle.

8. Create a sphere object using the Create, NURBS Primitives, Sphere menu command.

9. Select the Move tool and drag the sphere upward in the Front view to the top of the candle wick.

10. Click on the Select by Component button in the Status Line.

11. Drag over all the top CV points in the Front view and move them upward in the Front view using the green Y-axis manipulator.

12. Select the very top CV point on the sphere and drag it up and to the left in the Front view.

   The edited sphere looks like a simple candle flame, as shown in Figure 5-4.

13. Select File, Save Scene As and save the file as **Primitive candle.mb**.

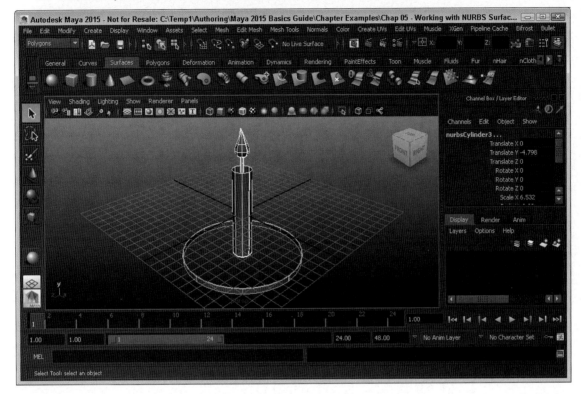

Figure 5-4
Primitive candle

Lesson 5.1-Tutorial 2: Add Isoparms

1. Create a cone object using the Create, NURBS Primitives, Cone menu command.

2. Right-click on the cone object and select Isoparms from the pop-up marking menu.

3. Then, click and drag from the bottom circle upward about halfway up the cone.

   A yellow dotted line appears where the new isoparm is located.

4. Select Edit NURBS, Insert Isoparms.

   A new isoparm is added to the object.

5. Right-click on the cone object and select Isoparms from the pop-up marking menu again.

6. Drag over the bottom circle and the new isoparm to select them both.

   The isoparms turn yellow when selected.

7. Select Edit NURBS, Insert Isoparms, Options.

8. Select the Between Selections option and set the # Isoparms to Insert value to 5. Then click the Insert button.

   Five new isoparms are created and equally spaced between the two selected isoparms, as shown in Figure 5-5.

9. Select File, Save Scene As and save the file as **New isoparms.mb**.

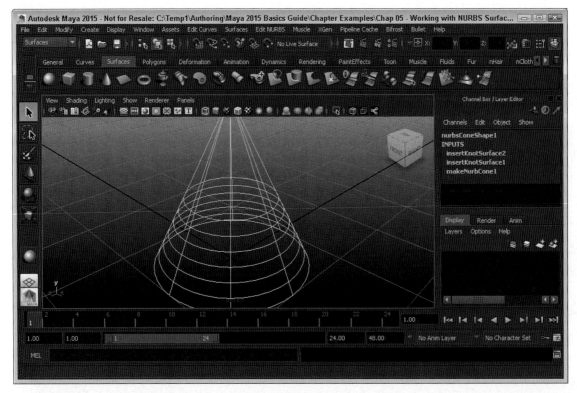

Figure 5-5
New isoparms

Lesson 5.2: Edit NURBS Surfaces

Once a NURBS surface is created, you can edit its surface directly by selecting and transforming its components. Transforming the object's CVs edits the basic shape of these primitives. To see an object's CVs, click the Select by Component Type button in the Status Line (or press the F8 key); select the primitive's CVs by right-clicking on the object and selecting Control Vertices from the marking menu. The selected CVs can then be transformed using the Move, Rotate, and Scale tools.

Selecting Components

NURBS surfaces can have many times the number of CVs as a NURBS curve, as shown in Figure 5-6, which can make it tricky to select the exact CVs you want. To help resolve this problem, the Edit NURBS menu includes a Selection menu. The Selection menu includes the Grow CV Selection, Shrink CV Selection, Select CV Selection Boundary, and Select Surface Border commands. These commands can really be helpful as you select NURBS surface components to edit.

Tip

> With a CV selected, you can use the arrow keys to select the adjacent CV.

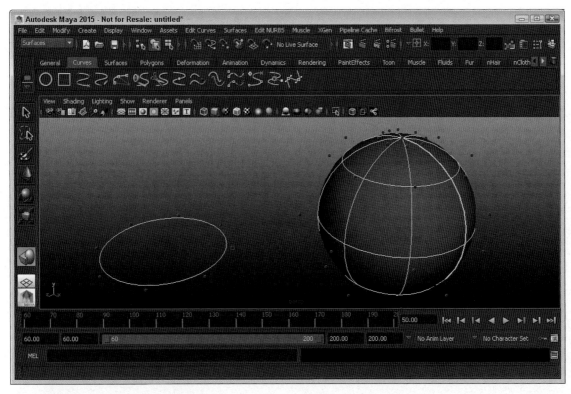

Figure 5-6
Circle CVs vs. Sphere CVs

Using the Surface Editing Tool

With the Edit NURBS, Surface Editing, Surface Editing tool selected, you can click on any point of the surface and a set of manipulators appears (as shown in Figure 5-7) that let you move the selected point. Dragging the Point Position handle moves the point and dragging the Slide Along Curve manipulator with the middle mouse button slides the Point Position handle along the isoparm. Clicking the Tangent Direction toggle switches between a U-align, V-align, and normal-aligned tangent. The Tangent Direction handle can also be manipulated to change the surface point's tangent. Clicking on one of the dotted axis lines aligns the tangent to that axis.

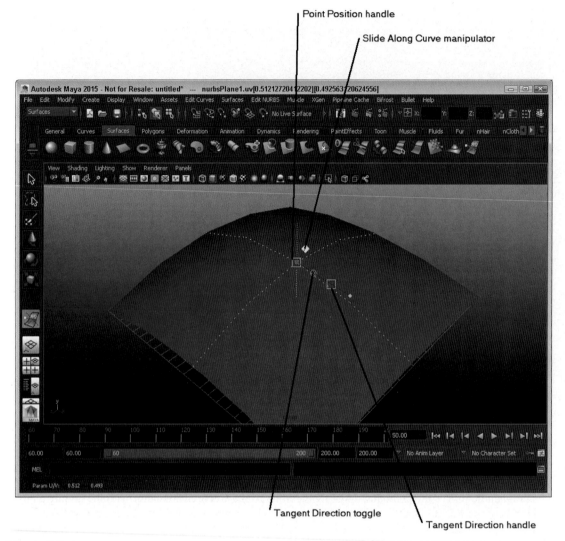

Point Position handle

Slide Along Curve manipulator

Tangent Direction toggle

Tangent Direction handle

Figure 5-7
Surface Editing tool

Using the Sculpt Geometry Tool

The Sculpt Geometry tool, available in the Edit NURBS menu, lets you push, pull, smooth, and erase surface CVs. Using the Tool Settings dialog box, shown in Figure 5-8, you can select the radius, opacity, and shape of the sculpt tool. When selected, a red manipulator shows you the size of the brush radius and an arrow pointing away from the radial circle shows how far the brush moves the surface. You can then paint on the surface of an object to deform the surface.

Tip

You can interactively change the brush radius by dragging with the b key held down; you can change the brush distance by dragging with the m key held down.

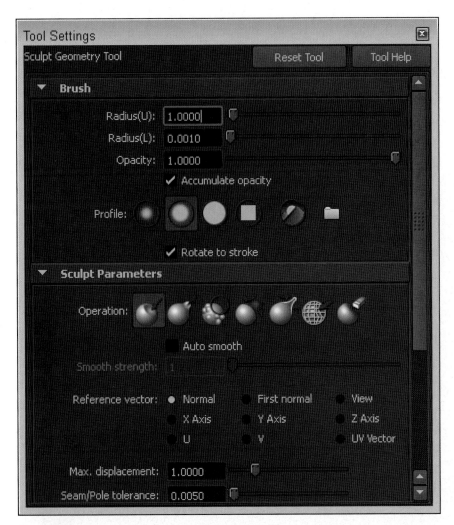

Figure 5-8
Sculpt Geometry tool options

Simplifying Surfaces

The Edit NURBS, Rebuild Surfaces menu command reduces the complexity of a surface. This option offers several different rebuild options and you can rebuild only the U or V direction.

Breaking and Smoothing Tangents

By default, NURBS surfaces are smooth across their surface because the tangent points between all the CVs are aligned, but if you want to create a hard edge, you can break the tangent for a selected isoparm using the Edit NURBS, Surface Editing, Break Tangents menu command. The Edit NURBS, Surface Editing, Smooth Tangents menu command may be used to smooth an isoparm that has been broken.

Lesson 5.2-Tutorial 1: Edit NURBS Components

1. Create a plane object using the Create, NURBS Primitives, Plane menu command.

2. Click on the Select by Component Type button in the Status Line (or press the F8 key).

3. Select the Move tool, hold down the Shift key and select the CVs at opposite corners of the plane object.

4. Then drag the two CVs upward using the green Y-axis manipulator.

    The surface of the plane object bends to follow the CVs' movements.

5. Hold down the Shift key and select the other two opposite corner CVs.

6. Drag these two CVs downward using the green Y-axis manipulator.

7. Press the 5 key to see this surface shaded, as shown in Figure 5-9.

8. Select File, Save Scene As and save the file as **Bent plane object.mb**.

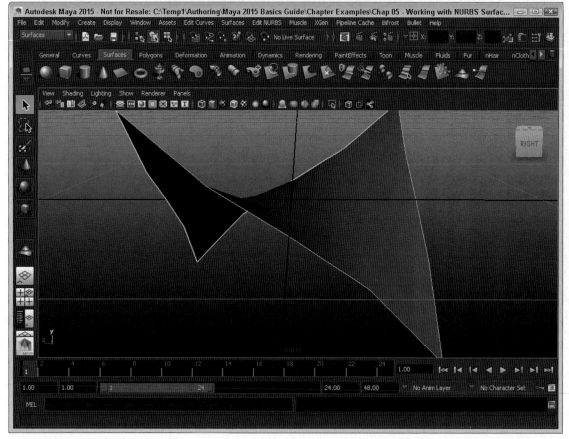

Figure 5-9
Bent plane object

Lesson 5.2-Tutorial 2: Use the Surface Editing Tool

1. Create a sphere object using the Create, NURBS Primitives, Sphere menu command.

2. Click on the Model View button from the Quick Layout buttons and select the Top View command from the pop-up menu.

3. Select the Edit NURBS, Surface Editing, Surface Editing Tool menu command.

4. Click on the left edge of the sphere and drag the Point Position handle to the left to elongate the sphere.

5. Then select and drag the Tangent Distance handle until it is on top of the Point Position handle.

6. Repeat Steps 4 and 5 for the right side of the sphere.

7. Click the Model View button again and select the Perspective view. Then press the 5 key to see the object shaded.

The sphere object looks like a football, as shown in Figure 5-10.

8. Select File, Save Scene As and save the file as **Football.mb**.

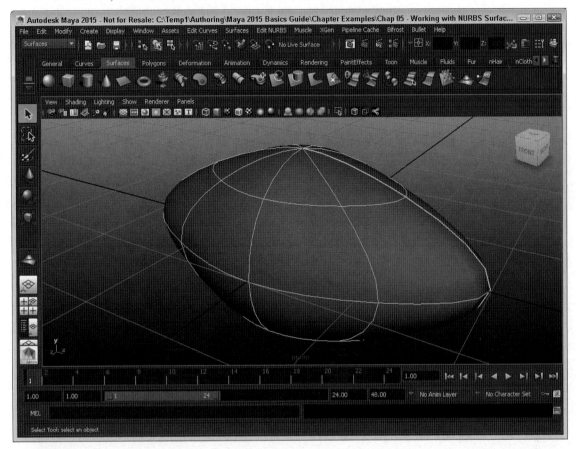

Figure 5-10
A football object

Lesson 5.2-Tutorial 3: Use the Sculpt Geometry Tool

1. Select the Create, NURBS Primitives, Cylinder, Options menu command to open the NURBS Cylinder Options dialog box. Set the Radius value to 5, the Height to 15, the Number of Sections to 20 and the Number of Spans to 10. Select the Both option for Caps and click the Create button.

2. Press the f key to zoom in on the selected plane object.

3. Select the Edit NURBS, Sculpt Geometry Tool menu command. Double-click on the tool in the Toolbox and select the Pull option from the Tool Settings panel.

4. Hold down the 'b' key and drag the tool radius to around 2.0. Then hold down the 'm' key and drag the Max Displacement value to around 2.0.

   Moving the cursor over the cylinder surface shows the size of the Radius and an arrow pointing out from the surface shows the Max Displacement.

5. Move the sculpt cursor to the side of the cylinder and drag several times to pull a section away from the surface. This pulled section is the character's nose.

6. Rotate the view until the pulled area is directly in front of the view. Select the Push option in the Tool Settings panel and drag below the pulled area to create a mouth.

7. Hold down the 'b' key and drag to set the Radius to about 1.0, and then drag in two places above the nose area to create some eye sockets.

8. Select the Create, NURBS Primitives, Sphere menu command and position the sphere in one of the eye sockets.

9. With the sphere still selected, choose the Edit, Duplicate menu command and move the duplicate sphere to the other eye socket.

   The simple character face object is shown in Figure 5-11.

10. Select File, Save Scene As and save the file as **Sculpted face.mb**.

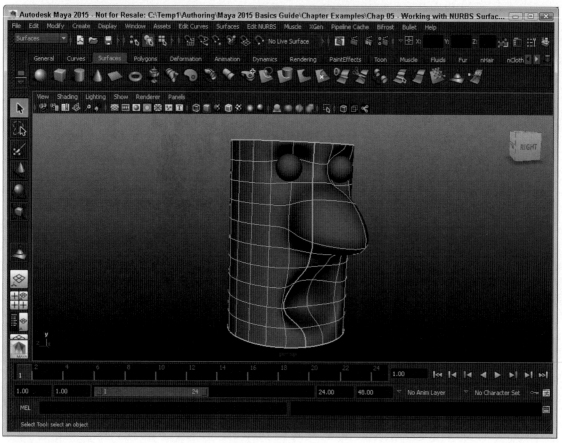

Figure 5-11
Sculpted face

Lesson 5.2-Tutorial 4: Create a Hard Edge

1. Create a sphere object using the Create, NURBS Primitives, Sphere menu command.

2. Right-click on the sphere and select Isoparm from the pop-up marking menu.

3. Drag over one of the vertical running isoparms to select it.

4. With an isoparm selected, choose the Edit NURBS, Surface Editing, Break Tangent menu twice.

5. Right-click on the sphere and select Control Vertex from the pop-up marking menu.

6. Select the center CV that lies on the previously selected isoparm and drag it away from the center of the sphere.

7. Press the 5 key to see the object shaded.

With the tangent broken for the given isoparm, extra CVs have been added to the object that make the selected isoparm a hard edge.

8. Select the Create, NURBS Primitives, Sphere menu command and position the sphere as one of the eyes.

9. With the sphere still selected, choose the Edit, Duplicate menu command and move the duplicate sphere to the other eye position.

10. Select File, Save Scene As and save the file as **Bird head.mb**.

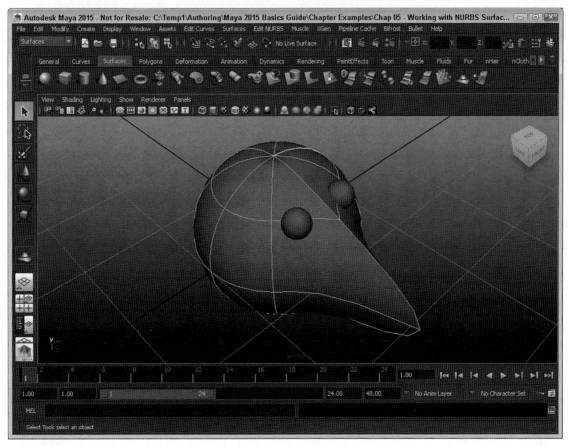

Figure 5-12
Bird head

Lesson 5.3: Apply Surface Operators

The Edit NURBS menu includes many actions that can be used to combine, align, offset, and blend NURBS surfaces. Most of these menu commands also have an options dialog box available.

Attaching and Detaching Surfaces

Two selected surfaces can be attached to one another using the Edit NURBS, Attach Surfaces menu command. The Connect option stretches to attach the closest edge of the last-selected NURBS surface to other surface, but the Blend option stretches both patches equally, as shown in Figure 5-13. If you select an isoparm, you can use the Edit NURBS, Detach Surfaces menu command to detach the isoparm and the patches that are attached to it from the original object.

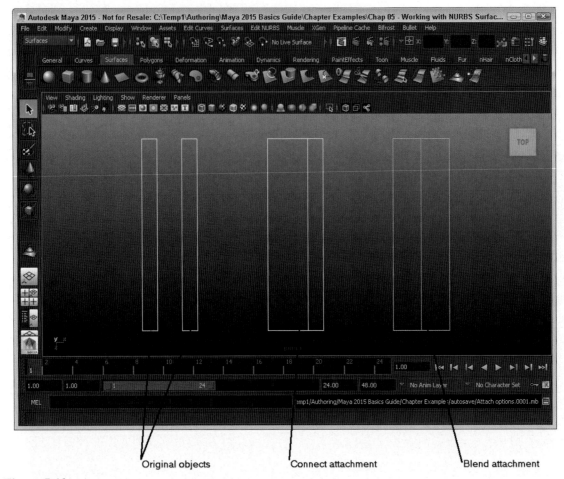

Figure 5-13
Attach options

Aligning Surfaces

With the isoparms on two surfaces selected, you can align the surfaces to each other. The Align Surfaces Options dialog box, shown in Figure 5-14, lets you choose to align a curve's position, tangent, or curvature. When the Position option is selected, you can select which surface to move: first, second, or both (which moves both surfaces halfway). With the Tangent or Curvature options selected, you can select to modify the tangents along the edge of either surface or both.

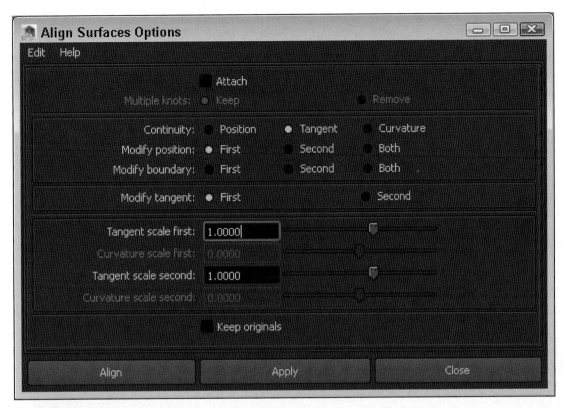

Figure 5-14
Align Surfaces options

Closing and Opening NURBS Surfaces

The Edit NURBS, Open/Close Surfaces menu command creates a closed surface from an open surface and vice versa. In the Open/Close Options dialog box, you can select to close the surface along the U, V or both directions, as shown in Figure 5-15. You can also select to ignore the existing shape, preserve the existing surface, or blend the existing surface.

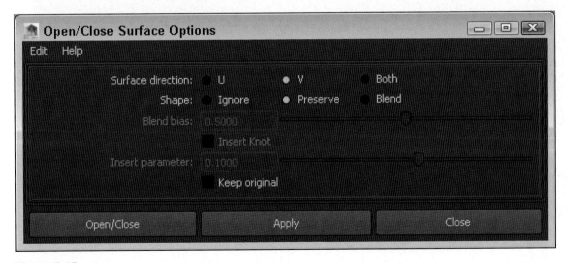

Figure 5-15
Open/Close Surface options

Extending Surfaces

With a NURBS surface selected, you can extend its open edges using the Edit NURBS, Extend Surfaces menu command. From the options dialog box you can select to extend the surface based on tangents or an extrapolation of the existing points. You can specify the distance to extend and the side (start, end, or both) and direction (U, V, or both). The Join to Original option makes the extensions part of the original surface.

Offsetting a Surface

Using the Edit, Duplicate command you can create a copy of a surface and then move it an offset distance or you can use the Edit NURBS, Offset Surfaces to do the same operation in one action. The options dialog box lets you specify the offset distance. Figure 5-16 shows a simple sphere that has been offset, forming a large sphere that encompasses the first.

Tip

You can also duplicate only a portion of an object using the Edit NURBS, Duplicate NURBS Patches menu command. This command only duplicates the selected NURBS patches.

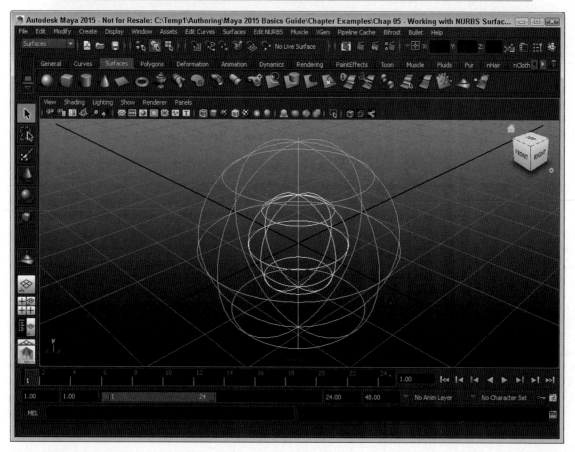

Figure 5-16
Offset sphere

Filleting Surfaces

If two surfaces intersect, you can create a **fillet** that smoothes the intersecting edges. The Edit NURBS, Surface Fillet menu offers three fillet options: Circular Fillet, Freeform Fillet, and the Fillet Blend tool. The Circular

Fillet option can be used to round the edges of two overlapping surfaces. The Freeform Fillet option uses a selected isoparm or a on-surface curve to mark where the fillet starts and ends. Figure 5-17 shows a fillet formed by selecting the isoparms on two intersecting plane objects.

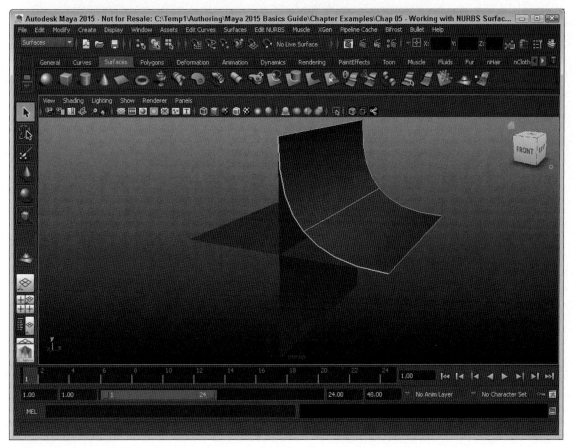

Figure 5-17
Freeform fillet

Blending Surfaces

Two surfaces can be blended together using the Edit NURBS, Surface Fillet, Fillet Blend tool. To use this tool, select two surfaces and choose the Fillet Blend tool menu command. The Help Line asks you to click on the isoparms for the first surface and press Enter, and then click on the isoparms for the second surface and press Enter to complete the blend. Figure 5-18 shows two torus objects blended together.

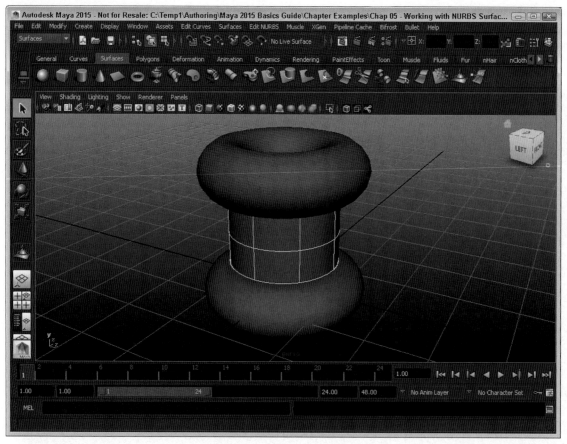

Figure 5-18
Blended torus objects

Lesson 5.3-Tutorial 1: Attach Surfaces

1. Select the Create, EP Curve Tool menu command and click several times in the view panel to create a simple NURBS curve. Press the Enter key to exit Curve Create mode.

2. Extrude the NURBS curve with the Surfaces, Extrude, Options menu command. Select the Distance option in the Extrude Options dialog box with an extrude length of 1.0, and then click the Extrude button.

3. Duplicate the extruded curve surface with the Edit, Duplicate menu command.

4. Drag the duplicated extruded surface upward with the Move tool.

5. Select both extruded surfaces and select the Edit NURBS, Attach Surfaces menu command.

6. Repeat Steps 3-5 two more times.

    The surface based off the NURBS curves has been created, as shown in Figure 5-19.

7. Select File, Save Scene As and save the file as **Attached NURBS surface.mb**.

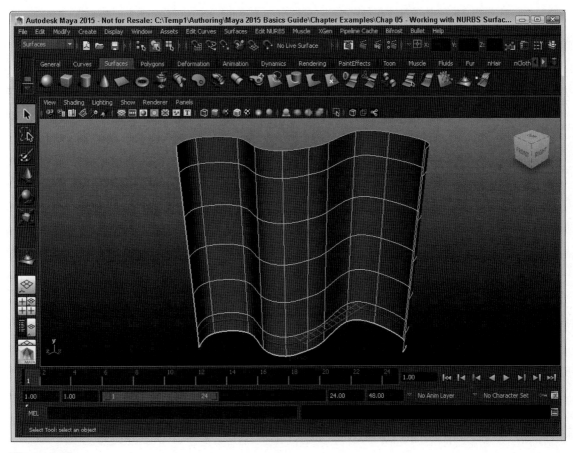

Figure 5-19
Attached surface

Lesson 5.3-Tutorial 2: Detach Surfaces

1. Create a sphere object using the Create, NURBS Primitives, Sphere menu command.

2. Right-click on the sphere and select the Isoparm option from the pop-up marking menu.

3. Hold down the Shift key and select each isoparm that runs from the top to the bottom of the sphere.

4. Select the Edit NURBS, Detach Surfaces menu command.

5. Select the Move tool and move each separate slice away from the center of the sphere.

   The Detach Surfaces menu command can be used to separate the sphere object into separate slices, as shown in Figure 5-20.

6. Select File, Save Scene As and save the file as **Segmented sphere.mb**.

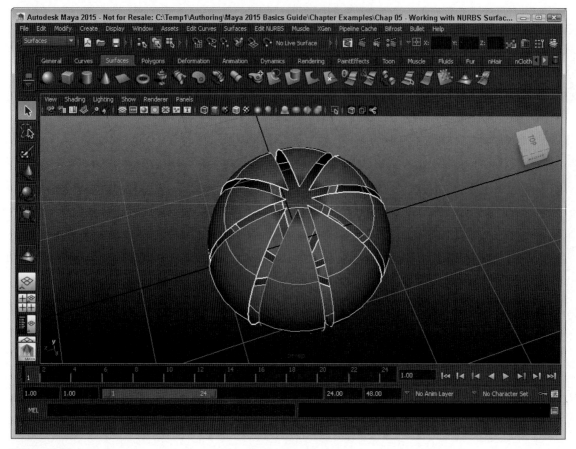

Figure 5-20
Segmented sphere.

Lesson 5.3-Tutorial 3: Open and Close a Surface

1. Create a torus object using the Create, NURBS Primitives, Torus menu command.

2. Select the Edit NURBS, Open/Close Surfaces menu command.

    Since the torus object is already a closed object, the Open/Close Surfaces menu command creates an open surface by removing a section of the object.

3. Select the Edit NURBS, Open/Close Surfaces menu command again.

    This time the torus is an open object, so the open surfaces are closed to resemble a flattened tire, as shown in Figure 5-21.

4. Select File, Save Scene As and save the file as **Flat tire.mb**.

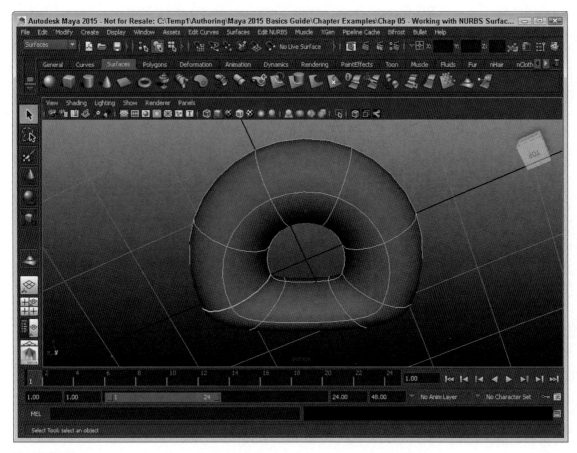

Figure 5-21
A closed torus surface.

Lesson 5.3-Tutorial 4: Offset Surface

1.   Create a cylinder object using the Create, NURBS Primitives, Cylinder menu command.

2.   With the cylinder object selected, choose the Edit NURBS, Offset Surfaces menu command six times.

     The surface is offset a distance of 1.0 from the original, as shown in Figure 5-22.

3.   Select File, Save Scene As and save the file as **Offset cylinders.mb**.

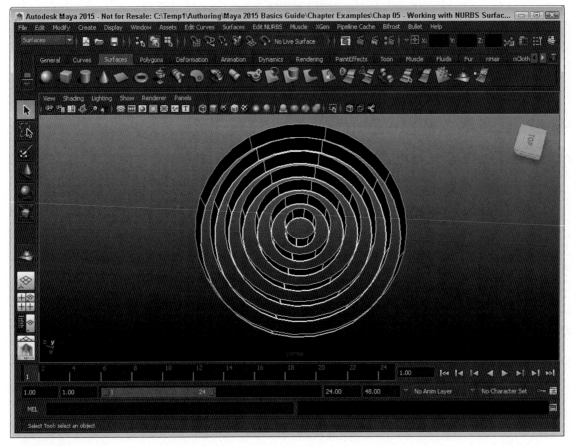

Figure 5-22
An offset cylinders

Lesson 5.3-Tutorial 5: Add a Circular Fillet

1. Create a cube object using the Create, NURBS Primitives, Cube menu command.

2. Hold down the Shift key and select the top and front surfaces of the cube.

3. Select the Edit NURBS, Surface Fillet, Circular Fillet, Options menu command.

4. Set the Radius value to –0.25 and click the Apply button.

   The corner between the two adjacent cube surfaces is rounded.

5. Select the front and bottom surfaces of the cube and repeat Step 4.

6. Repeat Step 4 again for the bottom and back and back and top surfaces.

   The cube has been rounded around the entire cube, as shown in Figure 5-23.

7. Select File, Save Scene As and save the file as **Cube with filleted corners.mb**.

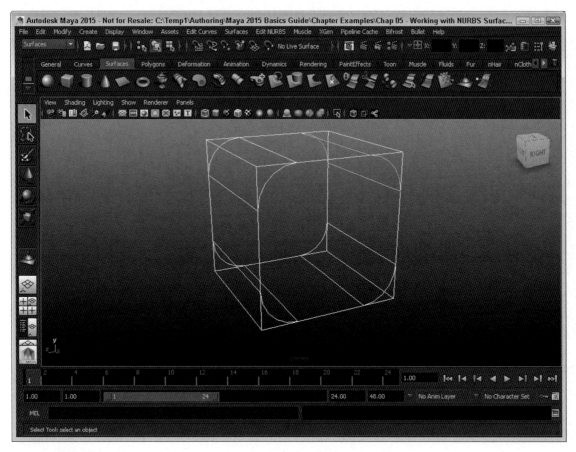

Figure 5-23
Cube with filleted corners

Lesson 5.3-Tutorial 6: Blend Two Surfaces

1. Create a cylinder object using the Create, NURBS Primitives, Cylinder menu command.

2. Select Edit, Duplicate to create a duplicate cylinder.

3. Click on the Move tool and move the duplicate cylinder upward and a little to the right. Then rotate it slightly in the Front view panel with the Rotate Tool.

4. With both objects selected, select the Edit NURBS, Surface Fillet, Fillet Blend Tool menu command.

   With the Fillet Blend tool active, the cursor changes and the Help Line gives instructions.

5. In the Front view panel, click on the bottom edge of the top cylinder object and press the Enter key.

6. Then click on the top edge of the bottom cylinder object and press the Enter key again.

   The two cylinders are blended together to create a new object. The blended objects look like a finger joint, as shown in Figure 5-24, and moving either of the cylinders causes the blend to move also.

7. Select File, Save Scene As and save the file as **Blended cylinders.mb**.

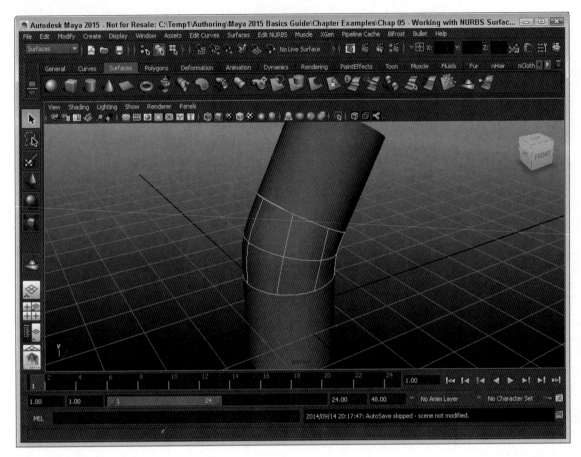

Figure 5-24
Blended cylinder

Lesson 5.4: Trim NURBS Surfaces

Mathematically speaking, NURBS surfaces do not contain any holes, but you can simulate a hole or a partial NURBS Surface by trimming the surface. The trimmed portion still exists, but it is hidden and is not displayed. Before a NURBS surface can be trimmed, it must have a curve on its surface that defines the trimming borders. These curves can be drawn on a surface when the surface is "live" or they can be projected onto the surface.

Drawing Curves on a NURBS Surface

A selected NURBS surface can be made "live" by clicking on the Make Object Live button in the Status Line. The button looks like a magnet, as shown in Figure 5-25. The live object is displayed using dark green lines. Once live, you can use any of the curve drawing tools found in the Create menu and the resulting curve is snapped to the surface of the live object. Click on the Make Object Live button again to exit Live mode.

Figure 5-25
Make Live toggle button

Projecting Curves onto a NURBS Surface

In addition to drawing a curve on a NURBS surface, you can also project an existing curve onto a surface. To do this, select both the curve and the receiving object and select the Edit NURBS, Project Curve On Surface menu command. Using the Project Curve on Surface Options dialog box, shown in Figure 5-26, you can select to project the curve using the Active view or using the Surface normal. Once projected, you can change the position of the curve using the manipulator that appears.

Caution

Be aware that projecting a curve onto a solid NURBS object projects it onto both sides of the object.

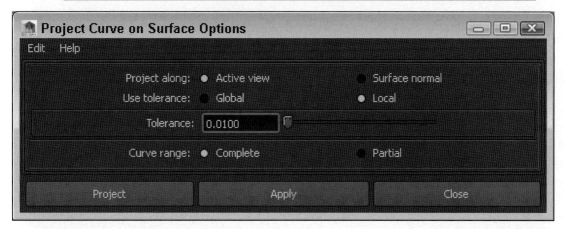

Figure 5-26
Project Curve on Surface options

Marking Intersecting Surfaces

A final way to draw a curve on a surface is to mark where two surfaces intersect. If two selected surfaces intersect, you can use the Edit NURBS, Intersect Surfaces menu command to create a curve that marks the intersecting section. Figure 5-27 shows the intersections between two cylinders. In the Intersect Surfaces options dialog box, you can create intersecting curves based on the first surface or both surfaces. The created curve can be placed on the surface or free of the objects. You can also set a tolerance value.

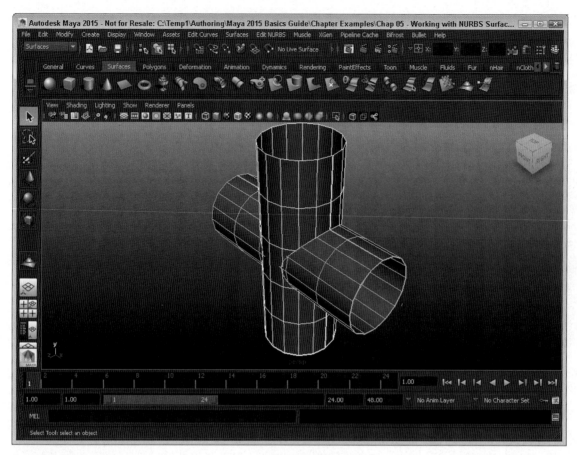

Figure 5-27
Intersecting surfaces

Trimming a Surface

A selected NURBS surface with a curve on its surface can be trimmed using the Edit NURBS, Trim tool. The Trim tool displays all surface isoparms as dashed lines, as shown in Figure 5-28. You can then click on the isoparms to keep as part of the object. Pressing the Enter key causes the unselected areas to be trimmed. The options dialog box includes an option to discard the section that you click on. A trimmed area can be undone using the Edit NURBS, Untrim Surfaces menu command.

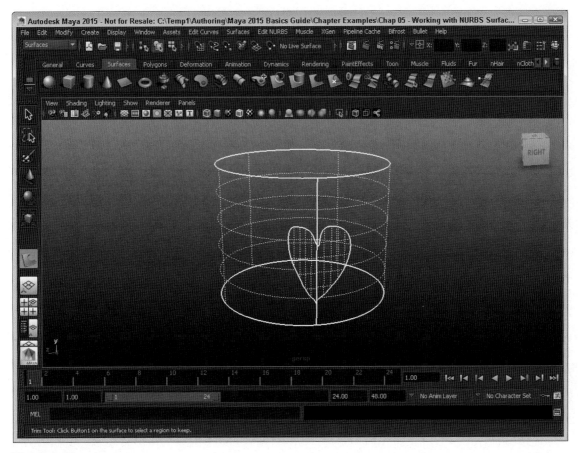

Figure 5-28
The Trim tool

Lesson 5.4-Tutorial 1: Draw and Trim a Surface

1. Create a sphere object using the Create, NURBS Primitives, Sphere menu command.

2. Click the Make the Selected Object Live button in the Status Line.

   The cylinder object appears dark green in the view panel.

3. Select the Create, EP Curve Tool and click on the sphere object to create a shape, but don't finish the shape. Press the Enter key to create the curve.

4. Select Edit Curves, Open/Close Curves to close the curve.

5. Click on the Make the Selected Object Live button in the Status Line again to exit Live mode.

6. Drag over the sphere object to select both the sphere and the drawn curve.

7. Select Edit NURBS, Trim Tool.

   All interior lines that make up the shape and the sphere are displayed as dashed lines.

8. Click on the sphere lines outside the shape and press the Enter key.

9. Press the 5 key to shade the object.

   The shape is trimmed from the sphere object, as shown in Figure 5-29.

10. Select File, Save Scene As and save the file as **Trimmed sphere.mb**.

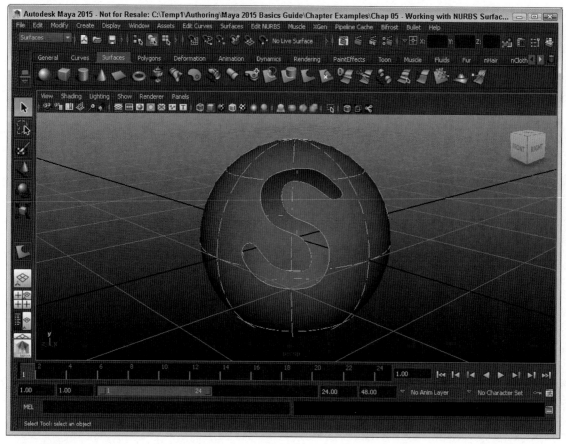

Figure 5-29
Trimmed cylinder

Lesson 5.4-Tutorial 2: Project and Trim a Curve

1. Create a cube object using the Create, NURBS Primitives, Cube menu command.

2. Create a circle object using the Create, NURBS Primitives, Circle menu command.

3. Select the Move tool and drag the circle object upward using the green Y-axis until the circle is above the cube.

4. Select the circle and the cube objects in the Top view panel.

5. Choose the Edit NURBS, Project Curve on Surface menu command.

   A manipulator appears that lets you precisely position the location of the projected curve.

6. Select the cube object and choose the Edit NURBS, Trim Tool menu command.

   All interior lines that make up the shape and the cylinder are displayed as dashed lines.

7. Click on the cube lines outside the circle and press the Enter key.

8. Press the 5 key to shade the object.

   The circle is trimmed from the cube object, as shown in Figure 5-30.

9. Select File, Save Scene As and save the file as **Trimmed cube.mb**.

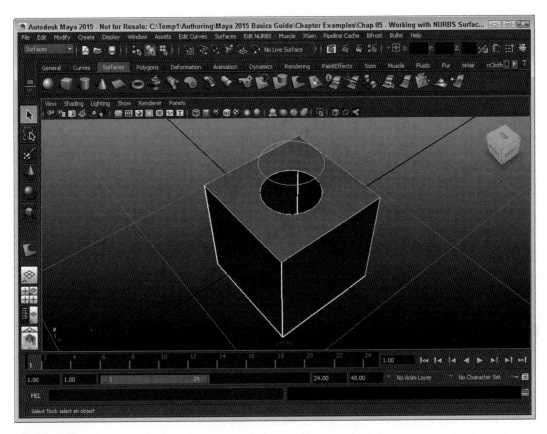

Figure 5-30
The trimmed cube

Lesson 5.5: Use Boolean Tools

When NURBS surfaces overlap, you can use the Edit NURBS, Booleans menu to access one of three tools that can be used to add, subtract, or locate the intersection between the two objects. With any of these tools selected, you can click to select the first object or objects and then press the Enter key before clicking to select the second object or objects. The options dialog box (shown for the Union tool in Figure 5-31) for each of these tools lets you delete the inputs and exit the tool on completion.

Caution

The Boolean tools can only work on two NURBS surfaces at once.

Figure 5-31
NURBS Boolean Union options

149

Combining Surfaces with the Union Tool

When the Union tool is used on two overlapping surfaces, the intersecting lines are removed and the resulting object acts as a single object.

Removing Surface Parts with the Subtract Tool

The Subtract tool removes an overlapping portion of the second selected object from the first selected object. The order in which the objects are selected is important. Reversing the selection order changes the result.

Creating a Surface Intersection with the Intersect Tool

The Intersect Tool removes all but the intersecting portion of the two overlapping surfaces.

Lesson 5.5-Tutorial 1: Create Boolean Union Surfaces

1. Select File, Open Scene and open the file named Boolean.mb.

2. Select the Edit NURBS, Booleans, Union Tool menu command.

3. Then select the sphere object and press the Enter key.

4. Click on one of the cylinder objects and press the Enter key again to union the objects together.

5. Repeat Steps 2-4 for the other two cylinders.

    The final object is shown in Figure 5-32.

6. Select File, Save Scene As and save the file as **Boolean union.mb**.

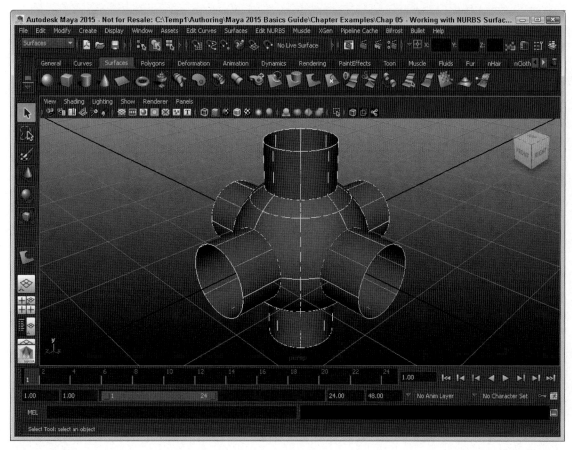

Figure 5-32
A Boolean union

Lesson 5.5-Tutorial 2: Create Boolean Subtract Surfaces

1. Select File, Open Scene and open the file named Boolean.mb.

2. Select the Edit NURBS, Booleans, Subtract Tool menu command.

3. Select the sphere object and press the Enter key.

4. Click on one of the cylinder objects and press the Enter key again to subtract one object from the other.

5. Repeat Steps 2-4 for the other two cylinders.

    The final object is shown in Figure 5-33.

6. Select File, Save Scene As and save the file as **Boolean subtract.mb**.

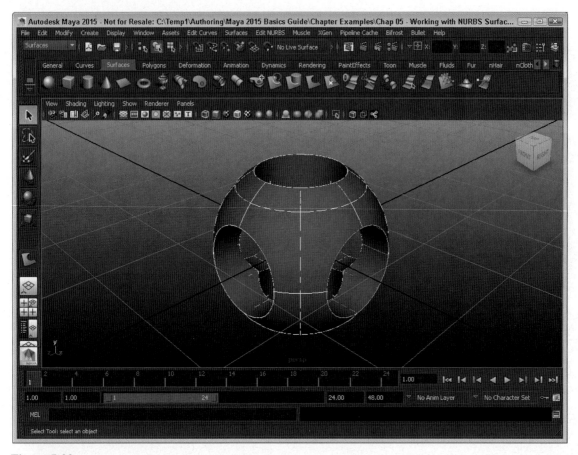

Figure 5-33
A Boolean subtract

Lesson 5.5-Tutorial 3: Create Boolean Intersect Surfaces

1. Select File, Open Scene and open the file named Boolean.mb.

2. Select the Edit NURBS, Booleans, Intersect Tool menu command.

3. Then select the sphere object and press the Enter key.

4. Click on one of the cylinder objects and press the Enter key again to intersect one object from the other.

5. Repeat Steps 2-4 for the other two cylinders.

    The final object is shown in Figure 5-34.

6. Select File, Save Scene As and save the file as **Boolean intersect.mb**.

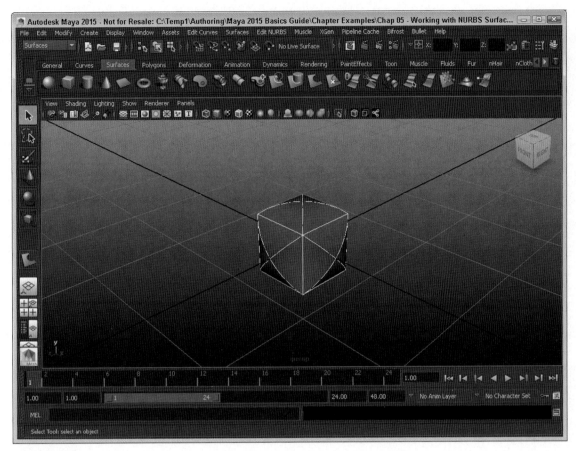

Figure 5-34
A Boolean intersect

Lesson 5.6: Stitch Surfaces Together

Another common way to combine two surfaces is with the Edit NURBS, Stitch menu commands. There are several different ways to stitch surfaces, including using the Stitch Surface Points command, the Stitch Edges tool, and Global Stitch. Figure 5-35 shows the effect of moving a row of stitched plane objects away from their stitched neighbors.

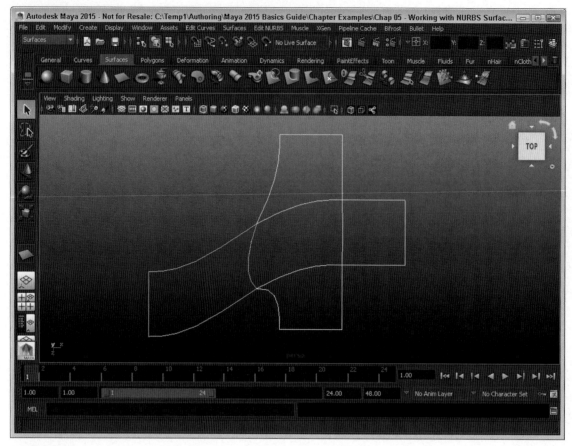

Figure 5-35
Stitched edges

Applying Global Stitch

When several surfaces are placed next to one another as you are modeling an object, they can be independently moved, causing gaps in your model. To prevent this, you can stitch the individual objects together using the Edit NURBS, Stitch, Global Stitch menu command. This creates an attachment between the objects so that moving one causes the other to move with it.

Stitching Surface Points Together

If two CVs are selected, you can use the Edit NURBS, Stitch, Stitch Surface Points menu command to connect the two points together. This moves the two points to the same location.

Stitching Surface Edges Together

It is more common to stitch entire edges than to stitch individual points. NURBS edges can be stitched using the Edit NURBS, Stitch, Stitch Edges tool. This tool instructs you to select a boundary edge isoparm line and then a second boundary isoparm that is moved to the location of the first isoparm edge.

Lesson 5.6-Tutorial 1: Apply Global Stitch

1. Select File, Open Scene and open the file named 6*6 planes.mb.

2. Select the Edit, Select All menu command.

3. Then select the Edit NURBS, Stitch, Global Stitch menu command.

4. In the Top view panel, select the middle 4*4 grid of plane objects.

5. With the Move tool, drag the selected plane objects upward in the Front view panel.

6. In the Top view panel, select the middle 2*2 grid of plane objects.

7. With the Move tool, drag the selected plane objects upward even further in the Front view panel.

> For the resulting hill-shaped object, shown in Figure 5-36, the unselected plane objects move along with their adjacent plane objects because they are stitched together.

8. Select File, Save Scene As and save the file as **Global stitch.mb**.

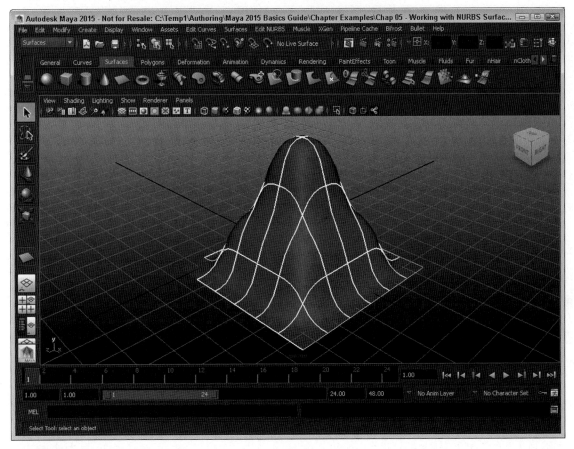

Figure 5-36
Global stitch

Lesson 5.7: Convert Objects

Each of the various modeling types includes several advantages. You can switch between the various object types using the Modify, Convert menu selections. Using these menu commands, you can convert NURBS objects to polygons and subdivision surfaces, polygons to subdivision surfaces, and subdivision surfaces to NURBS and polygons.

Note

You can't convert polygon objects directly to NURBS, but you can convert them to subdivision surfaces and then back to NURBS.

Converting NURBS to Polygons

You can convert NURBS objects to polygons using the Modify, Convert, NURBS to Polygons menu command. Using this command creates a converted polygon objects on top of the existing NURBS object. The Convert NURBS to Polygons Options dialog box, shown in Figure 5-37, lets you select to use triangles or quads for the converted polygon object. You can also select the tessellation method. The options include General, where you can specify the number of U and V spans; Count, where you can specify the number of polygons; Standard Fit, which lets Maya calculate the best conversion parameters; and Control Points, which simply uses the NURBS CVs as polygon vertices.

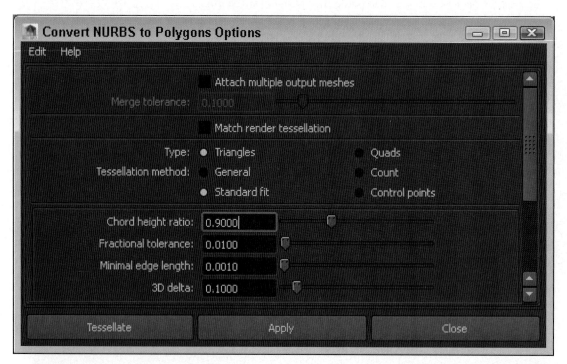

Figure 5-37
Convert NURBS to Polygons Options

Converting to Subdivision Surfaces

NURBS objects and polygon objects can both be converted to subdivision surfaces using the Modify, Convert, NURBS to Subdiv, and Polygons to Subdiv menu commands. All converted components make up the base (Level 0) level for the subdivision surface. The Options dialog box for these commands includes Maximum Base Mesh Faces and the Maximum Edges Per Vertex settings. Some complex geometries cannot be converted, such as when three polygon faces share an edge or adjacent faces have opposite-pointing normals. You should use the Polygons, Cleanup command if you are having trouble converting.

Converting Subdivision Surfaces to NURBS and Polygons

You can convert subdivision surfaces to NURBS and polygon objects using the Modify, Convert, Subdiv to NURBS and Subdiv to Polygons menu commands. Subdivision surfaces that are converted to NURBS splits the separate levels with different resolutions into separate NURBS objects. You can fix this with the Edit NURBS, Attach Surfaces and Stitch, Global Stitch commands. This makes the converted NURBS surface act as a single object. The Convert Subdiv to Polygons Options box offers four tessellation methods: Uniform, Adaptive, Polygon Count, and Vertices, as shown in Figure 5-38.

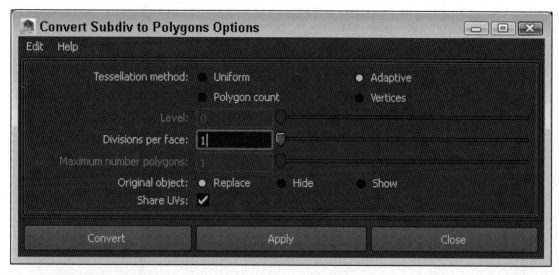

Figure 5-38
Convert Subdiv to Polygons option

Lesson 5.7-Tutorial 1: Convert NURBS to Polygons

1. Create a NURBS sphere object using the Create, NURBS Primitives, Sphere menu command.

2. Select the Modify, Convert, NURBS to Polygons, Options menu command.

3. In the Convert NURBS to Polygons Options dialog box, select the Quads option and the General tessellation method. Then set the Number of U and V parameters to 10 each and click the Apply button.

4. Move the converted sphere below the original.

5. Select the original NURBS sphere and select the Count tessellation method in the Convert NURBS to Polygons Options dialog box. Set the Count value to 1000 and click the Apply button.

6. Move this converted sphere next to the other converted sphere.

7. Repeat Steps 5 and 6 for the Standard Fit and Control Points tessellation methods in the Convert NURBS to Polygons Options dialog box.

   The converted spheres all have a different number of polygons, as shown in Figure 5-39.

8. Select File, Save Scene As and save the file as **Converted NURBS spheres.mb**.

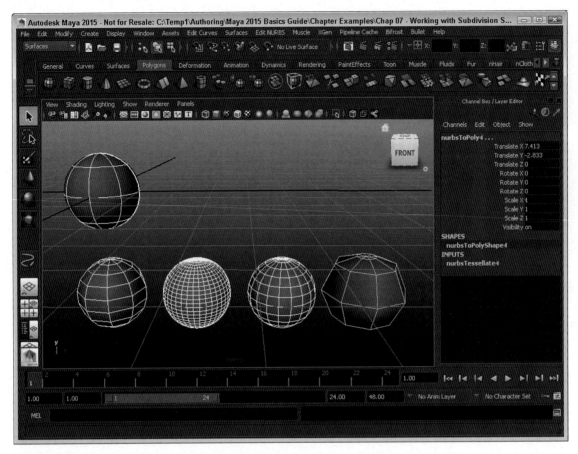

Figure 5-39
Converted NURBS spheres

Lesson 5.7-Tutorial 2: Convert NURBS to Polygons and Back

1. Create a NURBS cube object using the Create, NURBS Primitives, Cube menu command.

2. Select the Modify, Convert, NURBS to Polygons menu command.

3. With the cube selected, choose the Modify, Convert, Polygons to Subdiv menu command.

4. Select the Modify, Convert, Subdiv to NURBS menu command.

   Overusing the convert commands can result in some undesirable anomalies, as shown in Figure 5-40.

5. Select File, Save Scene As and save the file as **Overconverted cube.mb**.

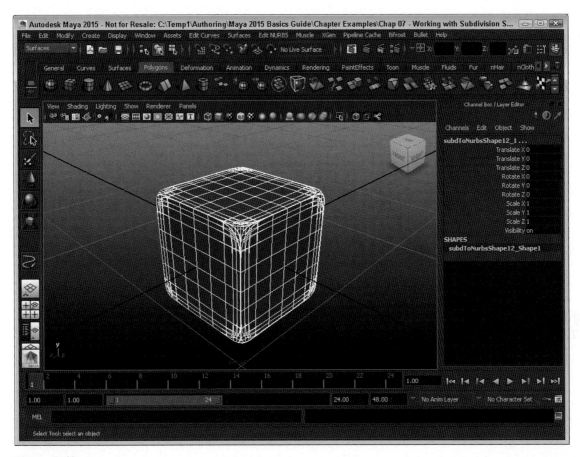

Figure 5-40
Overconverted cube

Chapter Summary

This chapter covers modeling with NURBS surfaces. NURBS is an acronym for Non-Uniform Rational B-Splines. NURBS are great for modeling organic models such as plants, trees, and other objects that flow smoothly from part to part. NURBS are created from curves that line each patch and can be edited by moving the object's CVs or Control Vertices. Maya includes several default NURBS primitives that offer a good starting point for creating complex models. This chapter also covers editing NURBS components and applying surface operators such attaching, filleting, trimming, and blending several objects together. Another way to combine two or more NURBS objects is with the Boolean operations. Stitching NURBS patches together makes them move together when adjacent patches are moved. The Convert commands let you change the selected object between the various modeling types.

What You Have Learned

In this chapter, you learned

* How to create NURBS primitives.

* How to insert an isoparm into a model.

* How to select NURBS components.

* How to use the Surface Editing and the Sculpt Geometry tools.

* How to work with tangents.

* How to attach, detach, and align NURBS surfaces.

* How to open, close, and extend NURBS surfaces.

* How to use NURBS operators such as offsetting, filleting, and blending.

* How to draw a curve on a NURBS surface and use it to trim an area.

* How to use the Union, Subtraction, and Intersection Boolean tools.

* How to stitch multiple NURBS patches together.

* How to convert between NURBS, polygon, and subdivision surfaces.

Key Terms From This Chapter

* **NURBS.** A 3D surface created from curves that define its area. An acronym that stands for Non-Uniform Rational B-Spline.

* **torus.** A circular primitive object with a circular cross section, shaped like a doughnut.

* **Isoparametric curve.** Representative lines that show the object's surface. Called isoparms for short.

* **NURBS patch.** The surface area that lies in between isoparms.

* **Surface Editing tool.** A tool that uses a manipulator to edit the surface curvature.

* **Sculpt Geometry tool.** A tool used to push and pull on an object's surface.

* **Filleting.** The process of smoothing the corner between two adjacent faces.

* **Trimming.** The process of cutting holes into a NURBS surface.

* **Boolean.** Operations used to combine surfaces by adding, subtracting, or intersecting two or more objects.

* **Stitching.** The process of attached adjacent patches together so they move without creating holes.

* **Convert.** A series of commands that lets you change one modeling type such as NURBS to another modeling type such as a subdivision surface.

Chapter 6

Creating and Editing Polygon Objects

IN THIS CHAPTER

6.1 Create polygon objects.

6.2 Edit polygons.

6.3 Use polygon operations.

6.4 Smooth polygon edges.

6.5 Use polygon Booleans ad triangulate polygons.

6.6 Create holes in polygons.

6.7 Work with edge loops, rings, and borders.

In addition to NURBS, Maya can model objects using **polygons**. Polygon surfaces are made from polygons that are positioned edge to edge and smoothed between the edges. You can model anything using polygons, but polygon models make it easier to work with individual faces, making them especially useful for modeling machine parts such as gears.

The components that make up a polygon include vertices, edges, and faces. Each polygon face also has two sides—one facing inward and one facing outward. A vector called the **normal** extends outward from the outward-facing face. This is the face that is shaded when the polygon is rendered.

Maya includes several polygon primitives, but you can also create polygons manually using the Create Polygon tool. The direction in which you create a polygon determines the normal's direction. You can determine this using your right hand. Just curl the fingers on your right hand in the direction that the vertices are created (either clockwise or counter-clockwise) and your thumb points in the direction of the face normal.

You can edit polygon objects by moving their components using similar tools that curves and NURBS use. There are also several useful commands found in the Edit Polygons menu that you can use to subdivide, split, and cut faces, merge vertices and edges, and delete components. The Edit Polygons menu also includes several polygon operations that you can use to **extrude**, **chamfer**, and **bevel** the polygon components.

Learning to work with normals gives you control over how a polygon object is smoothed and shaded. Triangulation is another aspect of polygon objects that controls how they are rendered. This chapter also covers several methods for creating holes in a polygon surface.

One popular modeling method is to align rows of polygons end to end in constructs called edgeloops. Maya includes selection tools and operations for working with edgeloops, rings and borders.

Lesson 6.1: Create Polygon Objects

There are a couple of ways to create polygon mesh objects. You can create and edit a polygon primitive or you can manually create a mesh one polygon at a time. Once you have created a polygon, you can add polygon objects together or detach them.

Creating Polygon Primitives

The easiest way to create polygon objects is with the Create, Polygon Primitives menu command. This menu includes the following polygon primitives: Sphere, Cube, Cylinder, Cone, Plane, Torus, Prism, Pyramid, Pipe, Helix, Soccer Ball, and Platonic Solids, as shown in Figure 6-1. Each of these polygon primitives has an Options dialog box, such as the Polygon Torus Options shown in Figure 6-2, in which you can enter precise dimensional values such as Radius and Height.

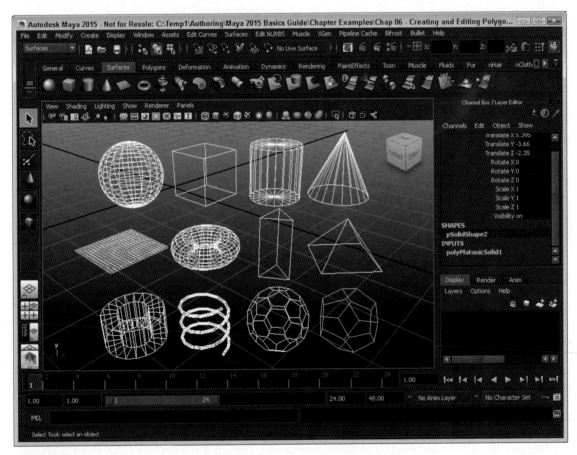

Figure 6-1
Polygon primitives

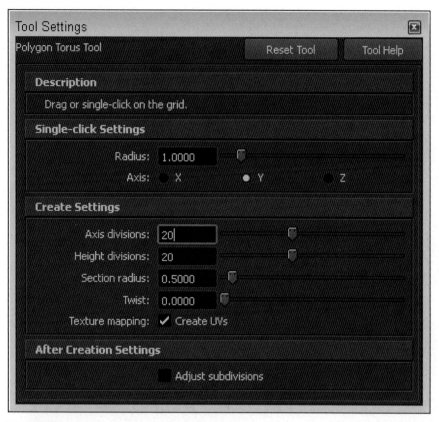

Figure 6-2
Polygon torus options

Creating Polygon Objects by Hand

A second way to create polygon objects is with the Mesh Tools, Create Polygon tool. This tool lets you create a series of connected polygons by clicking where the polygon vertices should be located. The polygonal surfaces that are created are *coplanar*, which means that all its vertices are on the same plane. Pressing the Delete key deletes the last vertex. Pressing the Insert key enters a mode in which you can select and move the existing vertices. Press the Insert key again to continue adding vertices. When the polygon is complete, you can press the Enter key to exit the tool or press the Y key to create another polygon.

Appending to a Polygon

With an existing polygon object selected, you can use the Mesh Tools, Append to Polygon tool. When this tool is selected, the polygon's edges appear thick, as shown in Figure 6-3. Click to select the edge that you want to append to, and then click to position the other vertices that make up the appended polygon. You can use the Delete and Insert keys with this tool, just like with the Create Polygon tool, to delete or edit vertices. When the appended polygon is finished, press the Enter key to exit the tool or the Y key to create more appended polygons.

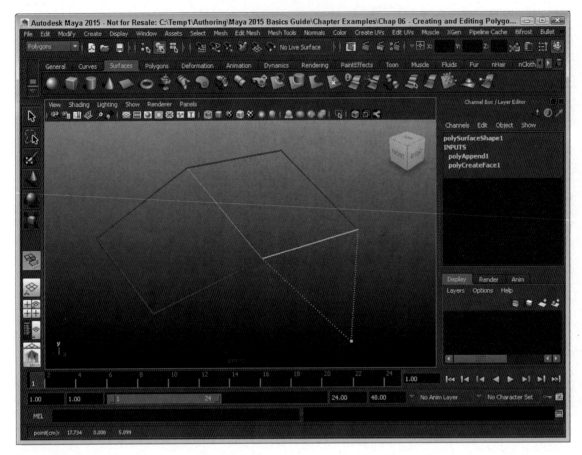

Figure 6-3
Append to polygon

Combining Polygons

The Mesh, Combine menu command combines two or more selected polygons together to make a single polygon object. Combined polygons are transformed together. You can undo the Combine command with the Mesh, Separate menu command.

Mirroring Polygon Objects

You can quickly create a duplicate copy of the existing polygon object using the Mesh, Mirror Geometry menu command. This command only works on objects; it cannot be used on components such as faces, segments, and vertices. The Polygon Mirror Options dialog box lets you specify the mirror direction and whether the mirrored object is merged with the original. Figure 6-4 shows a polygon cone primitive mirrored about its +Y-axis.

Note

Use the Mesh, Mirror Cut menu command also to mirror objects. This command places a slicing plane in the view and mirrors the selected object on each side of the plane. This is useful for symmetrical models.

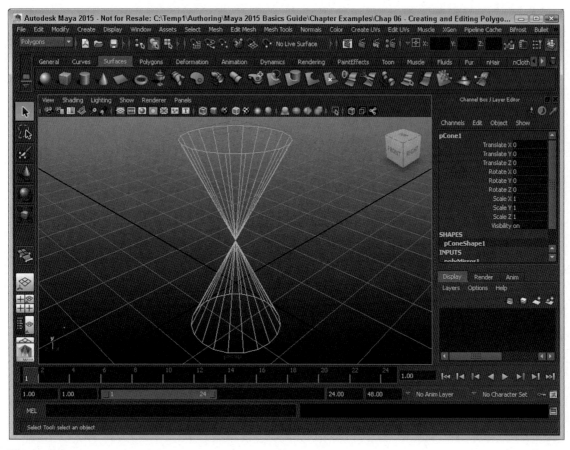

Figure 6-4
Mirrored polygon cone primitive

Duplicating Faces

If a polygon face or several faces are selected, you can use the Edit Mesh, Duplicate menu command to create a copy of the selected faces. The Duplicate Faces options dialog box lets you specify an offset value that you can use to offset the copy within the selected face, as shown in Figure 6-5. You can also define the transform values or a direction for the duplicated faces, or you can use the manipulator. The options dialog box also includes a Random setting that you can use to randomize the faces.

Tip

> The Mesh, Extract menu command works just like the Duplicate Faces menu command except that a copy isn't made and the selected faces are separated from the object.

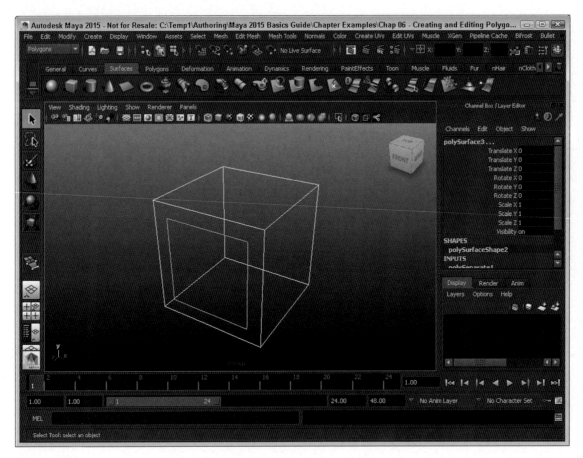

Figure 6-5
Duplicated face

Cleaning Up and Reducing Polygons

As you work with polygon objects, there is a good chance that you'll end up with some artifacts that may cause problems, such as non-planar faces, zero-length edges, and so on. You can remove all of these potential problems with the Mesh, Cleanup menu command. If the total number of polygons is too high, you can reduce the number with the Mesh, Reduce menu command. Figure 6-6 shows a polygon sphere primitive that has been reduced once, twice, and three times.

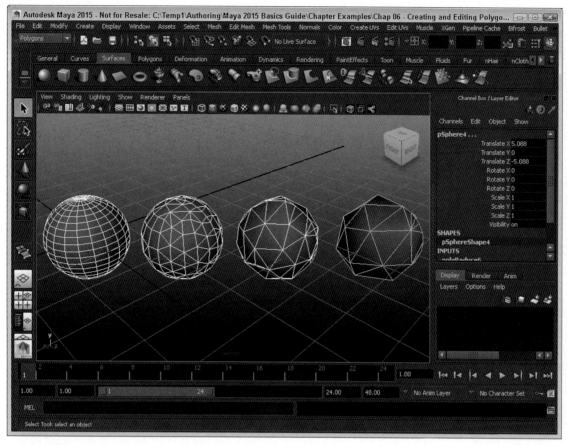

Figure 6-6
Reduced sphere primitives

Lesson 6.1-Tutorial 1: Create Polygon Primitives

1. Create a polygon sphere object using the Create, Polygon Primitives, Sphere menu command.

2. Enter a value of 2.0 for the TranslateY attribute in the Channel Box.

3. Create a polygon cone object using the Create, Polygon Primitives, Cone menu command.

4. Enter a TranslateY value of 0.3, a RotateZ value of 180, and a ScaleY value of 1.5 in the Channel Box.

   These attribute values raise the sphere and position the cone underneath it to resemble an ice cream cone, as shown in Figure 6-7.

5. Select File, Save Scene As and save the file as **Ice cream cone.mb**.

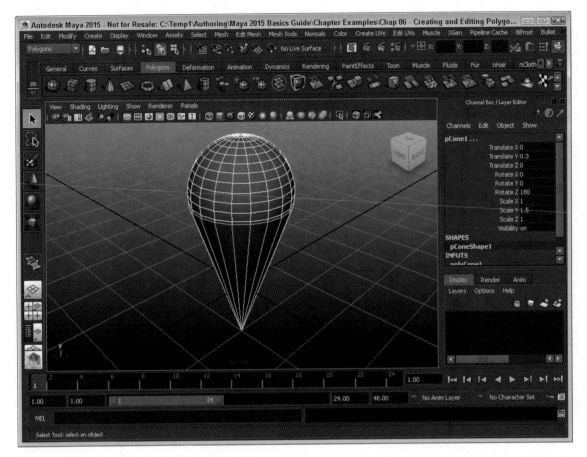

Figure 6-7
Ice cream cone made from polygon primitives

Lesson 6.1-Tutorial 2: Create a Polygon

1. Click on the Model View button from the Quick Layout buttons and select the Top View command from pop-up menu.

2. Click the Snap to Grid button in the Status Line.

3. Select the Mesh Tools, Create Polygon Tool menu command.

4. Click symmetrically around the origin five times to create a pentagon shape.

5. Press the Enter key to complete the polygon, as shown in Figure 6-8.

6. Select File, Save Scene As and save the file as **Pentagon.mb**.

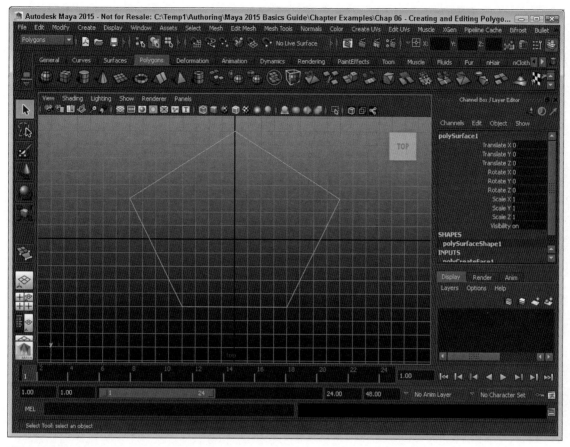

Figure 6-8
Manual polygon

Lesson 6.1-Tutorial 3: Append to a Polygon

1. Select the File, Open Scene menu command and open the Pentagon.mb file.

2. With the pentagon shape selected, choose the Mesh Tools, Append to Polygon Tool menu command.

    The lines of the pentagon are thicker.

3. Click on the bottom edge of the pentagon and then click at a point between and under the edge to make the point of a star.

4. Press the Y key to create another attachment.

5. Repeat Steps 3 and 4 for each edge in the pentagon until the star looks like that in Figure 6-9.

6. Select File, Save Scene As and save the file as **Star.mb**.

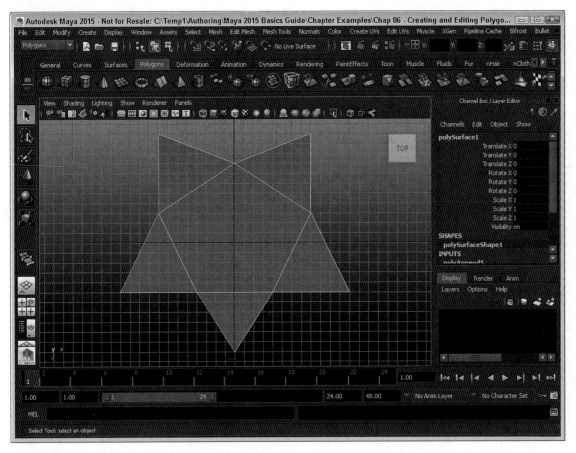

Figure 6-9
Polygon star

Lesson 6.1-Tutorial 4: Mirror an Object

1. Select the File, Open Scene menu command and open the Hammer.mb file.

2. Select both parts of the hammer.

3. Select the Mesh, Combine menu command.

    This command combines both hammer parts into a single object.

4. Select the Mesh, Mirror Geometry, Options menu command, and in the Polygon Mirror Options dialog box that appears, select the +Z option and click the Mirror button.

    The Mirror Geometry menu command creates a copy of the hammer, as shown in Figure 6-10.

5. Select File, Save Scene As and save the file as **Mirrored hammer.mb**.

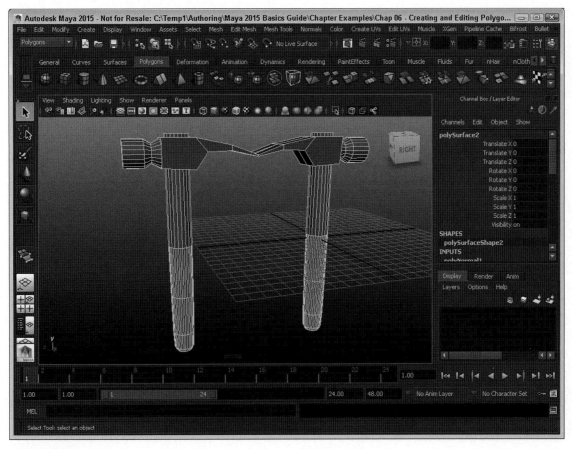

Figure 6-10
Mirrored hammer

Lesson 6.1-Tutorial 5: Offset Faces

1. Create a polygon cube object using the Create, Polygon Primitives, Cube menu commands.

2. Right-click on the cube object and select the Face option from the pop-up marking menu.

3. Drag over the entire cube to select all its faces.

4. Select the Edit Mesh, Duplicate, Options menu command, and in the Duplicate Face Options dialog box that appears, set the Offset value to 0.1, and the Z-axis Translate value (the third column) to 0.5.

5. Click the Duplicate button.

    All of the faces that make up the cube are duplicated, offset, and moved away from the original as if the cube were pulled apart, as shown in Figure 6-11.

6. Select File, Save Scene As and save the file as **Exploded cube.mb**.

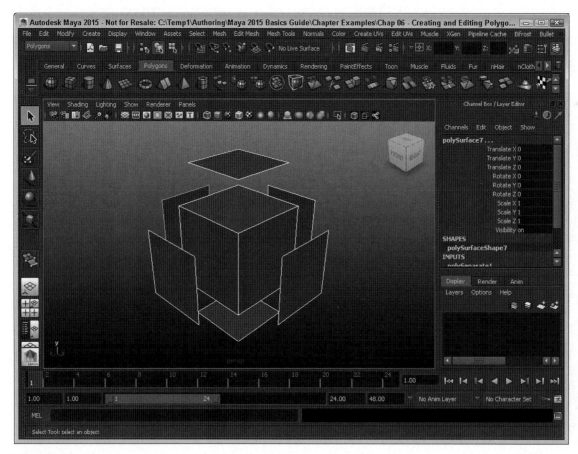

Figure 6-11
An exploded cube

Lesson 6.2: Edit Polygons

You can edit polygons by selecting and transforming their components. In addition to transforming components, the Edit Polygons menu includes many commands for working with polygon components.

Selecting Polygon Components

When the Select by Components button on the Status Line is enabled, all vertices that make up a polygon are displayed. From the right-click pop-up marking menu, shown in Figure 6-12, you can select to work with vertices, edges, or faces. The Select menu, shown in Figure 6-13, includes several commands that help you select the exact components to work with. The commands include Grow Selection Region, Shrink Selection Region, Select Selection Boundary, and Select Contiguous Edges, as well as several commands to convert the current selection between the various component types.

Note

Another common polygon component is UV, which is used to place textures on polygon objects. The UV component is discussed in Chapter 7, "Assigning Materials and Textures."

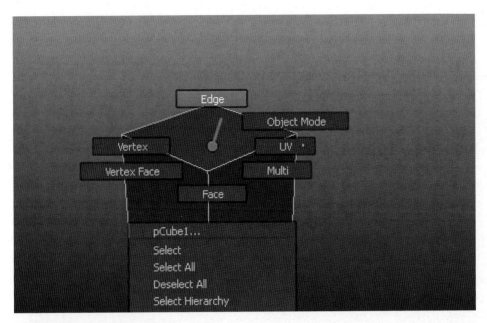

Figure 6-12
The polygon marking menu

Figure 6-13
The Select menu for the Polygons menu set

Subdividing and Splitting Polygon Faces

The real benefit of polygons becomes apparent as many appended polygons are combined to represent a surface. Areas of detail require more polygons than areas of less detail. You can add more polygons to an area by selecting an object's faces or edges and using the Edit Mesh, Add Divisions menu command. This command subdivides all selected faces into Quads or Triangles using the Subdivision Level value. Figure 6-14 shows a simple polygon cube that has been duplicated and subdivided to different levels.

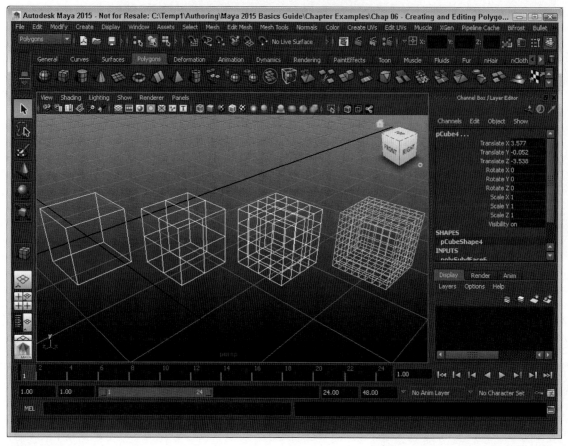

Figure 6-14
A subdivided cube

If you want to subdivide a polygon face with more control, you can use the Mesh Tools, Cut Faces tool. To use this tool, you must first select a polygon object; then click on the edge where you want the split to occur, and then click near a neighboring edge and drag to position exactly where the split is. You can make many splits at a single time by continuing to click near a neighboring edge. Pressing the Delete key deletes the last split point and the Insert key toggles on and off an editing mode wherein you can reposition the split points. Finally, pressing the Enter key completes the split operation. Figure 6-15 shows a plane face in the process of being split.

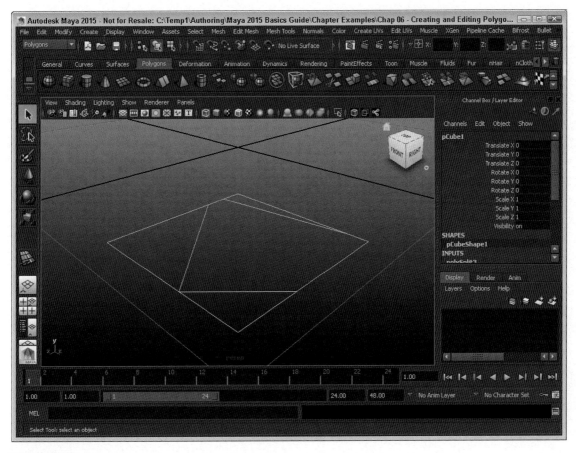

Figure 6-15
A split cube face

Cutting Faces

Another interactive way to subdivide polygon faces is to use the Mesh Tools, Cut Faces tool. You'll need to select a polygon object or face to cut before selecting this tool. Once a polygon face or object is selected, you can click at the point where the cut is to be located and drag to rotate the interactive cutting guide. When you release the mouse, the polygon face is cut where the guideline is located, as shown in Figure 6-16.

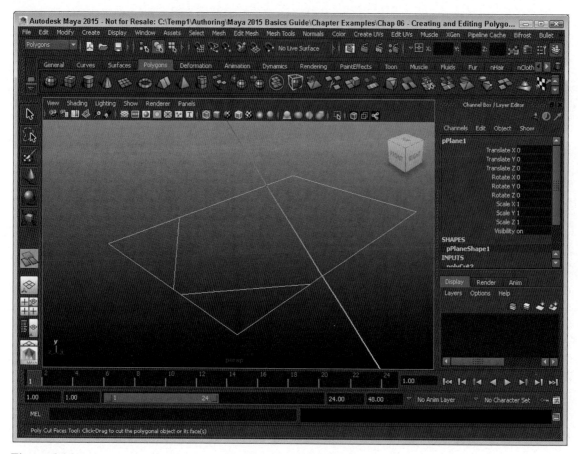

Figure 6-16
A cut face

Merging Vertices

You can simplify a polygon by merging its vertices together using the Mesh Tools, Merge Vertex tool menu command. The two selected vertices must be within the specified Distance value and they must belong to two polygons that are combined in the same polygon object. Figure 6-17 shows four vertices in a plane object that have been merged together.

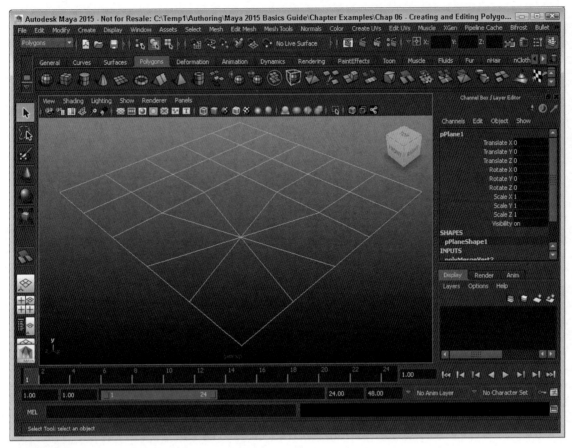

Figure 6-17
Merged vertices

Merging Edges

The easiest way to merge the edges of two polygons that are part of the same object is with the Mesh Tools, Merge Edge tool menu command. This command merges all edges that are within the specified Threshold value. You can also manually merge edges with the Merge Edge tool. This tool allows to you select two edges and then press the Enter key to combine them. When the first edge is selected, it is highlighted orange and all available edges that can be merged appear magenta, as shown in Figure 6-18. You can set the edges to meet at the location of the first edge, the second edge, or in the middle of the two.

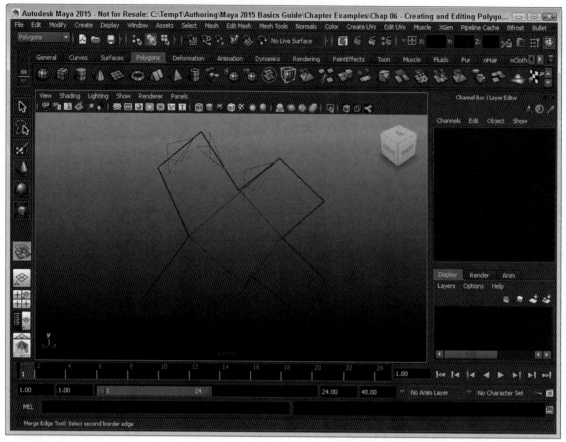

Figure 6-18
Merged edges

Deleting Components

You can delete interior vertices and edges using the Mesh, Delete Edge/Vertex menu command. For polygon objects, selecting a vertex and pressing the Delete key doesn't work on intersecting vertices. The Delete Edge command also deletes the adjoining vertices. Another method for deleting edges and faces is to select them and use the Edit Mesh, Collapse menu command. This command collapses the selected edges or faces into a single vertex.

Lesson 6.2-Tutorial 1: Create a Mushroom

1. Create a polygon sphere object using the Create, Polygon Primitives, Sphere menu command.

2. Enter a value of 0.5 for the TranslateY value in the Channel Box.

3. Click on the Select by Component Type button in the Status Line, and then right-click and select the Face option from the pop-up marking menu.

4. Drag over the lower half of the sphere in the Front view panel and press the Delete key.

5. Click the Select by Object Type button on the Status Line and choose the Mesh, Fill Hole menu command.

   Half of the sphere faces are deleted, leaving a large open hole. The Fill Hole command replaces the hole with a single polygon.

6. Right-click on the sphere and select Edge from the pop-up marking menu. Then select all of the edges along the bottom of the hemisphere.

Tip

> The easiest way to select all of the bottom edges is to drag over the final row of polygons in the Front view panel and then to hold down the Ctrl/Command key while selecting the final row of faces, leaving just the edges.

7. Select the Scale tool and drag the center handle to reduce the size of the bottom circle. Then move it slightly upward in the Front view panel with the Move tool.

8. Create a polygon cone object using the Create, Polygon Primitives, Cone menu command.

9. Set the ScaleX and ScaleZ values in the Channel Box to 0.25.

    This cone becomes the thin stem for the mushroom, as shown in Figure 6-19.

10. Select File, Save Scene As and save the file as **Mushroom.mb**.

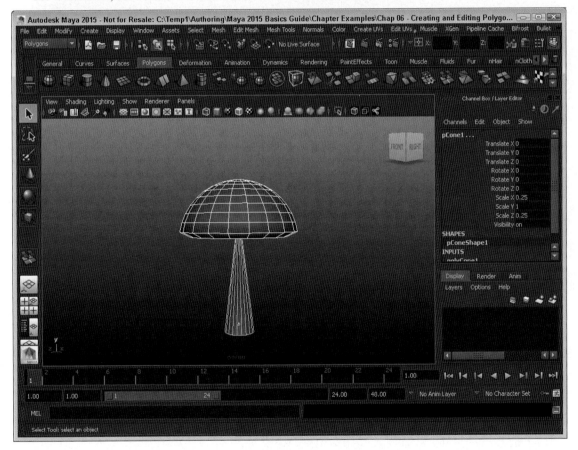

Figure 6-19
A polygon mushroom

Lesson 6.2-Tutorial 2: Split Faces

1. Select the File, Open Scene menu command and open the Capital M.mb file.

2. Click on the Snap to Grids button in the Status Line.

3. With the *M* shape selected, choose the Mesh Tools, Cut Faces tool and click on each interior corner point until the entire shape is made of rectangles.

4. Hold down the Shift key and use the Select tool to select all of the interior faces that make up the letter *M*.

5. Right- click on the shape and select Face from the right-click pop-up menu.

    This command splits all of the polygons that make up the letter, as shown in Figure 6-20.

6. Select File, Save Scene As and save the file as **Split letter faces.mb**.

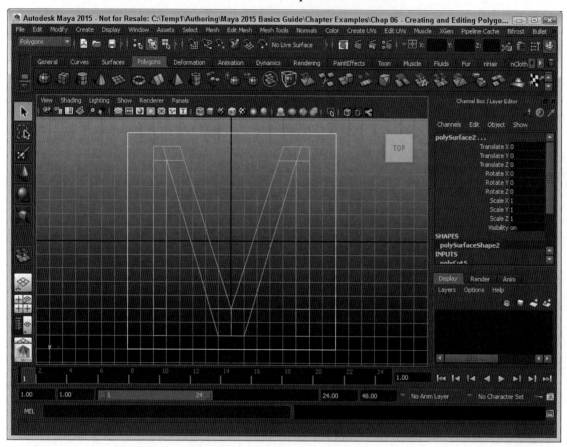

Figure 6-20
Split-letter faces

Lesson 6.2-Tutorial 3: Merge Vertices and Edges

1. Select the File, Open Scene menu command and open the Compass.mb file.

2. Select the top square, right-click, and select Vertex from the pop-up marking menu.

3. Drag over the top two vertices and select the Mesh Tools, Merge Vertex tool, Options menu command. Set the Distance value to 8.0 and click the MergeVertex button.

    This command combines the top two vertices, making the square into a triangle that points away from the center square.

4. Repeat Steps 2 and 3 for all the outer squares.

5. Right-click and select the Object Mode option from the pop-up marking menu. Then, choose all the polygon shapes and choose the Mesh, Combine menu command.

6. Select the Mesh Tools, Merge Edge Tool, Options menu command and set the Threshold value to 6.0, and then click the Sew button.

All of the edges within the Threshold value are merged, as shown in Figure 6-21.

7.   Select File, Save Scene As and save the file as **Merged compass.mb**.

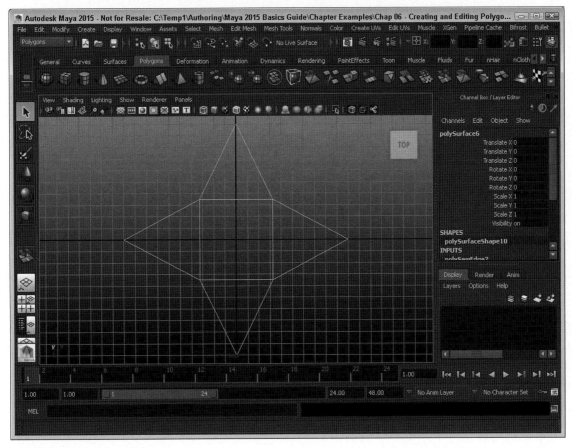

Figure 6-21
A merged compass

Lesson 6.3: Use Polygon Operations

With certain polygon components selected, you can use one of the many polygon operations found in the Edit Polygons menu. These operations let you extrude, chamfer, and bevel the selected components.

Extruding Vertices

The Edit Mesh, Vertex Extrude menu command raises the selected vertex along its normal a given length and create new faces that equal a specified width value. Figure 6-22 shows a single vertex of a plane object extruded.

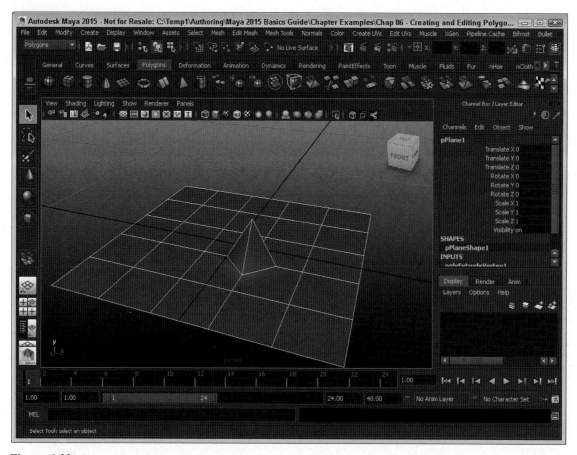

Figure 6-22
An extruded vertex

Extruding Edges and Faces

In addition to vertices, faces and edges can also be extruded. The menu commands for these operations include Edit Mesh, Edge Extrude, and Face Extrude. For both of these operations, you can specify Offset, Taper, and Twist values, as well as complete transform values. An easier way to manipulate the extrusion is with the manipulator that appears when the operation is used. With this manipulator, you can move and scale the extruded edge or face. Figure 6-23 shows an extruded face rising from a plane object.

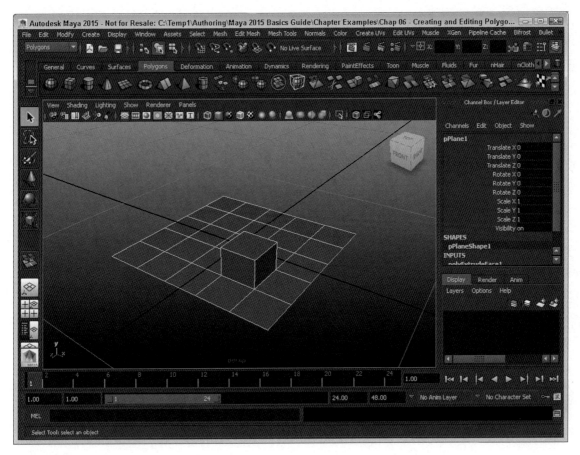

Figure 6-23
An extruded face

Chamfer a Vertex

Chamfering a vertex replaces each vertex with a face and connects the face component with the other adjacent faces. This is useful when you need to round an object. The Edit Mesh, Vertex Chamfer, Options dialog box includes an option to delete the face and to specify the width of the face that is created in place of the vertex. Figure 6-24 shows a single vertex of a cube object that has been chamfered.

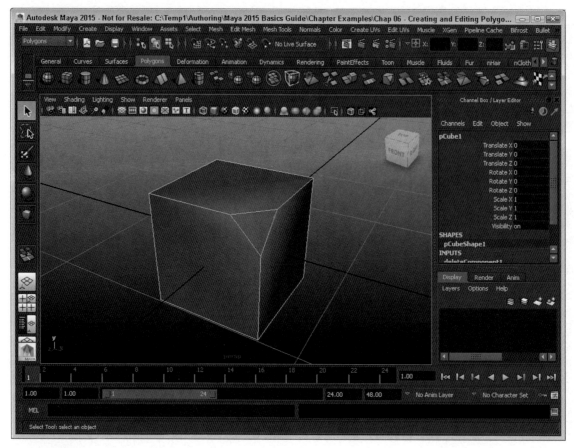

Figure 6-24
A chamfered vertex

Beveling an Edge

A bevel operation is similar to a chamfer, except it is applied to edges. You can make an edge into a face with the Edit Mesh, Edge Bevel menu command. In the Bevel Options dialog box, you can specify Offset and Roundness values. You can also apply the Bevel command to vertex and face components. Figure 6-25 shows a single edge of a cube object that has been beveled.

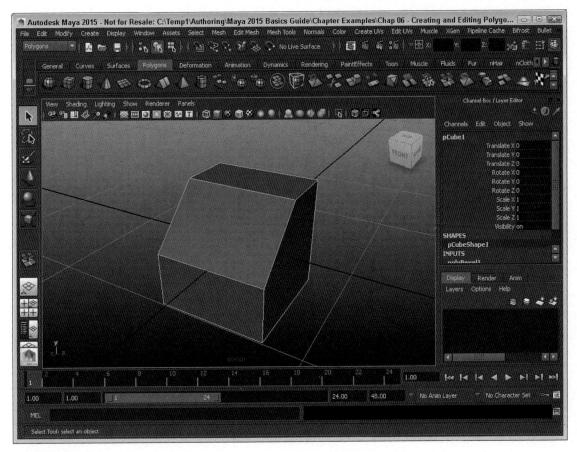

Figure 6-25
A beveled edge

Poking a Face

The Edit Mesh, Face Poke menu command adds a vertex to the center of the selected polygon face and subdivide the face using this new vertex. The vertex is also raised from the surface as if someone poked it from underneath. This operation is similar to the Extrude Vertex menu command, except it is applied to face components. Figure 6-26 shows a single face of a plane object that has been poked.

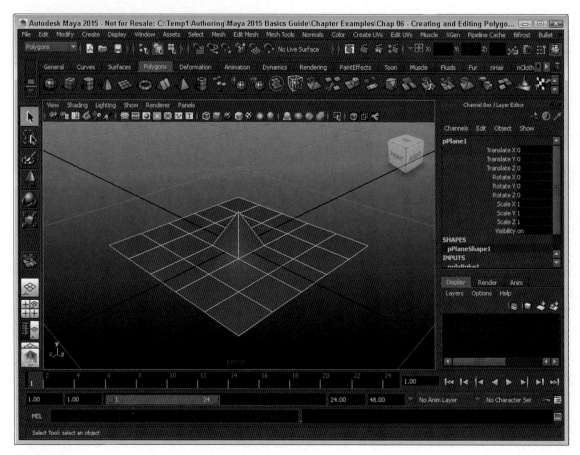

Figure 6-26
A poked face

Creating a Wedge

The Edit Mesh, Face Wedge menu command rotates a selected face using a selected adjacent edge, and the rotated face is connected with the series of segmented faces to its original location. This creates a wedge-like effect rising from the surface of the selected face. In the Polygon Wedge Face Options dialog box, you can select the Wedge Angle and the number of Wedge Divisions. Figure 6-27 shows a wedge rising from a plane object.

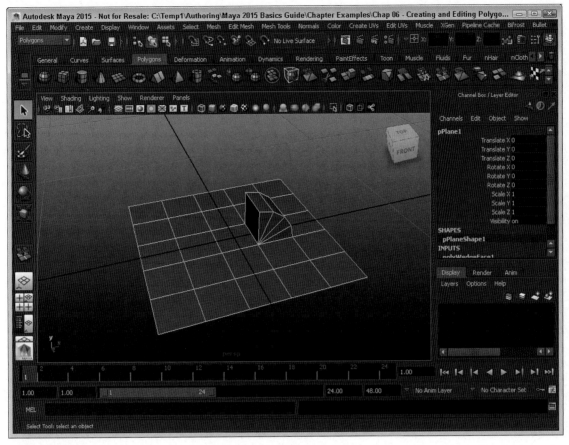

Figure 6-27
A wedged face

Lesson 6.3-Tutorial 1: Extrude Cube Vertices

1. Create a polygon cube object using the Create, Polygon Primitives, Cube menu command.

2. Select Vertex from the right-click pop-up marking menu and drag over the entire cube to select all of its vertices.

3. Select the Edit Mesh, Vertex Extrude menu command.

    Each vertex is extruded, creating a star object like the one shown in Figure 6-28.

4. Select File, Save Scene As and save the file as **Extruded vertex star.mb**.

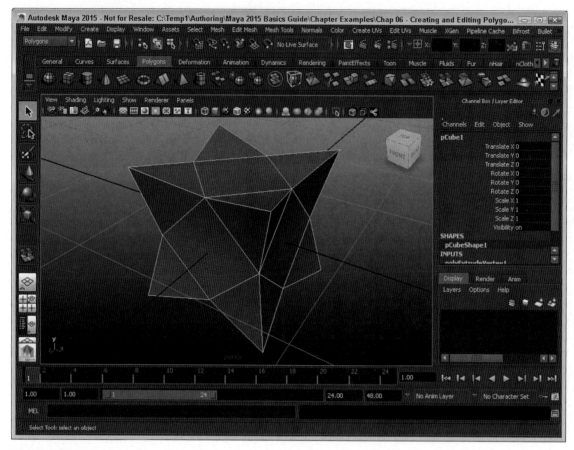

Figure 6-28
An extruded vertex star

Lesson 6.3-Tutorial 2: Extrude Cube Edges and Faces

1. Create a polygon cube object using the Create, Polygon Primitives, Cube menu command.

2. With the cube object selected, choose Edit, Duplicate and move the duplicate cube to the right with the Move tool.

3. Right-click on the left cube and select Edge from the right-click pop-up marking menu and drag over the entire cube to select all of its edges.

4. Select the Edit Mesh, Edge Extrude menu command. Select the blue Z-axis and drag it away from the cube object to extrude its edges.

5. Right-click on the right cube and select Face from the right-click pop-up marking menu and drag over the entire cube to select all of its faces.

6. Select the Edit Mesh, Face Extrude menu command. Select the blue Z-axis and drag it away from the cube object to extrude its faces.

   The cube on the left has extruded edges and the cube on the right has extruded faces. Notice the difference between the two shown in Figure 6-29.

7. Select File, Save Scene As and save the file as **Extruded cube.mb**.

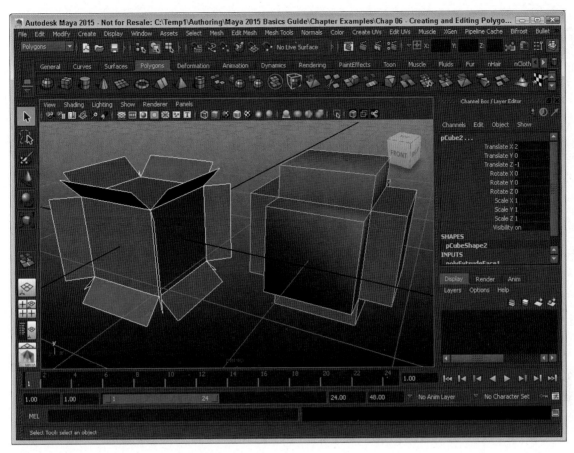

Figure 6-29
An extruded cub.

Lesson 6.3-Tutorial 3: Chamfer Vertices

1. Create a polygon cube object using the Create, Polygon Primitives, Cube menu command.

2. Right-click on the cube and select Vertex from the right-click pop-up marking menu and drag over the entire cube to select all of its vertices.

3. Select the Edit Mesh, Vertex Chamfer menu command.

   All vertices on the cube are chamfered, revealing several holes.

4. Drag over the entire cube to select it and choose Mesh, Fill Hole.

   All the chamfered holes are now filled, revealing a cube with octagonal sides, as shown in Figure 6-30.

5. Select File, Save Scene As and save the file as **Chamfered cube.mb**.

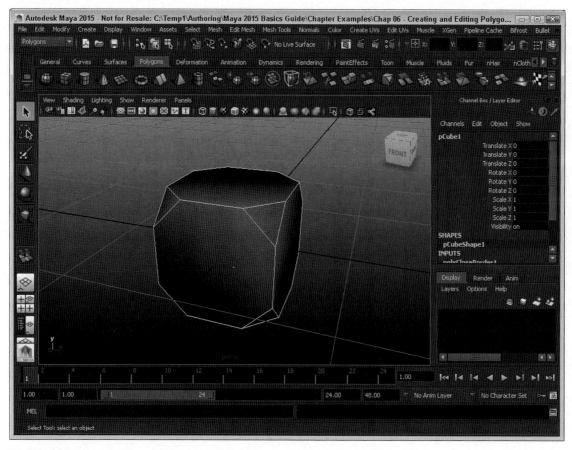

Figure 6-30
A chamfered cub.

Lesson 6.3-Tutorial 4: Bevel Edges

1. Create a polygon cube object using the Create, Polygon Primitives, Cube menu command.

2. Right-click on the cube and select Edge from the right-click pop-up marking menu and drag over the entire cube to select all of its edges.

3. Select the Edit Mesh, Edge Bevel menu command.

    All edges on the cube are beveled, as shown in Figure 6-31.

4. Select File, Save Scene As and save the file as **Beveled cube.mb**.

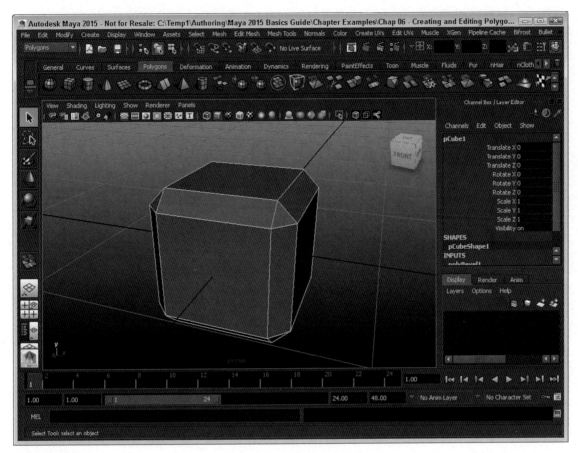

Figure 6-31
A beveled cube

Lesson 6.3-Tutorial 5: Poke Faces

1. Create a polygon sphere object using the Create, Polygon Primitives, Sphere menu command.

2. Set the SubdivisionAxis and SubdivisionHeight values in the Channel Box to 10.

3. Right-click on the sphere and select Face from the right-click pop-up marking menu and drag over the entire sphere to select all of its faces.

4. Select the Edit Mesh, Face Poke menu command.

5. A manipulator appears. Drag the blue Z-axis handle to pull the faces away from the sphere center.

   a. Each face of the sphere is raised like a spike, as shown in Figure 6-32.

6. Select File, Save Scene As and save the file as **Poked sphere.mb**.

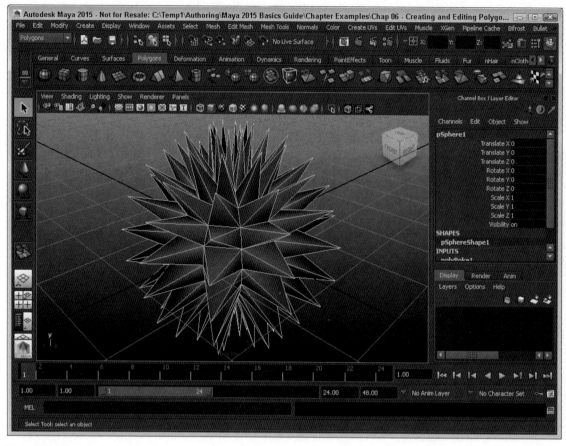

Figure 6-32
A poked sphere

Lesson 6.3-Tutorial 6: Wedge Faces

1. Create a polygon cube object using the Create, Polygon Primitives, Cube menu command.

2. Right-click on the cube and select Face from the right-click pop-up marking menu and drag over one of the side faces to select it.

3. Right-click on the cube and select Edge from the right-click pop-up marking menu and drag over the lower edge of the selected face with the Shift key held down, so that both the face and edge are selected at the same time.

4. Select the Edit Mesh, Face Wedge menu command.

    A wedge extends outward from the selected face.

5. Repeat steps 2-4 for the other side faces.

    Each face of the cube extends outward, as shown in Figure 6-33.

6. Select File, Save Scene As and save the file as **Wedged cube.mb**.

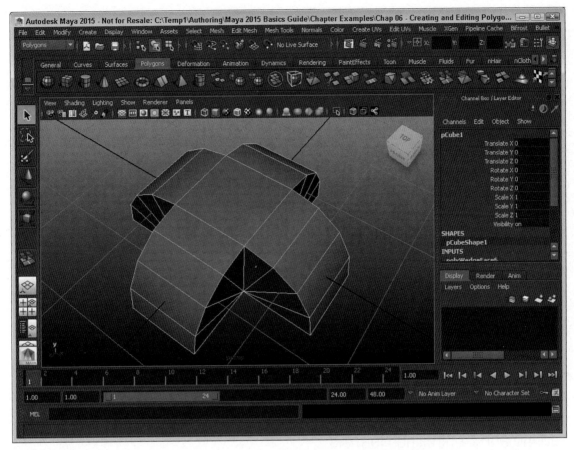

Figure 6-33
Wedged cube

Lesson 6.4: Smooth Polygon Edges

Learning to control the normals of a polygon object saves you many headaches down the road. The Polygons menu also includes a couple of smoothing commands.

Showing Normals

If some faces on your object aren't displayed in shaded view, you may have some misplaced normals. This is common for imported objects. To see an object's normals, select Display, Polygon Components, Normals. This menu command adds a single vector that extends from the center of each polygon face. Figure 6-34 shows the normals for a polygon sphere.

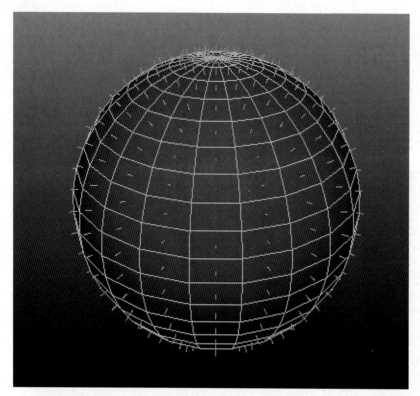

Figure 6-34
Sphere normals

Reversing and Controlling Normals

If you select a number of face components, you can reverse their normal direction using the Normals, Reverse menu command, but it is more likely that you'll want to unify the direction of all of the normals, which you can do using the Normals, Conform menu command. This points all normals in the direction of the majority of the face normals.

Normals define how the light bounces off the surface of an object. Using the Normals, Vertex Normal Edit Tool menu command, you can control the precise direction that the normals point.

Softening and Hardening Edges

You can make each selected edge hard using the Normals, Soften/Harden menu command. In the Polygon Soften/Harden Edge Options dialog box, you can set an angle value. If the angle between the normals of adjacent polygon faces are greater than this angle value, the edge between them is smoothed. If the angle is less than the designated value, the edge is hard with a sharp corner.

Smoothing Polygons with Subdivisions

To smooth a selection of faces, you can use the Mesh, Smooth menu command. This method subdivides the selected faces depending on the Subdivision Levels value found in the Polygon Smooth Options dialog box. Be aware that higher Subdivision Levels values produce a huge number of polygons. Figure 6-35 shows a polygon cone object that has been smoothed with the Mesh, Smooth menu command.

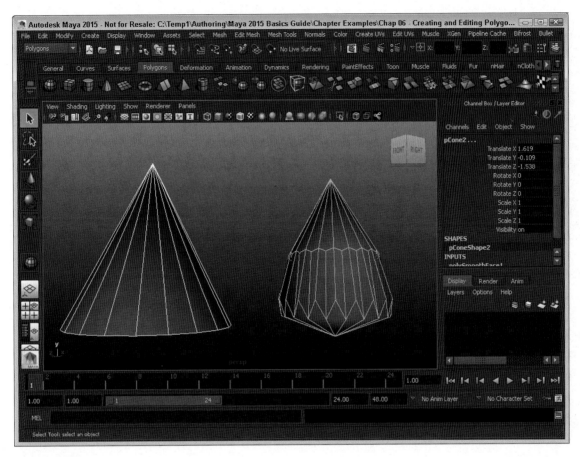

Figure 6-35
A smoothed cone

Creating a Smooth Proxy

Smoothing an object can create a dense mesh of polygon that makes it difficult to edit; using the Mesh, Smooth Proxy menu command to creates a smooth dense object, but leaves the original object in place. Editing the components of the original object changes the smoothed object also. Using a smooth proxy makes it easier to edit the dense smoothed mesh. You can also move and scale the proxy object independent of the smoothed object and in a shaded view; the proxy object is semi-transparent, allowing the smooth object to be seen.

Tip

> If the Smooth Proxy object is selected, you can use the
> Ctrl+~ hotkey to switch between the normal polygon and
> the smooth proxy display.

Adding a Crease to a Smoothed Polygon

Applying a smooth proxy operation to a polygon model causes the entire surface to be smoothed, but if you want to selectively maintain some hard edges, you can use the Mesh, Smooth Proxy, Crease tool to add a hard crease to the selected edges, as shown in Figure 6-36. To use this tool, choose the tool and select the polygon proxy edges that you want to crease and then drag with the middle mouse button to adjust the crease amount.

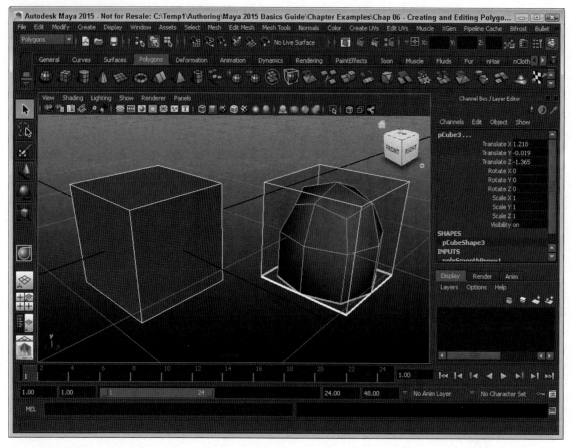

Figure 6-36
A smoothed proxy cone with a crease on one end.

Smoothing Polygons with Vertex Averaging

Another way to smooth polygon faces is with the Mesh, Average Vertices menu command. This command moves the selected vertices to form a smooth surface without adding more polygons to the mesh.

Note

> Yet another polygon smoothing method is to use the Smooth option in the Mesh Tools, Sculpt Geometry tool, Options menu command.

Lesson 6.4-Tutorial 1: Conform Normals

1. Select File, Open Scene and open the Sphere with reversed normals.mb file.

2. Select the sphere and choose the Display, Polygon Components, Normals menu command to display the normals.

    All of the normals in the center of the sphere are reversed and point inward.

3. With the sphere selected, choose the Normals, Conform menu command.

    The normal for each face is changed to point the same direction.

4. Select File, Save Scene As and save the file as **Conformed normals.mb**.

Lesson 6.4-Tutorial 2: Smooth Faces

1. Select File, Open Scene and open the Poked sphere.mb file.

2. Right-click on the sphere and select Face from the right-click pop-up marking menu and drag over the entire sphere to select all its faces.

3. Select the Mesh, Smooth menu command.

    Each face is subdivided and smoothed, turning the spikes into bumps, as shown in Figure 6-37.

4. Select File, Save Scene As and save the file as **Bumpy sphere.mb**.

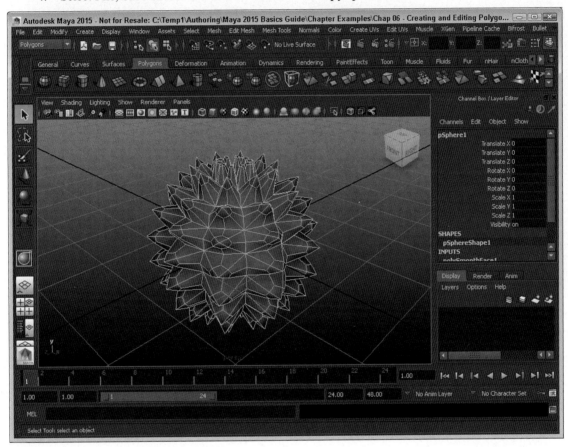

Figure 6-37
A bumpy sphere

Lesson 6.4-Tutorial 3: Smooth Faces

1. Select File, Open Scene and open the Turtle.mb file.

2. With the turtle object selected, choose the Mesh, Smooth Proxy, Subdiv Proxy menu command.

    The original object remains as a proxy, but a smoothed version appears underneath the original colored magenta.

3. Move the original object above the smoothed object.

4. Select and drag some of the components of the original object.

    As the components of the original object are moved, the underlying smoothed object is affected, as shown in Figure 6-38.

5. Select File, Save Scene As and save the file as **Smoothed turtle.mb**.

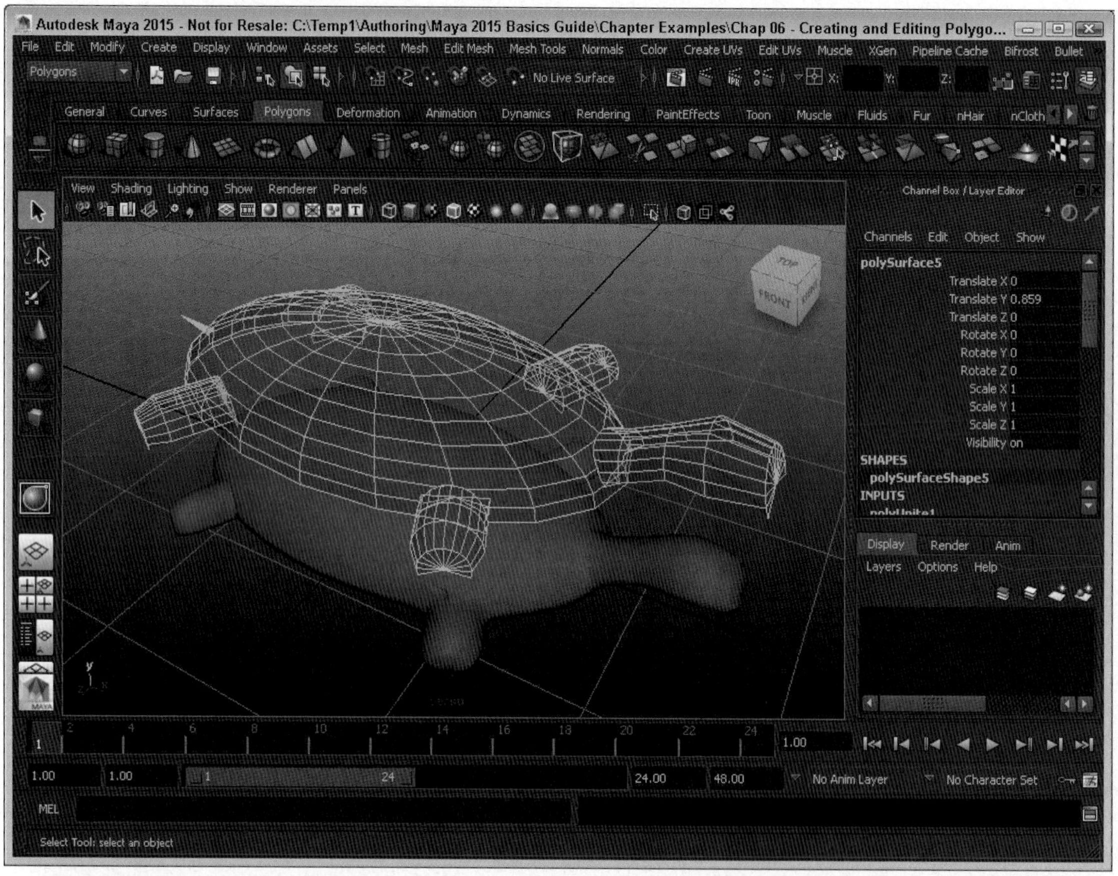

Figure 6-38
Smoothed proxy

Lesson 6.4-Tutorial 4: Smooth Faces with Vertex Averaging

1. Create a polygon sphere object using the Create, Polygon Primitives, Sphere menu command.

2. Click on the Four Views button in the Quick Layout Buttons.

3. Click on the Select by Component Type button in the Status Line.

4. Drag over the lower half of the sphere faces in the Front view and press the Delete key.

    Deleting the lower half of the sphere's faces creates a perfect hemisphere.

5. Drag over the last row of faces in the Front view to select them and choose the Edit Mesh, Face Extrude menu command. Then drag the blue Z-axis manipulator to extrude the selected faces.

6. Click on the Select by Object Type button in the Status Line and choose the Mesh, Smooth menu command.

    The object is smoothed and the number of polygons is increased.

7. Select the Mesh, Average Vertices menu command to apply an additional smoothing.

    The Average Vertices menu command smoothes the object even more without adding to the complexity of the object, as shown in Figure 6-39.

8. Select File, Save Scene As and save the file as **Smoothed sun.mb**.

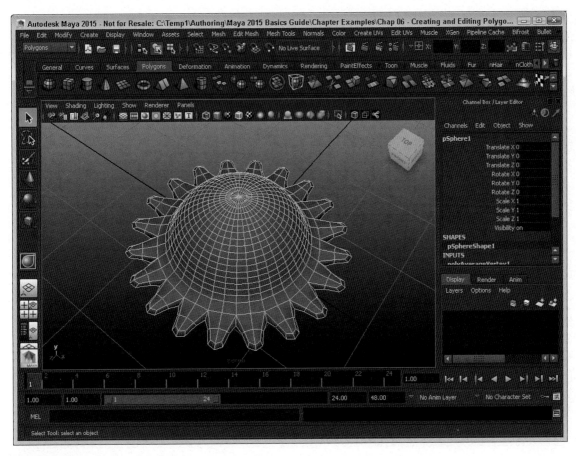

Figure 6-39
Smoothed sun

Lesson 6.5: Use Polygon Booleans and Triangulate Polygons

When two polygon surfaces overlap, you can use the Mesh, Booleans menu to compute the union, difference, or intersection between the two objects. To use the Union, Difference, or Intersection commands, just select the two polygon objects and select the desired command. Figure 6-40 shows the various Boolean operations performed on a polygon sphere and a polygon cone.

Tip

To produce the smoothest Boolean operations, make sure the surfaces that are being combined have a sufficient number of faces.

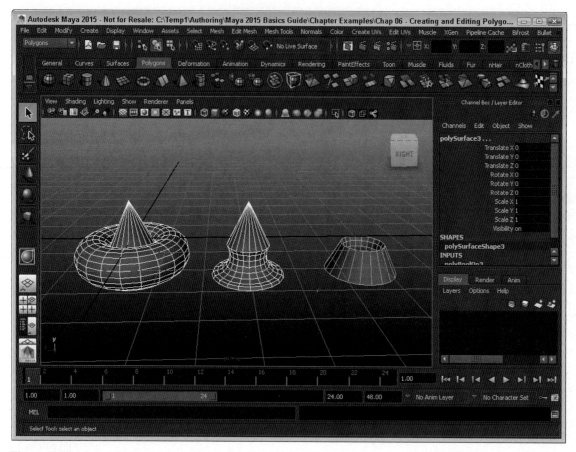

Figure 6-40
Polygon Boolean operations

Combining Polygon Objects

When the Mesh, Booleans, Union menu command is used on two overlapping surfaces, the intersecting lines are removed and the resulting object acts as a single object.

Finding the Difference Between Objects

The Mesh, Booleans, Difference menu command removes an overlapping portion of the second selected object from the first selected object.

Creating an Intersection Object

The Mesh, Booleans, Intersection menu command removes all but the intersecting portion of the two overlapping surfaces.

Triangulating Polygon Faces

If you create a polygon manually, you can accidentally create a surface that is non-planar. Non-planar surfaces are surfaces that have vertices that aren't on the same place. This condition can cause problems when they are rendered. The Mesh, Triangulate menu command divides all selected polygon faces into triangles. This ensures that all faces are co-planar. Figure 6-41 shows a simple polygon plane object that has been triangulated.

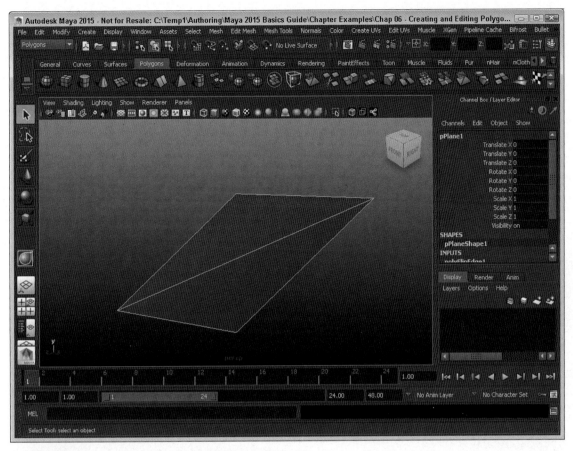

Figure 6-41
A triangulated plane object

Switching Polygon Faces to Rectangles

If you prefer to work with rectangles, you can use the Mesh, Quadrangulate menu command. This reduces the number of faces by half.

Flipping Triangle Edges

If you use the Triangulation command and the added edge for a face runs the wrong way, you can flip its direction by selecting the edge and using the Edit Mesh, Flip Triangle Edge menu command. This command cannot be used on border edges, though.

Lesson 6.5-Tutorial 1: Create a Button from Booleans

1. Create a polygon cylinder object using the Create, Polygon Primitives, Cylinder menu command.

2. Click on the polyCylinder1 input node in the Channel Box and change the Radius value to 15, the Height value to 1, and the SubdivisionAxis value to 36.

3. Create another cylinder object using the Create, Polygon Primitives, Cylinder menu command.

    The large, flat cylinder is the button and the smaller cylinders are used to cut out the buttonholes using a Booleans operation.

4. Click the Four Views button from the Quick Layout buttons.

5. Change the Radius value for the new cylinder to 1.0.

6. Move the new cylinder with the Move tool halfway towards the upper-right corner of the button.

7. Duplicate the new cylinder object with the Edit, Duplicate menu command (Ctrl/Command+d) and drag the blue Z-axis manipulator to move the duplicate downward in the Top view panel.

8. Select both smaller cylinders, duplicate them, and drag them to the left in the Top view panel using the red X-axis manipulator.

9. Select the button object and then one of the smaller cylinders, and then choose the Mesh, Booleans, Difference menu command.

10. Repeat Step 9 for the other three smaller cylinders.

    The Booleans operation removes the smaller cylinders from the larger button face, as shown in Figure 6-42.

11. Select File, Save Scene As and save the file as **Boolean button.mb**.

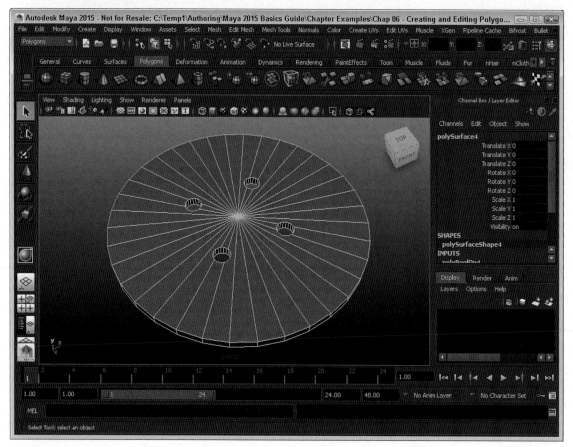

Figure 6-42
A Boolean button

Lesson 6.5-Tutorial 2: Triangulate Non-Planar Polygons

1. Create a polygon plane object using the Create, Polygon Primitives, Plane menu command.

2. Click on the polyPlane1 input node in the Channel Box and change the SubdivisionWidth and SubdivisionHeight values to 1.

3. Right-click on the plane object and select Vertex from the pop-up marking menu.

4. Select and move the right vertex upward with the Move tool.

5. Select and move the left vertex downward with the Move tool.

    This movement makes the plane object non-planar.

6. Select the entire plane object and choose Mesh, Triangulate.

7. Right-click on the plane object and select Edge from the pop-up marking menu.

8. Select the center triangulated edge and choose Edit Mesh, Flip Triangle Edge.

    The center triangulated edge is flipped to run between the opposite two vertices, as shown in Figure 6-43.

9. Select File, Save Scene As and save the file as **Triangulated plane.mb**.

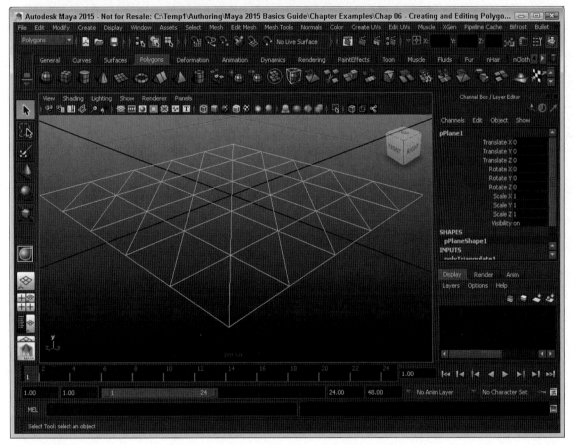

Figure 6-43
A triangulated plane

Lesson 6.6: Create Holes in Polygons

There are several ways to create a hole in a polygon object. Perhaps the easiest is to just select and delete a polygon face component. Be aware that deleting a polygon face makes the interior of the polygon object visible.

Splitting a Vertex

The Edit Polygon menu also includes a Split Vertex menu command. This command creates a separate vertex for each edge coming into the selected vertex. These vertices can then be selected independently and moved away from the others to create a hole in the geometry. Figure 6-44 shows a single vertex that has been split. Each split vertex has then been moved away from its original position.

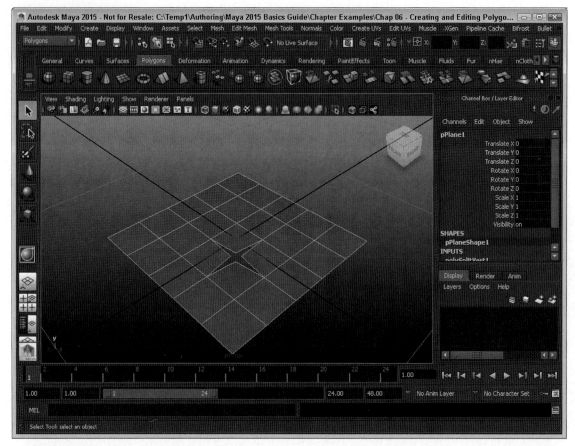

Figure 6-44
A split vertex

Extracting Faces

If a polygon face or several faces are selected, you can use the Mesh, Extract menu command to separate the selected faces from the polygon object. The Extract Options dialog box lets you specify an offset value that you can use to offset the face within the selected face. You can also define the transform values or a direction for the duplicated faces. The dialog box also includes a Random value that you can use to randomize the faces. Figure 6-45 shows a plane object with several extracted faces.

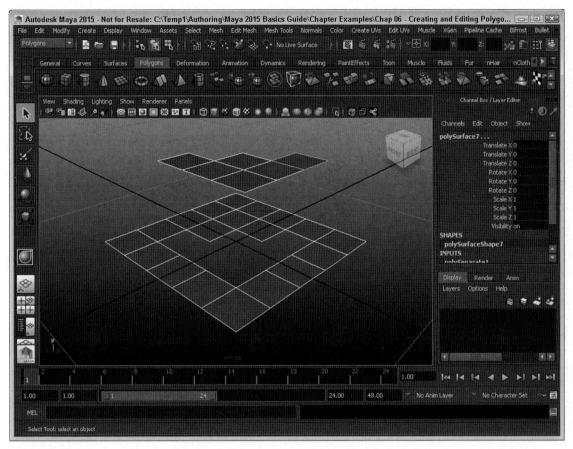

Figure 6-45
Extracted faces

Using the Make Hole Tool

Use the Mesh Tools, Make Hole tool to create a hole within a single polygon object's face. The face used to make the hole must be part of the polygon object and it must project within a single face on the object. In Component mode, select the Make Hole tool and click on the face that receives the hole and then on the face that makes the hole and then press the Enter key. If the face to make the hole is positioned away from the other face, new polygons are created to meet the hole. The Tool Options dialog box includes several merge modes, including Project First, Project Middle, or Project Second. Figure 6-46 shows one plane object cutting a hole into another one.

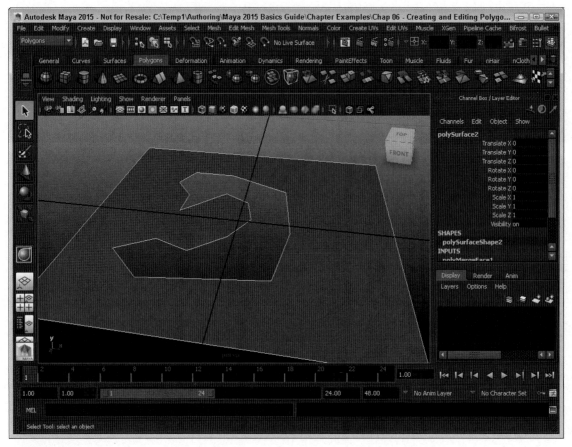

Figure 6-46
Creating a hole

Filling Holes

To fill a hole that may have been created by deleting a face, you can use the Mesh, Fill Hole command. This command patches all holes in the current object.

Tip

Using the Fill Holes command likely fills the hole with a non-planar polygon. You can fix this with the Mesh, Cleanup menu command or by selecting the new polygon and using the Mesh, Triangulate or Quadrangulate commands.

Lesson 6.6-Tutorial 1: Add Holes to a Cube

1. Create a polygon cube object using the Create, Polygon Primitives, Cube menu command.

2. Right-click on the cube object and select Face from the pop-up marking menu. Then drag over the entire cube to select all of its faces.

3. Select the Edit Mesh, Face Duplicate, Options menu command to open the Duplicate Face Options dialog box.

4. Set the Offset value to 0.2 and the Translate Z-axis value to 0.1. Then click the Duplicate button.

The Duplicate Faces menu command creates and moves a slightly smaller duplicate face away from the center of the cube. These faces can create holes in the cube.

5. With all objects selected in Object mode, choose the Mesh, Combine menu command.

6. Select the Mesh Tools, Make Hole Tool menu command.

7. In Component mode, click on the cube face and then on its matching duplicated face while holding down the Shift key and press the Enter key.

   A hole is cut in the underlying cube, but the hole won't be visible until you make the view panel shaded using the 5 key.

8. Repeat Step 6 and 7 for each cube face.

   The final cube is shown in Figure 6-47.

9. Select File, Save Scene As and save the file as **Cube with holes.mb**.

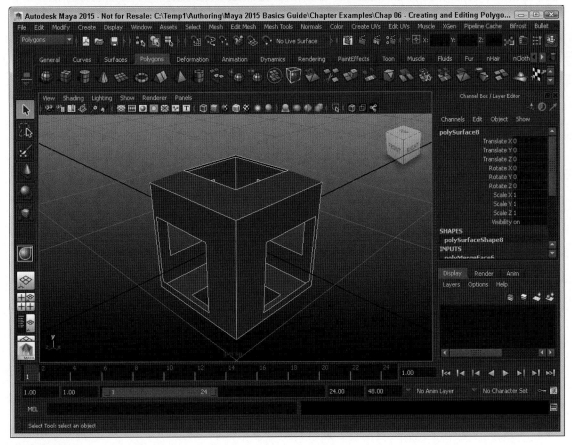

Figure 6-47
Cube with holes

Lesson 6.7: Work with Edge Loops, Rings, and Borders

For many models, the capability to select edge loops, rings, and borders is helpful. For example, cutting a hole in a torso and selecting the border edge enables you to quickly extrude those edges to create an arm. An edge loop is a group of edges that are aligned end to end, an edge ring is a group of edges that are aligned parallel to one another in a column, and a border includes the edges that surround a hole in the polygon model, as shown in Figure 6-48.

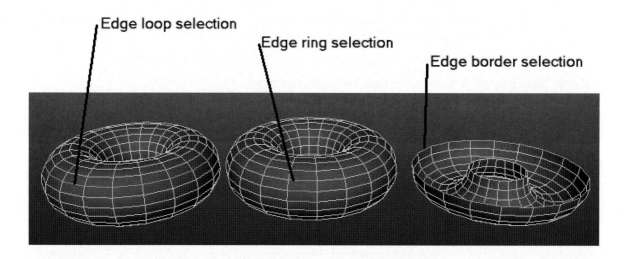

Figure 6-48
Edge loop, ring, and border selections

Selecting Edge Loops, Rings, and Borders

You can select each of these selection types by double-clicking on one edge contained within the loop or border with the appropriate tool. The Select Edge Loop, Select Edge Ring, and Select Border Edge tools are in the Edit menu.

Converting Selections

Using the Select, Convert Selection options, you can convert an existing selection of components to the desired selection, including edge loops, edge rings, face paths, and contained faces and edges.

Using the Duplicate Edge Loop Tool

The Mesh Tools, Offset Edge Loop tool is used to quickly create two additional edge loops on either side of the selected edge. Selecting this tool and clicking on an edge makes duplicate edge loops appear on either side of the selected edge. These duplicate edges appear as dashed lines, as shown in Figure 6-49, and you can drag to move them closer or further from the selected edge. Releasing the mouse button places the new duplicate edge loops.

Duplicate edge loops

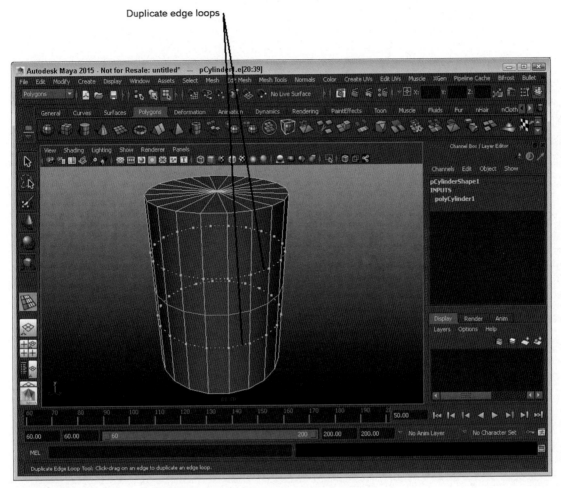

Figure 6-49
Duplicate edge loops

Using the Split Edge Ring Tool

The Mesh Tools, Multi-Cut tool adds a single edge ring next to the selected edge. You can drag this edge ring into position like the Duplicate Edge Loop tool and then place it when the mouse button is released. If you disable the Auto Complete option in the Tools Setting dialog box, you can click on different oriented edges to define the path of the edge ring. Figure 6-50 shows an edge ring that follows just such a unique path.

Custom edge ring

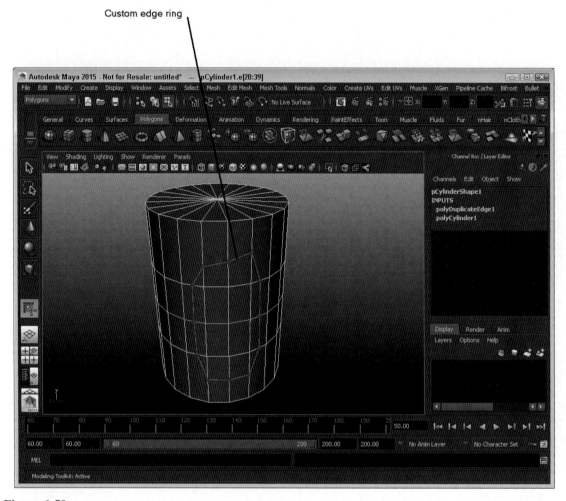

Figure 6-50
Customized edge ring

Lesson 6.7-Tutorial 1: Add Edge Loops to a Face

1. Select File, Open Scene and open the Simple face.mb file.

    This face was created using Subdivision Surfaces and converted to polygons. The Sculpt Geometry tool was then used to indent the eyes and nose.

2. Select the Mesh Tools, Offset Edge Loop Tool, Option menu command.

3. In the Polygon Duplicate Edge Tool Options dialog box, disable the Auto Complete option and click the Enter Tool and Close button.

4. Select the single horizontal edge in the center of the eye socket and press the Enter key to make the edge loop. Repeat for the opposite eye.

    The Duplicate Edge Loop tool adds two radial edge loops surrounding the eyes.

5. Select the Mesh Tools, Multi-Cut Tool, Option menu command.

    The Tool Settings window opens to the right of the view panel.

6. Disable the Auto Complete option in the Tool Settings window.

210

7. Click on several horizontal edges that run along the right side of the nose. Then select several vertical edges under the nose and some more horizontal edges that run along the left side of the nose.

   A simple edge ring is added that surrounds the nose.

8. Select the Mesh Tools, Offset Edge Loop Tool, Option menu command again. This time, enable the Auto Complete option and click the Enter Tool and Close button.

9. Click on the new edge ring that surrounds the nose and drag to create two new edge rings that are positioned close to the existing edge ring.

   The face with its new edge loops and rings is shown in Figure 6-51.

10. Select File, Save Scene As and save the file as **Edge loop face.mb**.

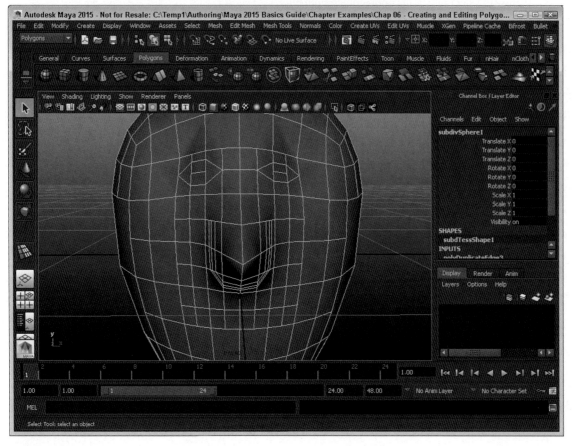

Figure 6-51
Face with edge loops

Chapter Summary

This chapter covers modeling with polygons. All polygon modeling commands are found in the Polygons and Edit Polygons menus. Maya includes several default polygon primitive objects as well as a Create Polygon tool that you can use to create custom polygons. You can edit polygons by moving their vertex, face, or edge components. There are also numerous polygon operations for working with polygon components, including extrude, chamfer, bevel, and merge. Boolean operations provide a way to combine polygon objects using union, difference, and intersection methods. There are also tools for making holes in polygons and tools to working with edge loops.

What You Have Learned

In this chapter, you learned

*   How to create polygon primitives.

*   How to create a custom polygon with the Create Polygon tool.

*   How to append polygons with the Append to Polygon tool.

*   How to duplicate a polygon face.

*   How to clean up and reduce a polygon object.

*   How to select the various polygon components.

*   How to subdivide a polygon face.

*   How to split and cut a polygon face.

*   How to merge vertices and edges and delete components.

*   How to display and reverse face normals.

*   How to soften and harden normals.

*   How to smooth polygons and to use a smooth proxy.

*   How to add creases to a smooth proxy.

*   How to use Booleans.

*   How to triangulate polygons.

*   How to split a vertex.

*   How to extract faces.

*   How to use the Make Holes tool.

*   How to fill existing polygon holes.

*   How to select edge loops, edge rings, and borders.

*   How to create edge loops and edge rings.

Key Terms From This Chapter

*   **Polygon.** A co-planar surface created from three or more linear edges.

*   **Normal.** A vector extending perpendicular from the surface of a polygon used to determine the polygon's inner and outer faces.

*   **Appending.** The process of attaching a polygon to an existing polygon.

*   **Reduce.** An operation that reduces the total number of polygons in a model.

*   **Cleanup.** An operation that removes potential trouble parts of a polygon model such as unattached vertices.

*   **Subdividing.** An operation for splitting all polygon faces into two or more faces.

*   **Extruding.** An operation that moves the selected component perpendicular from its current position.

*   **Chamfer.** An operation that replaces the selected vertices with polygon faces.

*   **Bevel.** An operation that replaces an edge with a polygon face.

* **Poking.** An operation that adds a vertex to the center of the selected face and attaches edges to the new vertex.

* **Wedge.** A model structure created by rotating a face about an edge and connecting it to the original face's position.

* **Smooth proxy.** A smoothed copy of an original polygon object.

* **Booleans.** A set of operations for combining two polygon objects together using a union, difference, or intersection.

* **Edge loop.** A series of edges that run end to end across the surface of a polygon object.

* **Edge ring.** A series of parallel edges that run across the surface of a polygon object.

* **Border.** A series of edges that line a polygon hole.

Chapter 7
Assigning Materials and Textures

IN THIS CHAPTER

7.1 Apply materials.

7.2 Use the Hypershade.

7.3 Work with materials.

7.4 Work with textures.

7.5 Position textures.

7.6 Use utilities nodes.

7.7 Paint in 3D.

Modeling geometry is only one aspect of creating a realistic object. Another critical aspect involves dressing objects with the correct materials and textures. Using materials and textures, you can change attributes such as the color, transparency, and shininess of an object.

Materials are often referred to as **shaders** in Maya. Materials control how the light interacts with the object's surface. Material nodes are combined to make up a shading group and can be applied to objects in the scene. A single material can consist of many different rendering nodes. Each node contributes to the final rendering.

Textures are the image files that can act as input nodes for the various material attributes such as color or transparency. For example, a wood material may have a texture node that includes colors, another texture node to define its shininess, and a relief texture node that defines its surface bumps. In addition, each node has several attributes that define its description. You can change node attributes in the Attribute Editor.

You can view all of the details on material and texture nodes in an interface called the **Hypershade**. You can connect nodes together so that the output of one node becomes the input of another. The Connection Editor connects attributes together. You can also drag materials with the middle mouse button and drop them on objects to apply the materials.

The Hypershade has access to all the various render nodes using the **Create Bar** and the Work Area is used to view and connect nodes together. All attributes for the selected node are displayed in the Attribute Editor. The available nodes include Materials, 2D and 3D textures, and an assortment of utility render nodes that enable you to do things like control the placement of textures.

You can create effective materials by understanding the differences between all of the various materials and textures.

The Texturing menu includes a 3D Paint tool that lets you paint colors using the Artisan and Paint Effect brushes directly on 3d objects. This tool also lets you paint other attributes, such as transparency and **bump maps**.

Lesson 7.1: Apply Materials

When an object is first created, a default material is applied to it; this is the Lambert1 material. You can see this material using the Lambert1 tab in the Attribute Editor, as shown in Figure 7-1. You can replace this default material with a new material and, once it's applied, you can edit the material's attributes—such as Color, Transparency, and Specularity—in the Attribute Editor.

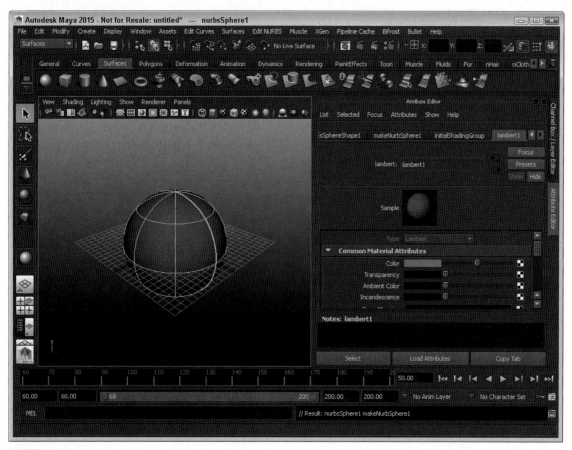

Figure 7-1
Default material node

Applying New Materials

When an object is selected in the view panel you can apply a new material to the object using the Lighting/Shading, Assign New Material menu command. The Lighting/Shading menu command is available when the Rendering menu set is selected. This opens a submenu of several material and environment options, as shown in Figure 7-2. Selecting a material from the menu creates a new shading group and material nodes that you can view in the Attribute Editor. You can view the material attributes for the selected object using the Lighting/Shading, Material Attributes menu command.

Note

If the Lighting/Shading, Assign New Material, Automatic Attribute Editor menu command is enabled, assigning a new material automatically opens the Attribute Editor.

Figure 7-2
A sample of the available materials

Renaming Materials

Although the material node is named by default using the material name followed by a single-digit number, you can enter a new name for the material in the Attribute Editor. Renaming materials is a good way to easily find them again if you plan on reusing them within the scene.

Applying Existing Materials

Maya keeps track of all the materials applied to different objects in the scene. You can apply an existing material to another object in the scene using the Lighting/Shading, Assign Existing Material menu command, which includes the names of all the currently used materials.

Changing Material Attributes

Most of the attributes found in the Attribute Editor for a material node consist of a color swatch, a value slider, and a button to open the Create Render Node dialog box, as shown in Figure 7-3. The color swatch shows the current color that is applied to the attribute. For attributes such as Color, the color represents the actual color that is displayed, but for other attributes, like Transparency, the color represents a value with black being a minimum value and white being the maximum value. Clicking the color swatch opens a Color Chooser in which you can select a new color. The Create Render Node dialog box, shown in Figure 7-4, lets you select textures to replace solid colors. Each texture node has its own set of attributes.

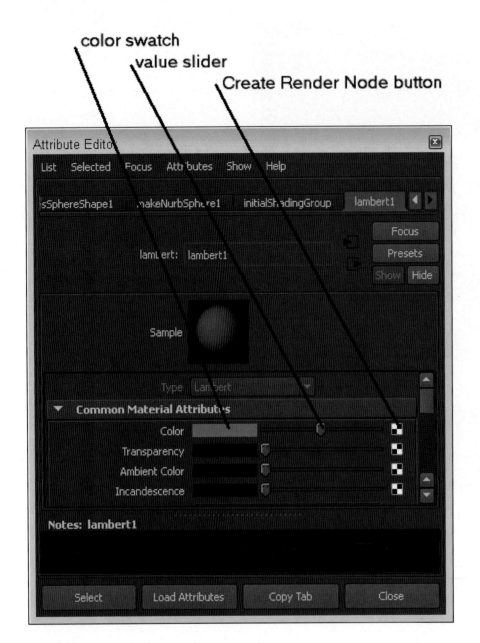

Figure 7-3
Material attribute controls

Figure 7-4
The Create Render Node dialog box

Moving Between Nodes

If you replace the Color attribute of a material with a texture, the Create Render Node button is also replaced with an Input Connection button. Clicking this button opens attributes for the Input node, which in this case is the texture node. Using the Input and Output Connection buttons (see Figure 7-5), you can move forward and backward through all of the nodes that make up the entire material.

Input Connection button —
Output Connection button —

Figure 7-5
Input and Output Connection buttons

Rendering Materials

To see a rough view of the material and textures applied to an object, press the 6 key, but be aware that the view panel displays only a limited set of material properties, such as color, texture, and transparency. To see all of the material details, such as bump maps, you'll need to render the scene using the Render View interface (shown in Figure 7-6), which you can open using the Window, Rendering Editors, Render View menu command.

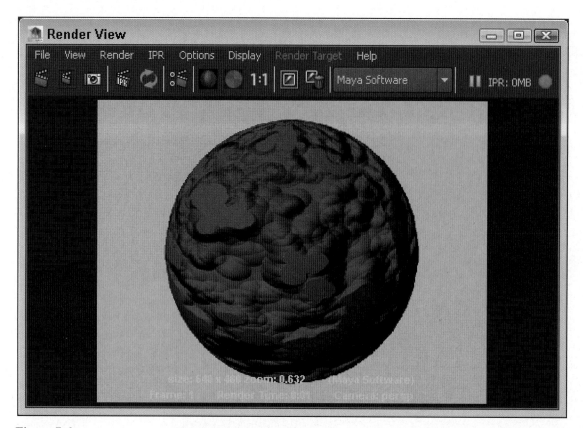

Figure 7-6
Render View interface

Lesson 7.1-Tutorial 1: Apply a Material

1. Create a sphere object using the Create, NURBS Primitives, Sphere menu command.

2. Click on the Menu Sets drop-down list to the far left of the Status Line and select the Rendering menu set.

3. With the sphere selected, choose the Lighting/Shading, Assign New Material, Phong menu command.

4. Press the 6 key to enable the view panel to display textures.

    Applying this new material opens the Attribute Editor and display the material node. The object in the view panel is displayed using this new material.

5. In the Attribute Editor, type the name **Shiny red** for this material.

6. Click on the color swatch for the Color attribute and choose a red color in the Color Chooser, and then click the Accept button.

    Figure 7-7 shows the shiny red material applied to the sphere.

7. Select File, Save Scene As and save the file as **Shiny red sphere.mb**.

Figure 7-7
Shiny red sphere

Lesson 7.1-Tutorial 2: Apply and Render a Texture

1. Create a sphere object using the Create, NURBS Primitives, Sphere menu command.

2. With the sphere selected, choose the Lighting/Shading, Assign New Material, Blinn menu command. In the Attribute Editor, click on the Create Render Node button for the Color attribute.

3. Select the Checker option in the Create Render Node dialog box.

4. Press the 6 key to enable the view panel to display textures.

    The Create Render Node dialog box automatically closes, and the Checker node is made active in the Attribute Editor.

5. In the Attribute Editor, click on the Go to Output Connection button.

    Clicking the Go to Output button causes the blinn1 node to be selected in the Attribute Editor.

6. Click on the Create Render Node button for the Bump Mapping attribute, and click on the Fractal button in the Create Render Node dialog box.

    Although a bump map has been added to the sphere material, no change is shown in the view panel.

7. Select the Render, Render Current Frame menu command.

    The Render View window opens, and the current view panel is rendered showing the applied bump map.

8. Select File, Save Scene As and save the file as **Checkered bumpy sphere.mb**.

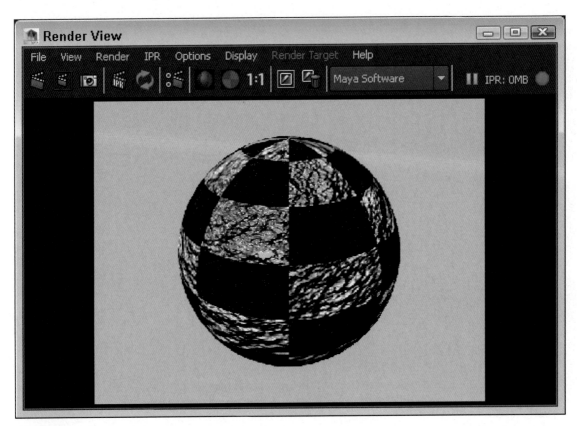

Figure 7-8
A rendered checkered sphere

Lesson 7.2: Use the Hypershade

The Hypershade, shown in Figure 7-9, is the interface wherein you can see and work with the entire network of nodes that make up a material. It is useful when you begin to create custom materials. These custom materials can then be applied to objects in the scene directly from the Hypershade. You can access the Hypershade using the Window, Rendering Editors, Hypershade menu command. The Hypershade interface consists of a menu, a toolbar, and three different panes—the Create Bar, and the upper and lower tabbed panes.

Figure 7-9
The Hypershade

Using the Create Bar

The pane on the left of the Hypershade is the Create Bar, as shown in Figure 7-10. The Create Bar is the source of available rendering nodes similar to the Create Render Node dialog box. Each of the categories of nodes can be selected using sections that can be expanded and collapsed as needed. Some of the available node categories include Surface, Volumetric, 2D and 3D Textures, Lights, General Utilities, and Glow Each category lists and displays a thumbnail for the available nodes.

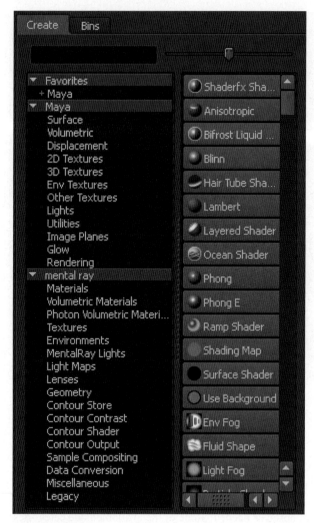

Figure 7-10
The Create Bar

Using the tabbed panes

Clicking on a node in the Create Bar adds the selected node to the tabbed panes in the Hypershade. The upper tabbed pane includes tabs that you can use to view only a specific category of rendering nodes for the current scene, including Materials, Textures, Utilities, Lights, Cameras, Shading Groups, Bake Sets, and Projects. Above the tabs on the upper pane is a text field where you can search for specific nodes. Figure 7-11 shows the Hypershade with the Textures tab selected. This shows all of the textures currently used in the scene. The lower tabbed pane includes a Work Area tab that is used as a scratch pad to connect the various nodes. You can also use the Tabs menu to create new tabs and manage the existing tab sets.

Tip

> You can use the buttons on the right end of the toolbar to show only the upper tabbed pane, only the lower tabbed pane, or both.

Toggle Create Bar
Show Top Tabs Only
Show Bottom Tabs Only
Show Top and Bottom Tabs

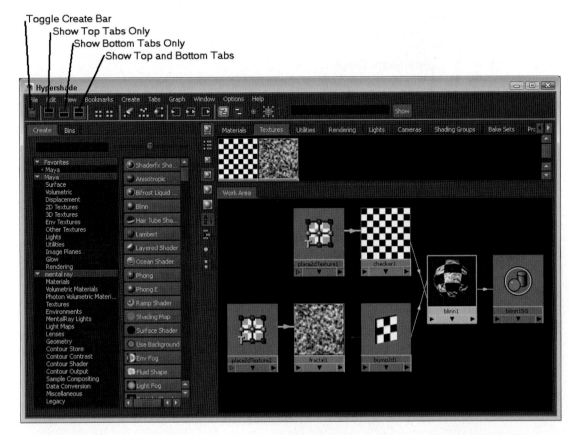

Figure 7-11
Scene textures

Using the Work Area

The Work Area tab, shown in Figure 7-12, is where you'll spend most of your time creating custom materials. You can select nodes within the Work Area by clicking on them; you can also drag over several nodes with the mouse or hold down the Shift key while clicking to select multiple nodes. Selected nodes are highlighted yellow or surrounded with a yellow border. You can move selected nodes within the Hypershade by dragging them. You can use the Alt/Option key together with the middle and right mouse buttons to pan and zoom selected nodes within the Hypershade. The Clear Graph toolbar button erases all nodes in the Work Area. The Rearrange Graph toolbar button lines up all nodes within the Work Area pane and the Graph Materials on Selected Objects toolbar button displays the nodes for the selected object.

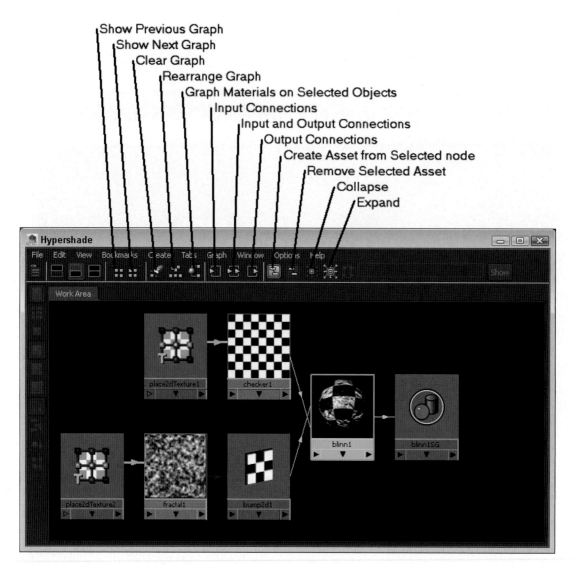

Show Previous Graph
Show Next Graph
Clear Graph
Rearrange Graph
Graph Materials on Selected Objects
Input Connections
Input and Output Connections
Output Connections
Create Asset from Selected node
Remove Selected Asset
Collapse
Expand

Figure 7-12
The Work Area tab

Working with Nodes

Each active node in the Hypershade is represented by a rectangular icon that displays the current settings for the material or texture. These icons are updated as you make changes to the node's attributes. Double-clicking on a node opens and displays all its attributes in the Attribute Editor. Double-clicking with the Ctrl/Command key held down lets you rename the node.

Connecting Nodes

Clicking on a node in the Create Bar makes the node appear in the Work Area. You can connect nodes together to create complex materials. These connections are displayed in the Hypershade as arrowed lines. The different colors represent different types of data. To connect two nodes, drag one node with the middle mouse button and drop it on the node to which you want to connect it. Doing so causes a pop-up menu to appear (like the one shown in Figure 7-13), from which you can select from several common attributes to connect to. If the attribute you want to connect to isn't on the pop-up menu, you can select Other to open the Connection Editor.

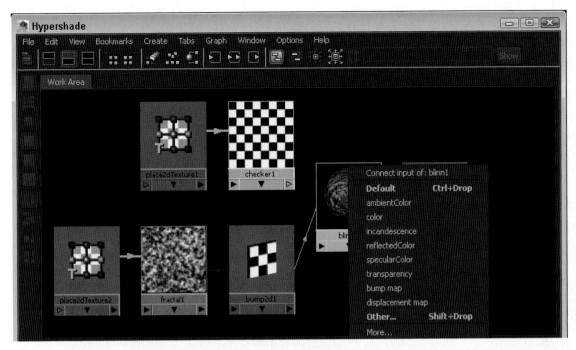

Figure 7-13
The Connection pop-up menu

Using the Connection Editor

The Connection Editor, shown in Figure 7-14, includes two panes—one for the Output node and one for the Input node. If you accessed this interface using the Hypershade pop-up menu, the name of the two nodes are at the bottom of each pane. You can reload a pane by selecting its node in the Hypershade and clicking the Reload Left or Reload Right buttons. Selecting an attribute in each pane establishes a connection between the two.

Figure 7-14
The Connection Editor

Dragging Materials to Objects

You can apply material nodes in the Hypershade to objects in the view panels by dragging the node with the middle mouse button and dropping it on the object in the view panel that it is to be assigned to. You can also assign materials to the selected object by right-clicking on the node and selecting Assign Material to Selection from the pop-up menu.

Lesson 7.2-Tutorial 1: Create a Custom Material

1. Create a sphere object using the Create, NURBS Primitives, Sphere menu command.

2. Select the Window, Rendering Editors, Hypershade menu command to open the Hypershade interface.

3. In the Hypershade's Create Bar, expand the Surface, 2D Textures and 3D Textures categories..

4. Then locate and click on the Blinn material node, the Grid 2D texture node, and the Crater 3D texture node.

    Each of these nodes appear in the Work Area tab.

5. Maximize the Work Area tab by clicking on the Show Bottom Tabs Only button in the toolbar.

6. Drag the Crater texture with the middle mouse button and drop it on top of the Blinn1 material node. In the pop-up menu that appears, select the Color attribute.

7. Drag the Grid texture with the middle mouse button and drop it also on top of the Blinn1 material node. In the pop-up menu that appears, select the Specular Color attribute.

8. Click on the Rearrange Graph button on the toolbar to arrange the nodes.

9. Select the sphere object in the view panel, right -click on the Blinn1 material, and select the Assign Material to Selection from the pop-up menu.

    Figure 7-15 shows the resulting material in the Hypershade's Work Area tab.

10. Select File, Save Scene As and save the file as **Custom material.mb**.

Figure 7-15
A Custom material

Lesson 7.2-Tutorial 2: Use the Connection Editor

1. Create a sphere object using the Create, NURBS Primitives, Sphere menu command.

2. Select the Window, Rendering Editors, Hypershade menu command to open the Hypershade interface.

3. Click on the Lambert material node and the Cloth 2D texture node.

    Each of these nodes appear in the Work Area tab.

4. Drag the Cloth1 texture with the middle mouse button and drop it on top of the Lambert2 material node. In the pop-up menu that appears, select the Other menu option.

    This command causes the Connection Editor to appear with the Cloth1 node in the left pane and the Lambert2 node in the right pane.

5. In the left pane, locate and click on the Out Color R attribute and, in the right pane, locate and click on the Color R attribute.

This command links the red channel of the cloth texture to the red channel of the Lambert material.

6. Click the Close button to exit the Connection Editor.

7. Drag the Lambert2 material with the middle mouse button and drop it on top of the sphere in the view panel.

Figure 7-16 shows the resulting material in the Hypershade's Work Area tab.

8. Select File, Save Scene As and save the file as **Red channel connection.mb**.

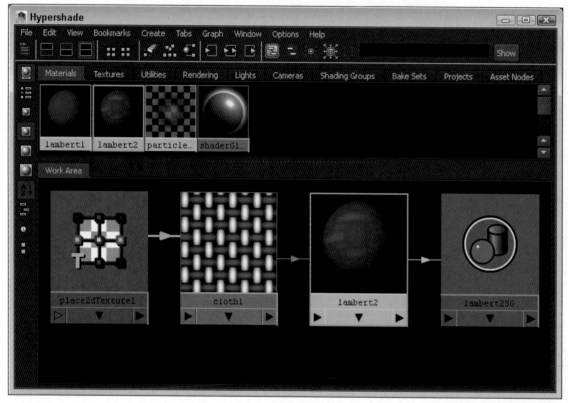

Figure 7-16
Another custom material

Lesson 7.3: Work with Materials

The first category in the Hypershade Create Bar is Surface. Each Surface node includes attributes that define such material properties as color and transparency. You can edit these attributes in the Attribute Editor. In addition to the standard surface materials, Maya also includes support for volumetric and displacement materials. Figure 7-17 shows all the nodes available in the Surface and Volumetric Materials categories.

Figure 7-17
Material nodes

Learning the Surface Materials

Maya includes the following ten different surface materials (or shaders), but the Unlimited version includes some additional nodes:

* **Anisotropic**. This material has elliptical specular highlights.

* **Blinn**. This material has soft circular highlights and is good for metallic surfaces.

* **Lambert**. This material has no highlights and is useful for cloth and non-reflective surfaces.

* **Layered Shader**. This material can combine several shaders into one and allows you to apply several materials to a single object.

* **Phong**. This material includes a hard circular highlight and is good for glass surfaces.

* **Phong E**. This material is similar to the Phong Shader, but it is optimized to render faster.

* **Ramp Shader**. This material gives you control over a gradient ramp.

231

* **Shading Map**. This material allows you to change the colors that are rendered and can be used to render cartoons.

* **Surface Shader**. This material allows you to connect an attribute to the surface material attributes.

* **Use Background**. This material allows you to alter the shadows and reflections of an object.

A key difference between these different surface materials is how the light is reflected off its surface. This is most evident in the specular highlights.

Changing Material Color

One property that is common for most surface materials is color. You can see the current color for a selected surface material node in the Attribute Editor. Dragging the Color Slider changes the color's brightness, and clicking on the color swatch opens the Color Chooser dialog box, as shown in Figure 7-18, wherein you can select a new color. The Color Chooser can display color values in RGB or HSV. The Color Chooser also includes a Blend rollout, where you can create new colors by blending four corner colors and a Palette rollout by scrolling to the bottom of the Color Chooser dialog box.

Figure 7-18
The Color Chooser

Changing Material Transparency

Another common surface material attribute is transparency. The Transparency attribute includes a color swatch and a slider. Setting the Transparency color to pure black will makes an object opaque and setting the color swatch to pure white makes it completely transparent.

Using Other Material Attributes

Surface materials include many other attributes. The following is a small sampling of some of the common material attributes:

* **Type.** Lets you change the material Shader.

* **Ambient Color**. Lightens the material's color, but has no effect when black.

* **Incandescence.** Color emitted from the object like a light bulb.

* **Diffuse**. Represents the purity of the color.

* **Translucence**. How much light shows through an object.

* **Specular color**. The color of the specular highlights.

* **Reflectivity**. Defines how reflective a surface is.

* **Reflected color**. The color that is reflected by the object.

* **Eccentricity**. Controls the size of the specular highlights.

* **Roughness**. Determines the blurriness of the specular highlights.

Layering Materials

You can use the Layered Shader material to create advanced materials by layering several materials together, as shown in Figure 7-19. To create a layered material, select and drag the materials that you want onto the Layered Shader node with the middle mouse button and select the Default menu option in the pop-up menu. This connects the material as a layer and the material is included in the Attribute Editor. The material at the left in the Attribute Editor is the top-most material and all materials need to be at least partially transparent in order to see the materials underneath.

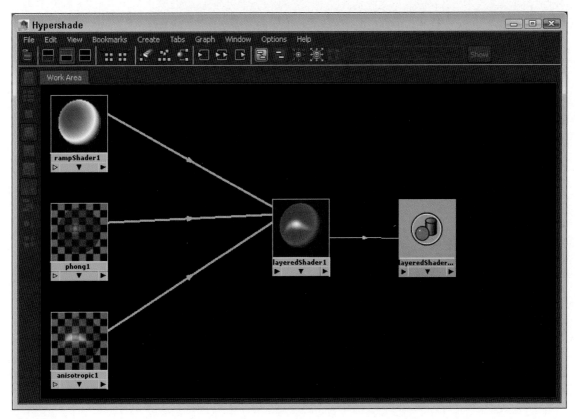

Figure 7-19
A layered material

Figure 7-20
The Attribute Editor for the Layered Shader

Using the Ramp Shader

The color section for the Ramp Shader material in the Attribute Editor includes a rectangle that represents the gradient ramp, as shown in Figure 7-21. Click on the rectangle at the location where you want to add a new color. A small circle appears above the rectangle and a small square appears below. If you select the circle, you can change its color by clicking the Selected Color swatch and if you drag the circle, you can reposition the color. If you click the square, the color is deleted. You can also create gradient maps for the Transparency, Incandescence, Specular Color, Specular Shading, Specular Roll Off, Reflectivity, and Environment attributes.

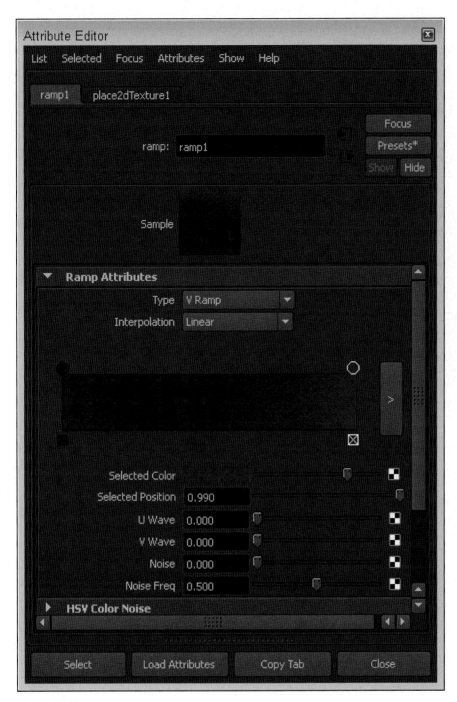

Figure 7-21
The Attribute Editor for Ramp Shader

Using the Shading Map

The Shading Map material has attributes for a Color and a Shading Map Color. It uses the Shading Map Color texture to determine the shading for the Color. For example, if you use a Ramp texture as the Shading Map Color, all the bright spots on the object are set to one end of the ramp and the darker spots get the lower part of the ramp, as shown in Figure 7-22.

Figure 7-22
Shading Map material

Lesson 7.3-Tutorial 1: Change Color and Transparency

1. Create a sphere object using the Create, NURBS Primitives, Sphere menu command.

2. Select the Window, Rendering Editors, Hypershade menu command to open the Hypershade interface.

3. Click on the Blinn material node in the Create Bar.

4. In the Attribute Editor, click the color swatch for the Color attribute.

    The Color Chooser opens.

5. Drag the color locator dot in the color wheel over to the orange color and drag the brightness slider up towards the top.

    The color in the Attribute Editor and Hypershade is automatically updated.

6. Click the Accept button to close the Color Chooser.

7. Drag the slider for the Transparency attribute to the right.

8. Select the sphere object in the view panel, right-click on the Blinn1 material in the Hypershade and select Assign Material to Selection from the pop-up menu.

    The sphere object is updated with the orange transparent material, as shown in Figure 7-23.

9. Select File, Save Scene As and save the file as **Orange transparent sphere.mb**.

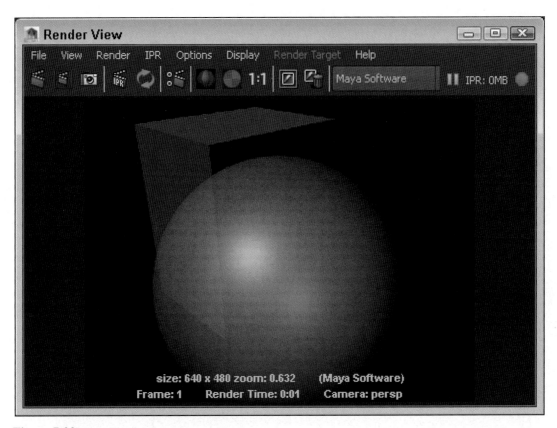

Figure 7-23
Orange transparent sphere

Lesson 7.3-Tutorial 2: Layer Materials

1. Create a sphere object using the Create, NURBS Primitives, Sphere menu command.

2. Select the Window, Rendering Editors, Hypershade menu command to open the Hypershade interface.

3. Click on the Layered Shader material node in the Create Bar.

4. Drag the Anisotropic material with the middle mouse button and drop it on the Layered Shader node in the Work Area. Then select the Default menu option in the pop-up menu.

5. Repeat Step 4 with the Phong and Ramp Shader materials.

6. Click the Rearrange Graph button in the Hypershade toolbar to rearrange the nodes.

7. Select the Layered Shader node and change its Color attribute to black and drag the slider for its Transparency attribute to the right.

8. Select the Anisotropic node and drag its Transparency slider half way to the right.

9. Select the Phong node, set its Color to a bright purple, and drag the slider for its Transparency attribute half way to the right.

10. Select the Ramp Shader node and change the Selected Color attribute to red. Click in the middle of the gradient ramp bar and select white and then click on the right end of the gradient ramp bar and select a blue color.

11. Change the Color Input attribute to Brightness.

The resulting layered material includes an elliptical highlight, compliments of the Anisotropic material, a normal circular highlight from the Phong material, and a gradient ramp of colors from the Ramp Shader material, as shown in Figure 7-24.

12. Select the sphere object in the view panel, right -click on the Layered Shader material in the Hypershade and select Assign Material to Selection from the pop-up menu.

13. Select File, Save Scene As and save the file as **Layered material with ramp.mb**.

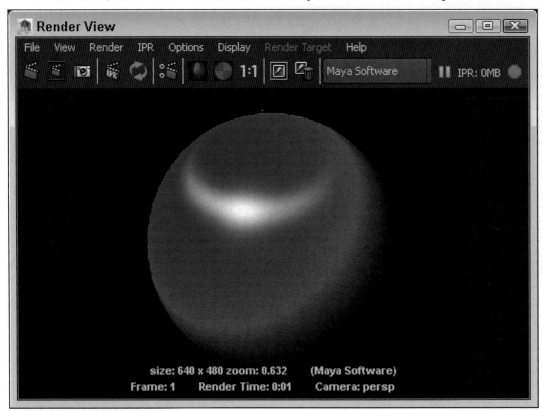

Figure 7-24
Layered material with ramp

Lesson 7.3-Tutorial 3: Use a Shading Map

1. Create a sphere object using the Create, NURBS Primitives, Sphere menu command.

2. Select the Window, Rendering Editors, Hypershade menu command to open the Hypershade interface.

3. Click on the Shading Map material node in the Create Bar.

4. Drag the Blinn material with the middle mouse button and drop it on the Shading Map node in the Work Area. Then select the Default menu option in the pop-up menu.

5. Select the ShadingMap1 node in the Hypershade and in the Attribute Editor, click on the Create Render Node button for the Shading Map Color attribute.

6. In the Create Render Node dialog box, choose the Checker node.

7. Click the Rearrange Graph button in the Hypershade toolbar to rearrange the nodes.

8. Select the Blinn1 node and change its Color attribute to a light purple color.

   The checker texture is used to represent the light purple shading for the Blinn material, as shown in Figure 7-25, creating a set of black and white stripes.

238

9. Select the sphere object in the view panel, right -click on the Blinn1 material in the Hypershade and select Assign Material to Selection from the pop-up menu.

10. Select File, Save Scene As and save the file as **Striped sphere.mb**.

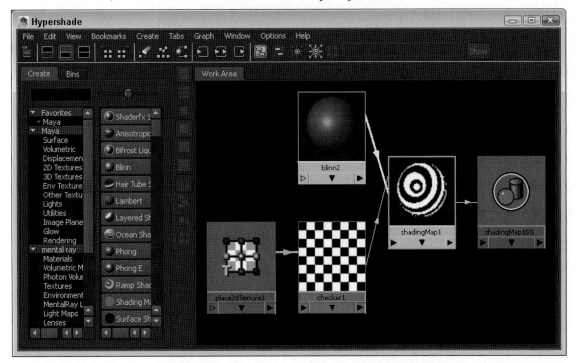

Figure 7-25
A striped sphere

Lesson 7.4: Work with Textures

Once a material node is created, you can connect texture nodes to it as inputs to the material's color, bump maps, transparency, specular highlights, and so on. You can apply many textures from the Create Bar, but you can also connect any image file using the File texture node. Texture nodes include several categories: 2D textures, 3D textures, Environment textures, and Others. Figure 7-26 shows the available 2D Texture nodes and Figure 7-27 shows the available 3D Texture nodes.

Figure 7-26
2D Texture nodes

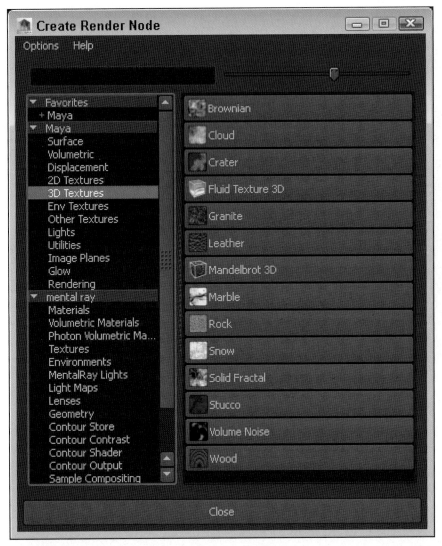

Figure 7-27
3D Texture nodes

Connecting Texture Nodes

You can connect textures to materials by dragging them with the middle mouse button and dropping them on a node in the Work Area. The pop-up menu that appears lets you select what the texture appears as. The pop-up menu options include many of the common material attributes.

Applying Textures as Color

When textures are applied as a material's color, the texture image is wrapped around the object. Selecting the texture node displays its attributes in the Attribute Editor. Many texture nodes must be connected with a utility node—for instance, a 2D texture node must be connected to a place2dTexture utility node, as shown in Figure 7-27. These utility nodes let you control the placement on the texture map on the object. When you click on a texture node in the Create Bar, Maya automatically adds and connects the necessary utility nodes in the Work Area.

Tip

If a texture's utility node isn't visible in the Hypershade, select the texture and click the Input Connections button.

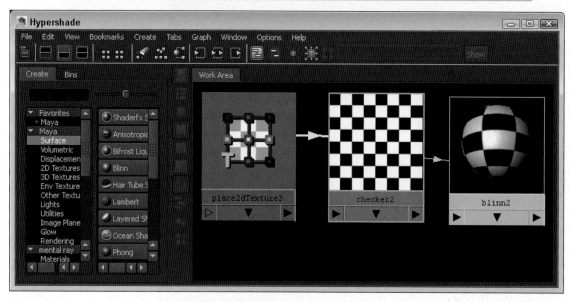

Figure 7-28
Texture map and utility node

Mapping Textures to Attributes

Applying a texture to a material attribute like Transparency causes the white areas to become transparent and the black areas to remain opaque, as shown in Figure 7-29. This works the same way for most of the other attributes—including specularity, reflection, and incandescence—as well.

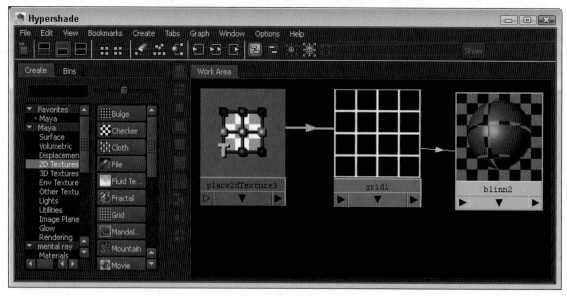

Figure 7-29
Texture-controlling transparency

Adding Relief

You can use textures to affect the relief of a surface using bump maps. Bump maps cause white textured areas to appear indented and black areas to appear "flat," as shown in Figure 7-30. You can use bump maps to add some relief to an object's surface. Connecting a texture as a bump map automatically adds a utility node that controls the amount of relief. The Bump Depth attribute controls how far the surface is indented and can be a negative value. Another way to add relief is with a Displacement map. Connecting a texture as a Displacement map uses the Displacement material node. Displacement maps actually alters the surface geometry, which affects the shadows, but bump maps do not affect the object's surface or shadows.

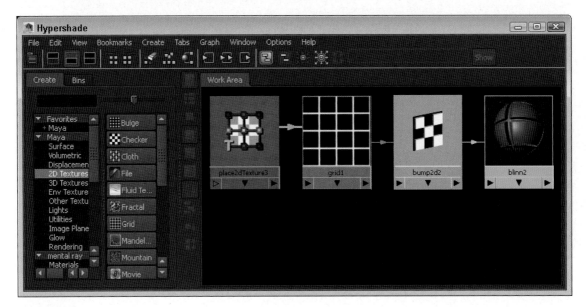

Figure 7-30
A Bump map

Loading File Textures

You can also use custom image files as textures using the File texture node. Once this node is connected to a material attribute, you can select it in the Work Area and, in the Attribute Editor, you can click on the File button by the Image Name field. This opens a file dialog box, from which you can select the image file to load and use as a texture. Figure 7-31 shows an image of a mountain stream mapped onto the surface of a cube.

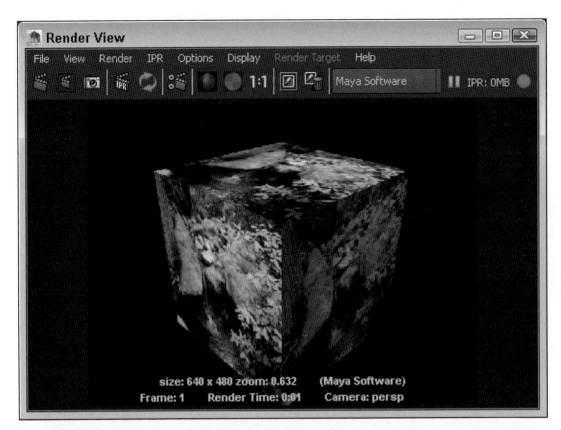

Figure 7-31
An image-mapped cube

Layering Textures

You can layer several textures on top of one another using the Layered Texture node found in the Other Textures category, as shown in Figure 7-32. With this node selected, you can drag and drop several textures onto the Layered Texture node with the middle mouse button and select the Default pop-up menu option. Each separate texture is listed within the Attribute Editor. You can change their position by dragging them using the middle mouse button. The Layered Texture node includes an Alpha value that blends between the layered textures, and you can select from many different Blend modes, such as Over, In, Out, Add, Subtract, and Multiply.

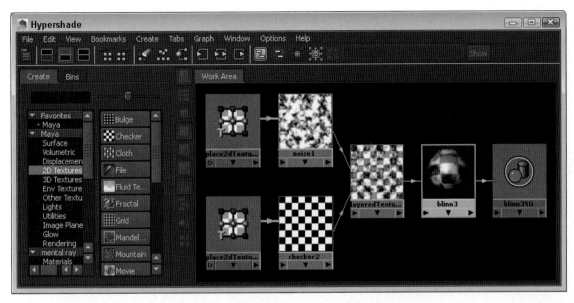

Figure 7-32
A layered texture

Lesson 7.4-Tutorial 1: Apply Textures

1. Create a sphere object using the Create, NURBS Primitives, Sphere menu command.

2. Select the Window, Rendering Editors, Hypershade menu command to open the Hypershade interface.

3. Click on the Blinn material node in the Create Bar.

4. Drag the Crater texture node with the middle mouse button and drop it on the Blinn1 node in the Work Area. Select Color from the pop-up menu.

5. Drag the Grid texture node with the middle mouse button and drop it on the Blinn1 node in the Work Area. Select Specular Color from the pop-up menu.

6. Drag the Noise texture node with the middle mouse button and drop it on the Blinn1 node in the Work Area. Select Bump Map from the pop-up menu.

   The Blinn1 material is updated.

7. Click on the Rearrange Graph button in the Hypershade toolbar.

8. Select the sphere object in the view panel, right -click on the Blinn1 material in the Hypershade and select Assign Material to Selection from the pop-up menu.

   The sphere object is updated with the mapped textures, as shown in Figure 7-33.

9. Select File, Save Scene As and save the file as **Texture mapped sphere.mb**.

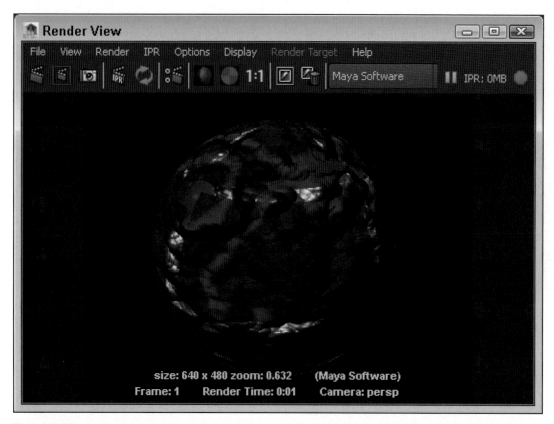

Figure 7-33
A texture-mapped sphere

Lesson 7.4-Tutorial 2: Load an Image Texture

1. Create a cube object using the Create, NURBS Primitives, Cube menu command.

2. Select the Window, Rendering Editors, Hypershade menu command to open the Hypershade interface.

3. Click on the Lambert material node in the Create Bar.

4. Drag the File texture node with the middle mouse button and drop it on the Lambert1 node in the Work Area. Select Color from the pop-up menu.

5. Click on the Load File button in the Attribute Editor and select the Coast from Diamond Head.jpg file and click the Open button.

   The image file is loaded and displayed in the File1 texture node in the Hypershade.

6. Click on the Rearrange Graph button in the Hypershade toolbar.

7. Select the cube object in the view panel, right -click on the Lambert1 material in the Hypershade and select Assign Material to Selection from the pop-up menu.

8. With the Lambert1 material selected in the Hypershade, drag the Ambient Color attribute halfway toward the right.

   All sides of the cube are wrapped with the image file texture, as shown in the Render View window in Figure 7-34.

9. Select File, Save Scene As and save the file as **Image file cube.mb**.

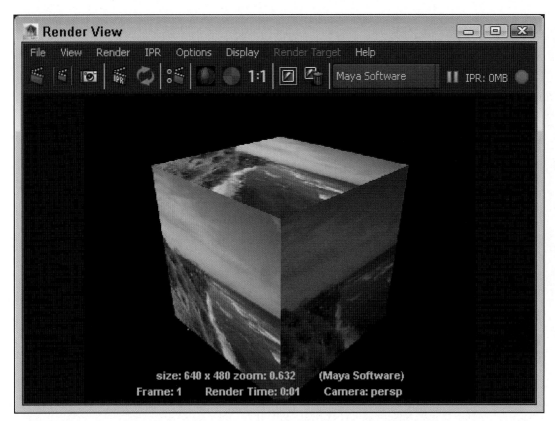

Figure 7-34
Image file cube

Lesson 7.5: Position Textures

When textures are applied to a material as colors or bump maps, Maya automatically creates a utility node that includes positional information for the texture. Using the attributes of this utility node, you can control the texture's offset, tiling, rotation, and how often it repeats. The Utilities category in the Create Bar includes utilities for 2D and 3D bump maps and texture placement.

Understanding Mapping Methods

In the Utilities section of the Create Bar in the Hypershade, you can select from three different mapping methods: Normal, Projection, and Stencil.

Using Normal Mapping

The Normal mapping method is the default and maps the texture using the UV coordinates created by default when the object was created. When Normal mapping is used, Maya connects the appropriate 2D or 3D placement utility node, as shown in Figure 7-35, in the Work Area. The attributes of this node controls the placement of the texture.

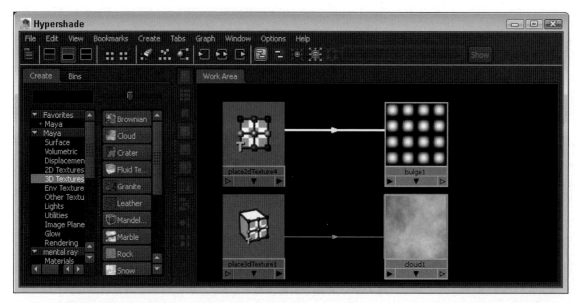

Figure 7-35
2D and 3D placement utility nodes

Using Projection Mapping

When the Projection Utility node is selected in the Create Bar when a texture node is connected, a Projection utility node is added to the Work Area, as shown in Figure 7-36. You can also select from several different projection types, including Planar, Spherical, Cylindrical, Ball, and Cubic.

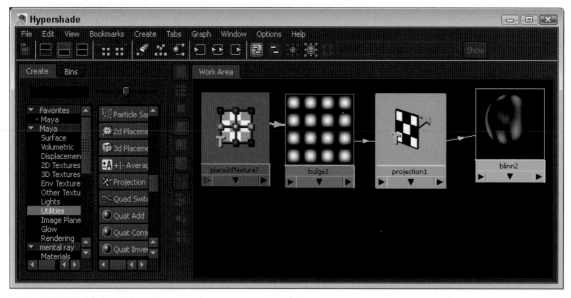

Figure 7-36
The Projection utility node

Using Stencil Mapping

The Stencil Utility node in the Create Bar of the Hypershade causes the texture to act like a mask to hide part of the texture. The Color Key attribute is the color that you want to mask. This color is replaced with the default color. You can access these attributes in the Attribute Editor when the Stencil utility node is selected. Figure 7-37 shows the Stencil node in the Hypershade.

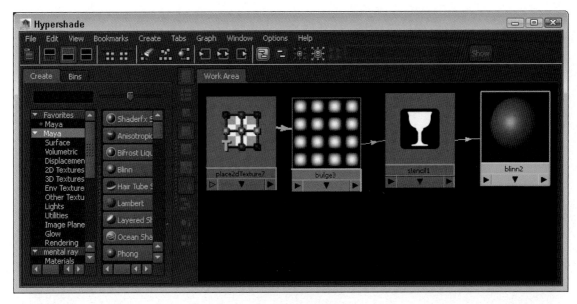

Figure 7-37
The Stencil utility node

Placing 2D Textures

Once textures have been applied to a NURBS object, you can reposition and reorient the textures using the Texturing, NURBS Texture Placement tool. This tool lets you select a face and change its attribute by dragging with the middle mouse button on the red manipulator handles, as shown in Figure 7-38, within the view panels. Moving the manipulator handles changes the attributes for the 2D Texture Placement node.

Tip

You can also access the NURBS Texture Placement tool using the Interactive Placement button in the Attribute Editor when the 2D Placement node is selected.

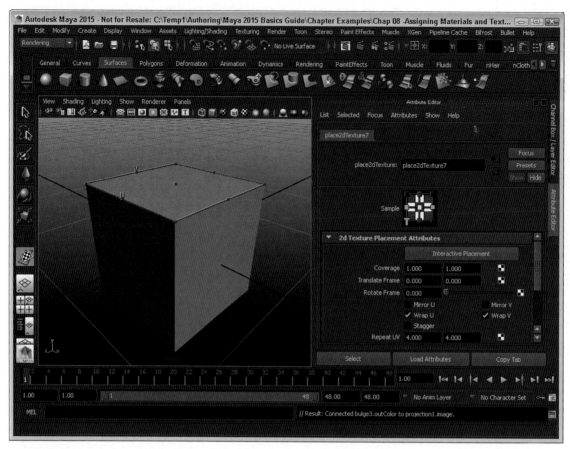

Figure 7-38
2D texture placement manipulator

Placing 3D Textures

The 3D Placement utility node includes a button that lets you interactively place the texture by moving a manipulator in the view panels. When this utility node is selected, you can click the Interactive Placement button in the Attribute Editor. This places a manipulator on the surface of the object, as shown in Figure 7-39. Drag the manipulator's handles to position the projected texture. There is also a Fit to BBox button that fits the texture to the object's Bounding Box.

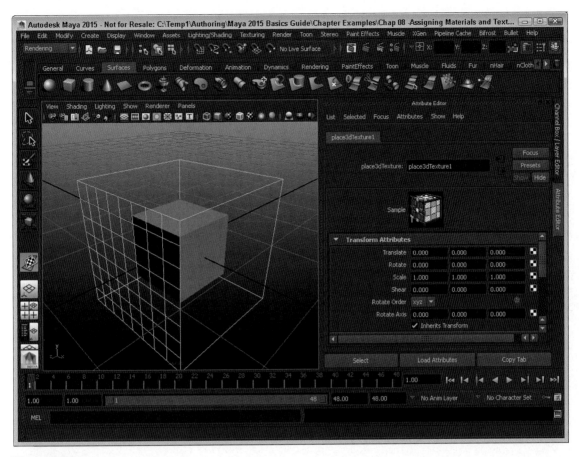

Figure 7-39
3D texture placement manipulator

Controlling Polygon Textures

Polygon and Subdiv surfaces use a different method for positioning textures. Each face of a polygonal object is divided into U and V coordinates that run from one corner to the opposite corner. The commands for controlling a polygon's UV coordinates are found in the Edit Polygons, Texture menu (and in the Subdiv Surfaces, Texture menu for Subdiv surfaces). Included in this menu are several mapping types, including Planar, Cylindrical, Spherical and Automatic.

Lesson 7.5-Tutorial 1: Position 2D Textures

1. Create a NURBS cube object using the Create, NURBS Primitives, Cube menu command.

2. Select the Window, Rendering Editors, Hypershade menu command to open the Hypershade interface.

3. Click on the Blinn material node in the Create Bar.

4. Click on the Create Render Node button for the Color attribute in the Attribute Editor.

5. Click on the Checker texture node.

6. Select the Checker1 texture node in the Attribute Editor and change the Default Color setting in the Color Balance section to red.

7. Click the Rearrange Graph button in the Hypershade toolbar.

8. With the cube selected, right-click on the Blinn1 material in the Hypershade and select the Assign Material to Selection from the pop-up menu.

9. Select the Texturing, NURBS Texture Placement Tool menu command and click on the top face of the NURBS cube

10. Drag each edge manipulator handle towards the center of the cube face with the middle mouse button.

   The sample sphere material in the Hypershade colors a portion of the sample sphere red, as shown in Figure 7-40.

11. Select File, Save Scene As and save the file as **Shifted checker map.mb**.

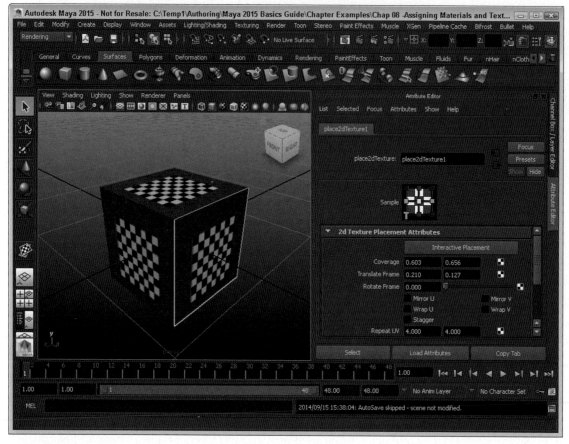

Figure 7-40
Shifted texture map

Lesson 7.5-Tutorial 2: Position 3D Textures

1. Create a NURBS sphere object using the Create, NURBS Primitives, Sphere menu command.

2. Select the Window, Rendering Editors, Hypershade menu command to open the Hypershade interface.

3. Click on the Blinn material node in the Create Bar.

4. Click on the Create Render Node button for the Color attribute in the Attribute Editor.

5. Click on the Marble 3D texture node.

6. With the sphere selected, right-click on the Blinn1 material in the Hypershade and select the Assign Material to Selection from the pop-up menu.

7. Click the Rearrange Graph button in the Hypershade toolbar.

8. Select the Place3dTexture1 utility node in the Hypershade.

9. Click the Fit to Group BBox button in the Attribute Editor.

10. Drag the light blue circle manipulator to rotate the texture.

The marbled veins shift in the sample material in the Hypershade, as shown in Figure 7-41.

11. Select File, Save Scene As and save the file as **Marbled sphere.mb**.

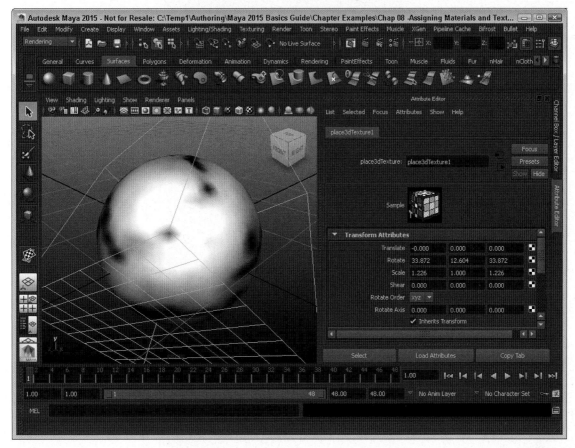

Figure 7-41
A marbled sphere

Lesson 7.6: Use Utilities Nodes

The Utilities category of the Create Bar includes many utilities that perform specialized functions. For example, the Blend Colors utility lets you blend two different textures or colors together.

Using the General Utilities

The General Utilities category in the Create Bar, shown in Figure 7-42, includes many nodes that are applied automatically when needed, such as the Bump 2d, Bump 3d, 2d and 3d Placement, Projection, and Stencil. It also includes several miscellaneous utilities used to display different colors based on a given situation, such as the Distance Between, Condition, Height Field, Light Info, Multiply Divide, or Average.

Figure 7-42
General utility rendering nodes

Using the Color Utilities

The Color Utilities, shown along with the other Utilities includes nodes that can alter several color properties of a texture. These utilities include Blend Colors, Clamp, Contrast, Gamma Correct, and more.

Using the Switch Utilities

The Switch Utilities category in the Create Bar includes nodes that can apply different materials to patches in the same object.

Lesson 7.6-Tutorial 1: Blend Colors

1. Create a NURBS sphere object using the Create, NURBS Primitives, Sphere menu command.

2. Select the Window, Rendering Editors, Hypershade menu command to open the Hypershade interface.

3. Click on the Blinn material node in the Create Bar.

4. Click on the Create Render Node button for the Color attribute in the Attribute Editor.

5. Click on the Blend Colors utility node in the Color Utilities category.

    The Blend Colors node includes two colors that are blended together to create a purple color. Using this node gives you the ability to set animation keys for the colors. Figure 7-43 shows the nodes for this material.

6. Drag the Rock texture from the Create Bar with the middle mouse button and drop it on the blendColors1 node, select Color1 from the pop-up menu. Then, drag the Marble texture from the Create Bar with the middle mouse button and drop it on the blendColors1 node, select Color2 from the pop-up menu.

    The texture placement nodes are added automatically. You can also blend textures using the Blend Colors node.

7. Click the Rearrange Graph button in the Hypershade toolbar.

8. With the sphere selected, right-click on the Blinn1 material in the Hypershade and select the Assign Material to Selection from the pop-up menu.

9. Select File, Save Scene As and save the file as **Blended textures.mb**.

Figure 7-43
Blended textures

Lesson 7.7: Paint in 3D

The Texturing, 3D Paint tool lets you paint directly on a 3D surface using several different modes with Artisan or Paint Effects brushes. You can also paint other attributes including bumps, transparency, and specular color. To see the 3D Paint tool settings, click on the Show Tool Settings button on the right end of the Status Line.

Assigning a Paint Texture

Before you can paint on an object, the object must be selected, have a material besides the default applied, and have a paint texture assigned to it. To assign a paint texture to an object, select the Texturing, 3D Paint tool, open the Tool Settings, and click on the Assign/Edit Textures button in the File Textures section. This button opens a simple dialog box, shown in Figure 7-44, where you can specify the dimensions of the paint texture.

Note

If the brush cursor displays a large red X, a paint texture hasn't been assigned to the object, and you won't be able to paint.

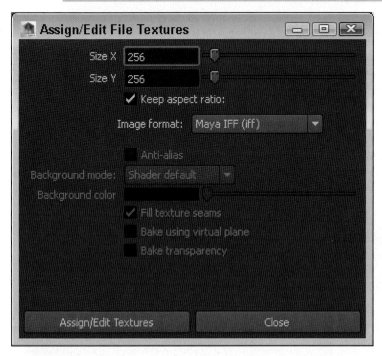

Figure 7-44
The Assign/Edit File Textures dialog box

Selecting a Brush

The 3D Paint tool may use any of the Artisan or Paint Effects brushes. You can select these brushes from the Brush section of the Tool Settings panel, from which you can also set the Radius values for the selected brush. Holding down the B key while dragging in the view panel enables you to interactively change the brush radius. Figure 7-45 shows a simple paint stroke drawn on a sphere object.

Figure 7-45
Paint on an object

Applying Color

To change the paint color, click the Color swatch in the Color section of the Tool Settings panel and select a new color from the Color Chooser. You can also control the opacity of the painted color with the Opacity setting. The Flood Paint button colors the entire object using the Flood Color or colors only the selected components if the Selected option is enabled.

Using Different Paint Operations

Depending on the type of brush that is selected, the selected color can be painted, erased, or cloned with the Artisan brush or painted, smeared and blurred with a Paint Effects brush. These options are located in the Paint Operations section of the Tool Settings panel. This section also allows you to select a Blend mode. Figure 7-46 shows a sphere that was painted with one color, and then much of that color was erased using the Erase Paint Operation.

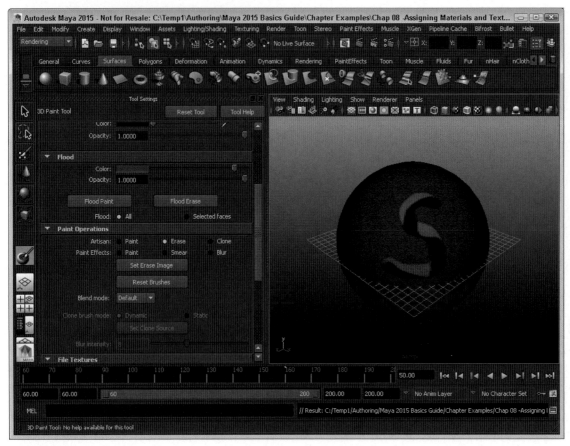

Figure 7-46
Erasing paint

Painting Other Attributes

In the File Textures section of the Tool Settings panel, you can choose the attribute to paint. The options include Color, Transparency, Incandescence, BumpMap, SpecularColor, Reflectivity, Ambient, Diffuse, Translucence, ReflectedColor, and Displacement. Figure 7-47 shows a simple cylinder with some painted bumps.

Note

You must add a new paint texture to the object with the Assign/New Textures button for each new attribute you paint.

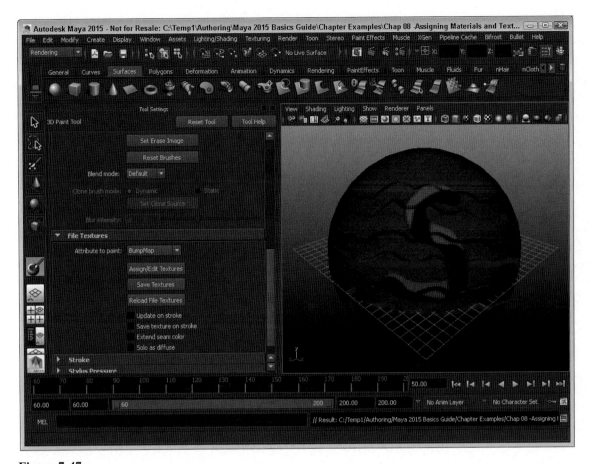

Figure 7-47
Painted bump maps

Lesson 7.7-Tutorial 1: Use the 3D Paint Tool

1. Open the Football.mb file using the File, Open Scene menu command.

2. With the football object selected, choose the Lighting/Shading, Assign New Material, Lambert menu command.

3. Click on the Color attribute in the Attribute Editor and select the brown color from the Color Chooser.

4. Select the Texturing, 3D Paint Tool menu command and double click on the 3D Paint tool in the Toolbox to open the Tool Settings panel.

5. In the Tool Settings panel, click on the Assign/Edit Textures button in the File Textures section. In the Assign/Edit Textures dialog box, click the Assign/Edit Textures button.

6. Click on one of the Artisan brushes in the Brush section.

7. In the Color section, click on the Color swatch and select a white color from the Color Chooser.

8. Hold down the B key and drag in the view panel to change the brush radius size.

9. Paint directly on the football to create some threads.

    The white colors painted on the football become part of the texture applied to the football material, as shown in Figure 7-48.

10. Select File, Save Scene As, and save the file as **Painted football.mb**.

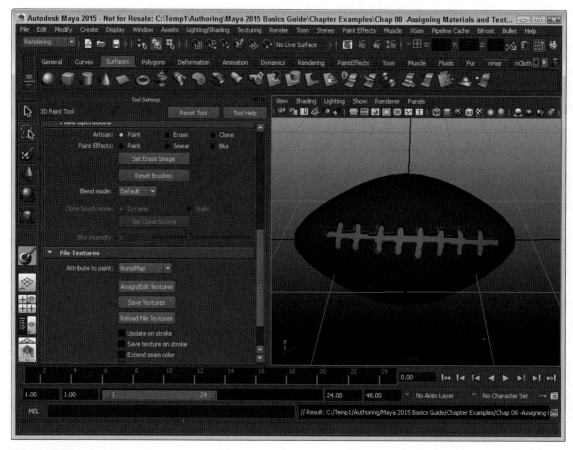

Figure 7-48
Football with painted threads

Chapter Summary

This chapter covers the basics of creating and applying materials and textures to objects. Materials and textures are defined in the Hypershade interface. This interface lets you connect various nodes to create an endless variety of custom materials. You can also apply textures to objects and position them using various placement utility nodes. The 3D Paint tool lets you apply paint using a brush directly on the surface of an object in the view panel.

What You Have Learned

In this chapter, you learned

*   How to apply new materials to objects.

*   How to view and change material attributes.

*   How to move between material nodes.

*   How to render materials.

*   How to use the Hypershade and the Create Bar.

*   How to connect nodes in the Hypershade.

*   How to use the Connection Editor.

*   How to apply materials by dragging them.

* How to use the various surface materials.

* How to change material colors.

* How to change a material's transparency.

* How to use the various material attributes.

* How to layer materials.

* How to use the Ramp Shader and the Shading Map.

* How to connect texture nodes.

* How to map textures to a specific attribute.

* How to add bump maps to an object.

* How to load file textures and layer textures.

* How to use the different mapping methods.

* How to use normal, projection, and stencil mapping.

* How to place 2D and 3D textures.

* How to use the various material utility nodes.

* How to assign a paint texture.

* How to use the 3D Paint tool.

Key terms From This Chapter

* **Material.** A set of surface properties that are assigned to an object to simulate various object materials.

* **Shader.** A complex set of connected material nodes that define a specific material.

* **Bump map.** A texture that is used to set the relief of a material where dark areas are raised and lighter areas are indented.

* **Hypershade.** A interface where materials and shaders are created.

* **Create Bar.** A selection list in the Hypershade where you can choose from default materials, textures and nodes.

* **Node.** A single set of material attributes that you can connect to other nodes to create a shader.

* **Connection Editor.** An interface for defining the connections between various nodes.

* **Anisotropic.** A material noted for its elliptical specular highlights.

* **Lambert.** A material with no highlights; useful for cloth and non-reflective surfaces.

* **Blinn.** A material with soft circular highlights; good for metallic surfaces.

* **Phong.** A material with a hard circular highlight; good for glass surfaces.

* **Texture.** A bitmap file that is wrapped around an object.

* **Mapping.** The method used to wrap a texture around an object.

Chapter 8

Adding Paint Effects

IN THIS CHAPTER

Several Maya's tools let you paint within the scene. These paint features include Paint Textures, Paint Weights, Paint to Select, Paint to Sculpt, and Paint Effects. Of all these paint features, **Paint Effects** is probably the most innovative and exciting. Using the Paint Effects tools, you can paint directly in the view panel, on a 2D canvas, or directly on a 3D object.

Paint Effects are applied using brushes. You can set the attributes—such as the size, color, thickness, and shape of the brush head—of these brushes. You can also select from several styles of brushes, including airbrushes, markers, oils, pencils, pens, and watercolors. In addition to the default preset brushes, you can create and save your own custom brushes.

Dragging a brush in the scene produces a **stroke**. These strokes can be simple strokes like a normal paintbrush would make or a growth stroke, which causes additional strokes to appear and extend from the base stroke. Using growth strokes, you can paint trees and flowers simply by drawing the base stem; Maya adds all the smaller limbs and branches automatically.

Several Paint Effect brushes are found in the Paint Effects shelf, but you'll find many more in the **Visor** interface. Brushes contained in the Visor include animal furs, clouds, feathers, flowers, glows, hair, and so on.

To apply a Paint Effect, a special panel mode is available called the Paint Effect panel. This panel includes several unique controls for accessing **alpha channels,** taking snapshots and editing the brush settings. The easiest way to move between this mode and the normal modeling mode is with the 8 key.

The Paint Effects menu also includes several commands for controlling brushes and their settings. Using the Preset Blending command, you can combine the settings of different brushes. The Make Paintable option lets you paint directly on the surface of the selected NURBS object and the **Auto Paint** feature paints on an object using a grid or random strokes.

Lesson 8.1: Use the Preset Brushes

Paint Effects in Maya are fun to play with, thanks to the variety of unique brushes that are available. You can start by playing with the available preset brushes, but you can also change the attributes of a brush to create a custom brush.

Accessing the Paint Effects Panel

If you select a Paint Effects brush and draw in one of the view panels, you'll only see lines. To see the actual paint strokes as they are being drawn, you need to change the view panel to Scene Painting mode. You can do this using the Panels, Panel, Paint Effects menu command. You'll be able to tell when a view is in Scene Painting mode because the Paint Effects toolbar appears at the top of the view panel. Figure 8-1 shows Scene Painting mode with several sample brush effects.

Tip

Pressing the 8 hotkey toggles the active view panel between Scene Painting mode and Normal mode.

Figure 8-1
Scene Painting mode

Using the Paint Effects Tool

The Paint Effects tool can paint in the view panel in Scene Painting mode. You can select this tool using the Paint Effects, Paint Effects Tool menu command. It is also selected automatically when a preset brush is selected. Using the Tool settings, you can configure the Pressure Mapping values for a graphics tablet.

Using Preset Brushes

Many preset brushes are found under the Paint Effects shelf, as shown in Figure 8-2. To select a preset brush, just click on its icon button in the shelf. To see the name of each brush, hold the mouse cursor over the top of the icon button and its name appears in the pop-up Help. Some of the sample brushes include Curly Hair, Bubbles, Crystals, Charcoal, Red Oil, Smear, Gold, Water Tube, Neon Blue, and Grass Clump.

Tip

    Don't miss the second row of Paint Effects brushes in
    the shelf.

Figure 8-2
Paint Effects shelf

Introducing the Visor

In addition to the presets found in the Paint Effects shelf, you can access a repository of preset Paint Effects brushes in the Visor dialog box, shown in Figure 8-3. The Visor includes a categorized look at the folders on your hard drive. Each folder contains thumbnails of the available content, including brushes. You can open the Visor dialog box using the Window, General Editors, Visor menu command. Sample Paint Effects folders in the Visor include categories such as animal, clouds, feathers, flowers, food, fun, galactic, hair, trees, and underwater.

Note

    You can also open the Visor by selecting the Paint
    Effects, Get Brush menu command.

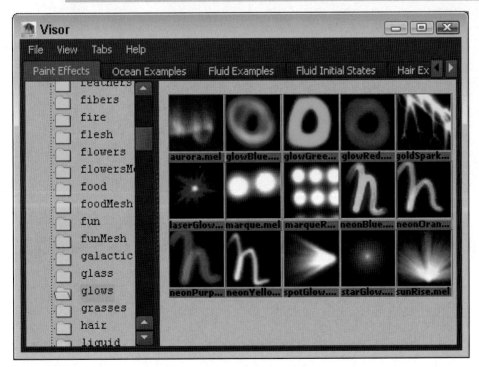

Figure 8-3
The Visor

Blending Presets

You can blend brush presets together so the shape of one brush is combined with the shading of another brush using the Paint Effects, Preset Blending menu command. To blend two brushes, select the first brush and then open the Brush Preset Blend Options dialog box and choose the percentage of shape and shading to use from the second preset. Then select the second preset. Figure 8-4 shows the shape of the Down Feather brush blended with the shading from the Crystal, Neon Blue, and Lightning brushes.

Note

Remember that the Paint Effects menu is found in the Rendering menu set.

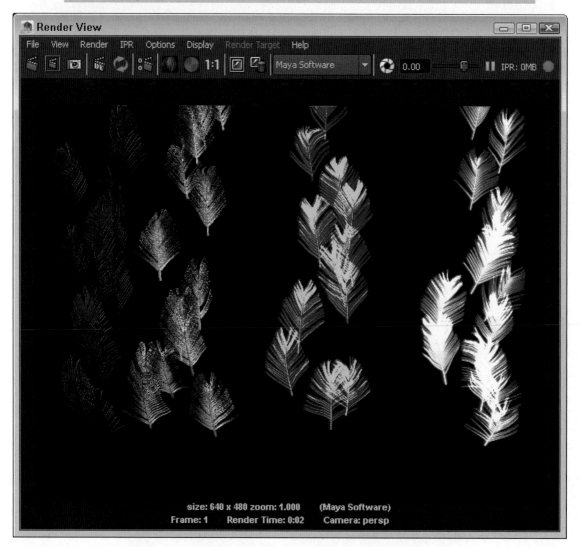

Figure 8-4
Blended Paint Effects

Redrawing the View

As you paint in the view panel, some Paint Effects are drawn as wireframe lines in order to save memory. You can set the display value for the selected Paint Effect using the Stroke Refresh panel menu. This menu appears in Scene Painting mode. The options include Off, Wireframe, and Rendered. You can cause the Paint Effects to be redrawn using the Redraw Paint Effects View button in the panel toolbar.

Clearing the View

If you want to delete the last-created stroke, you can simply use the Edit, Undo menu command. This clears the strokes in the order they were created. If you want to clear the entire view, you can use the Clear Canvas/Delete All Strokes panel toolbar button. This completely erases all Paint Effects, but doesn't delete any objects.

Lesson 8.1-Tutorial 1: Use a Paint Effects Brush

1. Select the Rendering menu set from the drop-down list to the left in the Status Line.

2. Select the Panels, Panel, Paint Effects panel menu command (or press the 8 key) to enter Scene Painting mode.

3. Click on the Paint Effects tab in the Shelf bar.

4. Click on the Crystals Brush icon in the Paint Effects shelf.

5. Drag in the view panel to create a shape made from crystals.

    The crystal shapes follow the drawn path, as shown in Figure 8-5.

6. Select File, Save Scene As and save the file as **Crystal paint effect.mb**.

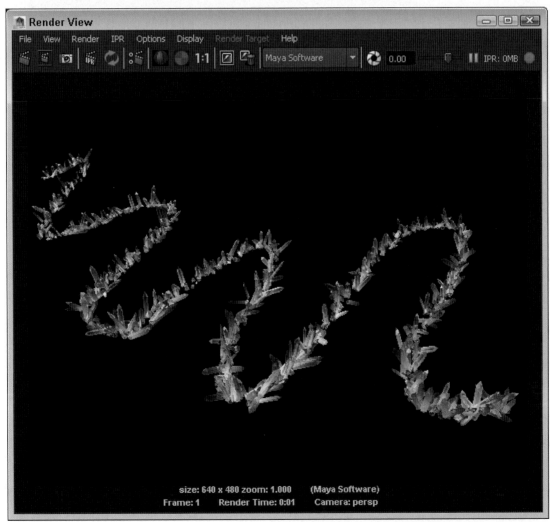

Figure 8-5
The Crystal Paint effect

Lesson 8.1-Tutorial 2: Use a Visor Brush

1. Select the Panels, Panel, Paint Effects menu command (or press the 8 key) to enter Scene Painting mode.

2. Select the Paint Effects, Get Brush menu command.

    The Visor dialog box opens.

3. Click on the Fun folder to the left.

    Thumbnails of the brushes contained within this folder are displayed.

4. Click on the Jumping Springs brush.

5. Drag in the center of the view panel to create a shape and zoom in on the created springs, as shown in Figure 8-6.

6. Select File, Save Scene As and save the file as **Jumping springs.mb**.

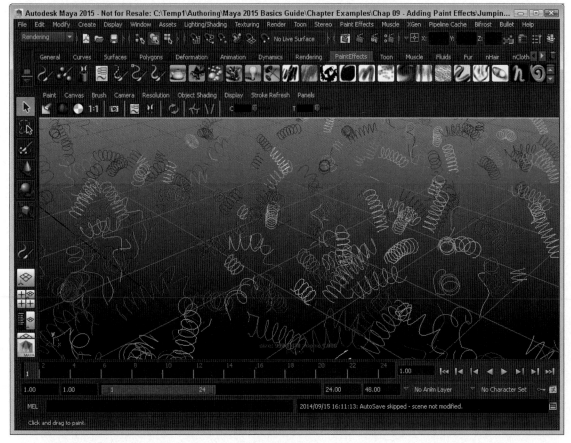

Figure 8-6
The Jumping Springs Paint Effect

Lesson 8.1-Tutorial 3: Blend Brushes

1. Select the Panels, Panel, Paint Effects menu command to enter Scene Painting mode.

2. Click on the Paint Effects tab in the Shelf bar.

3. Click on the Crystals Brush icon in the Paint Effects shelf.

4. Drag in the view panel to create a shape made from crystals.

5.   Select the Paint Effects, Preset Blending, Options menu command.

The Brush Preset Blend dialog box opens.

6.   Enter a Shading value of 100% and a Shape value of 0%.

This causes the blended brush to use all of the shading attributes of the next-selected brush and none of its shape attributes.

7.   Click on the Gold Brush icon in the Paint Effects shelf.

8.   Drag next to the existing set of crystals to reveal a set of gold crystals, as shown in Figure 8-7.

9.   Select File, Save Scene As and save the file as **Gold crystals.mb**.

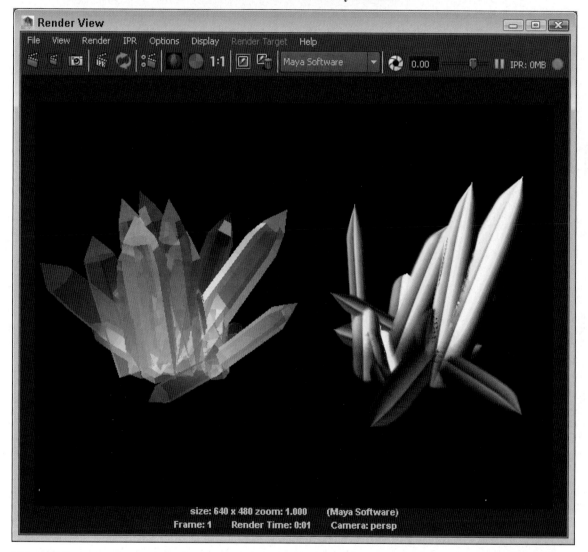

Figure 8-7
The Blended Paint Effect

Lesson 8.2: Create Custom Brushes

Preset brushes are great for starters, but you'll quickly want to know how to customize the brushes. Every brush pulls from a long list of attributes that you can alter to change the brush. You can the save customized brushes for later use.

Changing Template Brush Settings

When a preset brush is selected, the brush settings are copied to the Template Brush Settings dialog box, which holds the global settings for the brush. You can change the template brush settings at any time using the Paint Effects, Template Brush Settings menu command. This opens the Paint Effects Brush Settings dialog box, shown in Figure 8-8, where you can change brush attributes like the size, color, shadows, and glows. You can reset the current brush settings at any time with the Paint Effects, Reset Template Brush menu command.

Tip

```
The hotkey for opening the Template Brush Settings
dialog box is Ctrl+B.
```

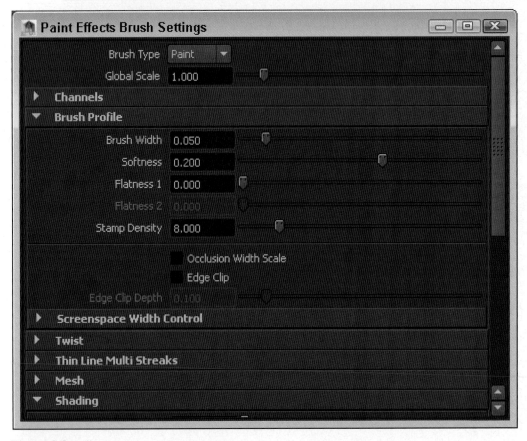

Figure 8-8
The Paint Effects Brush Settings dialog box

Using the Various Brush Types

The top of the Paint Effects Brush Settings dialog box includes a drop-down list from which you can select the brush type you want. The available options include Paint, Smear, Blur, Erase, Thin Line, and Mesh. The Paint brush type actually places color and the Erase brush type removes it. The Smear and Blur brush types alters the existing colors with a smear or blur effect. The Thin Line brush type divides the strokes into many thin lines like the Curly Hair brush. The Mesh brush type places random mesh objects about the scene like the Crystals and Tacks brushes. Figure 8-9 shows four brush strokes using the Red Oil brush. The second and third lines were done with the Smear and Blur brush types and in the bottom line the Erase brush type was used to erase some of the line. Figure 8-10 shows examples of the Thin Line and Mesh brush types.

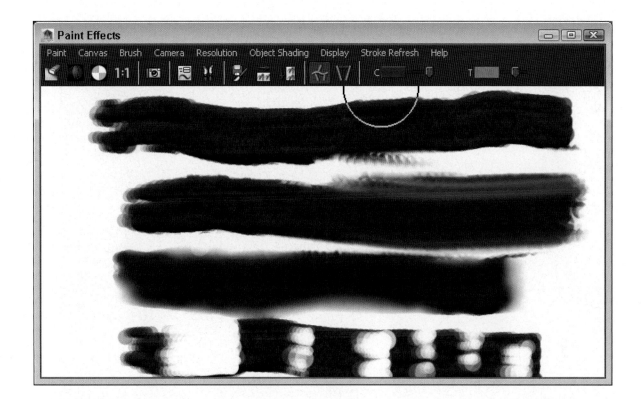

Figure 8-9
Brush types

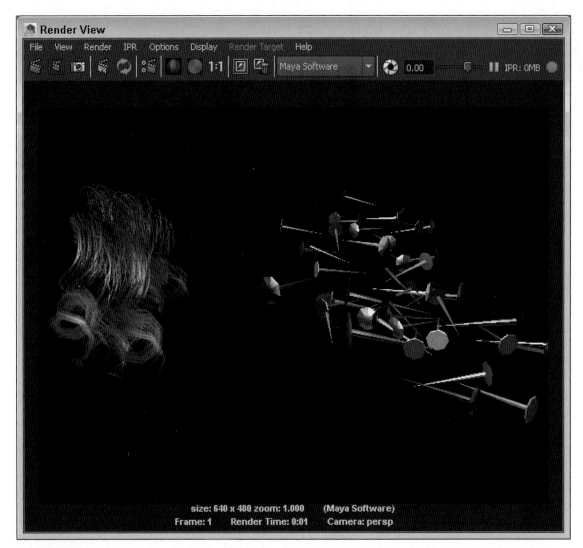

Figure 8-10
Curly Hair and Tacks brushes

Changing Brush Size

Use the Global Scale attribute to change the overall size of the brush. This attribute uniformly changes the size of the brush as indicated by the circular (or spherical) cursor that appears in the view panel. In the Brush Profile section of the Paint Effects Brush Settings dialog box, you'll find the Brush Width attribute. This affects the individual brush width, which can increase the size of a single blade of grass or spread the distance between individual brushes, as shown in Figure 8-11. Other attributes in this section include Softness, Flatness, and Stamp Density, which determines the thickness of a stroke.

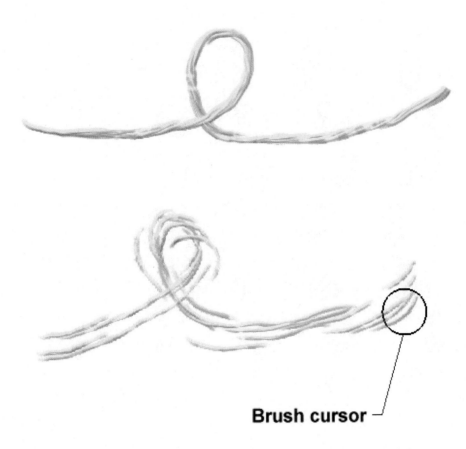

Brush cursor ⏤

Figure 8-11
Increasing brush width

Changing Brush Color

Each of the preset brushes has a color (or colors) that it uses. For example, the Red Oil brush has a red color defined as its primary color. The brushes' colors are found in the Shading section of the Paint Effects Brush Settings dialog box. Clicking on the color swatch lets you choose a new color in the Color Chooser. You can also choose colors for incandescence and transparency. Figure 8-12 shows the Vitamin E brush with several primary colors.

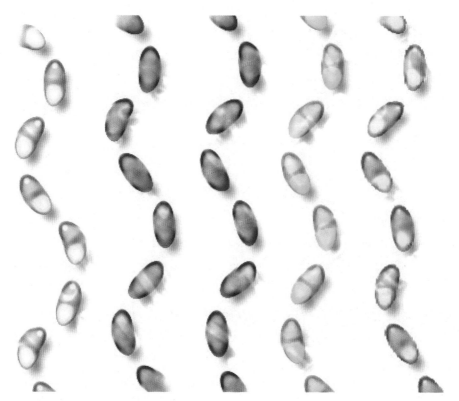

Figure 8-12
Changed colors with the Vitamin E brush

Enabling Illumination and Shadows

Using the Illumination section of the Paint Effects Brush Settings dialog box, you can choose whether the Paint Effects have no light cast on them, that the default lights illuminate them, or that real scene lights illuminate them. The Illuminated option lets you specify a Light Direction and you can change the settings for Specular, Specular Power, and Specular Color. The Shadow Effects section includes three options for fake shadows, including None, 2D Offset (which is a simple drop shadow), and 3D Cast. Fake shadows render quickly, but you can also enable real shadows by enabling the Cast Shadows options. Real shadows can take a long time to render. Figure 8-13 shows three lines painted with the Gold brush. The top one has no illumination, the middle one has standard illumination, and the bottom one has a blue specular color.

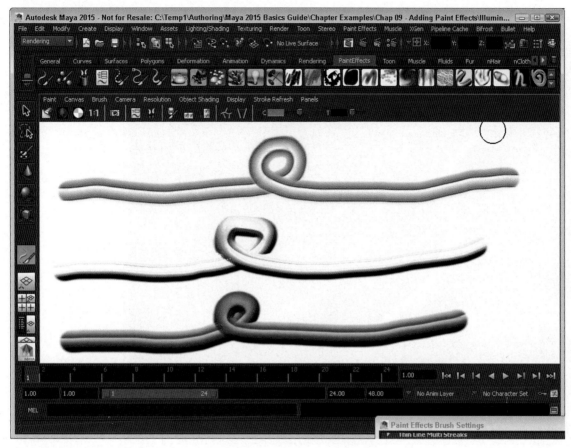

Figure 8-13
Altered illumination

Enabling Glows

The Glow section enables you to set the amount of glow that emanates, the glow color, and the glow spread. Several preset brushes use glows, including the Neon Blue, Galaxy, and Lightning brushes. Figure 8-14 shows the Green Snake brush with no glow enabled, with a normal glow enabled, and with a bright green glow enabled.

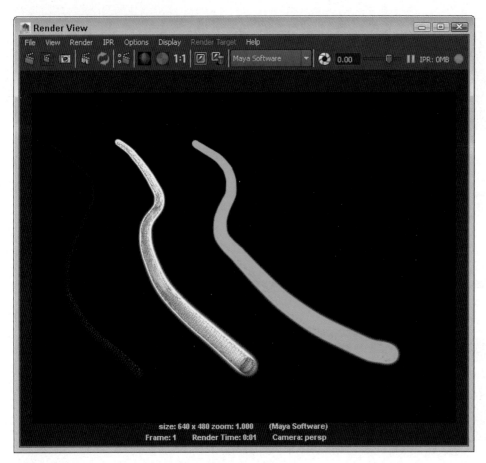

Figure 8-14
Enabled glows

Creating and Saving Custom Brushes

If you've tweaked a brush and you like its settings, you can save the custom brush to the Shelf or to the Visor using the Paint Effects, Save Brush Preset menu command. This opens a dialog box, shown in Figure 8-15, in which you can name the custom brush and give it a directory.

Figure 8-15
The Save Brush Preset dialog box

Lesson 8.2-Tutorial 1: Change Brush Size

1. Select the Panels, Panel, Paint Effects menu command to enter Scene Painting mode.

2. Click on the Simple Tree Brush icon in the Paint Effects shelf.

3. Drag in the view panel to create a line of trees.

4. Select the Paint Effects, Template Brush Settings menu command.

5. Change the Global Scale value to 0.5 and draw a parallel line in the view panel.

6. Repeat Step 5 for Global Scale values of 0.75, 1.0, and 1.25.

   The rows of trees gradually get larger as the Global Scale value is increased, as shown in Figure 8-16.

7. Select File, Save Scene As and save the file as **Rows of trees.mb**.

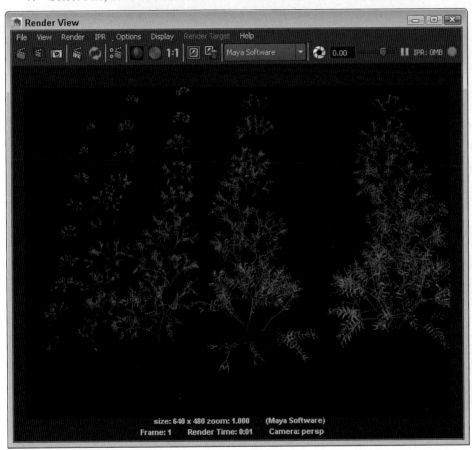

Figure 8-16
Rows of trees

Lesson 8.2-Tutorial 2: Change Brush Color

1. Select the Panels, Panel, Paint Effects menu command to enter Scene Painting mode.

2. Click on the Lightning Brush icon in the Paint Effects shelf.

3. Drag a vertical line in the view panel to create some lightning.

4. Select the Paint Effects, Template Brush Settings menu command.

5. Select the Shading section and click on the Color1 color swatch and change it to blue. Then change the Incandescence1 color to dark blue.

6. Select the Tube Shading section and change the Color2 and Incandescence2 colors to different tints of blue and dark blue.

7. Select the Glow section and change the Glow Color to a light blue color.

8. Drag again in the view panel to create another vertical line parallel to the first.

9. Repeat Steps 5-8 with the colors green, yellow, and red.

   The rows of lightning change from left to right, as shown in Figure 8-17.

10. Select File, Save Scene As and save the file as **Lightning colors.mb**.

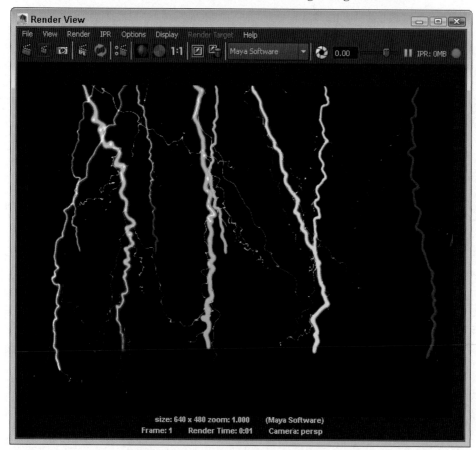

Figure 8-17
Lighting colors

Lesson 8.2-Tutorial 3: Add Shadows

1. Create a NURBS plane using the Create, NURBS Primitives, Plane menu command.

2. Select the Window, Frame Selection in All Views menu command (or press the f key) to zoom in on the plane object.

3. Select the Panels, Panel, Paint Effects menu command to enter Scene Painting mode.

4. Click on the Daisy Large Brush icon in the Paint Effects shelf.

5. Select the Paint Effects, Template Brush Settings menu command.

6. Select the Shadow Effects section, and then select the 3D Cast option in the Fake Shadow drop-down list.

7. Set the Global Scale value to 0.25.

8. Drag with the Paint Effects brush across the plane object.

9. Press the 5 key to see a shaded view of the plane object.

   The Scene Painting view shows several red arrows that cut through the scene. These arrows show the direction of the default lights. Notice how shadows are cast on the plane object, as shown in Figure 8-18.

10. Select File, Save Scene As and save the file as **Daisies with shadows.mb**.

Figure 8-18
Cast shadows

Lesson 8.2-Tutorial 4: Add a Glow

1. Select the Panels, Panel, Paint Effects menu command to enter Scene Painting mode.

2. Click on the Orange Pastel Scribble Brush icon in the Paint Effects shelf.

3. Select the Paint Effects, Template Brush Settings menu command.

4. Change the Global Scale value to 10.0 and, in the Glow section, change the Glow value to 0.5.

5. Drag in the view panel to create a circular pattern.

    The glow effect added to the Orange Pastel Scribble brush makes the brush brighter when it overlaps itself, creating an explosion effect, as shown in Figure 8-18.

6. Select File, Save Scene As and save the file as **Explosion.mb**.

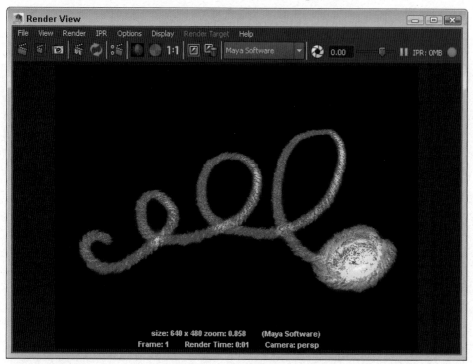

Figure 8-19
Explosion effect

Lesson 8.3: Paint in 2D

Sometimes drawing in the view panels with its perspective view isn't what you need. If you use Maya's **Paint Canvas**, you can draw and save images in 2D. The Paint Canvas is easy to identify because it has a white background and the canvas dimensions are displayed at the bottom of the view panel. You can use images you create with the Paint Canvas as textures or backgrounds.

Introducing the Paint Effects Canvas

Once the Paint Effects panel is visible, you can open the paint canvas using the Paint, Paint Canvas menu command. This displays the current view panel as a simple, orthogonal 2D canvas, as shown in Figure 8-20. Paint effects painted to the Paint Effects canvas cannot be edited and need to be saved before you return to the view panel. The Paint, Paint Scene menu command exits out of the paint canvas.

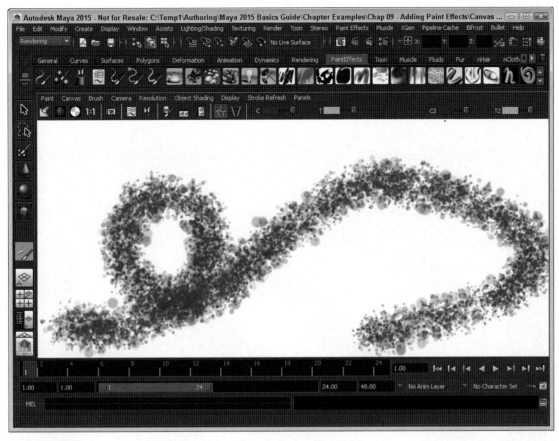

Figure 8-20
The Paint canvas

Changing the Canvas Size

The size of the paint canvas, along with its zoom amount, is shown in blue at the bottom of the canvas. The default canvas size is the size of the view panel window in pixels. You can change the size of the canvas using the Canvas, Set Size menu command. This opens a dialog box, shown in Figure 8-21, in which you can enter the new canvas dimensions.

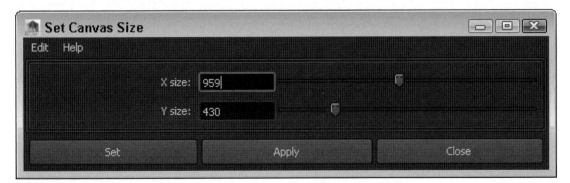

Figure 8-21
Set Canvas Size dialog box

Creating Seamless Textures

You can use the Paint Effects canvas to easily create **seamless textures**. Typical textures have seams that appear when they are repeated side by side. A seamless texture has opposite sides that match perfectly, so that the seams aren't evident. Enabling the Canvas, Wrap, Horizontally and Canvas, Wrap, Vertically panel menu commands makes any strokes that run off the edge of the canvas continue on the opposite edge, thereby create a seamless texture. Figure 8-22 shows a seamless texture created using a variety of brushes.

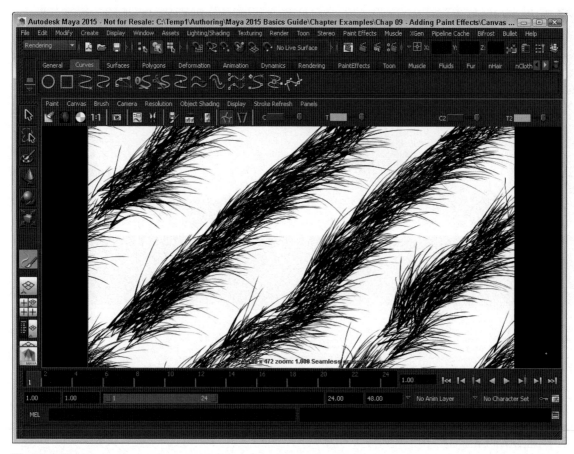

Figure 8-22
A seamless texture

Saving Textures

The Paint Effects Canvas lets you save any image drawn in the canvas with the Canvas, Save As menu command. The default image format is the Maya IFF format, but you can save the image in a number of different formats, including Cineon, EPS, GIF, JPEG, RLA, SGI, and so on. You can also save just a snapshot of the current image with the Paint, Save Snapshot menu command or with the Snapshot toolbar button. There is also a Canvas, Auto Save feature that you can enable.

Undoing the Last Stroke

You can use the normal Undo feature to undo any setting changes, but it cannot undo any brush strokes drawn in the paint canvas. The Canvas, Canvas Undo command undoes the last stroke added to the canvas.

Saving the Alpha Channel

Selecting the Display, Alpha Channel menu command in the panel menu or the Display Alpha Channel toolbar button displays the alpha channel for the canvas image, like the one shown in Figure 8-23. You can use alpha channels to represent transparency and to mask out unwanted areas. For an alpha channel, white areas appear black and black areas appear white. All other colors appear gray depending on their brightness.

Figure 8-23
Canvas alpha channel

Lesson 8.3-Tutorial 1: Create a Seamless Texture

1. Select the Panels, Panel, Paint Effects menu command to enter Scene Painting mode.

2. Select the Paint, Paint Canvas menu command.

3. Select the Canvas, Wrap, Horizontally and the Canvas, Wrap, Vertically panel menu commands.

4. Click on the Vine Gray Bud Brush icon in the Paint Effects shelf.

5. In the paint canvas, drag a diagonal line that moves from one corner of the canvas to the other.

   Notice how the vines that extend from either side of the canvas reappear on the opposite side, as shown in Figure 8-24.

6. Select Canvas, Save As and save the file as **Seamless vines.iff**.

Figure 8-24
Seamless vines

Lesson 8.3-Tutorial 2: Save an Image and Alpha Channel

1. Select the Panels, Panel, Paint Effects menu command to enter Scene Painting mode.

2. Select the Paint, Paint Canvas menu command.

3. Click on the Simple Tree Brush icon in the Paint Effects shelf.

4. Drag in the paint canvas to create a simple tree branch.

5. Click on the Flame Curly icon in the Paint Effects shelf.

6. Drag with the Flame brush over the top of the tree branch.

    The resulting image is shown in Figure 8-25.

7. Select Canvas, Save As and save the image as **Burning tree.iff**.

8. Click on the Display Alpha button in the panel toolbar.

    The alpha channel for the image is displayed, as shown in Figure 8-26. Notice how the transparent flames are partially visible.

9. Select Canvas, Save As and save the image as **Burning tree alpha.iff**.

Figure 8-25
A burning tree

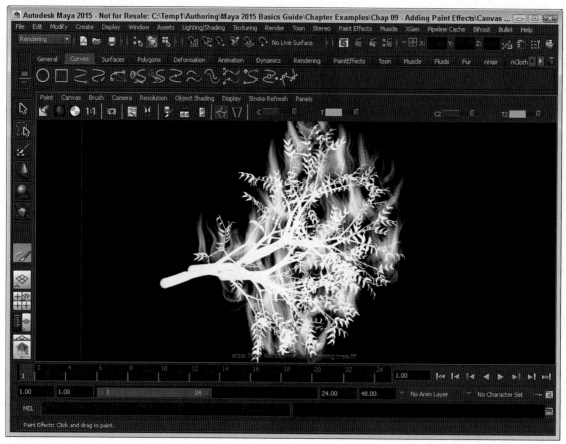

Figure 8-26
Alpha channel of the burning tree

Lesson 8.4: Paint on 3D Objects

Painting an image in 2D is fine for creating textures, but Maya also provides a way to paint directly on 3D objects.

Painting in a View Panel

In addition to painting on the Paint Canvas, the default is to paint directly in the scene. To access Paint Scene mode from the paint canvas, you can select the Paint, Paint Scene panel menu command. You can also paint in Modeling mode, but the strokes are only shown in wireframe. Figure 8-27 shows a simple sphere with two Paint Effects trees positioned next to it.

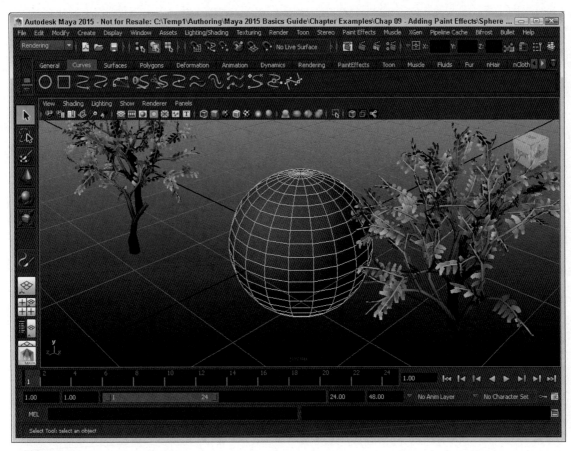

Figure 8-27
Combining models and Paint Effects

Painting on Objects

You can make selected NURBS objects paintable with the Paint Effects, Make Paintable menu command. This allows you to paint directly on the surface of the NURBS object. Paint Effects are painted on the View Plane by default, but you can switch to painting on 3D objects using the Paint Effects, Paint on Paintable Objects menu command. Figure 8-28 shows a NURBS sphere that has been made paintable and covered with the grass Paint Effect.

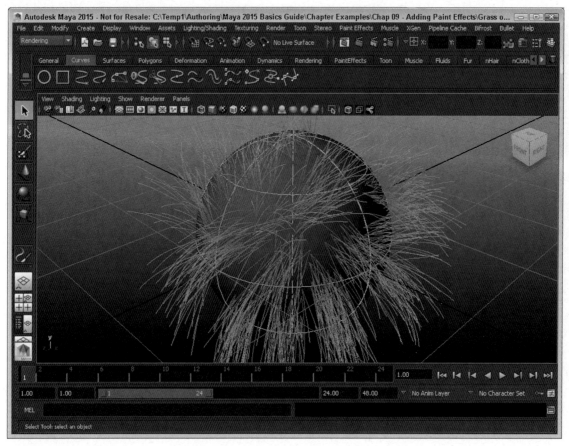

Figure 8-28
Paintable object

Auto-Painting an Object

With a NURBS surface selected, you can automatically apply paint strokes to its surface using the Paint Effects, Auto Paint, Paint Grid menu command. The Paint Grid Options dialog box lets you specify the number of spans in U and V to cover. The Auto Paint menu also includes a Random Paint option that randomly paint strokes on the object's surface. Figure 8-29 shows a simple NURBS torus object that has been auto-painted with a Neon Blue brush.

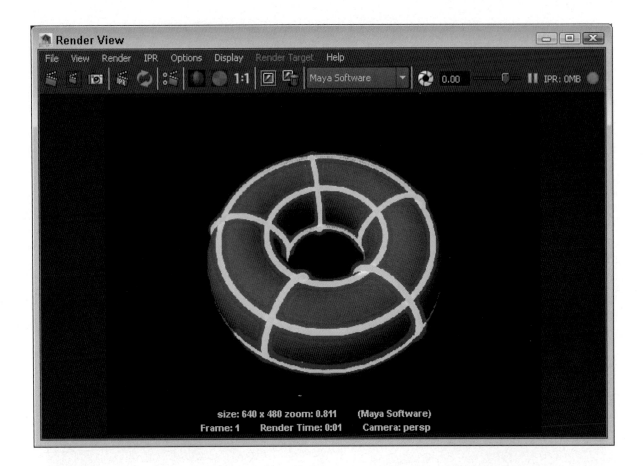

Figure 8-29
Auto- painted torus object

Saving Depth as a Grayscale Map

When Paint Effects are drawn in Scene Paint mode, they have a depth value that determines how close or far from the camera they are. You can save this depth information as a grayscale image using the Paint, Save Depth as Grayscale menu command. You can then use depth image maps as textures to control the placement of objects.

Lesson 8.4-Tutorial 1: Paint on Objects

1. Create a NURBS sphere object using the Create, NURBS Primitives, Sphere menu command.

2. With the sphere selected, choose the Paint Effects, Make Paintable menu command.

3. Select the Panels, Panel, Paint Effects menu command to enter Scene Painting mode.

4. Click on the Curly Flame Brush icon in the Paint Effects shelf.

5. Drag over the top of the sphere object.

    The flames from the brush are painted only on the sphere, as shown in Figure 8-30.

6. Select File, Save Scene As and save the file as **Flaming sphere.mb**.

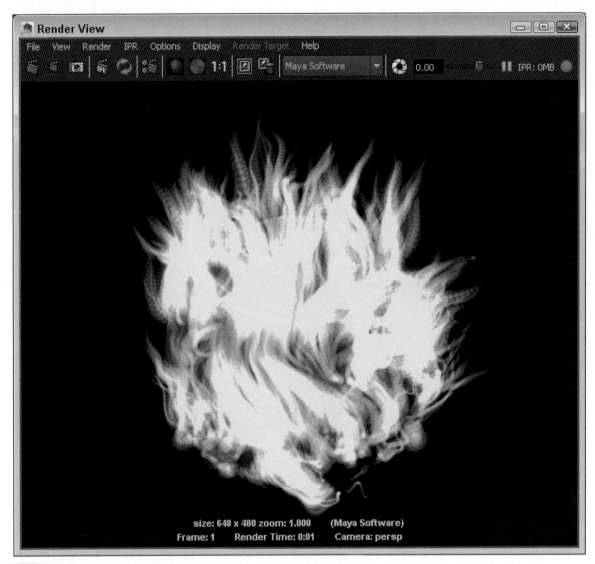

Figure 8-30
A flaming sphere

Lesson 8.4-Tutorial 2: Auto-Paint on Objects

1. Create a NURBS sphere object using the Create, NURBS Primitives, Sphere menu command.

2. With the sphere selected, click on the Cumulus Cloud Brush icon in the Paint Effects shelf.

3. Select the Paint Effects, Auto Paint, Paint Grid menu command.

    Clouds are automatically added to surround the sphere.

4. Select the sphere object again.

5. Click on the Lightning Brush icon in the Paint Effects shelf.

6. Select the Paint Effects, Auto Paint, Paint Random menu command.

7. Select the Panels, Panel, Paint Effects menu command to enter Scene Painting mode.

    The sphere surrounded with clouds and lightning are displayed, as shown in Figure 8-31.

8. Select File, Save Scene As and save the file as **Cloud and lightning sphere.mb**.

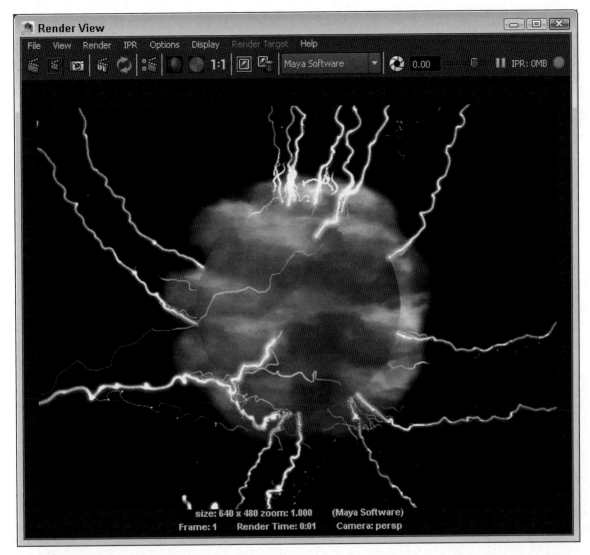

Figure 8-31
An auto-painted sphere

Lesson 8.5: Edit Paint Effects

You can edit paint strokes that have been drawn in the Modeling or Scene Painting mode once you select them using the Attribute Editor. Every stroke that is painted includes a tab in the Attribute Editor for the stroke, for the brush, and for the time.

Selecting Strokes

Before you can edit existing strokes, you need to select them. You can select a stroke using the Paint Effects Strokes selection mask by right-clicking on the Curves selection mask in the Status Line, or you can display all strokes as wireframe lines in Scene Painting mode by holding down the Ctrl/Command key. You can also use the Paint Effects, Select Brush/Stroke Names Containing menu command. This opens a dialog box, shown in Figure 8-32, in which you can type the name of the brush or stroke you want to select. Selected strokes appear light green and their tabs appear in the Attribute Editor. The Edit, Select All by Type, Strokes menu command selects all strokes.

Figure 8-32
The Select Brush/Stroke Names Containing dialog box

Editing Strokes

Once a stroke is selected, you can edit its stroke attributes or the brush attributes used to create it using the Attribute Editor or the Channel Box. Changes to the stroke are displayed immediately.

Converting Strokes to Polygons

If you really want to edit Paint Strokes, you can convert them to polygons with the Modify, Convert, Paint Effects to Polygons menu command. There are also options to convert Paint Effects to curves and to NURBS. Figure 8-33 shows a set of crystals created as a Paint Effect that have been converted to polygons.

Figure 8-33
Paint Effects converted to polygons

Changing the Default Light

Another way to change the Paint Effects is to edit the default light that they use. In Scene Paint mode, the default light is shown as four dark red arrows that point in the direction that the light is shining. If you hold down the Ctrl/Command key, you can select these light arrows. When selected, their attributes show up in the Attribute Editor, where you can change their light type, color, and intensity. You can also set the light's transform node.

Lesson 8.5-Tutorial 1: Select and Edit Strokes

1. Select the File, Open Scene As menu command, and then locate and open the Curly hair sphere.mb file.

   This file includes a NURBS sphere that has been auto-painted with the Curly Hair brush.

2. Select the Paint Effects, Select Brush/Stoke Names Containing menu command.

3. In the dialog box that appears, type **Hair** and click the Select Brushes button.

   The Curly Hair Brush node appears in the Attribute Editor.

4. Enter a value of 1.25 for the Global Scale.

   The brush used to create the Paint Effect are updated, as shown in Figure 8-34.

5. Select File, Save Scene As and save the file as **Curly hair sphere - short.mb**.

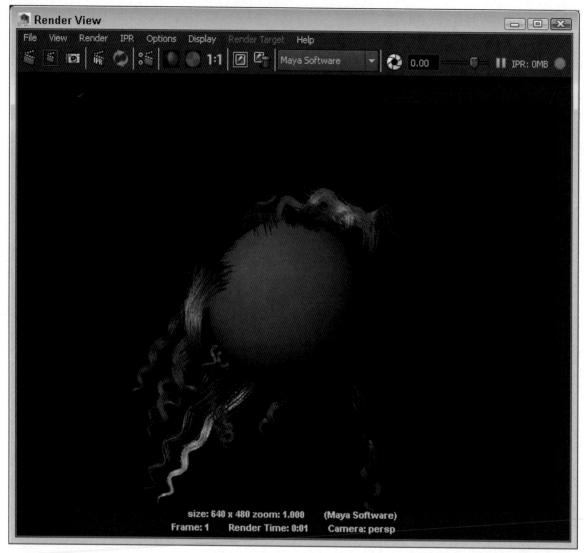

Figure 8-34
Edited brush values

Lesson 8.5-Tutorial 2: Convert Paint Effects to Polygons

1. Select the Panels, Panel, Paint Effects menu command to enter Scene Painting mode.

2. Click on the Light Bulb Brush icon in the Paint Effects shelf.

3. Drag in the view panel to create a bunch of light bulbs.

4. Select the Modify, Convert, Paint Effects to Polygons menu command

    All the light bulbs are now polygon objects, as shown in Figure 8-35, and you can edit them using the Edit Polygons menu options.

5. Select File, Save Scene As and save the file as **Polygon light bulbs.mb**.

Figure 8-35
Polygon light bulbs

Chapter Summary

This chapter covers Maya's innovative Paint Effects. Using one of the many preset brushes, you can quickly create Paint Effects such as flowers, trees, clouds, and buildings without having to model and texture objects. In addition to the presets, you can create custom brushes by blending effects of different brushes. The Paint Effects menu and Settings dialog box include many settings for controlling every aspect of the paint strokes, including size, color, glow, illumination, and so on. The Canvas interface lets you paint and save images in 2D or you can paint directly on 3D objects in the 3D scene. You can convert objects created with Paint Effects into polygon objects.

What You Have Learned

In this chapter, you learned

* How to access the Paint Effects panel.

* How to access the preset brushes found in the Visor.

* How to create new brushes by blending existing brushes.

* How to redraw and clear the current view.

* How to change the brush settings.

* How to use the Paint, Smear, Blur, and Erase brushes.

* How to change the brush size and color.

* How to enable brush illumination, glows, and shadows.

* How to create and save custom brushes.

* How to use the Paint Effects canvas.

* How to change the canvas size and enable seamless textures.

* How to save canvas images.

* How to save an alpha channel.

* How to paint on 3D objects.

* How to use the Auto Paint features.

* How to select and edit paint strokes.

* How to convert paint strokes to polygons.

Key Terms From This Chapter

* **Paint Effects.** An innovative Maya feature that lets you paint objects in the scene using brushes.

* **Brush.** An interface element used to create Paint Effects within a scene.

* **Visor.** A dialog box that holds presets that can be quickly selected, such as Paint Effects.

* **Stroke.** The resulting lines produced by dragging a brush in the scene.

* **Canvas.** A 2D interface where you can paint and save objects.

* **Seamless texture.** An image that allows strokes drawn on one edge of the canvas to be wrapped to the opposite edge.

* **Alpha channel.** An image that shows the transparency values of the scene as a grayscale image.

* **Auto Paint.** A painting mode that automatically applies strokes to the selected object.

Chapter 9
Using Cameras and Lights

IN THIS CHAPTER

9.1 Work with cameras.

9.2 Create a background.

9.3 Create and position lights.

9.4 Change light settings.

9.5 Create light effects.

Before moving on to animation and rendering, there are two more object types that you'll need to learn how to create and use—cameras and lights.

You can position cameras anywhere within the scene and then look at the current scene in a unique way. A single scene can contain several cameras, and cameras can be animated. Several types of cameras exist. The Camera and Aim camera type includes an Aim point that you can place at the location where the camera should be focused. The Camera, Aim and Up camera type includes two Aim points, one for aiming the camera direction and the other for controlling how the camera twists about its focus axis.

Camera attributes include **Angle of View, Focal Length,** and **Clipping Planes.** You can also set a camera to create a depth-of-field effect, which focuses on a specific point in the scene.

You can attach backgrounds to cameras and then render them using an **image plane**. Using this image plane, you can create a background consisting of a solid color, a texture, or a loaded image. Background images are rendered with the scene.

Lights are critical to the success of a scene and light placement and settings should be well-thought-out in order to convey the appropriate ambience. A typical lighting design includes a main light that provides most of the light for the scene and is used to create shadows, a background light that is positioned behind the main objects, and two or more secondary lights that are positioned in front of and to the sides of the scene objects, providing extra light.

There are several types of lights in Maya, each with its own advantages. They include Spot lights, Point lights, Directional lights, Volume lights, Area lights, and Ambient light. You can position lights using the transform tools and interactively change a light's settings using light manipulators. Attributes include Color, Intensity, and Decay.

You can enable shadows for lights using **depth maps** or **Ray Traced Shadows**. The difference is quality versus render speed. Depth maps are sufficient in most instances, but you might want to use Ray-Traced shadows when the scene requires a crisp, accurate shadow line.

You can also use lights to create a number of effects, including illuminated fog, glows, halos, and light effects.

Lesson 9.1: Work with Cameras

Behind every view panel is a camera that controls what is visible. By creating a custom camera, you can position the camera anywhere in the scene and change its settings.

Creating Cameras

Use the Create menu to create your own custom cameras. The Create, Cameras menu includes three camera types. The standard camera is used most often, but you can link the Camera and Aim camera to a point that can be aimed at a specific point in the scene. The Camera, Aim and Up camera is like the Camera and Aim camera, except it also includes a point for defining the camera's upward position. Figure 9-1 shows the icons for each of these cameras.

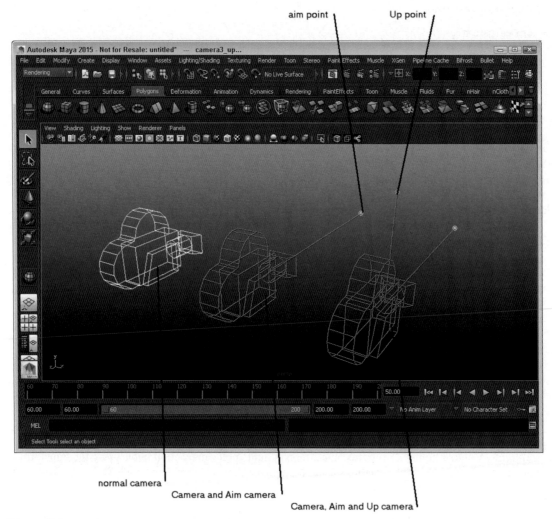

Figure 9-1
Camera icons

Changing Camera Settings

With a camera selected, you can change its settings using the Channel Box or the Attribute Editor. Use the View, Camera Attribute Editor panel menu command to get quick access to the current camera's settings, as shown in Figure 9-2. Sample attributes include the Angle of View, Focal Length, and Scale. Use the Near and Far Clip Planes options to set the nearest and farthest objects that the camera can see. When the viewing camera is selected, you can change its attributes and the view is updated.

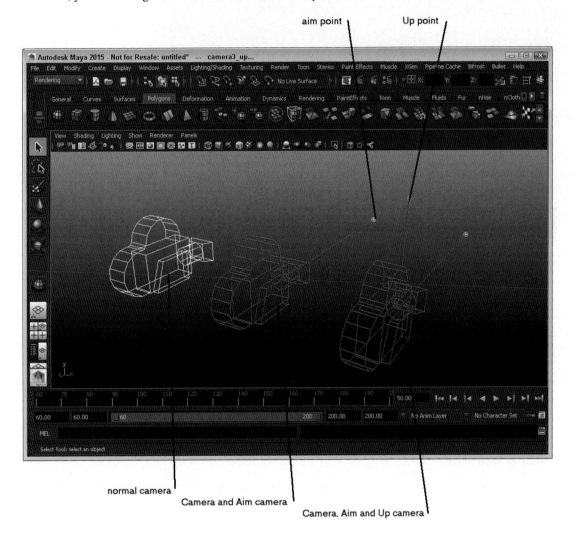

Figure 9-2
Camera settings

Selecting a Camera

You can easily select most objects in the scene by simply clicking on them, but the current camera is pointing at the scene and its icon cannot be clicked on in the current view panel. There are several ways to select the current camera. You can select its icon from a different view panel; open and select it from the Outliner with the Window, Outliner menu command; or select the View, Select Camera panel menu command.

Positioning Cameras

You can use the standard transform tools on cameras, but the Scale tool only changes the camera's icon size. You can rotate a Camera and Aim type camera by selecting and moving the camera's aim point. The top point of a Camera, Aim and Up type camera can be moved to twirl the camera about its center point. For precise camera positioning, you can always change the camera's transform node attributes in the Channel Box.

Looking Through a New Camera

With a camera selected, you can change the view panel so that the scene is seen through the new camera using the Panels, Look Through Selected panel menu command. You can force the current camera to look at a selected object using the View, Look at Selection panel menu command. Figure 9-3 shows a selected camera pointed at several objects and the camera view replacing the upper-right perspective view panel.

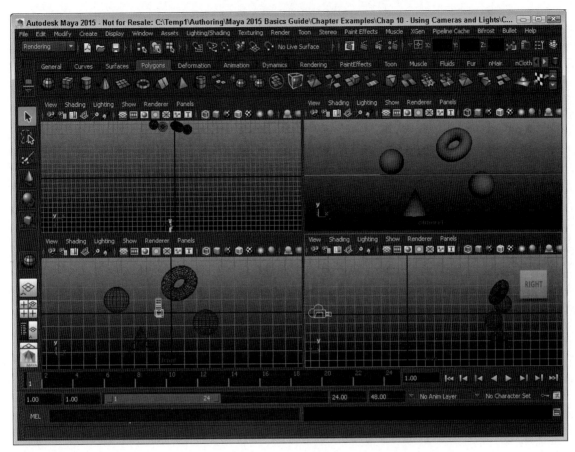

Figure 9-3
Camera view

Setting View Guidelines

When you work with a 3D scene, you can enable boundaries that marks the exact areas that appear within the rendered scene, as shown in Figure 9-4. The areas inside the boundaries are called **safe areas**. All areas within the safe-area boundaries are visible when the action or text is output to broadcast TV. The View, Camera Settings panel menu command is where you enable the Safe Action, Safe Title, and Resolution Gate boundary options.

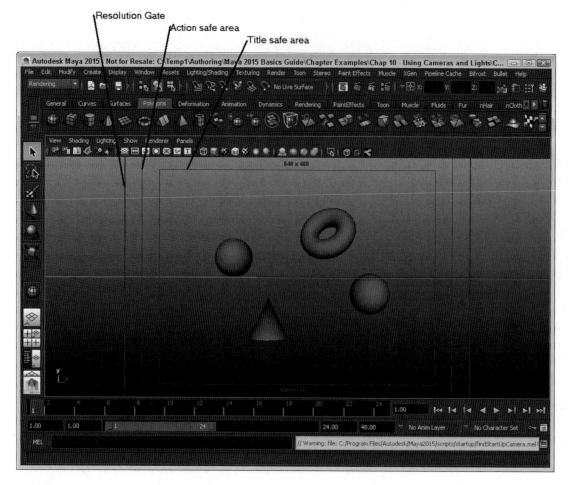

Figure 9-4
Safe boundaries

Changing the Depth of Field

You can set scene cameras to focus on a specific point within the scene, making all objects closer or farther from that point gradually blurred. This effect is known as a **depth-of-field** effect. In Maya, you can enable a depth-of-field effect in the Depth of Field section of the Attribute Editor. Once the effect is enabled, you can set attributes such as Focus Distance, which defines where the scene is in focus. Figure 9-5 shows a rendered scene of a row of simple trees with and without the Depth of Field option enabled.

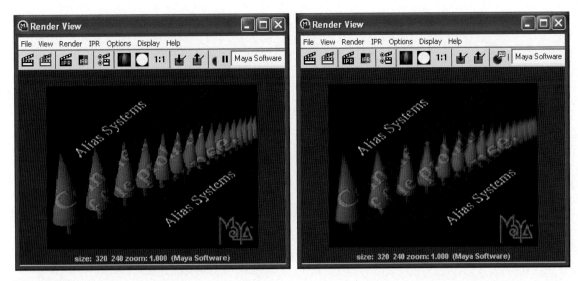

Figure 9-5
With and without depth of field

Lesson 9.1-Tutorial 1: Create a Camera

1. Select the File, Open Scene menu command and open the Simple chair.mb file.

2. Select the Create, Cameras, Camera menu command to create a new scene camera.

3. With the camera selected, position the camera with the Move tool so that it is pointing at the chair object.

4. With the camera still selected, choose the Panels, Look Through Selected panel menu command in the Perspective view panel.

    The perspective view is changed to the Camera1 view.

5. While using the other views and looking through the Camera1 view, continue to move and rotate the camera object in the other views until the chair is centered, as shown in Figure 9-6.

6. Select File, Save Scene As and save the file as **Centered chair.mb**.

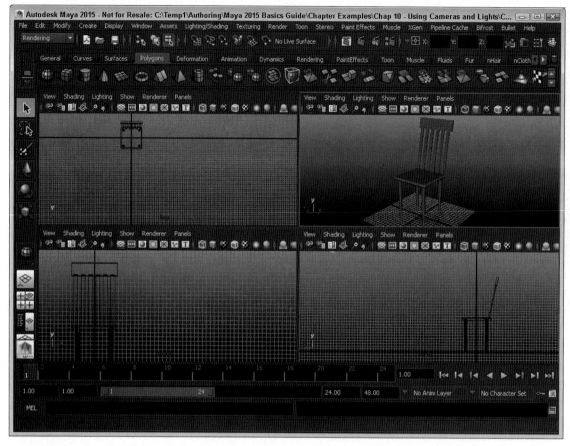

Figure 9-6
Centered chair

Lesson 9.1-Tutorial 2: Aim a Camera

1. Select the File, Open Scene menu command and open the Simple chair.mb file.

2. Select the Create, Cameras, Camera and Aim menu command to create a new scene camera.

3. With the camera selected, position the camera with the Move tool so that it is positioned a distance above and away from the chair object.

4. Using one of the other view panels, select the aim point and move it to the center of the chair.

5. Select the camera object again and choose the Panels, Look Through Selected panel menu command for the Perspective view.

    The aim point automatically controls the rotation of the camera so that it is pointing at the aim point, as shown in Figure 9-7.

6. Select File, Save Scene As and save the file as **Aimed chair.mb**.

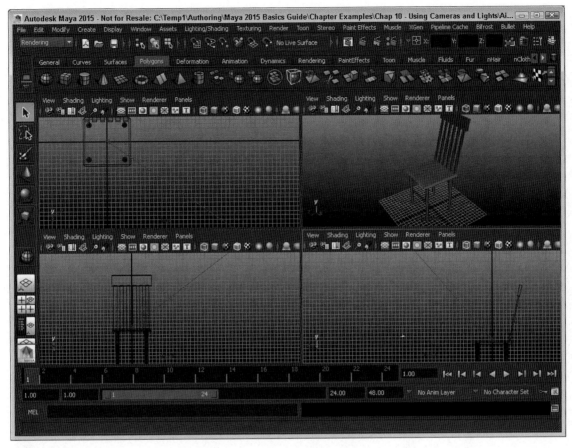

Figure 9-7
Aimed camera view

Lesson 9.1-Tutorial 3: Create a Depth-of-Field Effect

1. Select the File, Open Scene menu command and open the Row of chairs.mb file.

2. Select the Create, Cameras, Camera and Aim menu command to create a new scene camera.

3. With the camera selected, position the camera with the Move tool so that it is positioned a distance above and away from the chairs.

4. Select the aim point and move it to the center of the middle chair.

5. Select the camera object again and choose the Panels, Look Through Selected panel menu command for the Perspective view.

6. With the Camera1 view active, select the View, Camera Attribute Editor panel menu command or press the Ctrl/Command+A keys.

7. In the Depth of Field section, enable the Depth of Field option and set the Focus Distance value to be equal to the Focal Length value.

8. In the Environment section of the Attribute Editor, drag the Background Slider towards the right end to make the background light gray.

   By setting the Focus Distance value to be equal to the Focal Length value, the camera focus is at the aim point and all other points are blurry, as shown in Figure 9-8.

9. Select File, Save Scene As and save the file as **Depth of field chairs.mb**.

Figure 9-8
Depth-of-field effect

Lesson 9.2: Create a Background

Each camera is linked to an image plane that you can use to provide a scene background. You can set this background to display a solid color, a texture, or an image. The image plane is rendered along with the scene when the camera view is selected.

Setting the Background Color

With the current camera selected, the Background Color attribute can be found in the Environment section of the Attribute Editor, as shown in Figure 9-9. To change the background color, just click on the color swatch and select a new color in the Color Chooser.

Figure 9-9
Environment section

Adding an Image Plane

You can add image planes to a camera object and then the image planes hold a texture of an image that acts as the background for the scene. To create an image plane for a camera, you first need to select a camera and click the Create button in the Environment section of the Attribute Editor for the camera node. The image plane appears as a rectangle with an X through it, as shown in Figure 9-9.

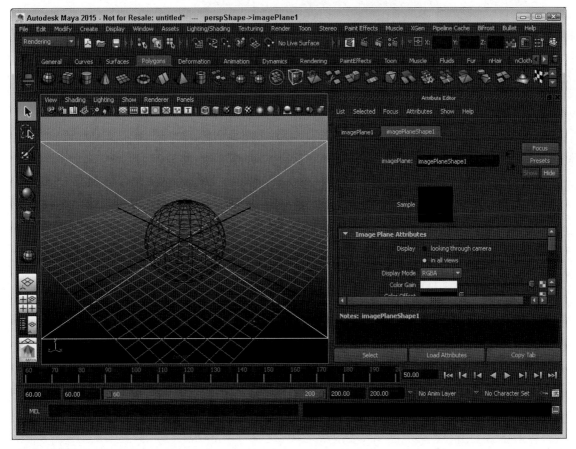

Figure 9-10
An image plane

Creating a Textured Background

The Type attribute in the Image Plane Attributes section for the Image Plane node includes two options—Image File and Texture. If you select the Texture option, you can click on Create Render Node button and select a texture to use for the background. Figure 9-11 uses the Checker render node as a background.

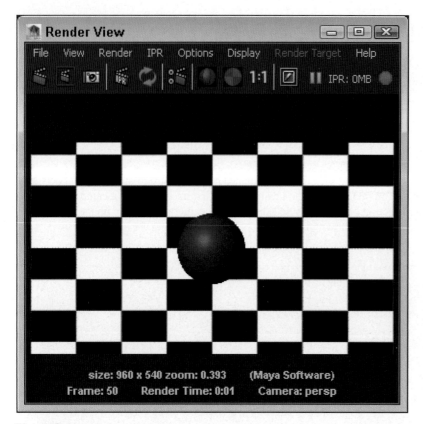

Figure 9-11
Texture background

Loading a Background Image

In addition to placing textures on an image plane, you can also select an image to be placed on the image plane. An easier way to load an image for the background is to use the View, Image Plane, Import Image panel menu command. This causes a file dialog box to open from which you can select the image to load. Figure 9-12 shows a rendered scene with an image background.

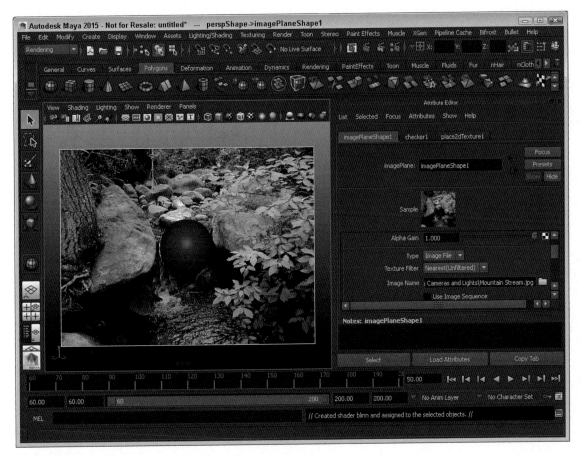

Figure 9-12
Image background

Positioning the Background

Images and textures that are loaded onto the image plane can be positioned using the attributes in the Placement section for the Image Plane node in the Attribute Editor. The Fit drop-down list allows you to select to fit the image using the Fill, Best, Horizontal, Vertical, or To Size options. The Fit to Resolution Gate and Fit to Film Gate buttons automatically fits the background. You can also offset and rotate the background image.

Tip

> You can select and access the image plane attributes
> using the View, Image Plane, Image Plane Attributes
> panel menu command.

Lesson 9.2-Tutorial 1: Change Background Color

1. Select the File, Open Scene menu command and open theHot air balloon.mb file.

2. Select the View, Select Camera panel menu command in the Perspective view panel.

3. Click on the Show Attribute Editor button in the Status Line or press the Ctrl/Command+A keys.

4. Click on the Background Color swatch in the Environment section of the Attribute Editor.

5. Select a light blue color in the Color Chooser and click the Accept button.

6. Click the Render the Current Frame button in the Status Line.

   The scene is rendered using the background color, as shown in Figure 9-13.

7. Select File, Save Scene As and save the file as **Background color.mb**.

Figure 9-13
Background color

Lesson 9.2-Tutorial 2: Change Background Texture

1. Select the File, Open Scene menu command and open the Hot air balloon.mb file.

2. Select the View, Select Camera panel menu command in the Perspective view panel.

3. Click on the Show Attribute Editor button in the Status Line or press the Ctrl/Command+A keys.

4. Click on the Create button in the Environment section of the Attribute Editor to create an image plane.

   An image plane is added to the current view.

5. Click the Type drop-down list and select Texture.

6. Click the Create Render Node button (which has a small checkered pattern on it) next to the Texture field.

   The Create Render Node dialog box appears.

7. Click the Cloud texture node.

8. Click on the place3dTexture1 node in the Attribute Editor and set all the Scale values to 50.

9. Click the Render the Current Frame button in the Status Line.

   The scene is rendered using the background texture, as shown in Figure 9-14.

10. Select File, Save Scene As and save the file as **Background texture.mb**.

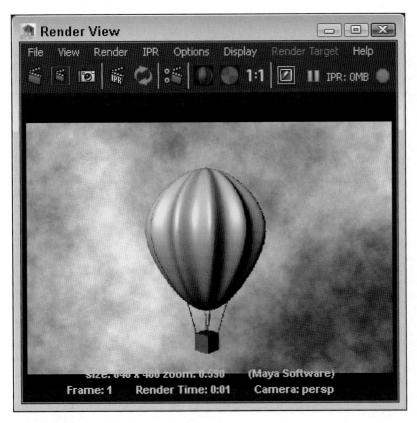

Figure 9-14
Background texture

Lesson 9.2-Tutorial 3: Add and Position a Background Image

1. Select the File, Open Scene menu command and open the Hot air balloon.mb file.

2. Select the View, Select Camera panel menu command in the Perspective view panel.

3. Click on the Show Attribute Editor button in the Status Line or press the Ctrl/Command+A keys.

4. Click on the Create button in the Environment section of the Attribute Editor to create an image plane.

   An image plane is added to the current view.

5. Click the Open File button next to the Image Name field.

6. In the File dialog box, locate and open the Coast from Diamond Head.jpg image.

7. In the Placement section, Click the Fit to Resolution Gate button.

8. Click the Render the Current Frame button in the Status Line.

   The scene is rendered using the background image, as shown in Figure 9-15.

9. Select File, Save Scene As and save the file as **Background image.mb**.

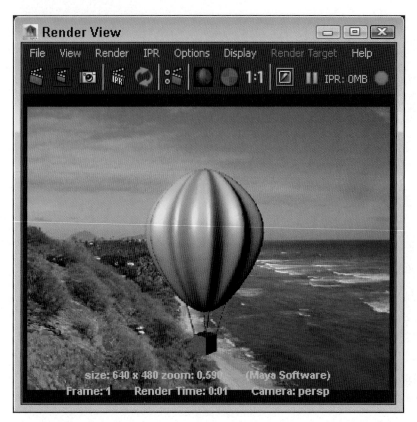

Figure 9-15
Background image

Lesson 9.3: Create and Position Lights

If you render a scene with only the default lights, the scene might appear flat. Proper use of lights can create ambience for the scene.

Using Default Lights

If no lights are present in a scene, Maya renders the scene using its default lights. Default lights can be enabled using the 5 key and are only meant to help render objects during the modeling phase, before you add any lights. Default lights can be disabled in the Render Options section of the Render Global Settings dialog box.

Understanding the Light Types

Maya includes several types of lights that you can use. One of the key differences between these light types is the shape of the light source and the direction that the light is cast. The light types include:

* **Ambient light.** Raises the overall light in the scene by increasing the brightness of all objects.

* **Directional light.** Casts light in parallel rays from a cylindrical source

* **Point light.** Casts light equally in all directions from a single point.

* **Spot light.** Casts light from a cone that can be positioned.

* **Area light.** Casts light equally from a specified area.

* **Volume light.** Casts light within a specified volume.

Figure 9-16 shows each of the light types.

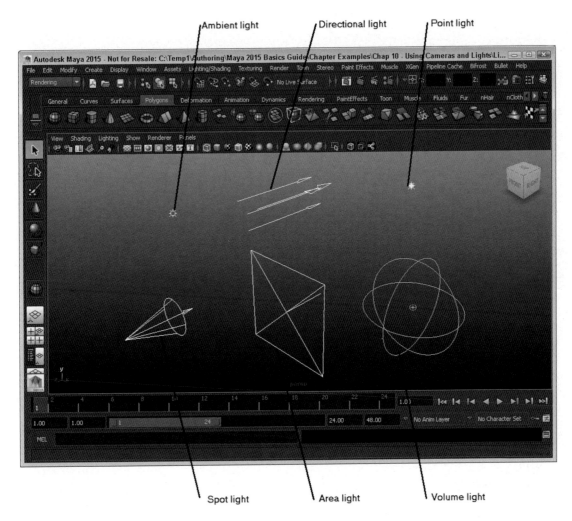

Figure 9-16
The Light types

Creating Lights

You can create any light type using the Create, Lights menu. You can also create lights using the Create Bar in the Hypershade. Each light type has an Options dialog box in which you can change settings prior to creating the light.

Manipulating Lights

When lights are created, their icon appears in the view panel. Clicking on the Display, Show, Light Manipulator menu command enables the light manipulator, shown in Figure 9-17. Clicking on the manipulator switches the attributes that can be changed. You can also switch between the attribute manipulators using the Display, Camera/Light Manipulator menu command. For all lights (except the Spot light), the first mode lets you change the light and aiming point's position and the second mode lets you set the light's pivot point.

Tip

```
You can enable the light manipulator by pressing the T
key.
```

Light manipulator   Pivot manipulator   Aiming point manipulator

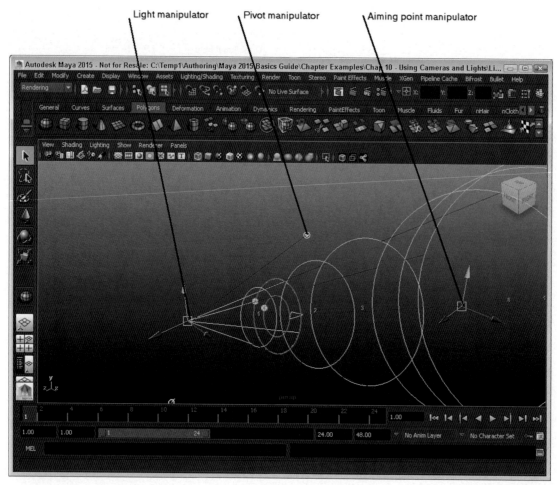

Figure 9-17
The light manipulator

Manipulating Spot Lights

Spot lights include many additional attributes that can be changed with the light manipulator. Clicking on the light manipulator switches between attributes for the Cone Radius, the Penumbra Radius, and the Decay. For each of these attributes, you can drag to change its value. Figure 9-18 shows a Spot light with the Decay manipulator enabled.

Decay manipulators

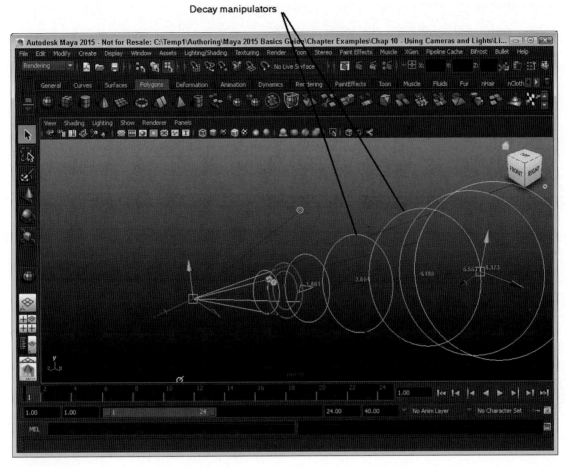

Figure 9-18
Decay manipulator

Lesson 9.3-Tutorial 1: Create and Manipulate a Light

1. Select the File, Open Scene menu command and open the Tree.mb file.

2. Select the Create, Lights, Spot Light menu command.

    A light icon is added to the scene at the origin.

3. Select the Scale tool and scale the light icon to increase its size.

4. Click on the Show Manipulator button in the Toolbox. The default manipulator lets you move the camera and aiming point.

5. With the light selected, change the Intensity value in the Channel Box to 2.0.

6. Select the Perspective view panel and press the 5 key to enable smooth shading, then press the 7 key to see the light effect.

7. Drag in the various views until the light is set a distance above and away from the tree and the aim point is at the tree's base, as shown in Figure 9-19.

8. Click the Render the Current Frame button in the Status Line.

    The scene is displayed using the spot light, as shown in Figure 9-20.

9. Select File, Save Scene As and save the file as **Spot light on tree.mb**.

315

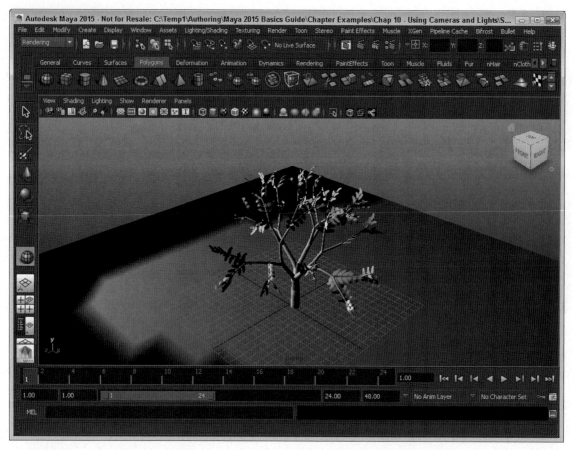

Figure 9-19
The Spot light

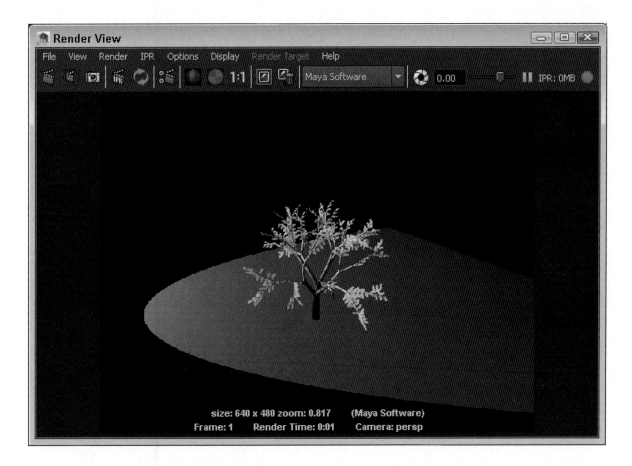

Figure 9-20
A rendered Spot light

Lesson 9.4: Change Light Settings

You can access a light's attributes in the Attribute Editor when the light is selected; you can also access these attributes by double-clicking on the light's icon in the Hypershade. Each light includes a Type attribute that you can use to switch between different light types.

Changing Light Color

Although most lights are white, lights can have color. Clicking on the color swatch in the Attribute Editor lets you change the light color in the Color Chooser. Figure 9-21 shows four Spot lights with different colors.

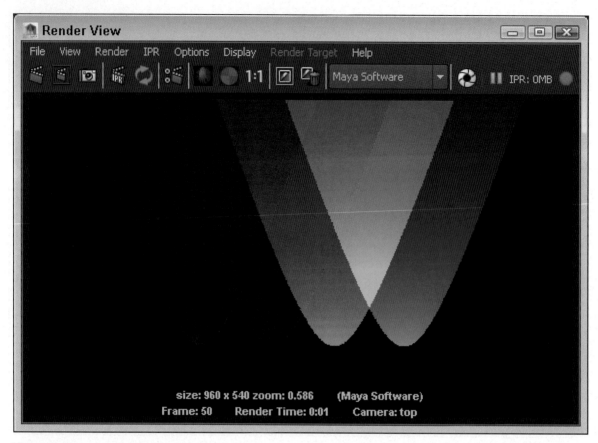

Figure 9-21
Colored spot lights

Changing Light Intensity and Decay

The brightness of a light is controlled by its Intensity attribute. For several light types (Area, Point, and Spot), you can select a Decay rate. This attribute defines how quickly the **light intensity** decreases over distance. The options include No Decay, Linear, Quadratic, and Cubic. Figure 9-22 shows each of the Decay types.

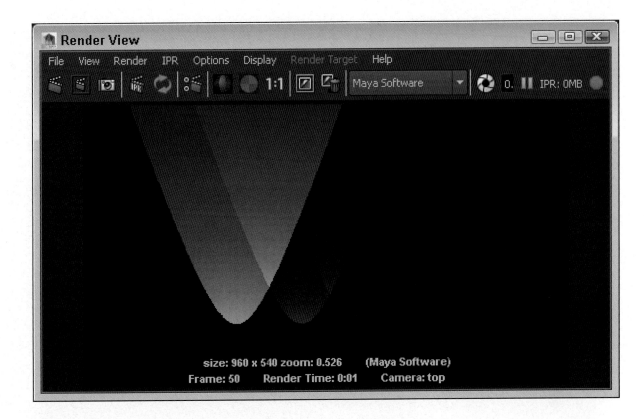

Figure 9-22
Decaying lights

Enabling Shadows

Maya includes support for two types of shadows—Depth Map shadows, which render quickly and are less accurately, and Raytraced shadows, which are more accurate but take longer to render. You can enable either shadow type with the Use Depth Map Shadows or the Use Ray Trace Shadows options. Figure 9-23 shows Depth Map shadows cast by a sphere of objects.

Figure 9-23
Depth Map shadows

Lesson 9.4-Tutorial 1: Change Light Color and Intensity

1. Select the File, Open Scene menu command and open the Spot light on tree.mb file.

2. Select the Spot light object.

3. Click on the Show Attribute Editor button in the Status Line or press the Ctrl/Command+A keys.

4. Click on the Color swatch in the Attribute Editor.

5. Select a bright yellow color from the Color Chooser and click the Accept button.

6. Increase the Intensity value to 3.0.

7. Right-click on the Perspective view panel and click the Render the Current Frame button in the Status Line.

    The scene is rendered using the yellow Spot light, as shown in Figure 9-24.

8. Select File, Save Scene As and save the file as **Yellow spot light on tree.mb**.

Figure 9-24
Yellow Spot light

Lesson 9.4-Tutorial 2: Enable Shadows

1. Select the File, Open Scene menu command and open the Spot light on tree.mb file.

2. Select the Spot light object.

3. Click on the Show Attribute Editor button in the Status Line or press the Ctrl/Command+A keys.

4. Click to open the Shadows section in the Attribute Editor.

5. Enable the Use Depth Map Shadows option.

6. Right-click on the Perspective view panel and click the Render the Current Frame button in the Status Line.

    The scene is rendered including shadows, as shown in Figure 9-25.

7. Select File, Save Scene As and save the file as **Shadowed spot light on tree.mb**.

Figure 9-25
Spot light and shadows

Lesson 9.5: Create Light Effects

You can add light effects to most lights in a scene using the Light Effects section of the Attribute Editor. These light effects can include fog, glows, halos, and **lens flares**. The key to several of these light effects is the Optical FX render node, found in the Glow section of the Utilities category of the Create Render Node dialog box. This render node includes the necessary settings to add glows, halos, and lens flares to a positioned light.

> **Note**
>
> Light effects aren't available for all light types, such as Ambient and Directional lights.

Creating Light Fog

If you look closely at the Attribute Editor for the selected light, you'll see that you can apply a render node to many attributes, including Color and Intensity. If you open the Light Effects section, you'll find several additional attributes, including Fog and Glow. To create one of the fog effects, you'll need to position the light where you want the illuminated fog to be and then click the Create Render Node button. This automatically adds the Light Fog render node to the light. For the Light Fog node, you can set Fog Color, Type, Radius, and Intensity options. Figure 9-26 shows a Fog light applied to a Point light in front of a sphere.

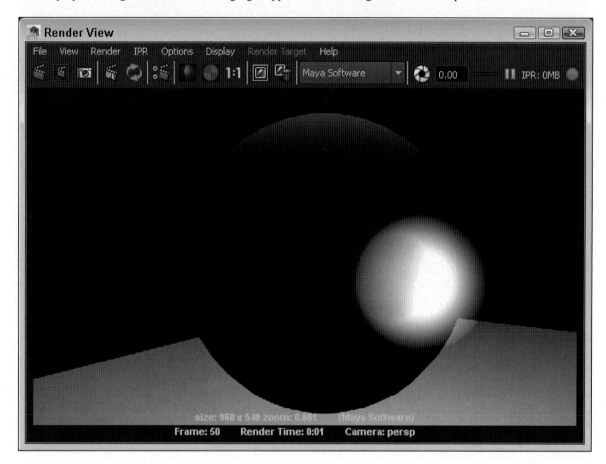

Figure 9-26
Fog light effect

Creating Glows and Halos

If you click the Create Render Node button for the Glow attribute, the Optical FX render node is added. The Optical FX render node includes attributes for creating glows and halos. The options for each include None, Linear, Exponential, Ball, Lens Flare, and Rim Halo. You can also set the number of star points, glow and halo colors, spread, and intensity. Figure 9-27 shows a five-point Rim Halo applied using a Point light.

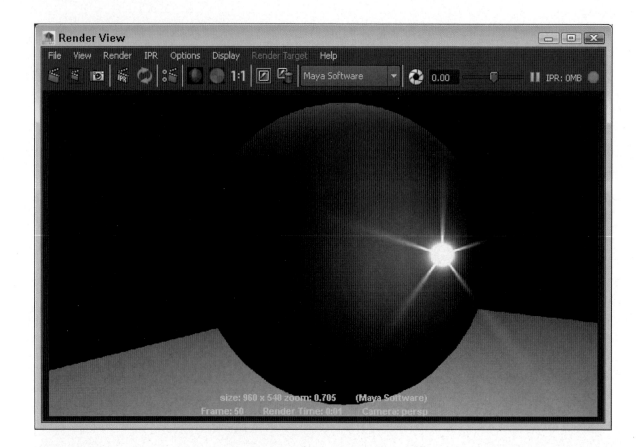

Figure 9-27
Halo light effect

Creating Lens Flares

Once you've added a glow or halo effect to a light, you can also enable a lens effect with the Lens Effect option. Lens flares have their own set of attributes, including Flare Color and Intensity. Figure 9-28 shows the same halo with the Lens Flare effect enabled.

Figure 9-28
Lens Flare light effect

Lesson 9.5-Tutorial 1: Enable Light Fog

1. Select the File, Open Scene menu command and open the Background image.mb file.

2. Select the Create, Lights, Point Light menu command.

3. Drag the Point light with the Move tool and position it in front of the balloon object.

4. Click on the Show Attribute Editor button in the Status Line or press the Ctrl/Command+A keys.

5. Open the Light Effects section in the Attribute Editor.

6. Set the Fog Radius value to 3.0.

7. Click on the Create Render Node button to the right of the Light Fog attribute.

   A Light Fog render node is added to the light and its attributes are opened in the Attribute Editor, as shown in Figure 9-29.

8. Right-click on the Perspective view panel and click the Render the Current Frame button in the Status Line.

   The scene is rendered, as shown in Figure 9-30.

9. Select File, Save Scene As and save the file as **Light fog on balloon.mb**.

Figure 9-29
Light Fog render node

Figure 9-30
Fog light on balloon

Lesson 9.5-Tutorial 2: Enable a Halo Light Effect

1. Select the File, Open Scene menu command and open the Background image.mb file.

2. Select the Create, Lights, Point Light menu command.

3. Drag the Point light with the Move tool and position it in front of the balloon object.

4. Click on the Show Attribute Editor button in the Status Line or press the Ctrl/Command+A keys.

5. Open the Light Effects section in the Attribute Editor.

6. Click on the Create Render Node button to the right of the Light Glow attribute.

    An Optical FX render node is added to the light and its attributes open in the Attribute Editor.

7. Enable the Active and Lens Flare options in the Optical FX Attributes section.

8. Right-click on the Perspective view panel and click the Render the Current Frame button in the Status Line.

    The scene is rendered, as shown in Figure 9-31.

9. Select File, Save Scene As and save the file as **Halo effect on balloon.mb**.

Figure 9-31
Halo light effect on balloon

Chapter Summary

This chapter covers cameras, background image planes, and lights. Cameras are non-visible objects placed in the scene that set the view of what is to be rendered. There are three camera types, including a camera with an aiming point. Cameras have special effects that you can use, including clipping planes and depth of field. Image planes are objects attached to a camera that hold a background that is rendered with the scene. This background can be a texture or a loaded image.

Lights add illumination and shadow effects to the scene. Of the six available light types, some have specialized features such as the Spot light, which allows you to set the amount of decay over time. You can also use lights to position special effects such as fog, glows, halos, and lens flares.

What You Have Learned

In this chapter, you learned

*   How to create, position, and use cameras.

*   How to change camera settings.

*   How to see a view through the selected camera.

*   How to create a depth-of-field effect.

*   How to set a background color.

*   How to create and use an image plane with a texture or an image.

* How to position a background image on an image plane.

* How to add a light to the scene.

* The different light types.

* How to use the various light manipulators.

* How to change a light's color, intensity, and decay values.

* How to enable shadows.

* How to create light effects such as fog, glows, and halos.

* How to add a lens flare to the scene.

Key Terms From This Chapter

* **Angle of View.** A camera's angle value used to set the width of the scene viewed through the camera. Sets the width of the view area.

* **Focal Length.** A camera setting used to determine where the camera's focus is located.

* **Near and Far Clipping planes.** Near and Far camera planes that define where objects are not visible.

* **Safe area.** A set of camera markings that denote where title and action areas are definitely visible.

* **Depth of Field.** A camera effect where objects farther away from the focus point become gradually blurrier.

* **Image plane.** A background plane where a background texture or image can be loaded.

* **Default lights.** A set of lights that are available by default as part of a new scene.

* **Light decay.** A light property that causes light intensity to gradually diminish as

* **Light intensity.** A value that denotes the power of a light source.

* **Depth map shadow.** A shadowing method created by saving the shadows into a bitmap that is projected onto the scene.

* **Ray trace shadows.** A shadowing method that computes shadows by following light rays as they move around the scene.

* **Lens flare.** A lighting effect that simulates the effect of pointing a camera at a light source.

Chapter 10
Animating with Keyframes

IN THIS CHAPTER

Simple 3D animation is surprisingly easy. Because Maya knows the exact location of objects in the 3D scene, it can quickly and easily interpolate the location of an object as it moves between two different points in space. These locations in space are called **keyframes** and they define intermediate positions of an object along its motion.

You can set keyframes for an object's position, rotation, scale, and any object attribute that is keyable. All keys, once created, are displayed along the **Time Slider** at the bottom of the interface. You can copy and paste these keys to other objects and then shift and scale them as needed.

Once an animation is created, you view it by scrolling through the time frames in the Time Slider. A preview of the animation is shown in the view panel. The Animation Controls are also useful in moving through an animation sequence. If the view panel is having trouble updating the scene fast enough, you can send snapshots of the current scene to a buffer using the **Playblast** feature.

There are several features that make it easier to visualize the animated objects. These features include motion trails, which show the trajectory of the object's motion, and **ghosting**, which shows copies of the animated object as it progresses in its motion.

Besides keyframing, another common way to animate objects is to attach an object to a motion path. The object then follows the path. This makes it easy to draw a curve that defines exactly where the object moves.

You can also edit animated scenes in the **Graph Editor,** where all object motions and attribute changes are shown as graphed curves and all keys are points. You can edit these curves and points by changing their smoothness and working with their tangents.

Another common editing interface is the **dope sheet,** which is useful in synchronizing the timing of different objects.

Lesson 10.1: Set Keyframes

You can animate using keys by positioning an object at its starting state and setting a key, and then changing it to its ending state and setting another key. Maya then interpolates between the two states for all the times in between the two keys. Keys enable you to create fairly complex animation sequences with a limited number of well-placed keys.

Note

All animation menu commands are found in the Animation
menu set.

Setting Keys

When an object is in the exact position, you can set a key for the current time using the Animate, Set Key menu command. You can also set keys by right-clicking on an attribute in the Attribute Editor or in the Channel Box and selecting Key Selected or Key All from the pop-up menu. Attributes that have keys set are shaded light brown in the Attribute Editor and in the Channel Box, as shown in Figure 10-1.

Tip

The S key is the hotkey for setting keys.

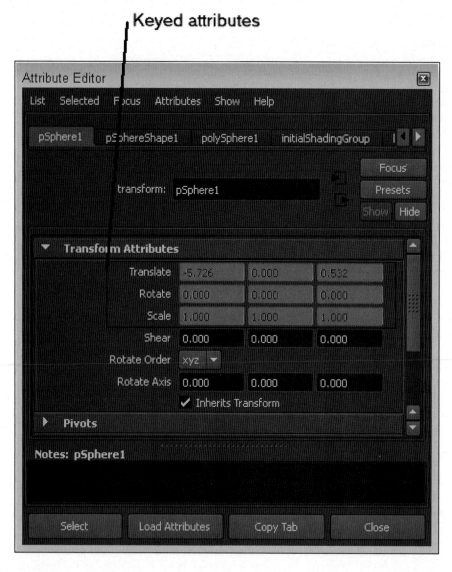

Figure 10-1
Keyed attributes

Using Auto Key

You can use **Auto Key** mode to automatically create keys for attributes that already have at least one key. To enable the Auto Key toggle, shown in Figure 10-2, click on the Auto Key button at the right end of the Range Slider. The button turns red when active. Once Auto Key is active, you can select a new time or update an attribute and the key is created automatically with needing to use the Set Keys menu command.

Caution

You need to create a keyframe for the selected object before enabling Auto Key or it won't work.

Figure 10-2
The Auto Key button

Selecting Keys

Keys for the selected object appear on the Time Slider as thin red lines. If you click on one of these red lines in the Time Slider, the current time is moved to that time and the key is selected. Selected keys are colored light blue, as shown in Figure 10-3. If you hold down the Shift key and drag over several keys, the selected time turns red and all of the keys within that segment are selected, as shown in Figure 10-4. You can shift or scale the selected time by dragging on the arrows positioned within and at either end of the selected area.

Tip

Using the Key Tick Size setting in the Timeline panel of the Preferences dialog box, you can increase the thickness of the keys displayed in the Time Slider. You can also change the key color in the Animation panel of the Colors dialog box, open with the Window, Settings/Preferences, Colors menu command.

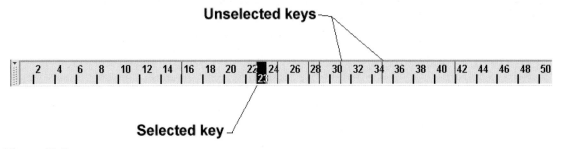

Figure 10-3
Time Slider keys

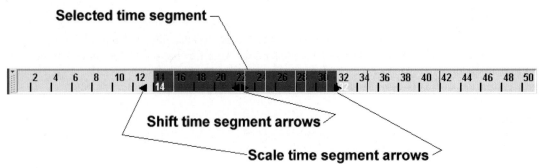

Figure 10-4
A selected time segment

Copying Keys

You can copy and paste a set of keys for the selected object between files using the Keys Clipboard. To copy the keys to the Clipboard, select the Edit, Keys, Cut Keys or Edit, Keys, Copy Keys menu command. The keys stay on the Clipboard as you close the current scene and open a new one. You can paste keys to the selected object using the Edit, Keys, Paste Keys menu command.

Deleting Keys

The Edit, Keys, Delete Keys menu command deletes all keys for the selected object. Any keys set for unselected objects remain intact.

Snapping Keys

The Edit, Keys, Snap Keys menu command causes all selected keys to be snapped to their nearest Value or Time. This is especially useful after scaling several selected keys. The Snap Keys Options dialog box, shown in Figure 10-5, lets you select to snap only the selected keys or all keys. You can also select to snap only Times, Values or Both.

Figure 10-5
Snap Keys Options dialog box

Lesson 10.1-Tutorial 1: Set Keys

1. Create a NURBS sphere object using the Create, NURBS Primitives, Sphere menu command.

2. With the Time Slider at frame 1, select the Animate, Set Key menu command.

    All transform attributes in the Channel Box are highlighted in light brown to show that they have keys associated with them.

3. Drag the time in the Time Slider to frame 25.

Note

> If frame 25 isn't visible, drag the right end of the Range Slider until the frame is visible. If the Range doesn't extend to frame 50, enter 50 in the text field to the right of the Range Slider.

4. Change the ScaleX, ScaleY, and ScaleZ attributes in the Channel Box to 5.0.

5. Select the Animate, Set Key menu command again.

6. Drag the time in the Time Slider to frame 50.

7. Change the ScaleX, ScaleY, and ScaleZ attributes in the Channel Box back to 1.0.

8. Select the Animate, Set Key menu command again.

9. Drag the Time Slider marker back and forth.

    The sphere increases and decreases in size as you drag the Time Slider.

10. Select File, Save Scene As and save the file as **Growing sphere.mb**.

Lesson 10.1-Tutorial 2: Use Auto Key

1. Create a NURBS sphere object using the Create, NURBS Primitives, Sphere menu command.

2. With the Time Slider at frame 1, click on the makeNurbsSphere1 input node in the Channel Box, click on the Start Sweep attribute, and then right-click and select Key Selected from the pop-up menu.

3. Click the Auto Key button in the lower-right corner of the interface.

4. Drag the time in the Time Slider to frame 25.

5. Change the StartSweep value to 180.

6. Drag the time in the Time Slider to frame 50.

7. Change the StartSweep value to 359.

8. Drag the Time Slider marker back and forth.

    The sphere slowly disappears as you drag the Time Slider, as shown in Figure 10-6.

9. Select File, Save Scene As and save the file as **Sweeping sphere.mb**.

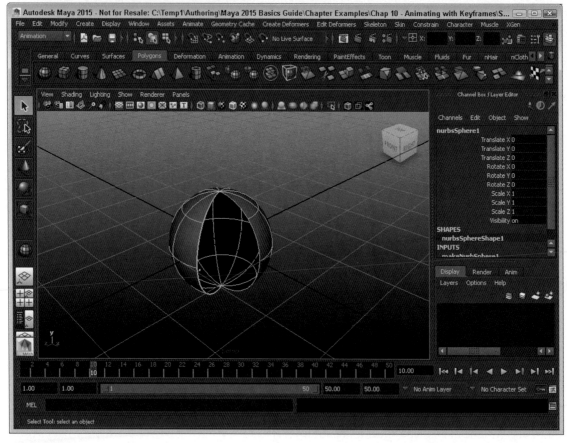

Figure 10-6
Sweeping sphere

Lesson 10.1-Tutorial 3: Move Keys

1. Create a NURBS sphere object using the Create, NURBS Primitives, Sphere menu command, and then create a NURBS plane object and scale the plane object to be larger than the sphere.

2. Select the sphere and click on the Select by Component Type button in the Status Line.

3. Drag over all the CVs that make up the lower portion of the sphere in the Front view to select them.

4. Select the Animate, Set Key menu command.

5. Drag the time in the Time Slider to frame 3.

6. Drag the CVs upward in the Side view and select the Animate, Set Key menu command again.

    This example shows that components as well as objects can be animated. By dragging the lower portion of CVs upward, the sphere is being squashed over three frames.

7. Click on the Select by Object Type button in the Status Line.

8. Select the sphere and move it upward in the Front view and select the Animate, Set Key menu command.

9. Drag the Time Slider to frame 10, move the sphere back down to the plane object, and select the Animate, Set Key menu command again (or press the s hotkey).

    The sphere is now falling onto the plane object.

10. Click on the Select by Component Type button in the Status Line again.

11. Select the same CVs that were selected earlier and drag over the set keys in the Time Slider with the Shift key held down.

12. Drag the selected keys to the right until the first key rests at frame 7.

    Dragging over the set keys with the Shift key held down turns the selected keys red and displays some black arrows that you can use to move or scale the selected keys.

13. Drag the Time Slider marker back and forth.

    The sphere falls to the base plane where it is squashed as it impacts with the plane object, as shown in Figure 10-7.

14. Select File, Save Scene As and save the file as **Falling sphere.mb**.

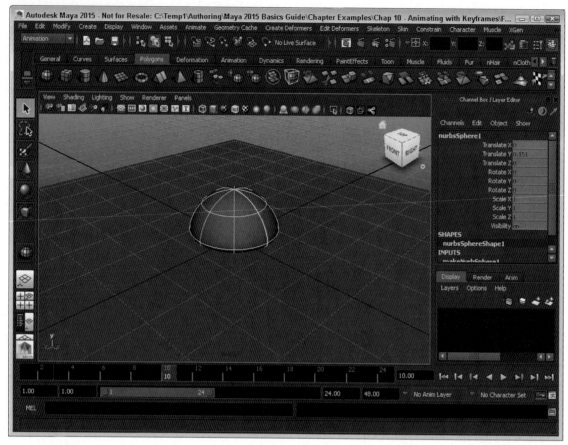

Figure 10-7
Animated squashed sphere

Lesson 10.2: View an Animation

Spending a lot of time rendering a final animation only to find out that you've made a mistake can be time consuming and frustrating. Preview animations can help eliminate mistakes early on.

Previewing Animation

Clicking the Play Forward button in the animation controls (shown in Figure 10-8) at the bottom of the interface cycles through the frames in the active view panel. You can also click on the Play Backwards button to see the animation in reverse. If you select and drag the Time Slider handle, the view panel is updated as you drag between the various frames.

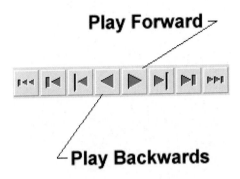

Figure 10-8
Animation controls

Looping an Animation

If you click on the Animation Preferences button, next to the Auto Key button, the Timeline panel of the Preferences dialog box appears, as shown in Figure 10-9. In this dialog box, you can set the number of frames that appear in the Time Slider. The Preferences dialog box also includes three Looping options—Once, Oscillate, and Continuous. The Once option plays the animation through once when the Play Forward button is clicked. Oscillate causes the animation to be played repeatedly forward and then backward, and the Continuous option plays the animation forward repeatedly.

Tip

You can also access the Looping options from a pop-up menu by right-clicking on the Time Slider or the Animation Controls.

Figure 10-9
Animation preferences

Enabling Ghosting

Ghosting is an animation technique in which you see an object's position in the previous and/or coming frames, as shown for the sphere in Figure 10-10. This is helpful when you work on the timing of an object's motion. To enable ghosting, select the Animate, Ghost Selected menu command. In the Ghost Options dialog box, shown in Figure 10-11, you can select exactly which frames are ghosted or how many frames before and after the current frame are shown. To disable ghosting, use the Animate, Unghost Selected or the Animate, Unghost All menu commands.

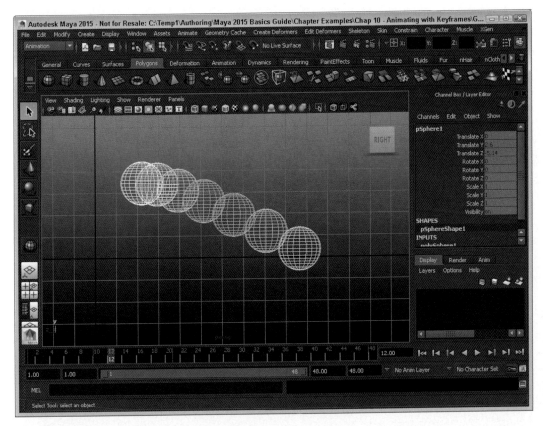

Figure 10-10
Ghosted objects

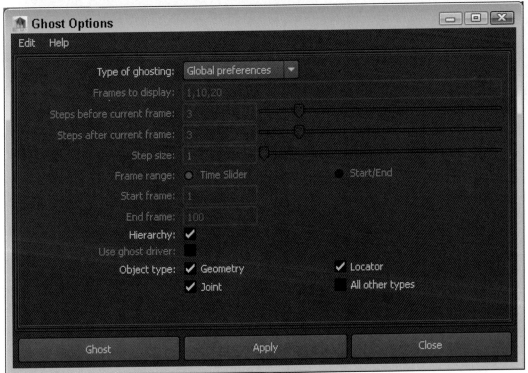

Figure 10-11
Ghost Options dialog box

Creating Motion Trails

A **motion trail** is the trajectory path that an animated object follows as it moves between frames, as shown in Figure 10-12. To create a motion trail, use the Animate, Create Motion Trail menu command. In the Motion Trail Options dialog box, you can set the start and end times for the motion trail and the Draw Style option to Line, Locator, or Points. You can also select or deselect Show Frame Numbers.

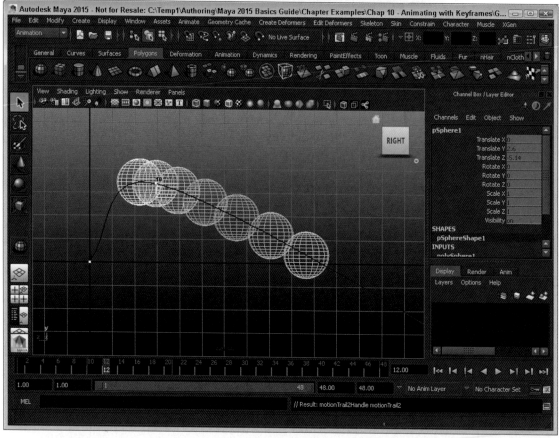

Figure 10-12
A motion trail

Using Playblast

The Window, Playblast menu command captures a screenshot of the active view panel for each frame. These frames are then stitched together to create a preview animation that is played in the default system movie player. Using Playblast is convenient, because complex scenes can take some time to update their view in the view panel. The Playblast Options dialog box, shown in Figure 10-13, lets you set the Time Range, Viewer, and Display Size options. You can also select to save the preview to a file.

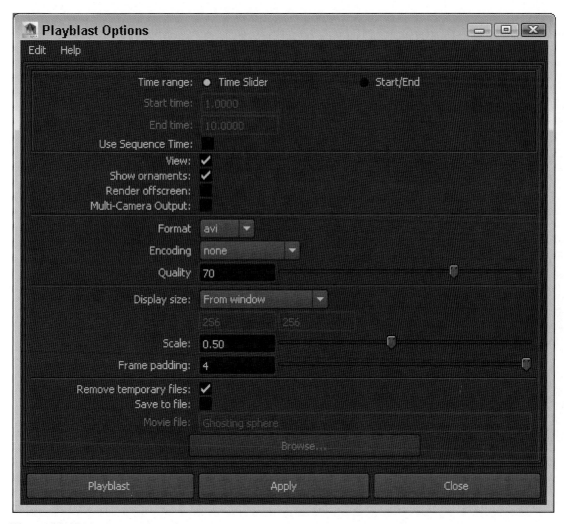

Figure 10-13
Playblast Options dialog box

Lesson 10.2-Tutorial 1: Preview an Animation

1. Select the File, Open Scene menu command and locate and open the Simple airplane.mb file.

2. Drag the Time Slider to frame 10.

3. With the airplane selected, choose the Animate, Ghost Selected, Options menu command.

4. In the Ghost Options dialog box, choose Custom Frame Steps from the Type of Ghosting list. Change the Step Size to 3 and click the Ghost button.

5. In the Animation Controls, press the Play Forward button.

    The animation loops over and over with ghosting enabled, as shown in Figure 10-14.

6. Select File, Save Scene As and save the file as **Airplane with ghost.mb**.

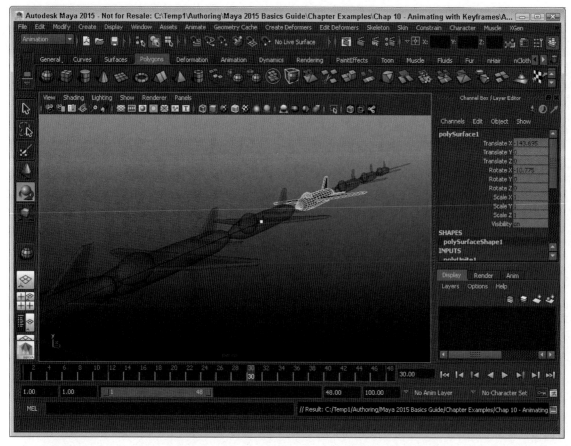

Figure 10-14
A ghosted airplane

Lesson 10.2-Tutorial 2: Use Playblast

1. Select the File, Open Scene menu command, locate and open the Simple airplane.mb file.

2. Select the Window, Playblast menu command.

    Every frame of the animation is captured in the Playblast buffer and the animated frames are shown in the default system video player, such as the Windows Media Player, as shown in Figure 10-15.

Figure 10-15
A Playblast preview

Lesson 10.3: Animate Using Motion Paths

Keyframing is easy to work with, but sometimes it can be easier to define a path and to have an object follow that path. **Motion paths** are curves that you can use to define how an object should move through the scene.

Creating Motion Path Keys

You can create a motion path by dragging objects about the scene and using the Animate, Motion Paths, Set Motion Path Key menu command. This command places a motion path key for the selected object for the current time frame. Moving the object to another location and using this command again creates another key, and a curve joining the keys is drawn. Each motion path key acts as a point on the curve. Figure 10-16 shows a sphere following a motion path with several motion path keys.

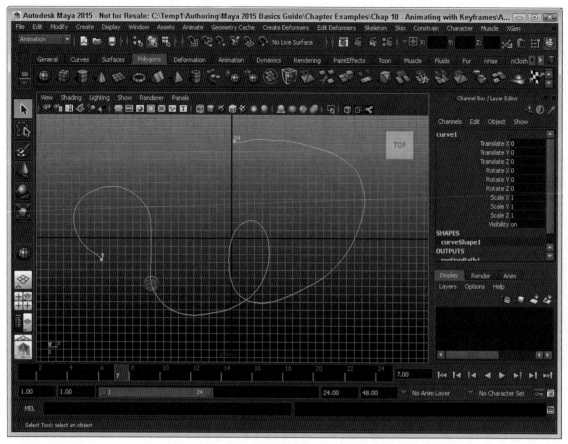

Figure 10-16
Motion path keys

Drawing a Motion Path

You can use any NURBS curve as a motion path. By default, the first point on the NURBS curve marks the starting point for the attached object. You can create motion paths using any of the curve creation tools found in the Create menu, including the CV Curve tool, the EP Curve tool, and the Pencil Curve tool.

Attaching an Object to a Motion Path

To attach an object to a motion path, you need to select the object or objects to attach and then select the NURBS path that you want to use for the motion path. The motion path curve should always be selected last. Select the Animate, Motion Paths, Attach to Motion Path menu command. Figure 10-17 shows a NURBS sphere that has been attached to the motion path. Clicking the Play Forward button shows the sphere following the entire path.

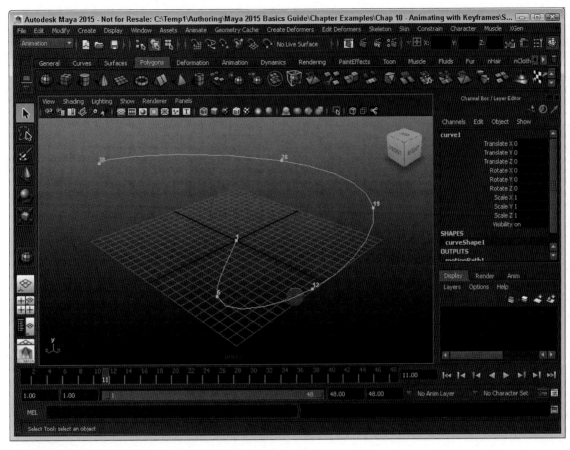

Figure 10-17
Attached sphere and motion path

Adjusting an Attached Motion Path

When an object is attached to a motion path, you can move the object along the motion path by dragging the Time Slider. To adjust the attached motion path, you can move the attached object with the Move tool and create a new motion path key with the Animate, Motion Paths, Set Motion Path Key menu command. Figure 10-18 shows an adjustment made to the existing attached path.

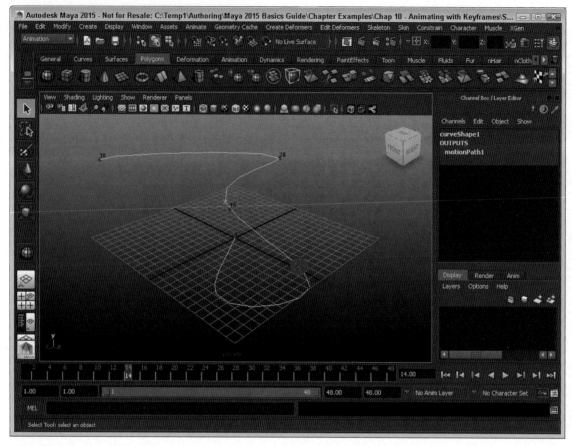

Figure 10-18
Adjusted motion path

Deforming an Object as it Follows a Motion Path

If an object follows a motion path, you can select the object and choose the Animate, Motion Paths, Flow Path Object menu command. This command causes a lattice to appear around the selected object. This lattice deforms as it moves along the motion path. By altering this lattice, you can control how the object deforms as it follows the motion path. Figure 10-19 shows a torus object that follows a motion path with a lattice surrounding it.

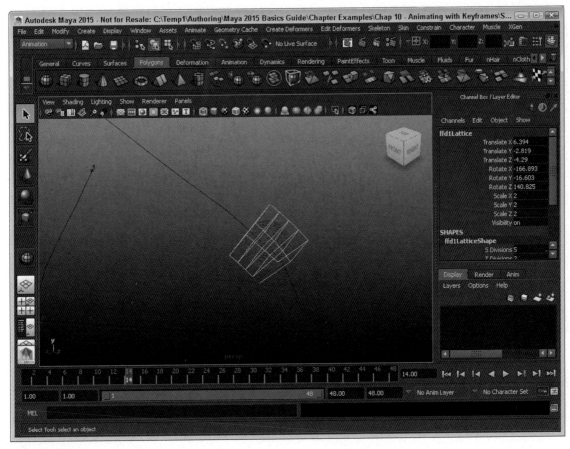

Figure 10-19
Deform lattice surrounding a object

Lesson 10.3-Tutorial 1: Create a Motion Path

1. Create a NURBS cone object using the Create, NURBS Primitives, Cone menu command,

2. Select the Animate, Motion Paths, Set Motion Path Key menu command.

3. Drag the Time Slider to frame 5 and drag the cone away from its current position.

4. Select the Animate, Motion Paths, Set Motion Path Key menu command again.

5. Repeat steps 3 and 4 several more times.

    Each key acts as a curve point for the motion path.

6. Press the Play Forward button.

    The cone object follows the motion path curve, as shown in Figure 10-20.

7. Select File, Save Scene As and save the file as **Motion path.mb**.

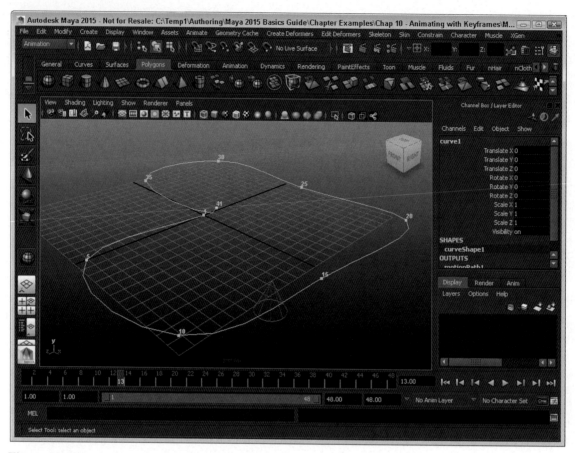

Figure 10-20
A motion path created by moving an object

Lesson 10.3-Tutorial 2: Draw a Motion Path and Attach an Object

1. Select the File, Open Scene menu command, locate and open the Shark.mb file.

2. Select the Create, Pencil Curve tool menu command.

3. Draw a path for the shark to follow in the Perspective view panel.

4. Select the shark object, and then hold down the Shift key and select the path curve.

5. Select the Animate, Motion Paths, Attach to Motion Path, Options menu command.

6. Disable the Follow option in the Attach to Motion Path Options dialog box and click the Attach button.

    The shark object is positioned at the beginning of the path curve.

7. Press the Play Forward button to see the shark follow the path.

    The shark object follows the curve, as shown in Figure 10-21.

8. Select File, Save Scene As and save the file as **Shark on path.mb**.

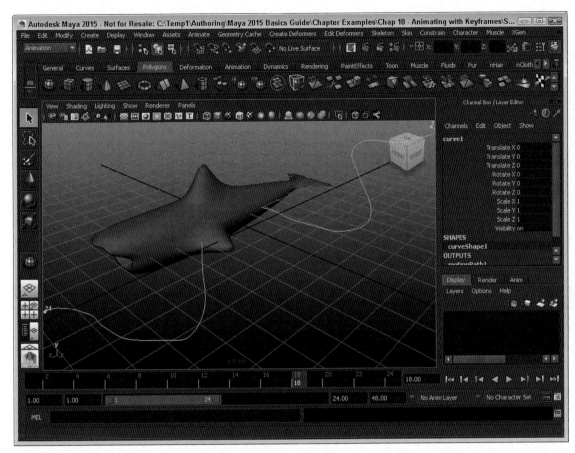

Figure 10-21
An animated shark following a path

Lesson 10.4: Edit Animation Curves

Fine-tuning an animation can be tricky using the view panels, but Maya makes all animations available as graphed lines in the Graph Editor. This makes tweaking animation curves easier.

Using the Graph Editor

The Graph Editor, shown in Figure 10-22, shows the change in animated attributes over time as graphed lines. Each key is represented as a point and the animation curve defines the movement of the attribute between the key points. Open the Graph Editor using the Window, Animation Editors, Graph Editor menu command. The nodes and keyable attributes are listed in the left pane. If an attribute is selected in the left pane, its animation curves are displayed in the right pane. Using the Shift and Ctrl/Command keys, you can select multiple attributes.

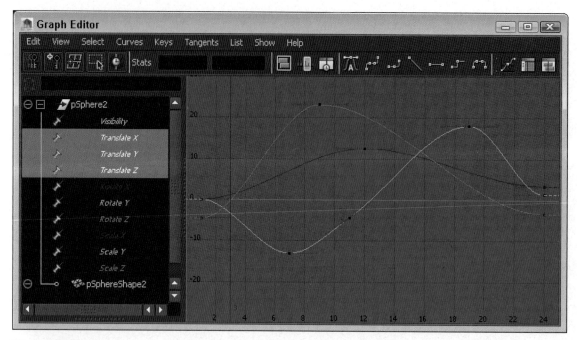

Figure 10-22
The Graph Editor

Framing Curves

The Graph Editor includes two buttons on its toolbar, as shown in Figure 10-23, that frame the selected curves. The Frame All button fits all the selected animation curves within the right pane, and the Frame Playback Range shows the entire range of frames for the current scene. These commands also appear in the View menu, along with options to Frame Selection, Center Current Time and Auto Frame. The Auto Frame option automatically frames the selected animation curve.

Tip

> You can also use the Alt/Option+middle and right mouse buttons to pan and zoom the animation curve pane.

Figure 10-23
Frame All (left) and Frame Playback Range (right) buttons

Editing Keys

You can select a key by dragging over it in the right pane. When a key is selected, its curve turns white and the key point turns yellow. A small square appears to the left of the attribute name for each curve that has a selected key, and the key's frame number and value appear in the top toolbar, as shown in Figure 10-24. Using the Shift key, you can select multiple keys at the same time. If the Move Nearest Picked Key tool is selected in the Toolbar, you can move the selected keys by dragging with the middle mouse button. You can enable the Time Snap and Value Snap buttons so that they snap the keys as they move.

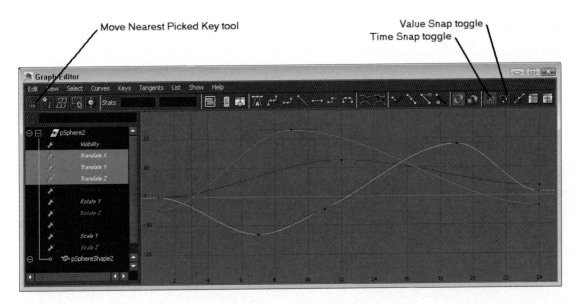

Figure 10-24
Selected keys

Smoothing and Simplifying Curves

You can smooth a curve in the Graph Editor with the Curves, Curve Smoothness menu command. The four settings are Coarse, which makes the lines between the keys straight lines, Rough, Medium, and Fine. Figure 10-25 shows the Graph Editor curves with a smoothness setting of Coarse. If an animation curve includes too many keys, you can use the Curves, Simplify Curve menu command to reduce the total number of keys.

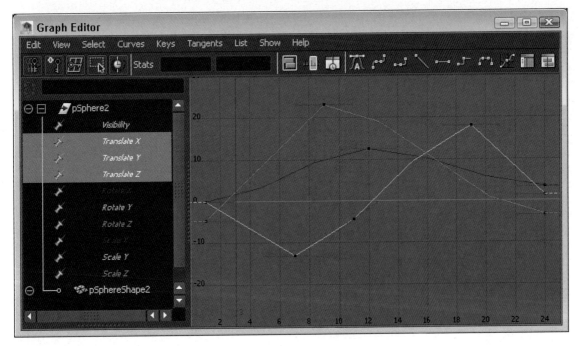

Figure 10-25
Coarse curves

Setting Infinity Conditions

Even if no keys are set when an object completes its keyed motions, you can set the motion to repeat or loop indefinitely. These are known as *infinity conditions*. You can set the infinity condition before the first key with the Curves, Pre Infinity menu command and the infinity condition for the animation curve after the last key with the Curves, Post Infinity menu command. The options include Cycle, Cycle with Offset, Oscillate, Linear, and Constant. To view the resulting curve affect, select the View, Infinity menu command and the curve motions are shown as dashed lines. Figure 10-26 shows a simple animated sequence with a Cycle Pre-Infinity setting and a Linear Post-Infinity setting.

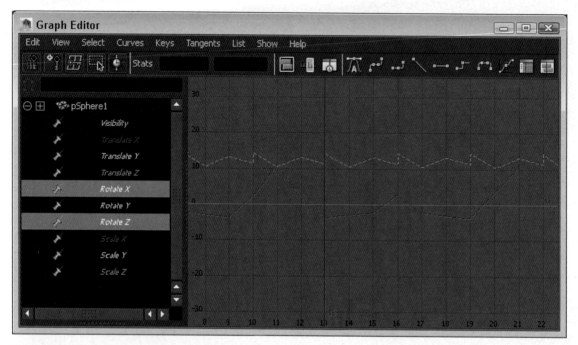

Figure 10-26
Pre- and Post-Infinity settings

Working with Tangents

The smoothness of the curve leading to and from the key points is determined by the key's **tangent points**. To see the tangents, select the View, Tangents menu command. Each tangent extends to either side of the key point. You can select and move tangent points using the middle mouse button. Both tangent points are in a straight line by default, but if you select the Keys, Break Tangents menu command, you can move each tangent independently. You can also select several tangent positions from the Tangents menu. The options include Spline, Linear, Clamped, Stepped, Flat, Fixed, and Plateau. Figure 10-27 shows the Graph Editor with the Tangents visible. Notice how the second set of keys has broken tangents.

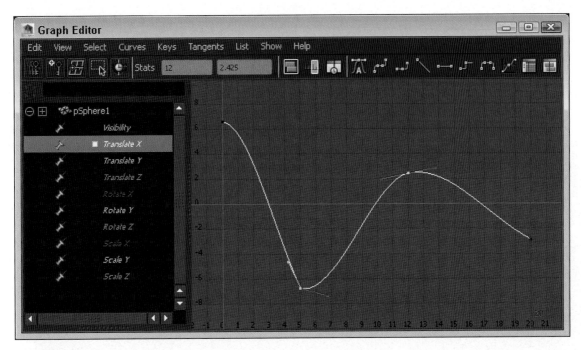

Figure 10-27
Graph Editor with tangents

Adding Keys

With a curve selected in the Graph Editor, you can add or insert keys to the curve by clicking on the Insert Keys tool button in the Graph Editor toolbar, shown in Figure 10-28. When the Keys, Add Keys tool is enabled, you can click on the curve at the location where you want the key with the middle mouse button. The Insert Keys tool lets you click and drag to position the new key. You can delete a key by selecting it and choosing the Edit, Delete menu command.

Figure 10-28
Insert Keys button

Lesson 10.4-Tutorial 1: Edit Animation Curves

1. Select the File, Open Scene menu command, locate and open the Animated airplane.mb file.

2. Select the airplane object.

3. Select the Window, Animation Editors, Graph Editor menu command.

   The Graph Editor opens and displays the animation curves for the airplane. The top red curve is the RotateX curve, and the lower red curve is the TranslateX curve, and the straight blue lines are the TranslateZ and ScaleZ curves.

4. Drag over the center key on the RotateX curve to select it.

5. With the Move tool selected, drag the key point upward with the middle mouse button.

6. With the key point still selected, choose the View, Tangents, On Active Keys menu command.

7. Select the Keys, Break Tangents menu command.

   This makes the tangents for the selected key point visible.

8. Drag over the left tangent point to select it and drag it with the middle mouse button downward.

9. Drag over the right tangent point and drag it also with the middle mouse button downward to form a sharp point.

   The animation in the curve editor now resembles Figure 10-29 and the rotating animation of the airplane now happens much quicker.

10. Select File, Save Scene As and save the file as **Curve edited airplane.mb**.

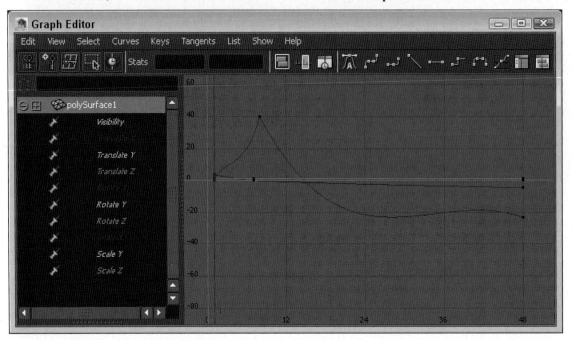

Figure 10-29
Curve edited airplane

Lesson 10.4-Tutorial 2: Repeat Motion

1. Select the File, Open Scene menu command, locate and open the Jumping bean.mb file.

2. Select the bean object.

3. Select the Window, Animation Editors, Graph Editor menu command.

4. Select the View, Infinity menu command.

   The Graph Editor displays dashed lines for the continuing motion of the selected object.

5. Select the Curves, Post Infinity, Cycle with Offset menu command.

   The Graph Editor changes the dashed lines to show the offset motion for the bean object, as shown in Figure 10-30.

6. Click the Play Forward button to see the entire animation.

7. Select File, Save Scene As and save the file as **Repeating jumping bean.mb**.

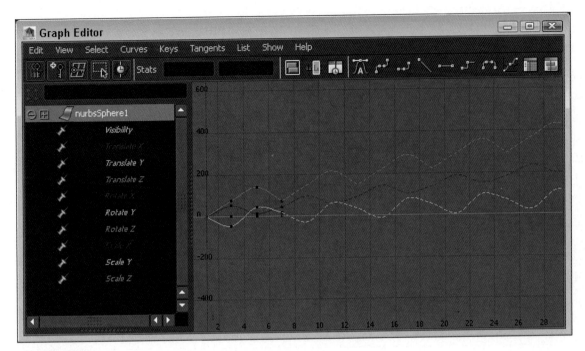

Figure 10-30
Repeating motion

Lesson 10.5: Control Animation Timing

The dope sheet is helpful when synchronizing several objects within the scene and matching object interactions to an audio file.

Using the Dope Sheet

The dope sheet shows all keys as small squares graphed at their location in time. You can select and move these keys using the middle mouse button. This makes it easy to synchronize the various keys between objects and sound. The dope sheet, shown in Figure 10-31, is opened using the Window, Animation Editors, Dope Sheet menu command.

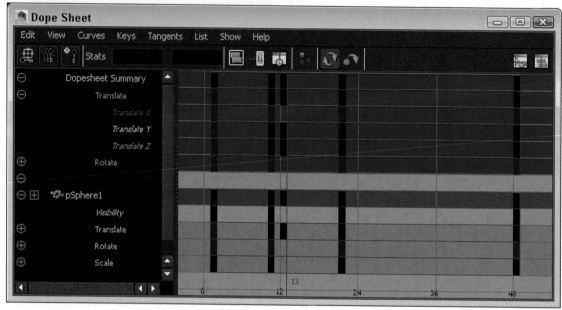

Figure 10-31
The dope sheet

Using the Dope Sheet Manipulator

The Select Keyframe Tool button lets you drag a manipulator over a section of the dope sheet. The keys within the selected area are selected and outlined with a light blue rectangle, as shown in Figure 10-32. The center of each edge has a handle that you can use to rescale the selected keys. Dragging the center handle lets you move the selected area to a new position. You can also cut and copy the selected keys with the Ctrl/Command+X and Ctrl/Command +C hotkeys and paste them in a new location with the Ctrl/Command +V hotkey. If keys are pasted in the middle of some keys, all existing keys are automatically shifted to accommodate the pasted keys. To temporarily remove the effect of keys, you can select the Keys, Mute menu command. Keys, Unmute restores any muted keys.

Select Keyferame tool   Dope Sheet manipulator

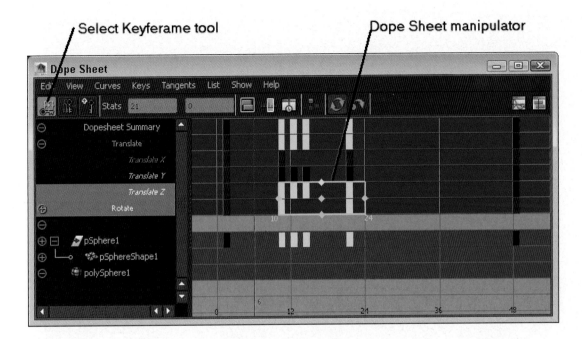

Figure 10-32
The Dope Sheet Manipulator

Adding Sound

You can import sound files into Maya using the File, Import menu command. Supported audio files include WAV and AIF formats. Once imported, the audio file appears in the Time Slider, where it is easy to synch with the keys. The imported sound file also appears in the dope sheet. Figure 10-33 shows an imported audio file in the Time Slider.

Tip

Dropping an audio file on the Time Slider automatically imports it.

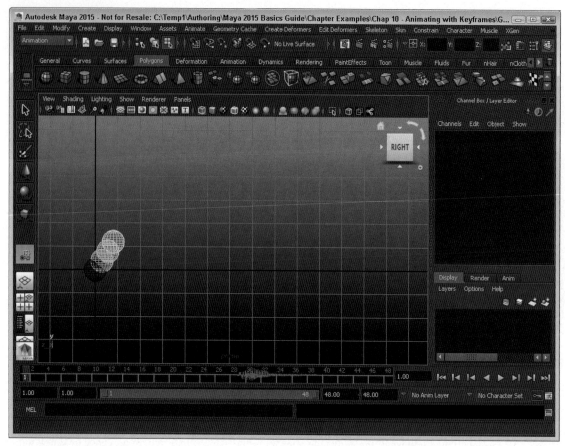

Figure 10-33
An imported sound file

Lesson 10.5-Tutorial 1: Use the Dope Sheet

1. Select the File, Open Scene menu command, locate and open the Newtons cradle.mb file.

2. Select the first sphere. Select the Rotate tool and drag on the blue Z-axis manipulator to rotate the sphere away from the other spheres. Select the Animate, Set Key menu command.

    This sets a key for the starting position of the first sphere.

3. Drag the Time Slider to frame 10. Rotate the sphere back into place next to the other sphere. Select the last sphere in the row. Select the Animate, Set Key menu command.

4. Drag the Time Slider to frame 20. Rotate the sphere away from the other spheres. Select the Animate, Set Key menu command.

5. Select the Window, Animation Editors, Dope Sheet menu command.

    The dope sheet displays all of the keys for the sphere as black rectangles.

6. Expand the nurbsSphere11 object and then expand the Rotate channel to see all the rotation keys.

7. Click on the Add Keys Tool in the Dope Sheet toolbar and drag with the middle mouse button the Rotate Z key in the first column of keys to Frame 30.

    This creates a new key with the same value as the one in the first column in frame 30.

8. In the view panel, select the first sphere object again and expand its channels in the dope sheet until the Rotate Z channel is visible.

9. With the Add Keys Tool button selected, drag the Rotate Z key in the second column with the middle mouse button to Frame 30. Then drag the Rotate Z key in the first column with the middle mouse button to Frame 40. Then edit the value for the last key in the Value field in the toolbar to match that of the first key, to 53.4.

    The additional keys cause the spheres to swing back and forth.

10. Click on the Play Animation button to view the resulting animation.

11. In the panel menu for the lower-left view panel, select the Panels, Panel, Dope Sheet to open the dope sheet within a view panel, as shown in Figure 10-34.

12. Select File, Save Scene As and save the file as **Animated Newtons cradle.mb**.

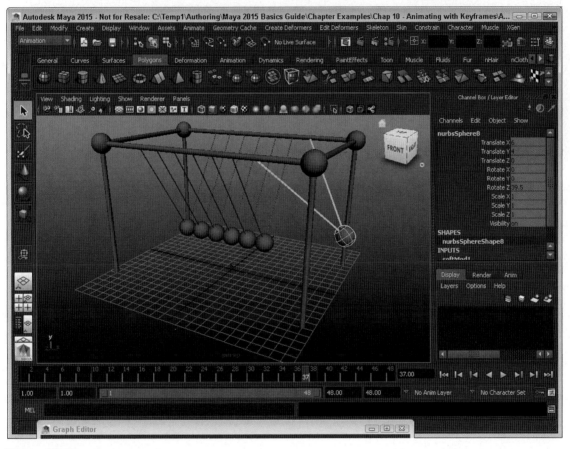

Figure 10-34
Animated Newton's cradle

Lesson 10.5-Tutorial 2: Add Sound

1. Select the File, Open Scene menu command, locate and open the Bouncing ball.mb file.

2. Select the File, Import menu command. Locate and import the Boing.wav file.

    The imported audio file appears in the Time Slider.

3. Select the Window, Animation Editors, Dope Sheet menu command.

    The dope sheet displays all of the keys for the sphere as black rectangles along with the audio file.

4. Click on the center keys for the NURBS sphere object to select them.

5. Drag them to the right to align them with the sound file.

The dope sheet shows the selected keys aligned with the start of the audio file, as shown in Figure 10-35.

6. Select File, Save Scene As and save the file as **Bouncing ball with sound.mb**.

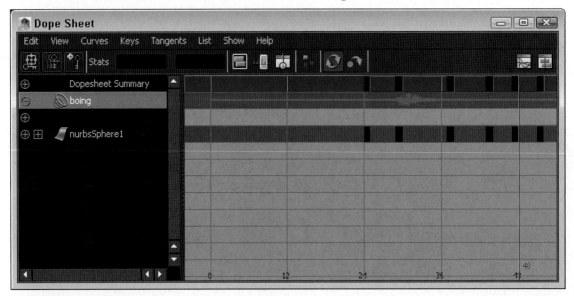

Figure 10-35
Added sound

Chapter Summary

This chapter covers the basics of animating scenes using keyframes. Keyframes define the state of scene objects for a given frame of animation. All keys appear on the Time Slider located at the bottom of the interface. You can play back any created animation using the Animation Controls and using the Playblast feature. Animations can also be created using motion paths. To edit animation keys and parameters, you can use the Graph Editor, which displays all keys as points and curves that can be easily edited. The dope sheet controls the timing of the animation and provides a way to add sound to an animation.

What You Have Learned

In this chapter, you learned

* How to set keyframes.

* How to use the Auto Key mode.

* How to select keys on the Time Slider.

* How to use the Time Slider menu to cut, copy, paste, delete, and snap keys.

* How to preview an animation.

* How to make an animation loop.

* How to enable ghosting and motion trails.

* How to use Playblast.

* How to create a motion path.

* How to attach an object to a motion path.

* How to edit an existing motion path and deform an object following a motion path.

*   How to use the Graph Editor.

*   How to frame curves in the Graph Editor.

*   How to edit keys in the Graph Editor.

*   How to smooth and simplify Graph Editor curves.

*   How to set Pre- and Post-Infinity conditions.

*   How to work with tangents and insert keys in the Graph Editor.

*   How to open the dope sheet.

*   How to add sound to an animation.

Key Terms From This Chapter

*   **Keyframe.** An animation setting that records the state of an object for a given frame.

*   **Auto Key.** The mode that automatically creates keys whenever an object moves or a parameter changes.

*   **Time Slider .** An interface element that displays all the frames and keys for the current animation.

*   **Looping.** A setting that causes an animation to repeatedly play.

*   **Ghosting.** A setting that makes multiple copies of the animated objects appear at regular intervals along a motion path.

*   **Motion trail.** A curve that shows the path of the animated object.

*   **Playblast.** A feature that plays the current animation in a separate media player.

*   **Motion path.** A created curve that defines the animation path that an object follows.

*   **Graph Editor.** An interface that displays all animation actions as graphed curves allowing editing and modification.

*   **Infinity conditions.** A setting that enables an animated sequence to repeat indefinitely.

*   **Tangents.** Handles that control the curvature of a curve near each key point.

*   **Dope sheet.** An interface used to display and edit the timing of an animation.

Chapter 11
Working with Characters

IN THIS CHAPTER

Animating characters is much easier if you take some steps to prepare your character to be animated. This process is called **rigging** and it involves applying constraints to the character so that it moves in a believable fashion without its arm bending backwards.

Part of the rigging process is to create an underlying skeleton that can be animated. The actual character model creates a skin that is positioned over the skeleton. The skin must be bound to the skeleton before the skeleton can control the skin.

Skeletons are created using the Joint tool. With this tool, you can click on the locations where the joints are to be located. Each new joint is attached in a hierarchical structure to the other joints. Each joint also has attributes that you can set using the Attribute Editor. One of these attributes lets you set limits to the joint's movement. By limiting the motion of the skeleton's joints, you can control how the character moves.

Another way to control a skeleton's movement is with **Inverse Kinematics** (IK). Inverse Kinematics enables you to animate the character by placing its hands and feet and letting the rest of the body follow these positions.

When the skin is created, it then needs to be bound to a skeleton. Maya includes two methods for binding skin—Smooth and Rigid. Once the skeleton is bound to a skin, you can control the skin by moving the various joints and bones of the skeleton.

You can also edit and deform a character's skin by using Influence objects and by painting skin weights.

Adding hair and fur to a character increases the realism of the character.

Lesson 11.1: Build a Skeleton

A character's skeleton consists of all the underlying bones and joints that are necessary to animate a character. A skeleton consists of bones, which are rectangular boxes that narrow from its parent joint to its child joint and joints; these joints are spheres at either end of the bone, as shown in Figure 11-1. The joints of the skeleton are connected to one another using parenting. Each skeleton can have only one root, which is the top-most parent.

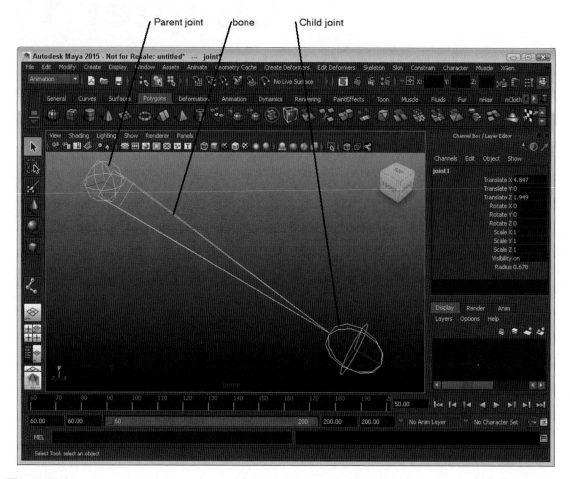

Figure 11-1
Bone and joints

Creating Joints

You can use the Joint tool (select Skeleton, Joint Tool) to create new bones and joints. Click in the view panel where the parent joint is and click again where the child joint is. A bone connects the two joints. You can then click again to create an attached bone and joint. When you've completed the entire joint chain, press the Enter key. When a joint is selected, all of its children bones and joints are automatically selected. When the Joint tool is selected, pressing the Delete key deletes the last bone and joint, the Insert key lets you move the last created joint, and the middle mouse button lets you reposition the last joint.

Inserting a Joint

Once you have created a joint chain, you can insert an attached joint chain using the Insert Joint tool (select Skeleton, Insert Joint Tool). With this tool selected, click on the joint that you want to share and drag to create a new joint. To enable your characters to have more motion, split a long bone into several smaller ones, like the one in Figure 11-2.

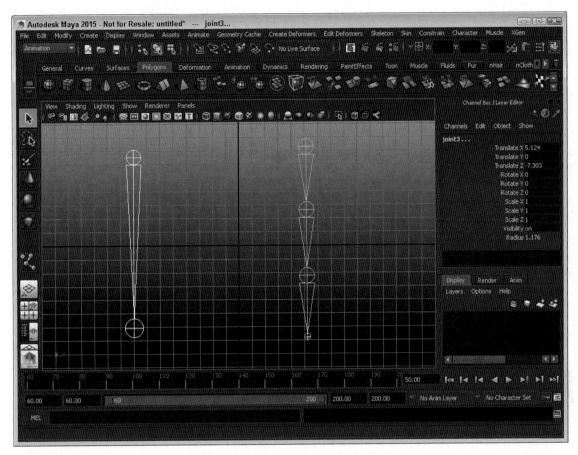

Figure 11-2
Inserting joints

Connecting a Joint Chain

You can connect a selected joint chain with a root joint to a selected joint in another chain with the Skeleton, Connect Joint menu command. To use this tool, select the root joint on one chain, hold down the Shift key, select the joint of another chain, and select the menu command. The Connect Joint Options dialog box includes two modes. The Connect Joint mode moves and aligns the root joint chain to the other chain, and the Parent Joint mode leaves both joints in place, creating a bone that connects the two joints. Figure 11-3 shows a skeleton before and after a chain has been connected.

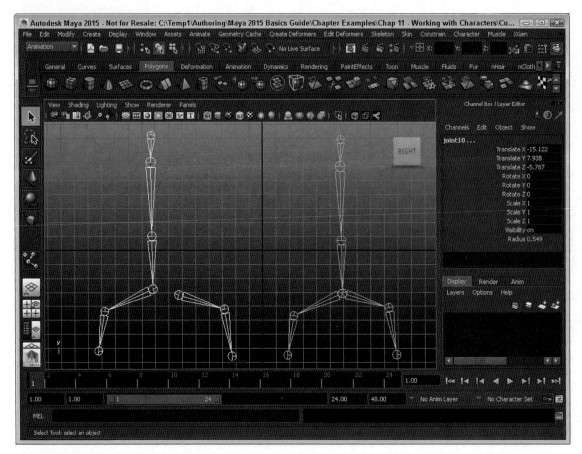

Figure 11-3
Connected chain

Removing and Disconnecting Joints

You can remove a joint from joint chain with the Skeleton, Remove Joint menu command and can be disconnected from a joint chain with the Skeleton, Disconnect Joint menu command. Root joints cannot be disconnected or removed, but you can delete the entire joint chain, including the root joint, with the Delete key.

Mirroring Joints

Many characters have a regular symmetry that you can quickly duplicate with the Skeleton, Mirror Joints menu command. To mirror a joint chain, you need to select one joint away from where it is connected. The Mirror Joint Options dialog box, shown in Figure 11-4, lets you choose the plane about which the mirror takes place.

Figure 11-4
Mirror Joint Options dialog box

Resetting the Root Joint

Although it may seem natural to have a skeleton start with the head joint, the pelvis is actually the best joint to be the root for human characters. If you've created your skeleton with the head as the root, you can reset it to the pelvis root joint with the Skeleton, Reroot Skeleton menu command.

Naming Joints

When joints are created with the Joint tool they are given the name "joint" followed by a number. If you don't name joints when created, it can become confusing to locate the correct joint later as you animate. Using the Attribute Editor, you can name the various joints.

Lesson 11.1-Tutorial 1: Create a Skeleton

1. Select the Front view panel.

2. Select the Skeleton, Joint Tool menu command.

3. Click at the top of the Front view panel and again to create a head joint.

4. Click again near the center of the view panel to create a torso joint, and then again to create a leg joint and again to the right to create a right foot joint.

5. Press the Enter key to end Joint Creation mode.

6. Select the center torso joint and choose the Skeleton, Reroot Skeleton menu command.

    This command flips the head joint and makes the torso the root for the skeleton.

7. Select the Skeleton, Insert Joint Tool and drag from the joint at the top of the torso out to the right to create an arm joint.

8. Repeat Step 7 for the left arm.

9. Select the joint between the right foot and leg, and then choose the Skeleton, Mirror Joint menu command.

    The right foot is mirrored and the new joint appears on top of the old one.

10. Drag the new foot joint to the left with the Move tool.

11. Open the Attribute Editor and select each joint and name it accordingly.

    The completed simple skeleton is shown in Figure 11-5.

12. Select File, Save Scene As and save the file as **Simple skeleton.mb**.

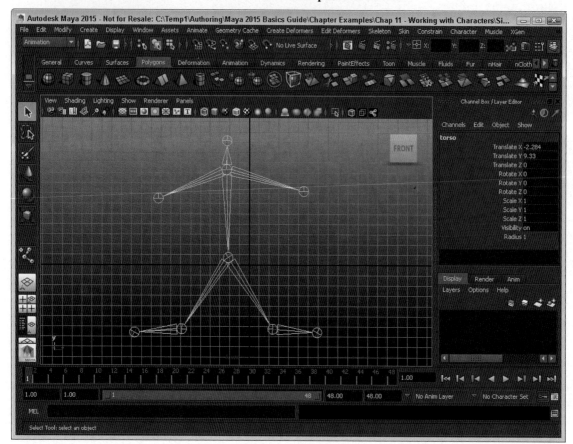

Figure 11-5
Simple skeleton

Lesson 11.1-Tutorial 2: Add a Tail to the Skeleton

1. Select the File, Open Scene menu command then locate and open the Simple skeleton.mb file.

2. Select the Skeleton, Joint Tool menu command.

3. Click in the view panel to create a joint chain with three bones and four joints. Press the Enter key to complete the chain.

4. In the Attribute Editor, name the joints for the tail.

5. Select the tail joint chain, hold down the Shift key, and select the pelvis1 joint. Then select the Skeleton, Connect Joint menu command.

    The tail joint chain is connected to the skeleton, as shown in Figure 11-6.

6. Select File, Save Scene As and save the file as **Skeleton with tail.mb**.

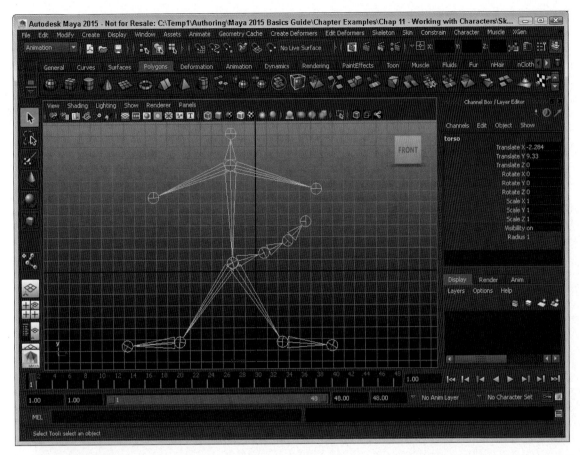

Figure 11-6
Skeleton with tail

Lesson 11.2: Edit Joint Attributes

Once you have created a rough skeleton, you can select the individual joints and define limits on how they can be moved and rotated. Applying correct limits helps ensure that your character moves in a realistic manner as it is being animated.

Inheriting Transforms

By default, all child joints move along with their parent. However, you can disable this action and have each joint move independent of its parent by disabling the Inherits Transform check box in the Transform Attributes on the Attribute Editor.

Orienting Joints

The Joint section of the Attribute Editor includes check boxes for specifying the degrees of freedom about which the joint can move. If any of these check boxes are disabled, the joint cannot rotate about the disabled axis. This section also lets you set the orientation for the joint, which is the angle that the bone points away from the joint. Preferred angle is the angle where the joint is most comfortable, and the stiffness defines how much force is required to move the joint from its preferred angle. You can return the selected joint to its preferred angle at any time with the Skeleton, Assume Preferred Angle menu command.

Labeling Joints

Each joint can be labeled, which is useful in location joints as you animate. To label a joint, select it and choose a label from the Type drop-down list in the Joint Labeling section of the Attribute Editor. The options in the Type list include all the major body parts, or you can select Other and type in your own. The Side marks the left or right side in parenthesis. Enable the Draw Label check box to make the label appear in the view panel, as shown in Figure 11-7.

Note

All joint labels are color-coordinated, based on their side.

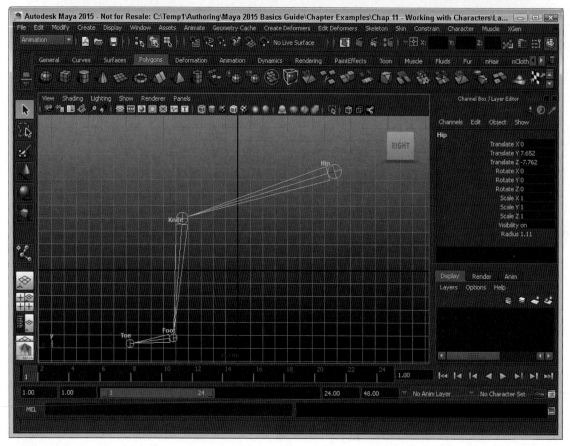

Figure 11-7
Labeled joints

Showing and Hiding Labels

Labels are useful in finding joints, but with many labels, they can get in the way. You can show and hide all labels using the Skeleton, Joint Labeling, Show/Hide All Labels menu command. The Skeleton, Joint Labeling, Toggle Selected Labels menu command shows or hides the labels for the selected joints. You can also rename all joints based on the labels or create labels based on the joint names with commands in the Skeleton, Joint Labeling menu.

Limiting Joints

The Limit Information section of the Attribute Editor (shown in Figure 11-8) lets you specify the translate, rotate and scale limits of the selected joint. For example, a knee joint can rotate forward to 90 degrees and backward about 75 degrees along the z-axis, but limiting its rotation for the X and Y axes keeps your animated character from having awkward bent legs by accident. For each dimension and transformation, you deselect its check box to keep its motion unlimited, or enable its limit and type in a value for its Maximum and Minimum limit values. Once limits are imposed, you can test them in the view panel by transforming the joint.

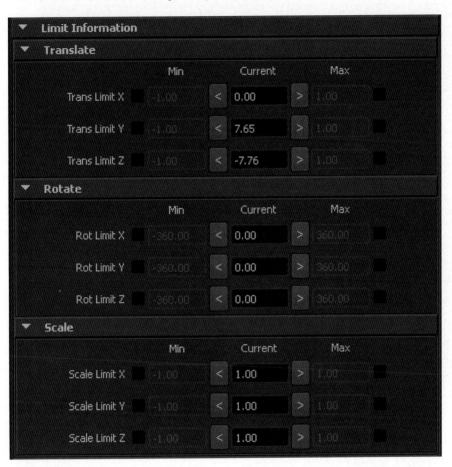

Figure 11-8
Limit Information

Displaying Joints

The Display section of the Attribute Editor lets you display a handle for the joint and move the handle away from the actual joint. Having a joint positioned away from the joint is helpful once you begin to animate the skeleton with a skin applied. Display Local Axis is also helpful. It displays axes around the joint as a quick reference. You can also set the default manipulator that appears when the joint is selected and the visibility of the joint and its children. Figure 11-9 shows a joint with the handle positioned away from the joint and the Local Axis option enabled.

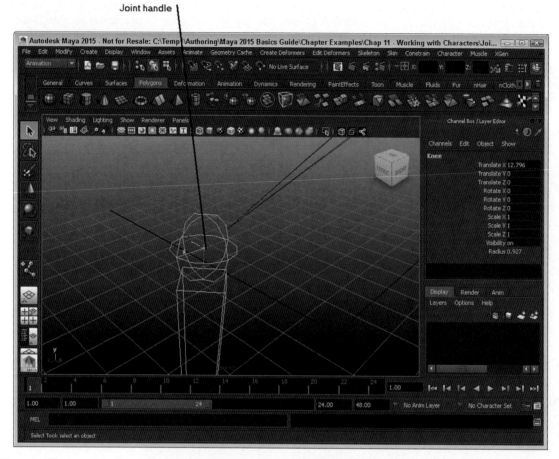

Figure 11-9
Joint handle

Lesson 11.2-Tutorial 1: Label Joints

1. Select the File, Open Scene menu command, and then locate and open the Simple skeleton.mb file.

2. Select the right hand joint and open the Attributes Editor.

3. In the Joint Labeling section, select the Hand options from the Type list and select Right from the Side list. Then, enable the Draw Label option.

4. Repeat Step 3 for the remaining joints.

    With the Draw Label option enabled, the text label appears for each labeled joint, as shown in Figure 11-10.

5. Select File, Save Scene As, and save the file as **Labeled skeleton.mb**.

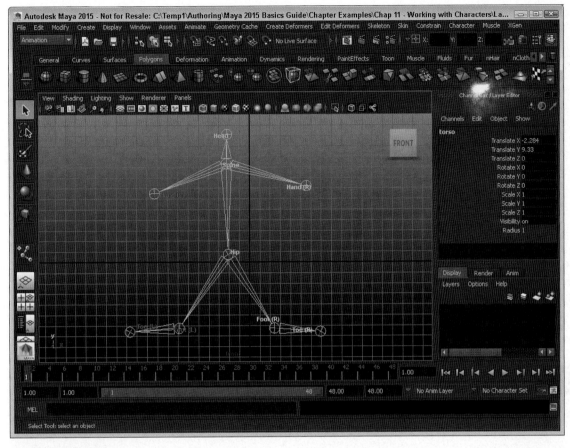

Figure 11-10
Labeled skeleton

Lesson 11.2-Tutorial 2: Limit Joint Motion

1. Select the Skeleton, Joint Tool menu command and click in the Front view to create a simple three-bone set of joints to represent an arm.

2. Select the elbow joint and open the Attributes Editor.

3. In the Limit Information section, enable the Minimum and Maximum Rotation Limit options for the z-axis.

4. Set the Minimum limit value to –90 and the Maximum limit value to 75.

5. Select the Rotate tool from the Toolbox and drag the blue z-axis manipulator to test the limits.

   With the limits enabled, the joint stops moving once a limit is reached, as shown in Figure 11-11.

6. Select File, Save Scene As, and save the file as **Limited arm.mb**.

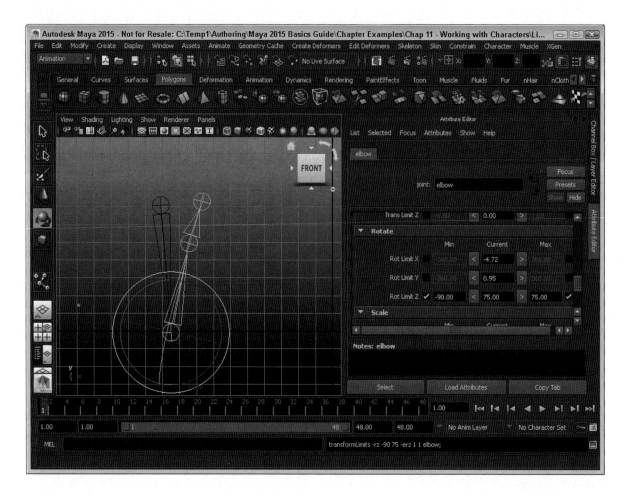

Figure 11-11
Limited arm movement

Lesson 11.3: Add Inverse Kinematics

Inverse Kinematics (IK) is a feature that you can add to skeleton that lets the child object control the motions of their parent object. Normal hierarchical motion is to move the child along with the parent. This motion is called **Forward Kinematics** (FK), but as characters walk and move, it is easier to animate a character by dragging their feet into position than by positioning their feet by rotating their upper leg. IK allows you to control a character's legs and arms by moving its hands and feet. FK lets you control a character's feet and hands by dragging its legs and arms.

Using the IK Handle Tool

You can use the IK Handle tool (select Skeleton, IK Handle Tool) to add IK to a skeleton. To do so, just select the tool and click on the parent joint followed by the last child joint in the limb. For example, to set up IK for the elbow, you'd select the shoulder joint and then the wrist joint. This overlays a light green triangle for the limb and add an IK handle to the last joint, as shown in Figure 11-11. If you move this handle, the bones follow naturally.

Tip

```
All skeleton bones that have an IK solution applied to
them appear light brown when unselected.
```

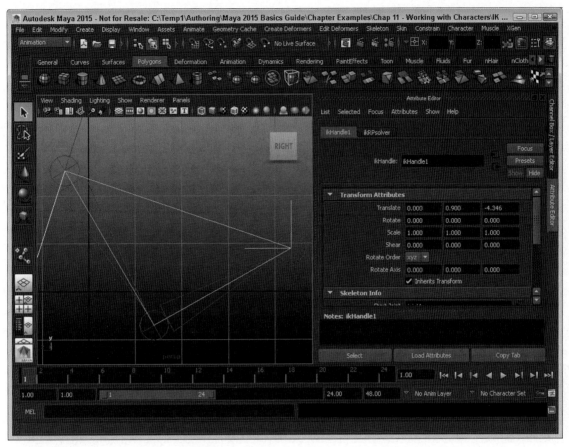

Figure 11-12
IK handle

Using the IK Spline Handle Tool

In addition to the IK Handle Tool, the Skeleton menu includes a second type of IK that you can apply to spline objects. This type of IK is useful for tails that are made from many bones in a straight line. It is applied to a joint chain the same way as the IK Handle Tool is—by selecting the first and last joints in the chain. The tool creates a NURBS curve that runs along the joint chain. Selecting and moving this curve's CV components causes the joint chain to move as well. Figure 11-13 shows a joint chain with an IK spline solution.

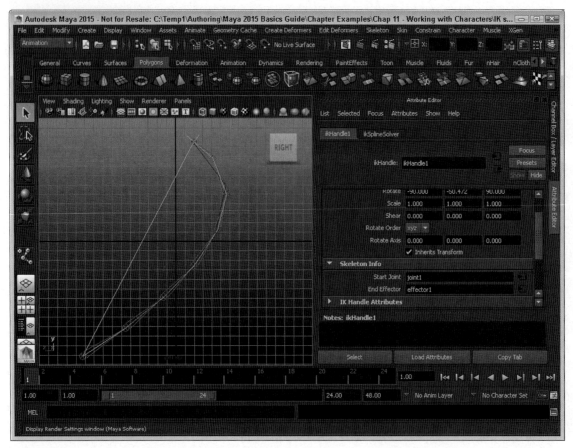

Figure 11-13
IK spline

Using the IK Manipulators

With the IK handle selected, you can enable a set of manipulators using the Show Manipulators button in the Toolbox. The manipulators include two circular discs that surround the start and end joints. These are used to Roll and Twist the IK chain, as shown in Figure 11-14. Sometimes when using the IK manipulators, it can become difficult to see where joints should be located with the skeleton in the way. To move a manipulator without having the skeleton follow, simply select the Skeleton, Disable Selected IK Handles menu command. Then the Skeleton, Enabled Selected IK Handles menu command snaps the skeleton to the manipulator's location.

Roll manipulator   Twist manipulator

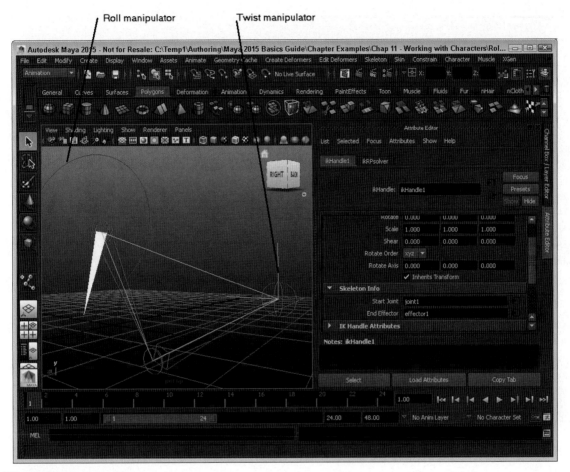

Figure 11-14
Roll and Twist manipulators

Switching Between FK and IK

As you animate, there may be times when you'll want to use Forward Kinematics to animate your character. With the IK handle selected, you can find the IK Blend attribute in the IK Solver Attributes section of the Attribute Editor; setting this attribute to 0.0 makes the control of the skeleton limb revert to FK. A setting of 1.0 uses the IK solution and anything in between blends between the two solutions.

Lesson 11.3-Tutorial 1: Add IK to a Skeleton

1. Select the File, Open Scene menu command then locate and open the Skeleton with tail.mb file.

2. Select the Skeleton, IK Handle Tool menu command.

3. Click on the pelvis joint and again at the bottom of the left foot joint.

4. Repeat Step 3 for the right foot.

   IK handles are created for each foot that move the body as the foot is moved. The left IK handle is shown in Figure 11-15.

5. Select File, Save Scene As and save the file as **Simple IK.mb**.

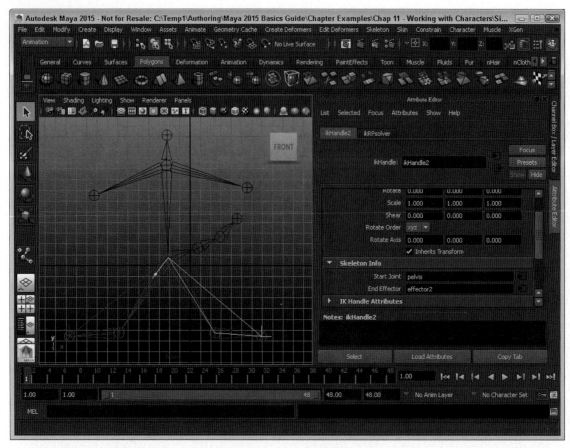

Figure 11-15
Simple IK

Lesson 11.3-Tutorial 2: Add IK Spline to the Skeleton Tail

1. Select the File, Open Scene menu command then locate and open the Simple IK.mb file.

2. Select the Window, Outliner menu command to open the Outliner. Click on torso and then on tail1 in the Outliner to expand them.

3. Select the Skeleton, IK Spline Handle Tool menu command.

4. Click on the tail1 in the Outliner and then on the tail4 joint in the view panel.

   This creates a NURBS curve that you can edit to control the tail's position, as shown in Figure 11-16.

5. Select File, Save Scene As and save the file as **Spline IK.mb**.

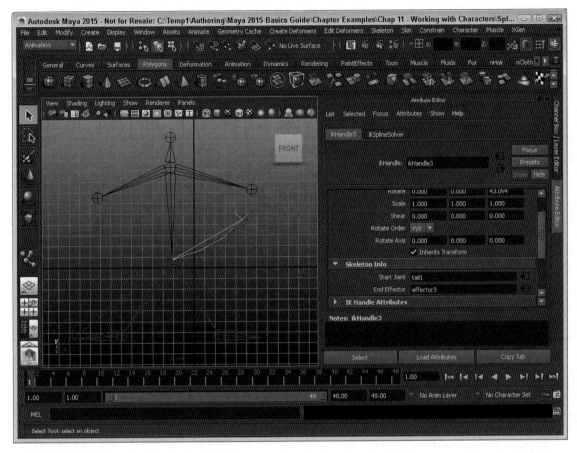

Figure 11-16
Simple IK spline

Lesson 11.4: Skin a Character

Skinning a character involves adding a surface to a skeleton hierarchy. This skin is bound to the skeleton and move as the underlying skeleton is moved. You can bound skin to a skeleton using two methods—Smooth Skinning or Rigid Skinning. Smooth Skinning displaces the skin around the joints and deform the skin in order to maintain a smooth appearance. Rigid Skinning requires that you set the points to deform as the joint is moved.

Creating Effective Skin

As you create a skin surface, remember that the skin only deforms and bends to the extent of the resolution of the skin surface, so when you create a skin object make sure that the number of spans and the number of sections is sufficient. Figure 11-17 shows two skeletons with smooth cylinder skins at different resolutions. The skin on the right deforms better than its counterpart on the left with minimal resolution.

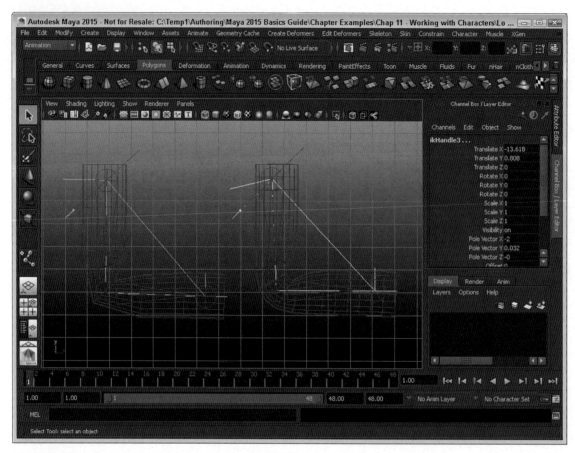

Figure 11-17
Skins require sufficient resolution

Positioning a Skeleton

Once the skin and the skeleton are created, you'll want to move the skeleton so that it lies in the center of the skin. Be sure to check all views for alignment. For the final rendered scene, you can hide the skeleton using the Display, Hide, Hide Kinematics, All menu command.

Binding Smooth Skin

With a skin and a skeleton created and aligned, you can create a smooth skin binding between the skin and the skeleton using the Skin, Bind Skin, Smooth Bind menu command. The skin must be selected first and then the skeleton. Once the skeleton and skin are bound, you can deform the skin by moving and rotating the underlying skeleton bones and joints. Figure 11-18 shows a simple cylinder that has been bound to a two-bone skeleton.

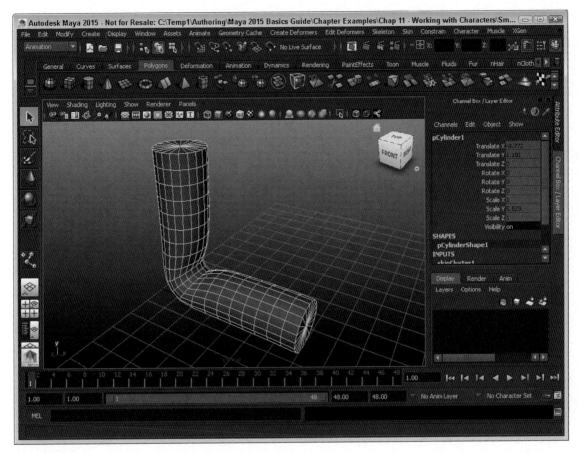

Figure 11-18
Smooth skin

Binding Rigid Skin

Binding to rigid skin works the same way as binding to smooth skin. First select the skin, and then select the skeleton and choose the Skin, Bind Skin, Rigid Bind menu command. Rigid skin bunches up at the joint when the skeleton is deformed, as shown in Figure 11-19. You can fix this bunching using deformers. Figure 11-20 shows a deformed cylinder with smooth skin (left) and rigid skin (right).

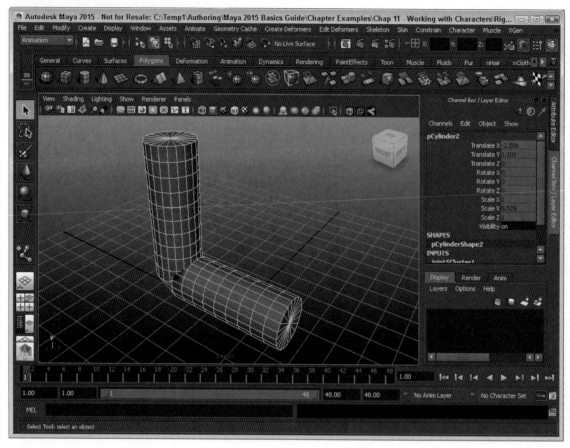

Figure 11-19
Rigid skin

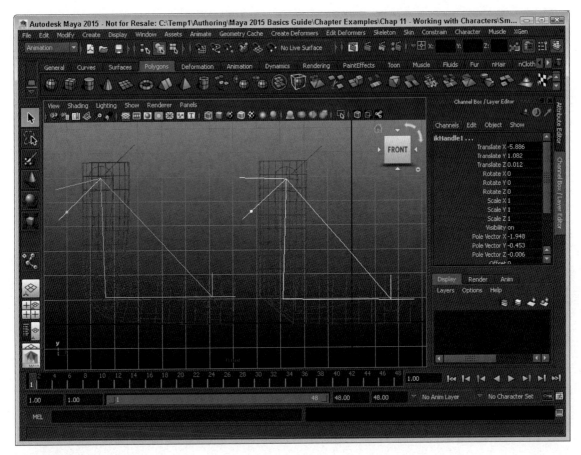

Figure 11-20
Rigid (right) versus smooth (left) skin

Returning to Default Pose

You can reset the position of your skin and skeleton at any time to its original pose that was used before the binding took place using the Skin, Go to Bind Pose menu command.

Detaching Skin

You can use the Skin, Detach Skin menu command to detach the selected skin object from its skeleton. This removes any deformations that were applied to the skin by moving the skeleton and return the skin to its shape before it was bound to the skeleton.

Animating Joints

Once a character is skinned and rigged, you can animate it by moving the various joints and IK handles.

Lesson 11.4-Tutorial 1: Position a Skin

1. Select the File, Open Scene menu command then locate and open the Sample IK.mb file.

2. Select the File, Import menu command, and then locate and import the Simple skin.mb file.

    The skin object is imported into the file with the IK skeleton. This skin was created by overlaying a primitive object on the skeleton, and then combining and applying a Smooth command to the primitives.

3. Scale the skin object to a size that roughly covers the skeleton object.

4. Click the Four Views button from the Quick Layout Buttons.

5. Select and move each joint to where it lies along the center of the skin objects in all views.

Tip

When moving the foot joint, be careful that you don't select the IK effector, or else all the IK joints will move.

Figure 11-21 shows the front view panel with the skin positioned over the skeleton.

6. Select File, Save Scene As and save the file as **Positioned skin.mb**.

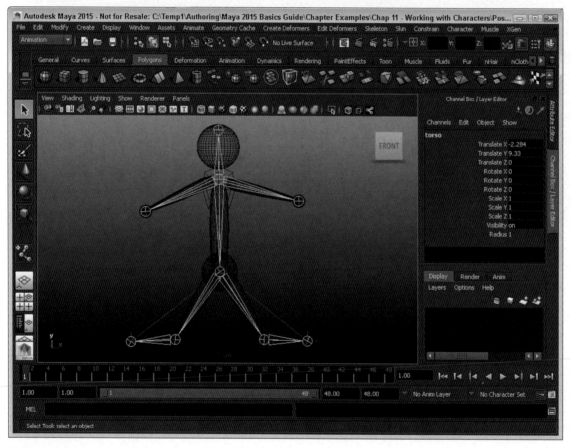

Figure 11-21
Positioned skin

Lesson 11.4-Tutorial 2: Bind Skin

1. Select the File, Open Scene menu command then locate and open the Positioned skin.mb file.

2. Select the skeleton object, hold down the Shift key, and select the skin object.

3. Select the Skin, Bind Skin, Smooth Bind menu command.

The skin turns magenta, showing its dependence on the skeleton, as shown in Figure 11-22.

4. Select File, Save Scene As and save the file as **Bound skin.mb**.

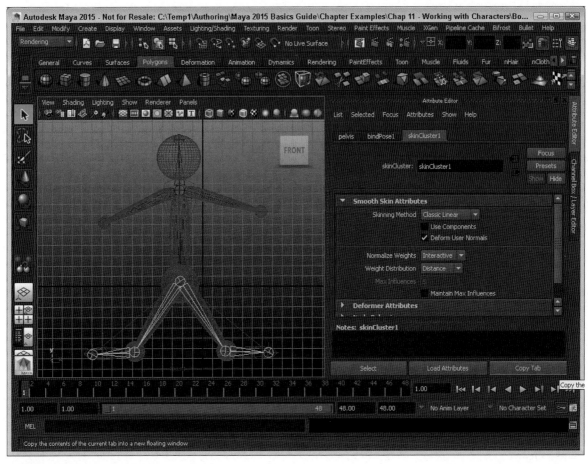

Figure 11-22
Bound skin

Lesson 11.4-Tutorial 3: Animate Joints

1. Select the File, Open Scene menu command then locate and open the Bound skin.mb file.

2. Select the IK effector for the left foot and choose Animate, Set Key to set a key.

3. Drag the Time Slider to frame 10 and enable the Auto Key button.

4. Move the left foot joint upward.

5. Drag the Time Slider to frame 20 and move the foot joint to its original position.

6. Repeat Steps 3 and 4 for frames 30 and 40 so that the characters foot taps up and down.

7. Repeat Steps 2–6 to set the keys to bop the character's head back and fourth.

8. Repeat Steps 2–6 to set the keys to swing the character's hips back and fourth.

9. Click the Play Forwards button to see the animation.

    One frame of the animation is shown in Figure 11-23.

10. Select File, Save Scene As, and save the file as **Animated character.mb**.

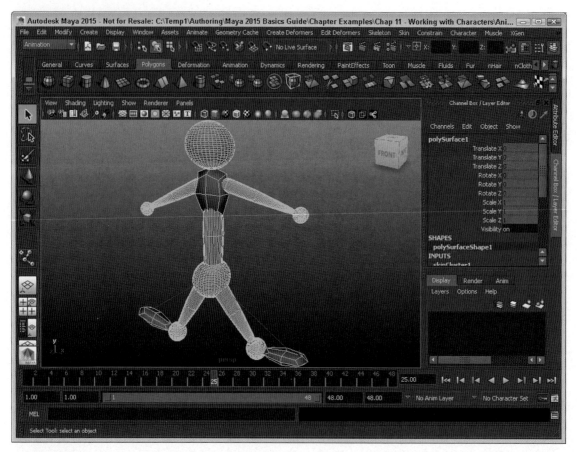

Figure 11-23
Animated character

Lesson 11.5: Edit a Skin

With a skin bound to a skeleton, you can control its movement using the skeleton, but as you begin to animate the character, you may notice some places where the skin isn't moving the way you'd like. To fix these problems, you may need to edit the skin. Maya provides several ways to edit both smooth and rigid skins, including influence objects and skin weights.

Adding Influence Objects

An influence object is a NURBS or polygon object that is placed near a skin object that pushes or pulls all nearby skin points to it. To add an influence object to a skin, select the skeleton and use the Skin, Go to the Bind Pose menu command, and then select the skin object, followed by the object that you want to use as the influence object and choose the Skin, Edit Smooth Skin, Add Influence menu command. Once an influence object is added to a skin, you can change the amount of skin deformation by moving the skin object closer to the influence object or by moving the influence object closer to the skin. Figure 11-24 shows an arm skin with a bulging muscle determined by the sphere influence object. You can remove influence objects using the Skin, Edit Smooth Skin, Remove Influence menu command.

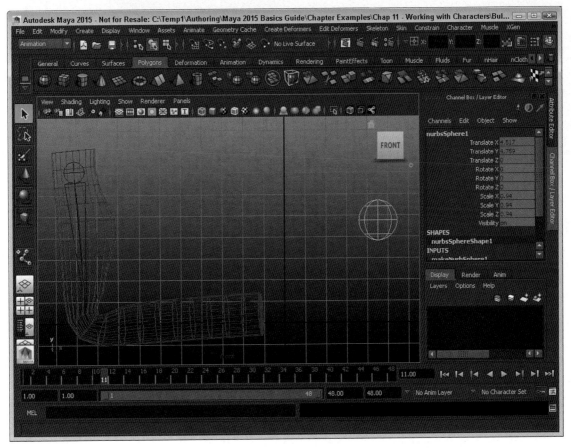

Figure 11-24
Influence object

Understanding Skin Weights

Another way to edit a skin is with skin weights. Each selected joint has an influence over the skin points that surround it. By changing this weighting, you can determine whether the skin is affected by the joint. A good example of this is the movement of a character's head. If the head skin is much larger than the bone that is used to control it, moving the head only moves those skin points near the top of the head and the neck where it is close to the bone, causing the character's head to remain stationary except for its neck and top. To fix this problem, you can set all points on the head to be affected by the head joint. You can view the weights for each skin point and each nearby joint in the Component Editor (shown in Figure 11-25), which you open using the Window, General Editors, Component Editor.

Figure 11-25
Component Editor

Painting Skin Weights

Although you can display and edit skin weights in the Component Editor, an easier way to change their value is with the Skin, Paint Skin Weights Tool. When this tool is selected, the Artisan brushes appear in the Tool Settings panel, and pressing the 5 key shows the skin weights for the selected joint in the view panel with white representing full weight and black representing no weight. The Tool Settings panel also offers options to replace, add, scale, or smooth skin weights. Figure 11-26 shows the weight values for Joint1, which is selected in the Tool Settings panel.

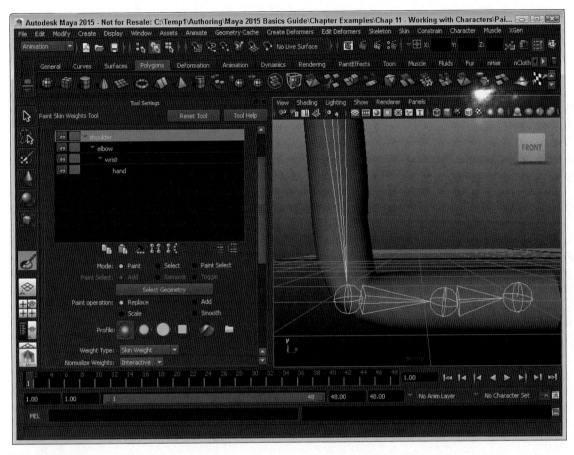

Figure 11-26
Painting skin weights

Resetting Skin Weights

If painting weights causes more problems, you can always return the skin weights to their default settings with the Skin, Edit Smooth Skin, Reset Weights to Default menu command.

Lesson 11.5-Tutorial 1: Add Influence Object

1. Select the File, Open Scene menu command, and then locate and open the Arm chain.mb file.

2. Select the Create, NURBS Primitives, Sphere menu command to create a sphere object. Move the sphere close to the upper arm.

3. Select the skeleton and choose the Skin, Go to Bind Pose menu command.

    The skeleton and skin return to the pose that they were in when the skin was bound to the skeleton.

4. Select the skin object, hold down the Shift key, and select the sphere object.

5. Choose the Skin, Edit Smooth Skin, Add Influence menu command.

    The sphere is now set to influence the skin points closest to it.

6. Select the elbow joint and press the S key to set an animation key. Then select the sphere object and press the S key again. Then click on the Auto Key button.

7. Drag the Time Slider to frame 10. Select and rotate the elbow joint to a 90-degree bend and drag the sphere object to the right.

8. Drag the Time Slider back and forth.

   The upper arm muscle bulges as the arm is bent, as shown in Figure 11-27.

9. Select File, Save Scene As, and save the file as **Bulging arm.mb**.

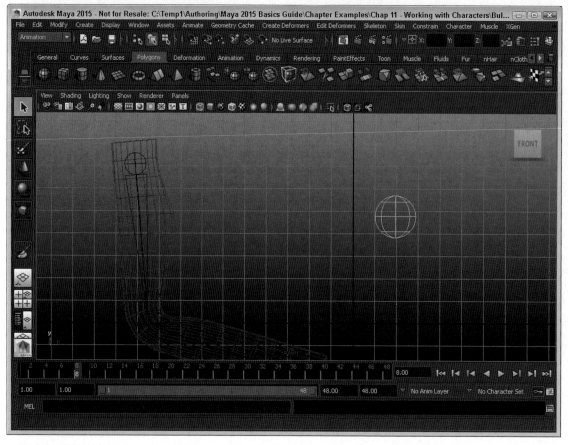

Figure 11-27
Bulging arm movement

Lesson 11.5-Tutorial 2: Paint Weights

1. Select the File, Open Scene menu command, and then locate and open the Arm chain.mb file.

2. Select the skin object and choose the Skin, Paint Skin Weights Tool menu command. Double-click on the Paint Skin Weights tool in the Toolbox to open the Tool Settings panel.

3. Press the 5 key to see the objects in shaded view.

   Each of the skin bones are listed in the Tool Settings panel, and the weights for the selected joint are displayed in black and white in the view panel.

4. In the Tool Settings panel, select the elbow joint and set the Radius value to 0.25.

5. Click on the eyedropper button in the Tool Settings panel and select the weight value above the elbow joint where the arm is still at full width, and then paint the vertices above the elbow where the arm starts to deform.

   The elbow has a more realistic line where the skin folds instead of the deep bend that was there before, as shown in Figure 11-28.

6. Select File, Save Scene As, and save the file as **Painted weights.mb**.

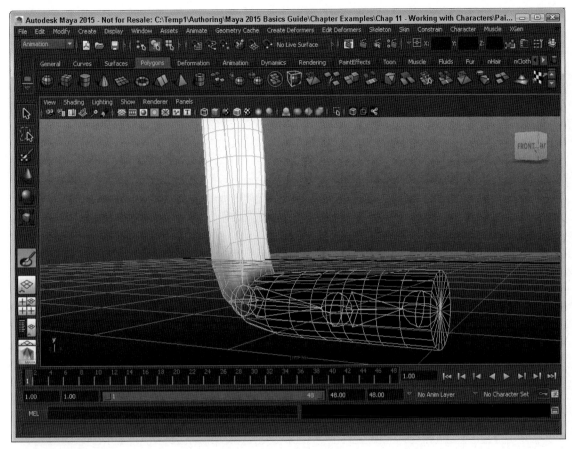

Figure 11-28
Painted weights

Lesson 11.6: Add Hair and Fur

Adding hair and fur to characters can do a lot to increase the realism of the character. Hair and fur are tricky because they deal with so many follicles that if they were treated as regular geometry objects, they would grind the processor to a halt. Hair instead is a separate system, much like particles, that together act together. They are also dealt with in a unique way when it comes to rendering by rendering the geometry first and then adding the hair.

Note

    Hair and fur features are part of the Maya Unlimited
    package.

Adding preset hair to an object

The easiest way to add hair and fur to a selected object is to choose one of the hair and fur presets. These presets have all the attributes already set to creating a unique hair and fur look. Several hair and fur presets are available in the Hair shelf, but you can find more in the Visor. Figure 11-29 shows the Duckling fur preset applied to a sphere object.

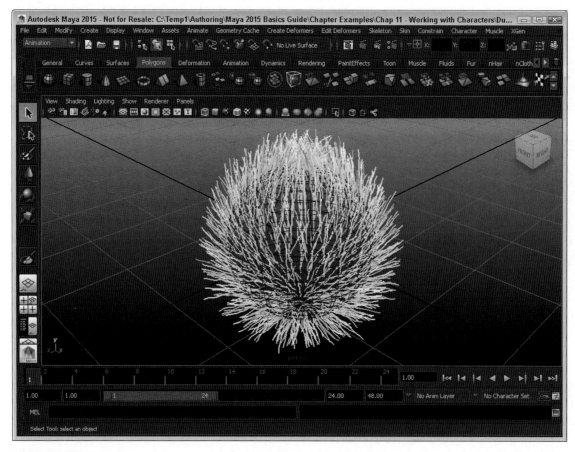

Figure 11-29
Duckling fur

Creating hair

Hair can be created on the selected object using the Hair, Create Hair menu command. This adds groups of hair to regular hair points around the surface of the object. If you open the Create Hair Options dialog box, there are options to Output hair as Paint Effects, NURBS Curves or a combination of both. You can also specify the Points Per Hair and the Length of the new hairs. Figure 11-30 shows a simple sphere with new hairs created using the Create Hair tool. Notice how the hairs all point out straight from the surface when first created.

Note

The Hair and Fur menus are located in the Rendering menu set.

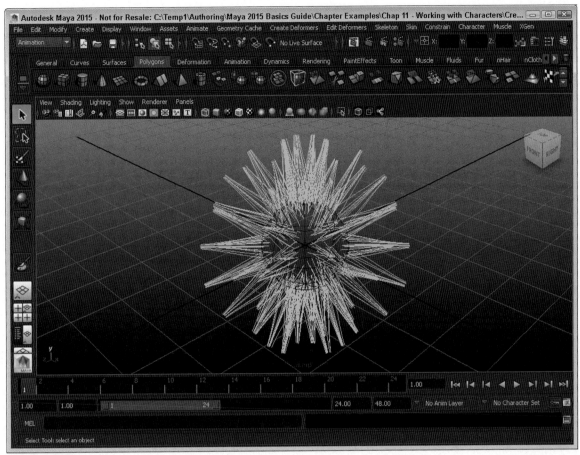

Figure 11-30
Creating hair

Style hair

Once hair is added to an object, you can use several tools in the Hair menu to style the hair. The Scale Hair Tool lets you drag in the view panel to change the hair's length. The Paint Hair Follicles tool lets you paint hair on the surface of the object using the configurable Artisan brushes. The Paint Hair Follicles Settings dialog box includes modes for painting and deleting hairs. The Paint Hair Textures tool includes options for painting baldness, color and specularity.

Making hair dynamic

Another property that you can set for hair is whether the hair is dynamic or static. Dynamic hair can be simulated to droop under the effects of gravity. New hair is set to be dynamic by default, but you can change it to be static in the Attribute Editor. To cause dynamic hair to fall naturally, select the Hair, Create Cache menu command. This causes the hair to fall naturally about the object it is attached to over the available range of frames. You can also select other objects for the hair to collide with using the Hair, Make Collide menu command. Figure 11-31 shows hair dynamically moved about the sphere object.

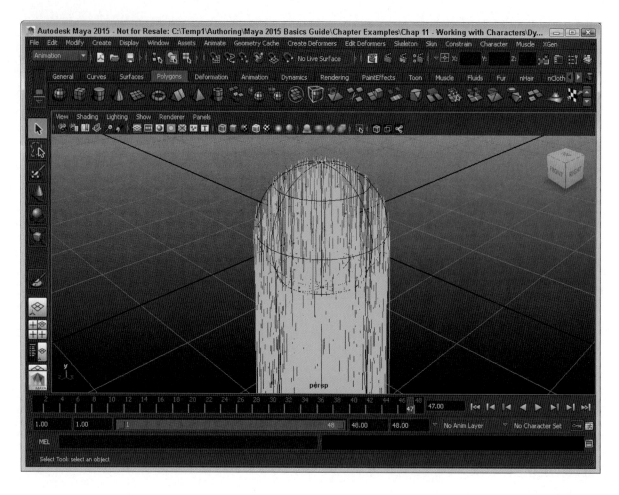

Figure 11-31
Dynamic hair

Creating and editing a fur description

Fur is handled using a different approach, which doesn't give you as much control over individual hairs. Each object that has fur is given a fur description using the Fur, Attach Fur Description menu command. If you select to Edit Fur Description, then all the fur attributes are displayed in the Attribute Editor where you can change everything from the Base and Tip Color to the Opacity, Curl, Scraggle and Clumping. You can also change these attributes using the Paint Fur Attributes Tool. This tool lets you paint various degrees of each of the attributes using the Artisan brushes. Figure 11-32 shows some scraggly fur painted on a sphere.

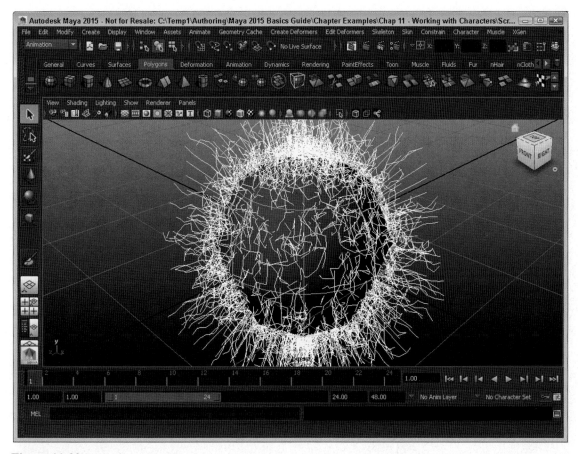

Figure 11-32
Scraggly fur

Rendering hair and fur

When hair and fur is displayed in the view panel, only a fraction of the total number of hairs are displayed. These hairs are only guides, but when the final hair system is rendered, the total number of hairs are interpolated between the displayed guides. To render the final object with hair, click on the Render Current Frame button on the Status Line. Figure 11-33 shows the sphere with the Duckling fur preset applied to it.

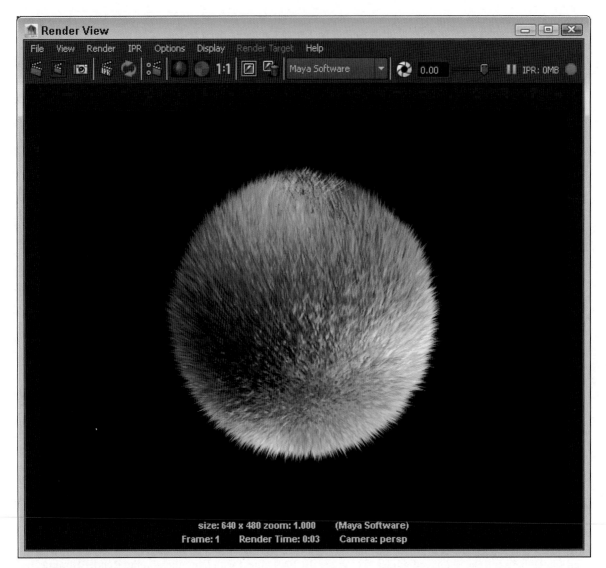

Figure 11-33
Rendered Duckling fur

Lesson 11.6-Tutorial 1: Add hair

1. Select the File, Open Scene menu command, and then locate and open the Simple face.mb file.

2. Select the back half of the head.

   The face object has been separated into a front part and the back half where the hair will be located.

3. Choose the Rendering menu set and choose the Hair, Create Hair, Options menu command. In the Create Hair Options dialog box, set the U and V Count values to 25 and the Randomization value to 1. Then click the Create Hairs button.

   Hair is added to the face object at regular intervals around the selected area.

4. Select the Hair, Scale Hair Tool menu command and drag in the view panel to reduce the length of the hair.

5. Select the Hair, Create Cache menu command.

All the hair is automatically set to be dynamic, so the Create Cache command causes the hair to fall about the head naturally.

6. Drag the Time Slider to frame 40 where the hair is relaxed.

7. Open the Attribute Editor and in the Clump and Hair Shape section, set the Hairs Per Clump value to 100.

8. Click the Render Current Frame button on the Status Line.

    The face is rendered with its dynamic hair, as shown in Figure 11-34.

9. Select File, Save Scene As, and save the file as **Simple face with hair.mb**.

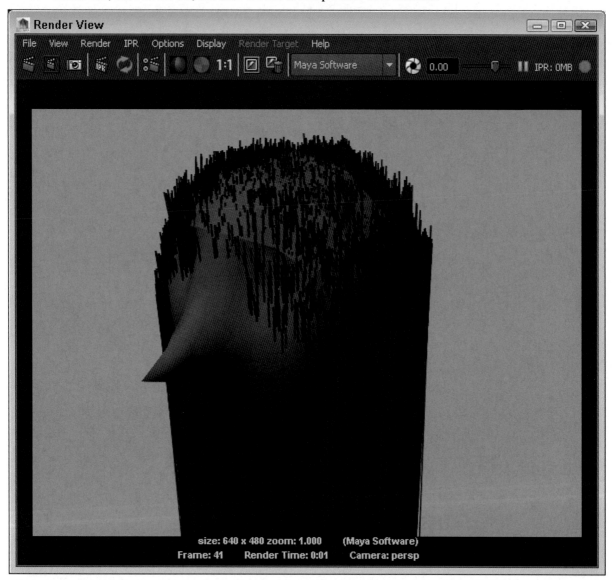

Figure 11-34
Simple face with hair

Chapter Summary

This chapter covers creating and rigging characters, starting with building a character skeleton using bones and joints. Once you establish the skeleton, you can connect several joints together and edit the joints in different ways. Inverse Kinematics lets you control the skeleton by positioning the end joints, thus causing the rest of the joints to follow. The second part of creating a character involves adding a skin to the skeleton that is deformed as the skeleton underneath is moved. You can edit skin by painting its weights. Another way to add realism to characters is with hair and fur.

What You Have Learned

In this chapter, you learned

*   How to build a skeleton using joints.

*   How to insert and connect a joint to an existing skeleton.

*   How to remove and disconnect a joint.

*   How to mirror a joint.

*   How to name, orient, and label joints.

*   How to show and hide joint labels.

*   How to limit joint movement.

*   How to add Inverse Kinematics using the IK Handle and IK Spline tools.

*   How to use the IK manipulators.

*   How to bind smooth and rigid skin.

*   How to detach skin from a skeleton.

*   How to add a skin influence object.

*   How to paint skin weights.

*   How to create and style hair.

*   How to make hair dynamic.

*   How to add fur to an object.

*   How to render hair and fur.

Key Terms From This Chapter

*   **Rigging.** The process of adding and configuring a skeleton to a character that is used to control its motion.

*   **Joint.** An object connected to a bone used to rotate and move skeleton bones.

*   **Bone.** An object that is connected between two joints and defines the rigid areas of a character.

*   **Skeleton.** A hierarchical set of bones and joints used to define the underlying structure of a character.

*   **Root joint.** The top joint in the skeleton hierarchy.

*   **Inverse Kinematics.** A physics definition that allows objects at the end of a skeleton hierarchy to control the motion and position of the entire skeleton.

*   **Forward Kinematics.** Physics that allows the position of child objects to be calculated when the

parent object is moved.

*   **IK Handle.** An IK solution that is used for parts such as arms and legs.

*   **IK Spline.** An IK solution that is used for parts such as tails.

*   **Skin.** The model that is placed over a skeleton that is bound to the skeleton and deformed by it.

*   **Smooth skin.** A skin object that deforms as its bound skeleton is moved.

*   **Default pose.** The skins original position when it was first bound to the skeleton.

*   **Influence object.** An object that controls the local deformation of a character skin.

*   **Skin weight.** The amount of control each vertex has when an adjacent bone is moved.

<h1 style="text-align:right"># **Chapter 12**</h1>

Animating with Dynamics

IN THIS CHAPTER

Dynamics is the physics of moving objects. Maya is smart enough to know all of the formulas for describing object motion and uses those to compute the position of objects that simulate real-world motions. For example, gravity is fairly easy to simulate by causing objects to fall downward. Likewise, you can simulate object collisions if you know the mass and velocity of the two colliding objects.

Particle objects are collections of small objects that act together to create dust, smoke, rain, and other effects. You can create **particles** using the Particle tool or using an **emitter,** which gives the particle's speed and direction.

Another way to control particles is with **fields**. Fields, like Gravity, Turbulence, and Vortex, provide forces to the dynamic systems. These forces can control particles or objects.

In addition to particles, you can force objects to interact with each other using rigid body or soft body dynamics. You can constrain **rigid body objects** using constraints like Nail, Hinge, and Barrier. A system of several rigid and **soft body objects** can be solved to determine the physical motions of the object based on physical laws.

Maya includes several effects that are scripted behaviors that use particles, glows, and dynamics to create fire, smoke, fireworks, and lightning.

Maya Unlimited includes some additional dynamic features for working with flowing cloth objects and fluids. You can use fluids to create gaseous objects such as clouds, fire, and explosions. In many ways, fluids behave just like particle systems including the use of emitters. Fluids, however, are confined to a specific volume defined by a container.

Lesson 12.1: Use Particles

Particles are a collection of small objects that act together as a single unit. They are useful for creating effects like dust, smoke, and clouds. A particle system can include a few objects or millions of objects. The more objects, the more time it takes to render and even display them in the view panels.

Creating Particles

You can begin creating particles by selecting Particles, Particle Tool. With the Particle tool selected, just click at the location where you want to place particles and press Enter when done. The Tool Settings panel for the Particle tool lets you name the particle collection, specify the number of particles to place with each click, and define the maximum radius within which the particles are placed. There is also a Sketch Particles option, which creates particles as you drag in the scene. The Sketch Interval value determines how close together the particles are. The Create Particle Grid option creates a grid of regularly spaced particles. The Particle Spacing value determines the spacing between each adjacent particle. The With Cursor option allows you click on opposite corners to create a particle grid and the With Text Fields option lets you enter the corner dimensions. Figure 12-1 shows a particle system created using each of these methods.

Note

The Particles menu is found in the Dynamics menu set.

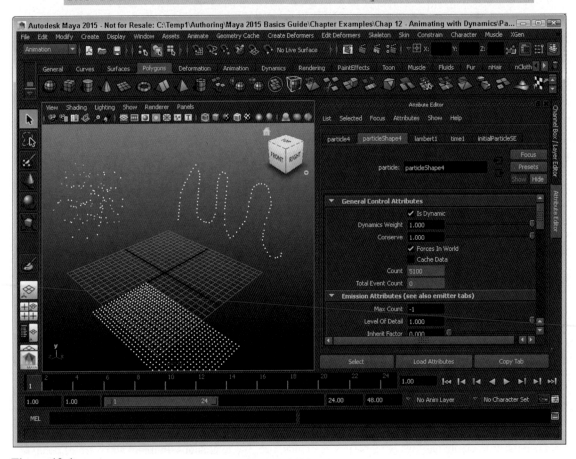

Figure 12-1
Particles options

Creating Surface Particles

If you select an object and choose the Modify, Make Live menu command, all of the particles that you create with the Particle tool are positioned on the surface of the object. Figure 12-2 shows a particle collection that is centered about a sphere.

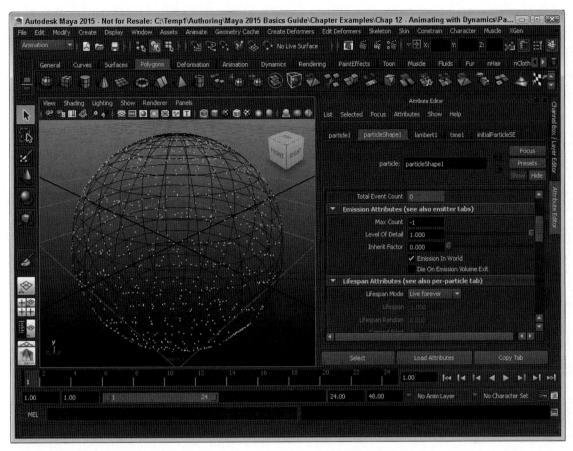

Figure 12-2
Particles about a sphere

Viewing Particle Attributes and Count

When a particle is selected, all particles in the set are selected and the Attribute Editor displays all of the various attributes for the particle collection. These attributes are split between a Transform node and a Shape node, just like other objects. In the Shape node for the selected particles set, the General Control Attributes section of the Attribute Editor includes a Count field that tells you how many particles make up the collection, as shown for a square array of particles in Figure 12-3.

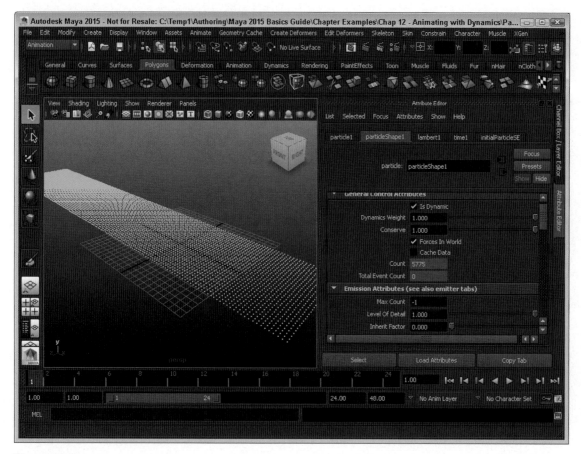

Figure 12-3
Particle's attributes

Setting Particle Lifespan

In the Lifespan Attributes section of the Attribute Editor, you can select a lifespan mode for the selected particle set. The options include Live Forever, Constant, and Random Range. If the Live Forever option is selected, the particles remain as long as the set is active. The Constant option lets you set a Lifespan value, which determines how many frames the particle stays around before disappearing; and the Random Range option randomly sets the lifespan of each particle in the set.

Changing Particle Render Type

In the Render Attributes section is a list of Render Types. Click the Render Type button to see additional attributes for the selected Render Type. The Render Types include the following:

* **MultiPoint.** Renders each particle as multiple points for a denser particle collection. Good for dust and smoke.

* **MultiStreak.** Combines each particle into several streaks for a denser particle collection.

* **Numeric.** Renders each particle using its particle number.

* **Points.** Makes each particle is simple point. You can set the Point size.

* **Spheres.** Renders each particle as a separate sphere.

* **Sprites.** Displays each particle as a rectangle that continually faces the camera. You can map images to these sprites.

* **Streak.** Renders each particle as a stretched point. The particle must be moving to be visible. The length of the streak depends on the speed of the particle. Good for rain and sleet.

* **Blobby Surface.** Renders each particle as a blobby sphere. When in close proximity, the blobby spheres run together like water drops.

* **Cloud.** Renders also as blobby spheres, except blurred to create the look of a cloud.

* **Tube.** Renders each particle as a tube.

Figure 12-4 shows a stream of particles rendered with the Blobby Surface and Cloud options selected.

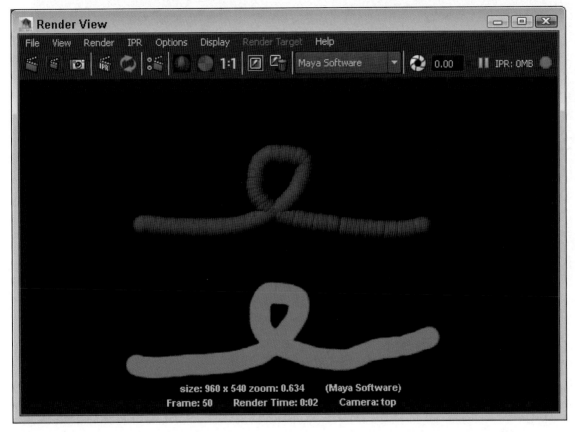

Figure 12-4
Particle shape rendered with Blobby Surface and Cloud

Using Instances

In addition to the default particle render types that you can set, you can also select any geometric object and use that as the particle's source object. To replace all of the particles with a geometric object, select the object then select the particle set and choose the Particles, Instancer (Replacement) menu command. This command replaces each particle with the geometric object. Changing the instanced geometry changes all of the particles also. Figure 12-5 shows a drawn path of particles that uses a cube object instance.

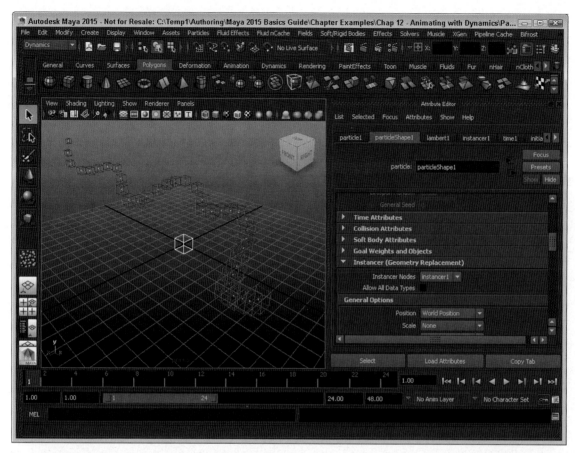

Figure 12-5
Particle instances

Cycling Instances

If you select the Particles, Instancer (Replacement), Options menu command, the Particle Instancer Options dialog box opens, as shown in Figure 12-6. This dialog box includes a list of instanced objects and several objects that you can add to the list by selecting an object and clicking the Add Selection button. You can set the particle system to cycle through the instanced objects in the list by selecting the Sequential option in the Cycle field. The Cycle Step Units can be set to Frames or Seconds, and the Cycle Step Size is the number of frames or seconds that must pass before the next object in the list replaces the current instances.

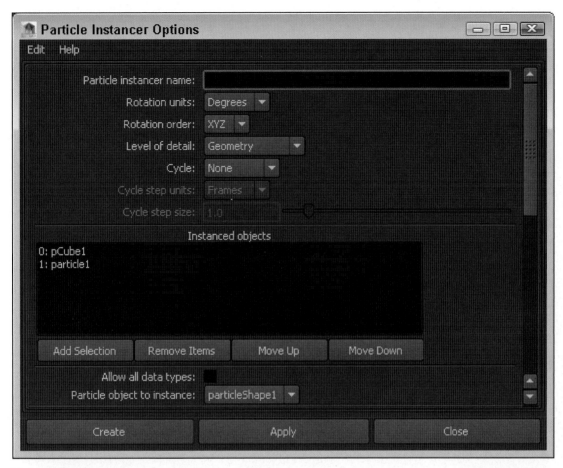

Figure 12-6
Particle Instancer Options dialog box

Lesson 12.1-Tutorial 1: Add Clouds to a Sphere

1. Create a NURBS sphere object with the Create, NURBS Primitives, Sphere menu command.

2. Select the Modify, Make Live menu command.

   The Make Live command causes all particles that are created to be positioned automatically on the surface of the live object.

3. Select the Particles, Particle Tool, Options menu command.

4. In the Particle Settings section of the Tool Settings panel, type the name **Clouds** then set the Number of Particles option to 5 with a Maximum Radius setting of 0.25.

5. Enable the Sketch Particles option and drag over the sphere to create the particles.

6. Press the Enter key when you're done creating particles.

   By setting the Maximum Radius value to 0.25, the particles are raised from the surface of the live object.

7. With the particle set selected, open the Attribute Editor.

8. Open the Render Attributes section of the Attribute Editor. In the CloudsShape node, select the Cloud option for the Particle Render Type attribute.

9. Below the Particle Render Type attribute, click on the Current Render Type button.

10. Set the Radius value to 0.15.

11. Right-click on the Perspective view panel to select it and click the Render Current Frame button in the Status Line.

The sphere is rendered surrounded by wispy clouds, as shown in Figure 12-7.

12. Select File, Save Scene As and save the file as **Cloudy globe.mb**.

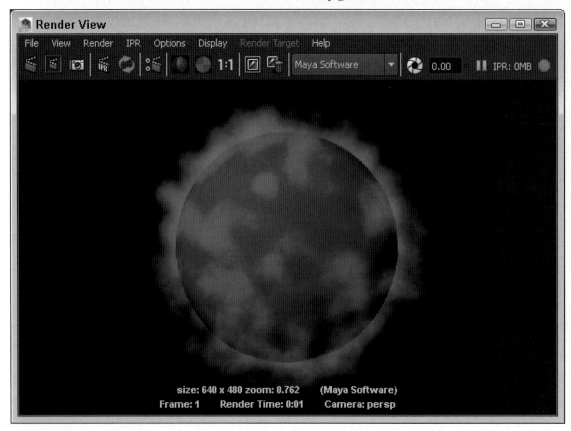

Figure 12-7
Cloudy globe

Lesson 12.1-Tutorial 2: Use an Instance

1. Select the File, Open Scene menu command, locate and open the Snowflake.mb file.

2. Select the Particles, Particle Tool, Options menu command.

3. In the Particle Settings section, type the name **Snowstorm** and set the Number of Particles option to 5 with a Maximum Radius setting of 10.0 and a Sketch Interval of 25.

4. Enable the Sketch Particles option and drag in the view panel.

5. Press the Enter key when you're done creating particles.

6. Select the Snowflake object, hold down the Shift key, and select the particles.

7. Select the Particles, Instancer (Replacement) menu command.

8. Select the original snowflake object and scale it down with the Scale tool.

Scaling the original snowflake scales all of the instanced particles also, as shown in Figure 12-8.

9. Select File, Save Scene As and save the file as **Snowstorm.mb**.

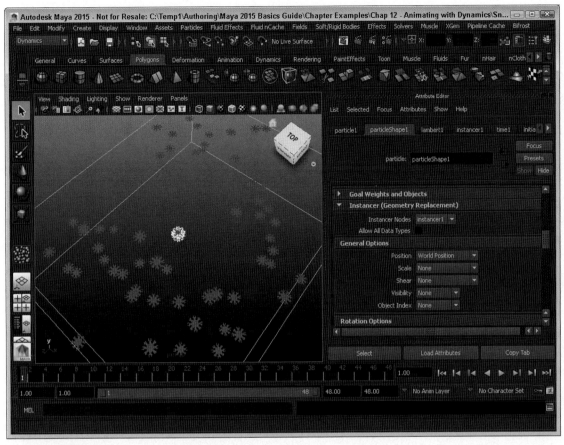

Figure 12-8
Instanced particles

Lesson 12.1-Tutorial 3: Cycle Instances

1. Select the Create, NURBS Primitives, Sphere menu command twice to create two sphere objects..

2. Click on the Select by Component Type button in the Status Line and stretch the end vertices of one of the spheres away from its center to create a football-shaped object.

3. Select the Particles, Particle Tool, Options menu command.

4. In the Particle Settings section, type the name **Sports ball storm** and set the Number of Particles option to 5 with a Maximum Radius setting of 5.0. Make sure that neither the Sketch Particles or the Create Particle Grid options are enabled.

5. Click randomly in the view panel to create a particle set that covers the entire view panel. Press the Enter key when you're done creating particles.

6. Select both sphere objects and select the Particles, Instancer (Replacement), Options menu command.

    The names of each of the selected spheres appear in the Particle Instancer Options dialog box.

7. Set the Cycle attribute to Sequential and the Cycle Step Units to Frames,

8. Select the particle set in the view panel and click the Create button.

9. Drag the Time Slider.

    Clicking the Create button causes all the particles to use the football-shaped instance, as shown in Figure 12-9. As you drag the Time Slider, the particles switch back and forth between the football and the normal sphere objects for each frame.

10. Select File, Save Scene As, and save the file as **Sports ball storm.mb**.

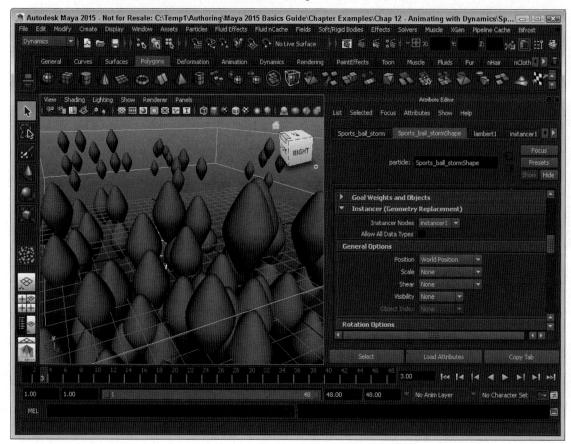

Figure 12-9
Raining footballs

Lesson 12.2: Create an Emitter

One of the key benefits of particles is that they can have motion. You can create this motion by moving the particle set with the Transform tools, but there are easier methods. An *emitter* is an object that creates and distributes particles at a regular rate.

Note

Although you can select individual particles, particles can only be transformed as an entire set.

Using an Emitter

An emitter sends particles into the scene. Emitters include attributes to define the number of particles created per second, as well as the particle's initial speed and direction. There are several types of particle emitters—Omni, Directional, Surface, Curve, and Volume. Dragging the Time Slider causes the particles to speed away from the emitter. Figure 12-10 shows three Omni emitters with different Rate values.

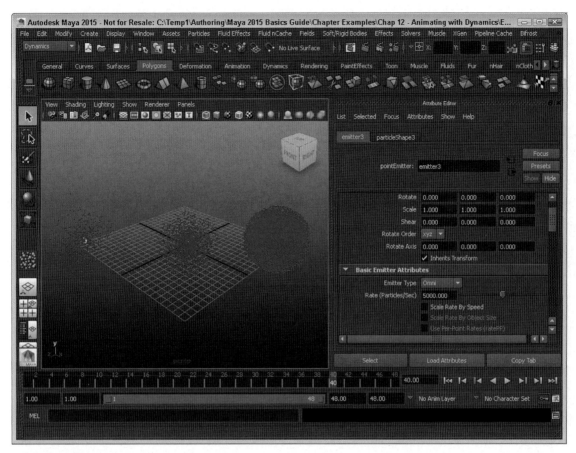

Figure 12-10
Emitters with different rates

Using a Directional Emitter

The Directional emitter type lets you set the direction that the particles move away from the emitter using the Direction X, Direction Y, and Direction Z attributes. Changing the Spread value causes the particles to spread randomly as they are emitted. A Spread value of 1.0 spreads the particles in the hemisphere. Figure 12-11 shows three directional emitters with increasing Spread values.

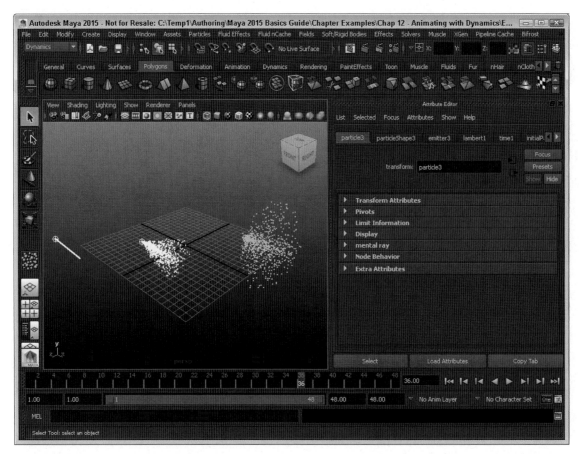

Figure 12-11
Directional emitters with different spreads

Using a Volume Emitter

The Volume emitter type can be cube, sphere, cylinder, cone, or torus shaped. For Volume emitters, you can set the particle's Sweep range and its speed Away From Center, Away From Axis, Along Axis, and Around Axis. Figure 12-12 shows a cubic, spherical, and cylindrical Volume emitters.

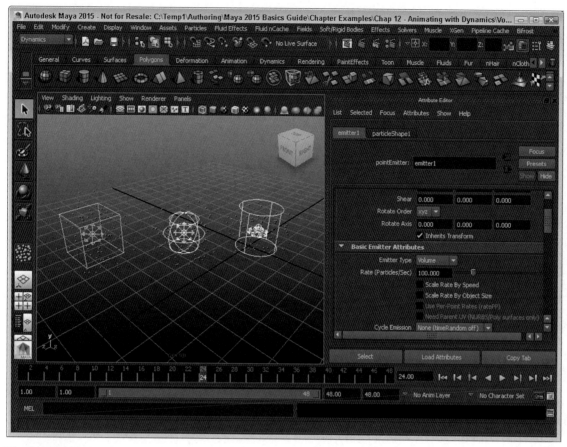

Figure 12-12
Volume emitters

Using an Object as an Emitter

In addition to the various emitter types, you can turn NURBS objects and curves into emitters using the Particles, Emit from Object menu command. This causes particles to be spawned from the surface of the selected object or curve. Figure 12-13 shows a NURBS object acting as an emitter with the emitter type set to Surface.

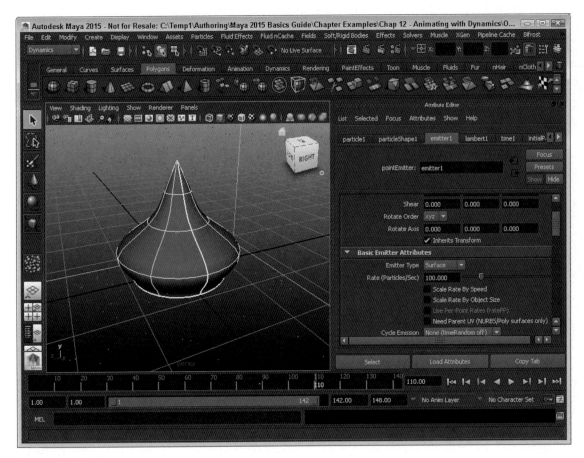

Figure 12-13
An object emitter

Changing Emitter Attributes

You can change the emitter's attributes in the Attribute Editor when the emitter is selected, but you can also change them using a manipulator, shown in Figure 12-14. With the emitter selected, click the Show Manipulator icon in the General Shelf and drag with the middle mouse button to change the attribute's value.

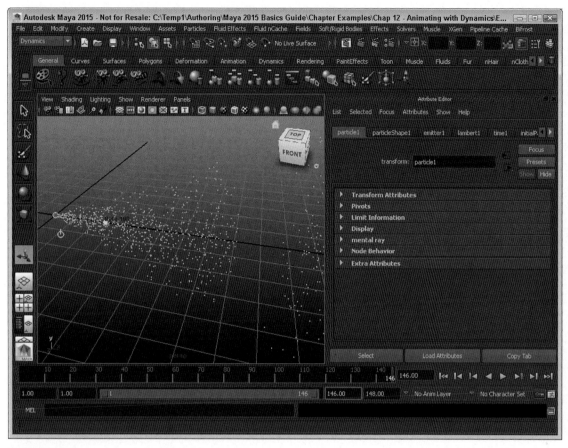

Figure 12-14
Emitter manipulator

Lesson 12.2-Tutorial 1: Create an Omni Emitter

1. Select the Create, Polygon Primitives, Cube menu command to create a cube object and move the cube away from the center of the view panel.

2. Select the Particles, Create Emitter menu command.

3. In the Attribute Editor, select Omni from the Emitter Type drop-down list and set the Speed value to 10.

4. Drag the Time Slider to see the particles.

5. Select the cube object, and then hold down the Shift key and select the particle set. Be sure to select the individual particles being emitted and not the emitter icon.

6. Choose the Particles, Instancer (Replacement) menu command.

   All the particles are replaced with cubes, as shown in Figure 12-15.

7. Select File, Save Scene As, and save the file as **Cube emitter.mb**.

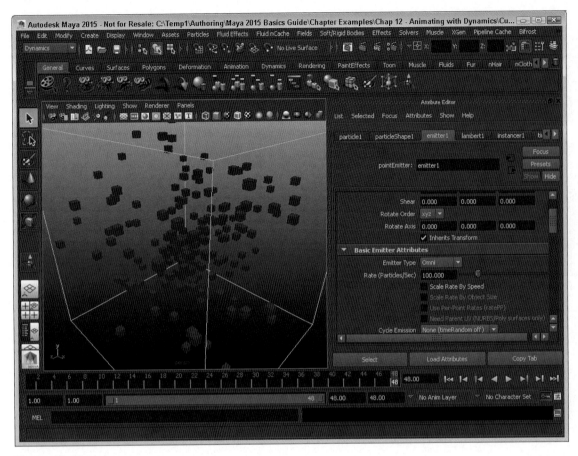

Figure 12-15
An Omni emitter

Lesson 12.2-Tutorial 2: Create a Directional Emitter

1. Select the File, Open Scene menu command and open the Simple tank.mb file.

2. Select the Particles, Create Emitter menu command and move the emitter to the end of the tank's gun.

3. In the Attribute Editor, select Directional from the Emitter Type drop-down list.

4. In the Distance/Direction Attributes section, set the Direction X value to 1.0 and the Spread value to 0.25.

5. Click on the Show Manipulator button in the Toolbox.

6. Click and drag the manipulator with the middle mouse button until the Rate value is over 500.

7. Drag the Time Slider to see the particles.

    The particles all speed away from the emitter, as shown in Figure 12-16.

8. Select File, Save Scene As and save the file as **Directional emitter on tank.mb**.

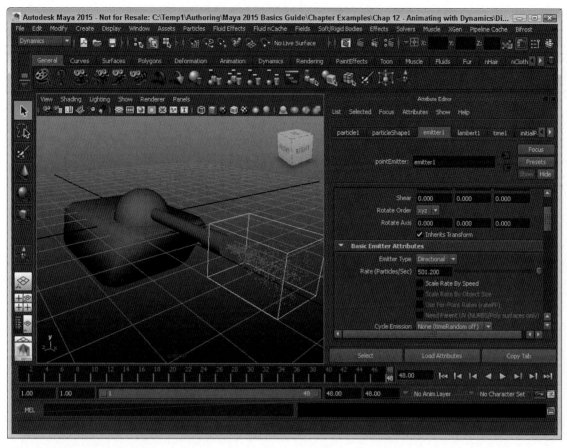

Figure 12-16
A Directional emitter on a tank gun

Lesson 12.2-Tutorial 3: Create an Object Emitter

1. Select the File, Open Scene menu command and open the Ceiling fan.mb file.

2. With the fan object selected, choose the Particles, Emit from Object, Options menu command.

3. In the Emitter Options dialog box, select Surface from the Emitter Type drop-down list, enable the Scale Rate By Object Size option, and set the Speed value to 10. Then click the Create button.

4. Drag the Time Slider to see the particles.

    The particles all speed away from the surface of the fan object, as shown in Figure 12-17.

5. Select File, Save Scene As and save the file as **Ceiling fan emitter.mb**.

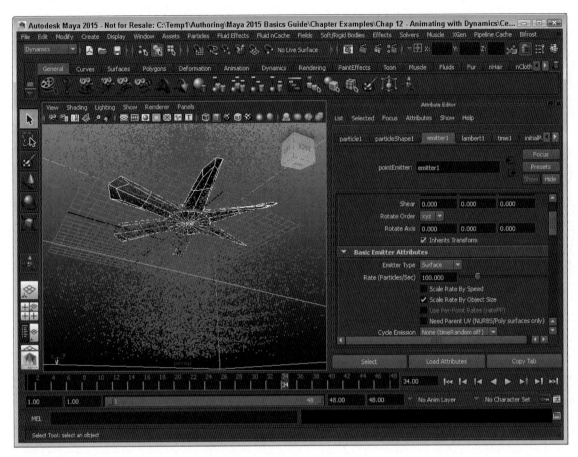

Figure 12-17
A cylinder emitter

Lesson 12.3: Create Fields and Goals

Fields define physical forces in the scene that objects and particles become subject to. You can also use **goals,** which are targets that the particles move towards.

Understanding Fields

Fields are a way of adding physical forces to the scene. All objects that are connected to a field are influenced by the field. Fields are created using the Fields menu command. Maya includes the following default fields:

* **Air**. This field represents airflow, such as a fan blowing.

* **Drag**. This field applies friction to a moving object.

* **Gravity**. This field simulates the Earth's gravity field. It causes object to accelerate in the direction of the field icon, which is typically downward in the negative Y-axis direction.

* **Newton**. This field pulls objects towards it.

* **Radial**. This field acts like a magnet repelling or attracting objects.

* **Turbulence**. This field randomly moves all particles within its influence.

* **Uniform**. This field pushes all objects in one direction with a consistent force.

* **Vortex**. This field pulls objects in a spiraling direction like a tornado or water down a drain.

*   **Volume Axis**. This field moves all objects within a given volume a specified direction.

You can set the strength of a selected field in the Attribute Editor.

Connecting Objects to a Field

All objects that are selected when a field is created are connected to the field and thereby are affected by it. You can connect objects to a field at any time using the Fields, Affect Selected Object menu command. The Fields, Use Selected as Source of Field menu command moves the field icon to the selected object and is useful for positioning fields.

Caution

When selecting particles to connect to a field or to a goal, be sure to select the actual particles and not the emitter.

Changing Field Attributes

When a Field is added to the scene, an icon is placed at the origin. You can move this icon using the Transform tools and modify the attributes for the field in the Attribute Editor. These attributes include Magnitude, Direction, and Distance. There is also a manipulator for these values that you can access using the Show Manipulator button, as shown in Figure 12-18.

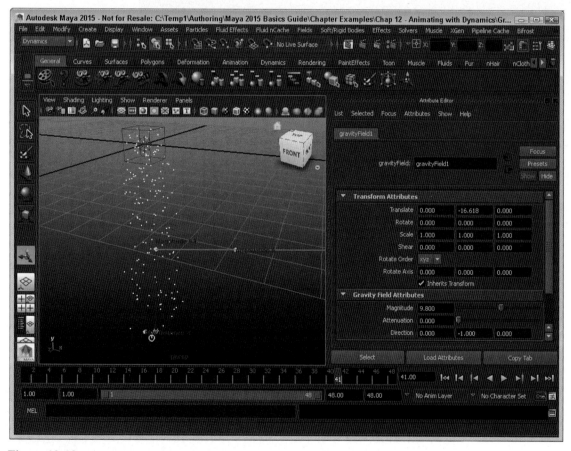

Figure 12-18
Gravity field and manipulator

Regulating Field Forces

When a field is applied to an object, it often takes a considerable force to get the object to first move, but if the force required to get the object moving continues to be applied, the object often accelerates out of the scene too quickly. If you enable the Use Max Distance attribute in the Distance section of the Attribute Editor for a field, a Falloff Curve section, shown in Figure 12-19, appears where you can define how the field's force diminishes as the object approaches its maximum distance.

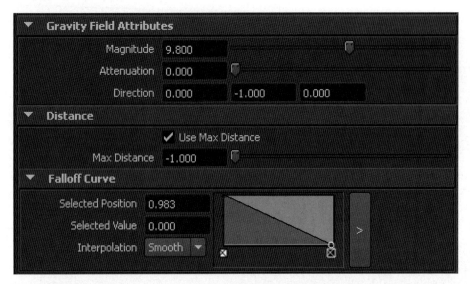

Figure 12-19
Falloff Curve section

Establishing Goals

A Maya goal is an object that a particle collection moves towards. You can use any object as the goal—it just needs to be connected to the particle object. To create a goal for a particle object, select the particle object then the object to be the goal, and then choose the Particles, Goal menu command. Figure 12-20 shows two equal emitters, but the one on the right has the sphere as its goal and all its particles are directed towards the goal. To create multiple goal targets, deselect all objects and repeat the steps with another goal object.

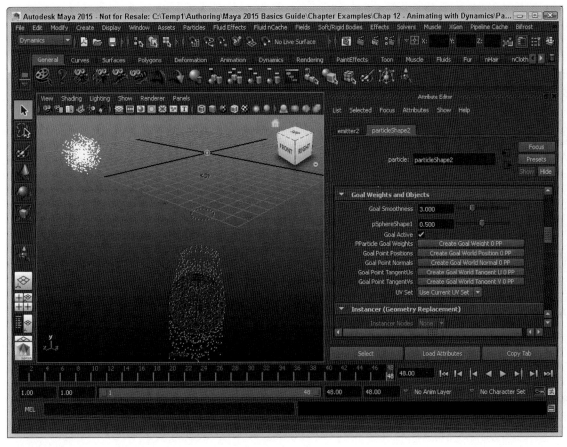

Figure 12-20
Particle goal

Lesson 12.3-Tutorial 1: Create a Vortex Field

1. Select the Particles, Create Emitter menu command.

2. In the Attribute Editor, select Omni from the Emitter Type drop-down list and set the Rate to 1000.

3. Drag the Emitter icon upward using the Move tool.

4. Select the Fields, Vortex menu command.

5. Drag the Time Slider to see the particles.

6. Select the particles, hold down the Shift key, and click on the Vortex field icon.

7. Select the Fields, Affect Selected Object menu command.

8. Set the Magnitude value to 50.

9. Drag the Time Slider to see the spiraling particles.

   The particles spiral around the Vortex field icon, as shown in Figure 12-21.

10. Select File, Save Scene As and save the file as **Spiral galaxy.mb**.

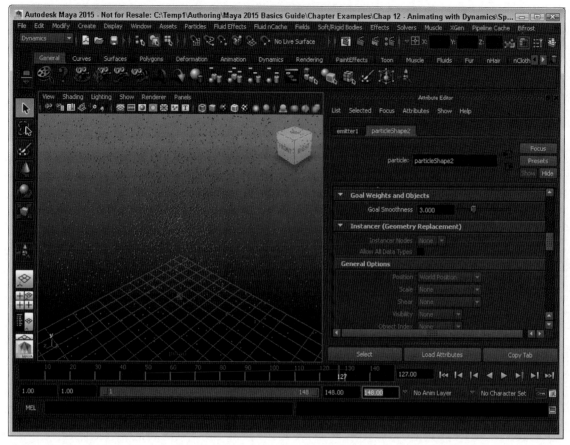

Figure 12-21
Vortex field

Lesson 12.3-Tutorial 2: Create a Goal

1. Select the File, Open Scene menu command and open the Bee and hive.mb file.

2. Select the Particles, Create Emitter menu command and move the emitter away from the hive object.

3. With the emitter selected, set the Rate to 5 and the Speed Random value to 5 in the Attribute Editor.

4. Drag the Time Slider to see the particles.

5. Select the bee object, hold down the Shift key, and select the particles, and then choose the Particles, Instancer (Replacement) menu command.

   All the particles change to the bee object.

6. Select the particles, hold down the Shift key, and select the hive object, and then choose the Particles, Goal menu command.

7. Drag the Time Slider.

   The bee particles move towards the hive goal object, as shown in Figure 12-22.

8. Select File, Save Scene As and save the file as **Hive goal object.mb**.

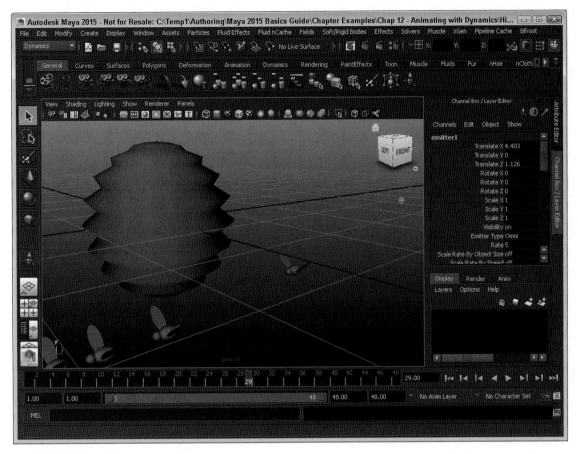

Figure 12-22
Goal object

Lesson 12.4: Manage Particle Collisions

Since Maya knows the position in 3D space of all objects, it is also aware of when two objects collide with one another. It can further instruct the particles to spawn new particles or tell an object how to respond to the collision.

Enabling Particle Collisions

You can enable collisions between a particle object and an object in the scene by selecting a particle object and Shift-selecting the collision object and choosing the Particles, Make Collide menu command. Figure 12-23 shows a simple directional emitter whose particles are bouncing off a plane object.

Note

Particles cannot be made to detect collisions with other particles.

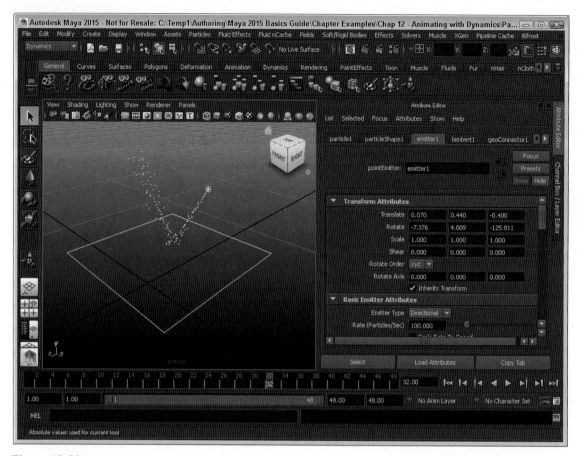

Figure 12-23
Particle collisions

Defining New Events

When a particle collides with an object, you can cause a new **event**—such as making the particle split or emit new particles—to happen. To create a new event, open the Particle Collision Events dialog box (shown in Figure 12-24) with the Particles, Particle Collision Events menu command. With the options in this dialog box, you can cause the event happen to all particles or to a given number of collisions.

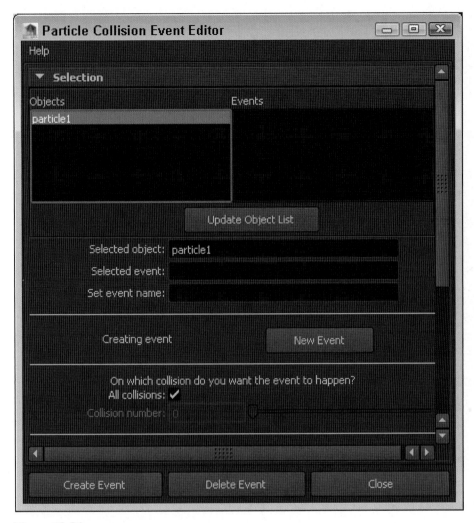

Figure 12-24
Particle collision Events dialog box

Creating Rigid Body Objects

In addition to particles, objects can also collide with other objects. A rigid body object is an object, such as a brick, that doesn't deform when forces act on it. The Soft/Rigid Bodies, Create Active Rigid Body menu command makes the selected object into a rigid body that can move when particles or other objects interact with it. The Soft/Rigid Bodies, Create Passive Rigid Body menu command makes the selected object a rigid body that is immovable, like the ground plane. The Rigid Options dialog box, shown in Figure 12-25, includes property values like Mass, Friction, Bounciness, and Damping.

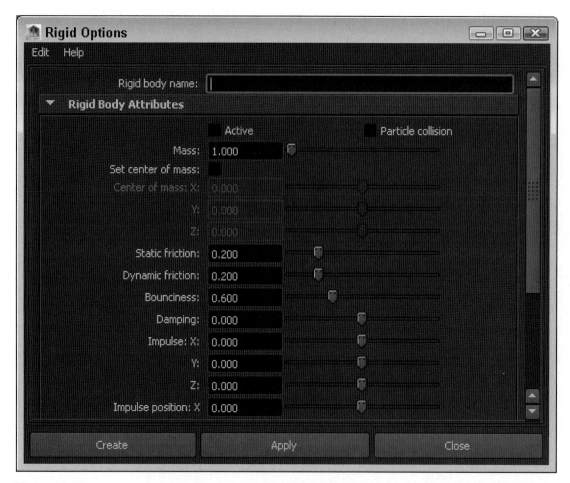

Figure 12-25
Rigid Options dialog box

Creating Soft Body Objects

A soft body object is one that deforms as it comes in contact with forces, much like a pillow. The Soft/Rigid Bodies, Create Soft Body menu command causes a selected object to inherit the properties of a soft body object. Soft body objects can be affected by field forces.

Lesson 12.4-Tutorial 1: Enable Particle Collisions

1. Select the File, Open Scene menu command and open the Pinball.mb file.

2. Select the Particles, Create Emitter menu command and move the emitter to the top of the pinball box.

3. In the Attribute Editor, set the Emitter Type to Directional, the Rate to 10, the Direction Y to –1, the Spread value to 0..25, and the Speed to 20.

4. Create a NURBS sphere with the Create, NURBS Primitives, Sphere menu command. Scale the sphere to fit within the pinball box.

5. Drag the Time Slider to see the particles.

6. Select the sphere object along with the particles and choose the Particles, Instancer (Replacement) menu command.

7. Select the particles, hold down the Shift key and select the pinball box, and then select the Particles, Make Collide menu command.

8. Drag the Time Slider to see the particles.

    The particles bounce around the box as they collide with the walls of the pinball box, as shown in Figure 12-26.

9. Select File, Save Scene As and save the file as **Bouncing particles.mb**.

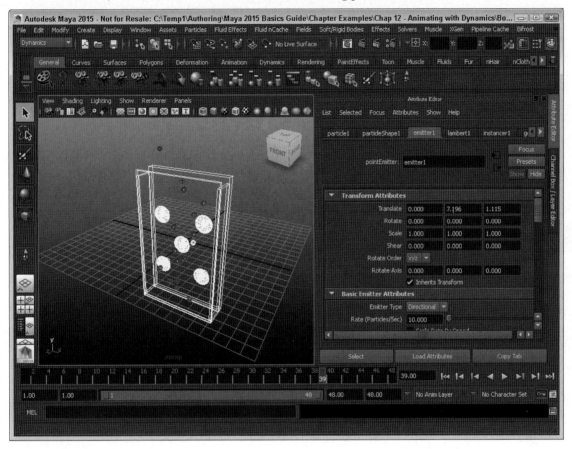

Figure 12-26
Colliding particles

Lesson 12.4-Tutorial 2: Add a Collision Event

1. Select the File, Open Scene menu command, and then locate and open the Bouncing particles.mb file.

2. Select the Particles, Particle Collision Events menu command.

    The Particle Collision Events dialog box opens.

3. Click the New Event button, enable the Emit button, set the Number of Particles to 100 and click the Create Event button.

    The particles emit new particles when they collide with the pinball box object, as shown in Figure 12-27.

4. Select File, Save Scene As and save the file as **Emit on collision.mb**.

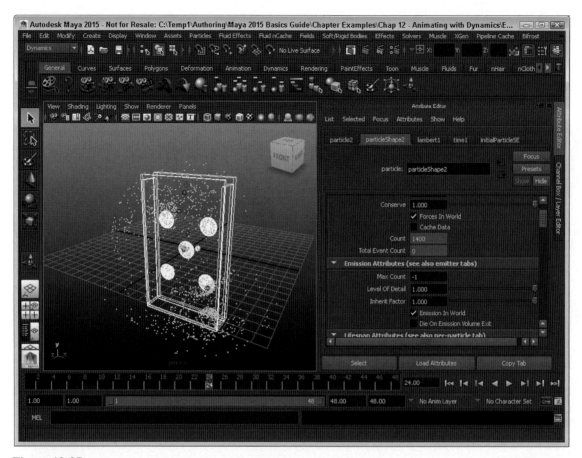

Figure 12-27
Emit on collisions

Lesson 12.4-Tutorial 3: Create Rigid Body Objects

1. Select the File, Open Scene menu command and open the Pinball.mb file.

2. Select all objects that make up the table and choose the Soft/Rigid Bodies, Create Passive Rigid Body menu command.

   By making the table into a passive rigid body, the table becomes immovable, but objects can still be affected by it.

3. Select all of the balls in the scene and choose the Soft/Rigid Bodies, Create Active Rigid Body menu command.

   Selecting the Create Active Rigid Body menu command with the ball objects selected makes the balls into moveable rigid body objects.

4. Select the cue ball and choose the Fields, Newton menu command. Then move the Newton field just behind the other balls and set its Magnitude value to 1000.

   With the Newton field positioned behind the other balls, the cue ball is pulled toward the field colliding with the other balls in the process.

5. Drag the Time Slider to see how the rigid body objects interact.

   Since all the balls are active rigid bodies, the collisions make them bounce off one another and off the walls of the table, as shown in Figure 12-28.

6. Select File, Save Scene As, and save the file as **Rigid bodies on billiard table.mb**.

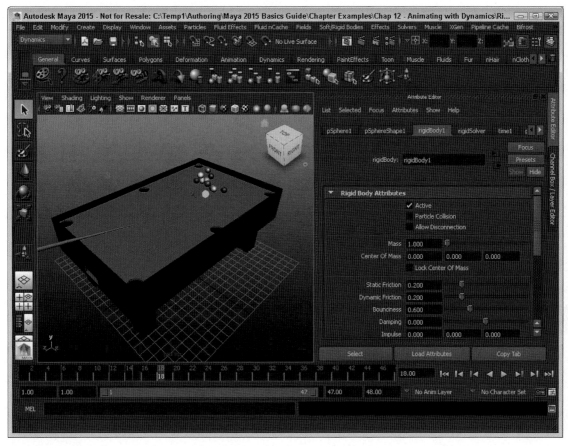

Figure 12-28
Billiard ball rigid bodies

Lesson 12.4-Tutorial 4: Create Soft Body Objects

1. Create a polygon plane object with the Create, Polygon Primitives, Plane menu command.

2. Scale the plane object up with the Scale tool.

3. Select the Soft/Rigid Bodies, Create Soft Body menu command.

4. Select the plane object and choose the Fields, Turbulence menu command.

5. Drag the Time Slider to see the rigid body objects interact.

   The plane object deforms under the Turbulence field, as shown in Figure 12-29.

6. Select File, Save Scene As and save the file as **Soft body.mb**.

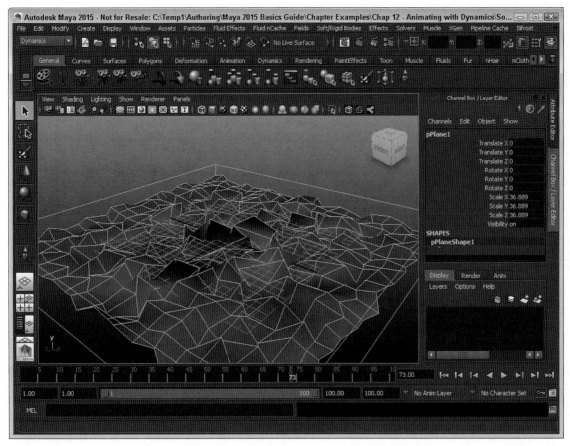

Figure 12-29
Soft body

Lesson 12.5: Constrain Motion

To control the simulations created from rigid bodies, Maya includes several different constraint types that are useful for resisting motions. The constraint types include nail, pin, hinge, spring, and barrier. They can all be selected from the Soft/Rigid Bodies menu.

Adding Constraints

You can use **constraints** to limit the motion of active rigid body objects. The Soft/Rigid Bodies, Create Constraint menu command creates a constraint for the selected rigid body object. The Constraint Options dialog box, shown in Figure 12-30, includes an option for selecting the Constraint Type.

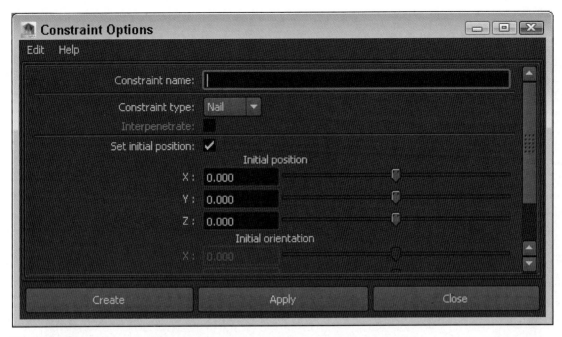

Figure 12-30
Constraint Options dialog box

Creating Nail and Spring Constraints

The Soft/Rigid Bodies, Create Nail Constraint menu command connects the selected object to a straight line that is linked to a nail that you can position anywhere in the scene. The object pivots around the nail at a distance defined by the line between the object and its nail, as shown in Figure 12-31. A spring constraint is created with the Soft/Rigid Bodies, Create Spring Constraint menu command. For a spring constraint, the line between the nail and the object can stretch.

Creating a Pin Constraint

The Soft/Rigid Bodies, Create Pin Constraint menu command connects two selected objects together so that they move together. Each object is connected to a pin using a straight line to its center, also shown in Figure 12-31. Each object can pivot about the pin, but the distance between the object and the pin stays constant.

Nail constraint

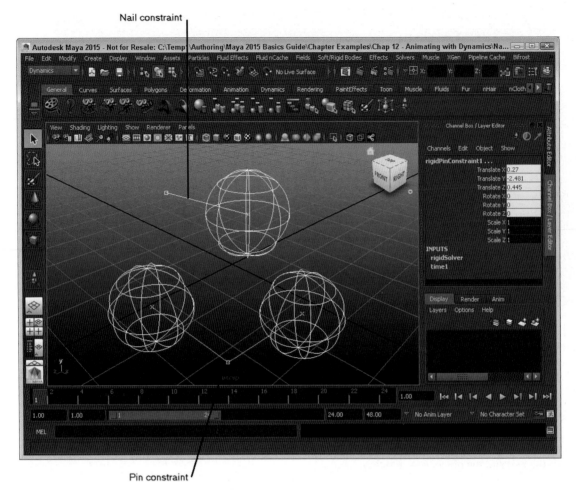

Pin constraint

Figure 12-31
Nail and Pin constraints

Creating a Hinge Constraint

The Soft/Rigid Bodies, Create Hinge Constraint menu command connects the center of a selected object to a hinge line that allows the object to pivot about a single axis, as shown in Figure 12-32.

Creating a Barrier Constraint

The Soft/Rigid Bodies, Create Barrier Constraint menu command connects the center of a selected object to a barrier line that the object cannot cross, also shown in Figure 12-32.

Hinge constraint

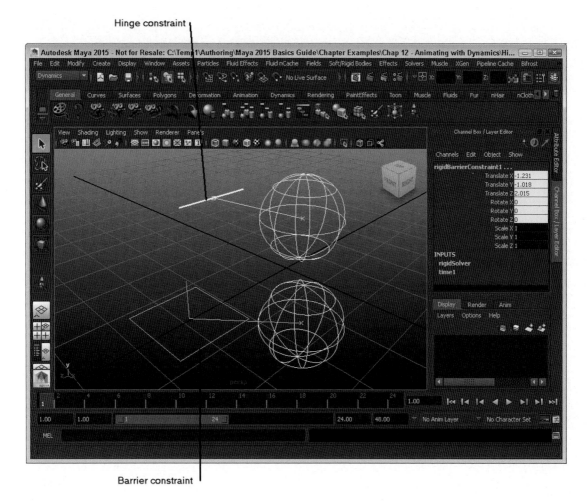

Barrier constraint

Figure 12-32
Hinge and Barrier constraints

Creating Springs

You can use the Soft/Rigid Bodies, Create Springs menu command on two selected objects to create springs between the two. This causes the two objects to move together and forces them toward each other as they are pulled apart. One of the objects must be a soft body object or a particle object. Springs are displayed as dashed lines between the two objects. Figure 12-33 shows the springs between two plane objects.

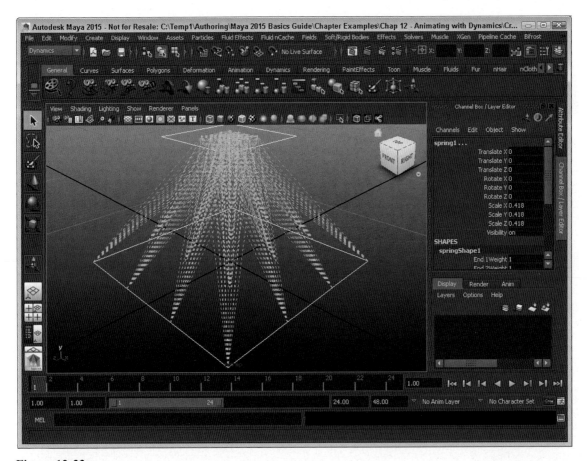

Figure 12-33
Springs between two plane objects

Lesson 12.5-Tutorial 1: Add a Constraint

1. Select the Create, NURBS Primitives, Sphere menu command twice to create two sphere objects.

2. Select the Create, NURBS Primitives, Plane menu command twice to create two plane objects.

3. Select and rotate one of the plane objects to form a 60 degree angle with the other plane object.

4. Move a sphere object above either side of the horizontal plane object.

5. Select both sphere objects and choose the Soft/Rigid Bodies, Create Pin Constraint menu command and drag the pin constraint upward.

    A straight line connects the center of each sphere with the pin.

6. Select both spheres and choose the Fields, Gravity menu command, and then move the gravity icon below the plane object.

    Each sphere turns magenta, telling you that each is connected to the Gravity field.

7. Select each of the plane objects and choose the Soft/Rigid Bodies, Create Passive Rigid Body menu command.

8. Drag the Time Slider to see how the spheres interact.

    The spheres begin to fall under the force of the gravity field, but one sphere is blocked by the plane object. The pin constraint also keeps the attached sphere from moving, as shown in Figure 12-34.

436

9. Select File, Save Scene As, and save the file as **Pin constraint.mb**.

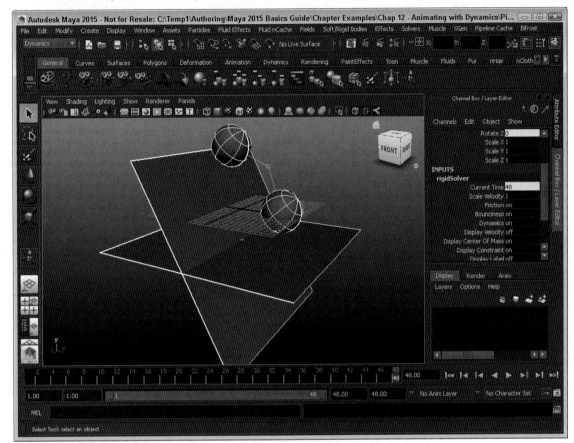

Figure 12-34
Two constrained spheres

Lesson 12.6: Create Effects

Maya includes a number of special effects that you can apply directly to an object or a selection of components. These effects are all found in the Effects menu and include Fire, Smoke, Fireworks, Lightning, Shatter, Curve Flow, and Surface Flow.

Creating Fire and Smoke

You can add the Fire effect to the selected object using the Effects, Create Fire menu command. The Fire Options dialog box includes settings for Fire Density, Intensity, Fire Spread, and Turbulence, as shown in Figure 12-35. A plane object on fire is shown in Figure 12-36. Similar to the Fire effect is the Smoke effect, but it requires a sprite image to be rendered. Some sample sprite images appear in the Gifts/smoke directory.

Note

The Smoke effect requires a series of sprite images be loaded into the ~~sourceimages~~ directory for the current project.

Figure 12-35
Fire effect options

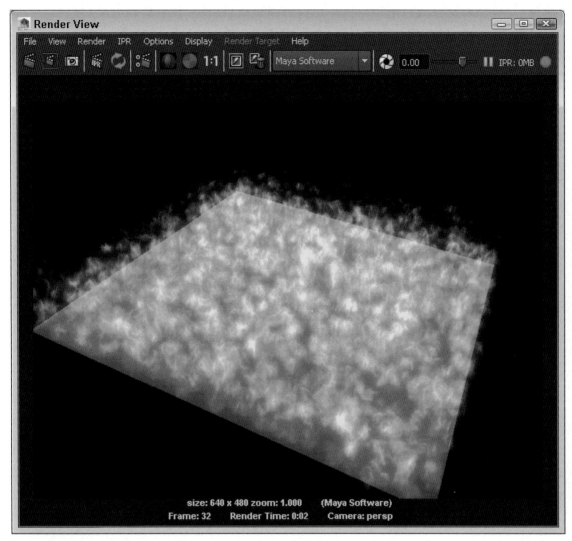

Figure 12-36
Rendered fire

Creating Fireworks

The Fireworks effect doesn't require an object be selected. The Effects, Create Fireworks adds a simple emitter to the scene. Dragging the Time Slider launches and displays the fireworks. Use the various attribute nodes to change the fireworks' colors and attributes. Figure 12-37 shows some rendered fireworks.

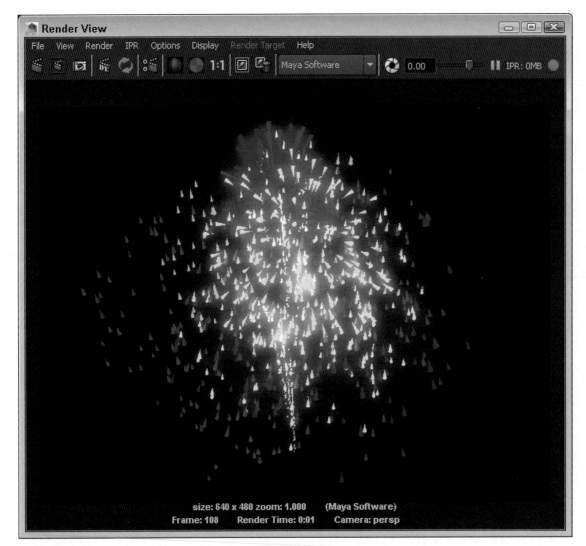

Figure 12-37
Fireworks

Creating Lightning

The Create Lightning effect can extend between several objects. The Lightning Options dialog box lets you specify whether the lightning spreads between all objects, in order, or from the first object. You can also specify the thickness, spread, and glow intensity of the lightening. Figure 12-38 shows a lightning arc between two cone objects.

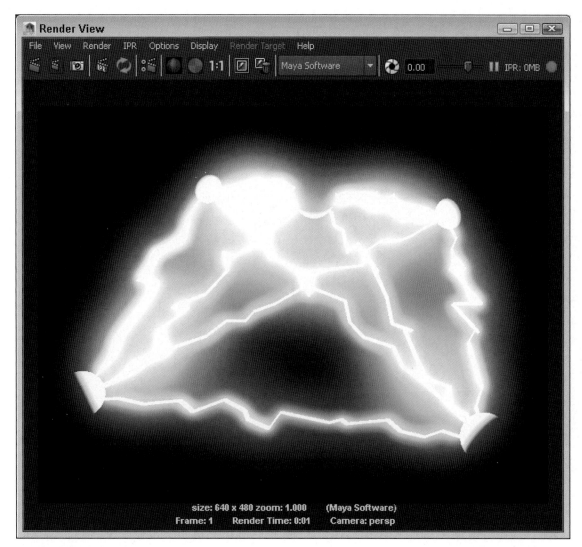

Figure 12-38
A lightning arc

Shattering Objects

The Create Shatter effect divides the selected objects into multiple separate objects, as shown in Figure 12-39. The Create Shatter Effect Options dialog box includes three tabs for Surface Shatter, Solid Shatter, and Crack Shatter. You can also specify the number of pieces that the object is broken into and the jaggedness of the shards.

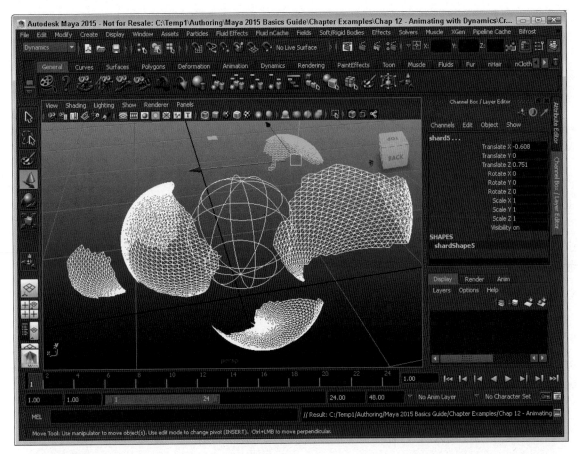

Figure 12-39
Shattered objects

Flowing Along a Curve

The Create Curve Flow effect lets you select a NURBS curve, and particle emitters are placed along the curve causing particles to follow the curve, as shown in Figure 12-40. Attributes for this effect include an Emission Rate, Particle Lifespan, and Speed. The Create Surface Flow effect allows particles to flow over a NURBS surface.

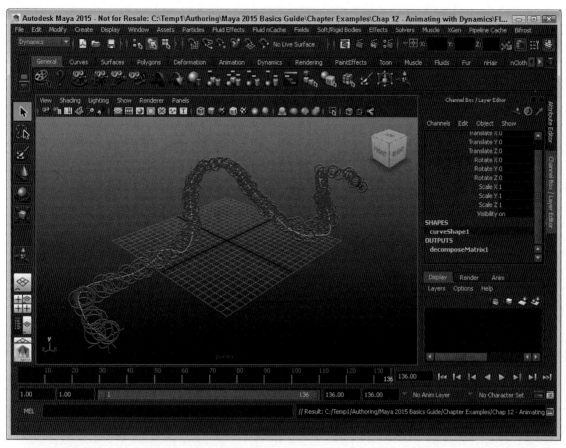

Figure 12-40
Particles flowing along a curve

Lesson 12.6-Tutorial 1: Create a Fire Effect

1. Create a polygon cylinder object with the Create, Polygon Primitives, Cylinder menu command.

2. Scale and rotate the cylinder object with the Scale tool to look like a log.

3. Select the Effects, Create Fire menu command.

4. Drag the Time Slider to see the flames rise.

   The cylinder object is engulfed in fire, as shown in Figure 12-41.

5. Select File, Save Scene As and save the file as **Log on fire.mb**.

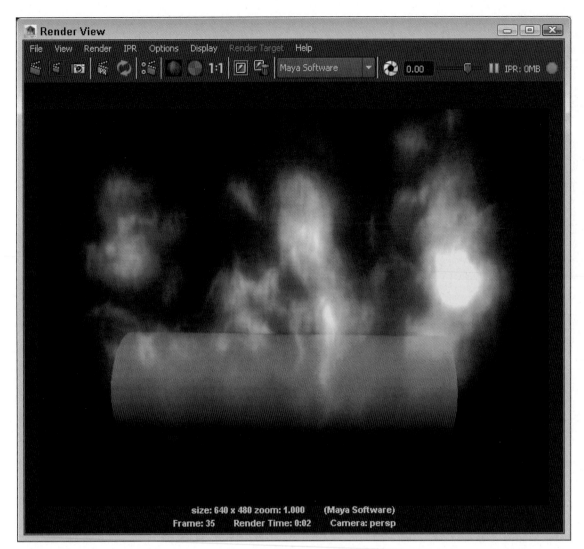

Figure 12-41
Fire effect

Lesson 12.6-Tutorial 2: Create Fireworks

1. Select the Effects, Create Fireworks menu command.

2. Enter a value of 200 in the End frame field for the Range Slider.

3. Drag the Range Slider to show the full 200 frames.

4. Click the Play Forwards button to see the fireworks.

    The fireworks explode on the view panel, as shown in Figure 12-42.

5. Select File, Save Scene As and save the file as **Fireworks.mb**.

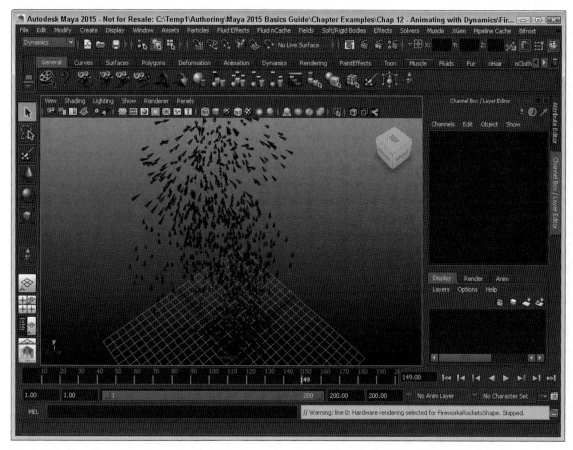

Figure 12-42
Fireworks

Lesson 12.6-Tutorial 3: Create Lightning

1. Create five NURBS sphere objects with the Create, NURBS Primitives, Sphere menu command.

2. Use the Move tool to move the five spheres away from each other and the center sphere above the rest.

3. Select all of the spheres and choose the Effects, Create Lightning menu command.

   Lightning objects and arcs connect each of the spheres, as shown in Figure 12-43.

4. Select File, Save Scene As and save the file as **Lightning.mb**.

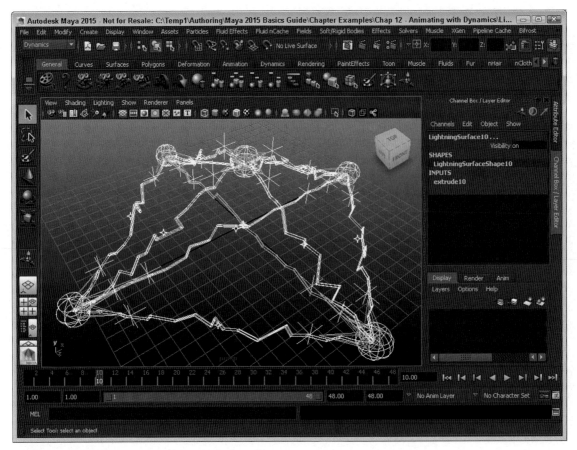

Figure 12-43
Lightning

Lesson 12.6-Tutorial 4: Create Curve Flow

1. Select the Create, Pencil Curve Tool menu command and draw in the view panel.

2. With the curve selected, choose the Effects, Create Curve Flow menu command.

3. In the Channel Box, set the Emission Rate to 1000.

4. Drag the Time Slider.

    The particles flow along the curve, as shown in Figure 12-44.

5. Select File, Save Scene As, and save the file as **Curve flow.mb**.

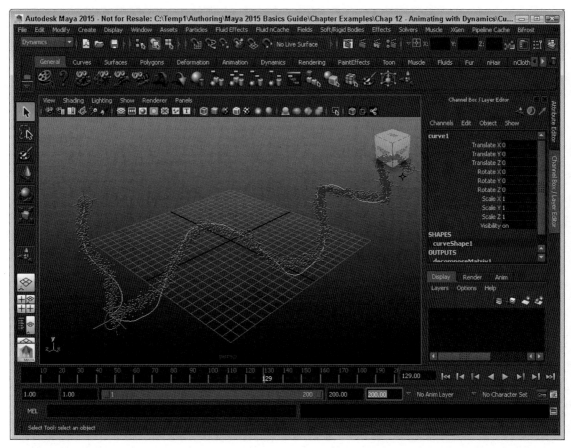

Figure 12-44
Curve flow

Lesson 12.7: Use Cloth and Fluids

Cloth and fluids are advanced features that can add a lot to the realism to a character or a scene. Each cloth and fluid object that is created automatically has all the controls and properties needed to dynamically simulate its motion. Both require a significant amount of computing power and should be used with restraint. Cloth added to a scene is automatically draped over collision objects and fluids include all the characteristics to create waves, splashes, and settling. You can also use fluids to create gaseous phenomenon such as clouds, fire, and explosions.

Note

The Cloth and Fluid Effects features are accessed from the nDynamics menu set.

Creating Cloth

There are several types of cloth objects that can you create. The simplest is to use the nMesh, Create nCloth menu command. This command converts the selected object into a cloth object. Cloth objects are automatically tessellated, as shown in Figure 12-45. You can create cloth objects, called *panels*, from a set of curves, and you can stitch several panels together to create a garment. Curves must be co-planar and closed in order to used to make a panel.

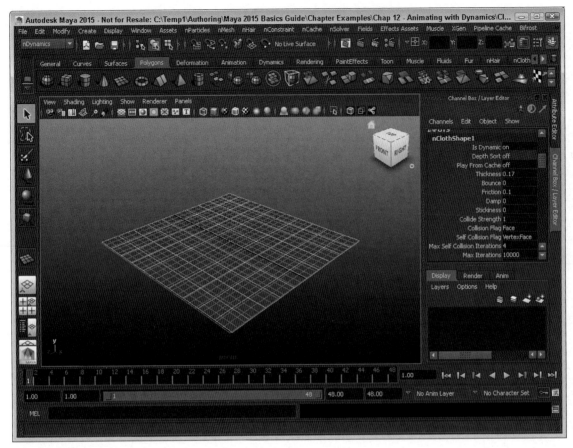

Figure 12-45
Cloth object and attributes

Creating a Cloth Collision Object

The dynamics of cloth aren't readily visible until the cloth object is draped over a collision object. To create a cloth collision object, simply select the object or objects that the cloth will be draped over and choose the nMesh, Create Passive Collider menu command. Once a collision object has been defined, you can drag the Time Slider and each frame of the cloth simulation is calculated and displayed. Figure 12-46 shows a simple cloth plane draped over a sphere collision object. Collision objects can be removed using the Cloth, Remove Collision Object menu command. You can add or remove specific objects from the collision set using the Cloth, Cloth Object Debug menu options.

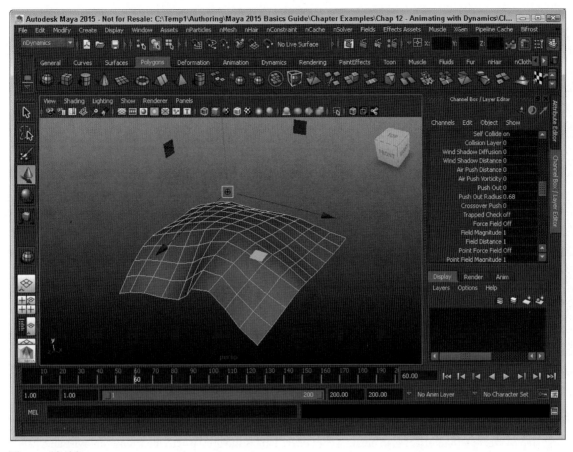

Figure 12-46
Cloth plane object draped over a collision sphere

Setting Cloth Object Properties

For the selected cloth object, you can set its physical properties using the nClothShape node in the Attribute Editor, as shown in Figure 12-47. The properties found here include Bend Resistance, Bend Rate, Stretch Resistance, Scale, Density, Thickness, Friction, and so on. You can add multiple property nodes to a cloth object using the Simulation, Properties, Create Cloth Property menu command. You can also paint cloth properties on the cloth object using the Simulation, Properties, Paint Cloth Properties tool. Once a cloth property has been changed, you need to delete the current simulation cache before the new dynamic motion is displayed. You can delete the current cache using the Simulation, Delete Cache menu command.

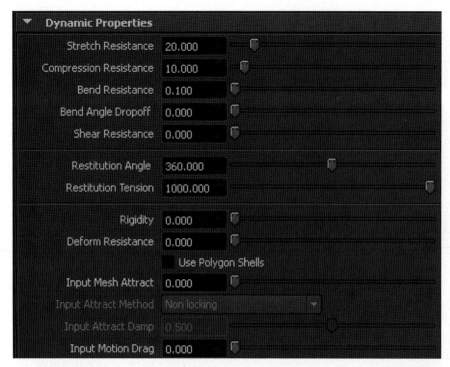

Figure 12-47
Cloth properties

Creating a Fluid Container

The first step to create a fluid effect is to create a container. This is the area where the fluids can exist and provides a boundary for the fluid. Each cell of the container is called a **voxel**. The number of voxels in a container determine the resolution of the fluid object. The Fluid Effects menu (located in the Dynamics menu set) includes commands for creating 2D and 3D containers. A 2D container has only one row of voxels. You can make a fluid collide with geometry objects by selecting both the fluid and the object and choosing the Fluid Effects, Make Collide menu command.

Creating a Fluid Emitter

An **fluid emitter** is similar to a particle emitter, except it is the source of the fluid. It must be located within the container. Dragging the Time Slider causes the defined fluid to flow into the existing container. As the fluid collides with the walls of the container, it flows back and forth as the container is slowly filled. You can add an emitter to a selected container using the Fluid Effects, Add/Edit Contents, Emitter menu command. There are also menu commands for creating a container and an emitter at once. Figure 12-48 shows a container being filled with fluid. Various emitter types are available including Omni, Surface, Curve, and Volume. Objects can also be used as emitters.

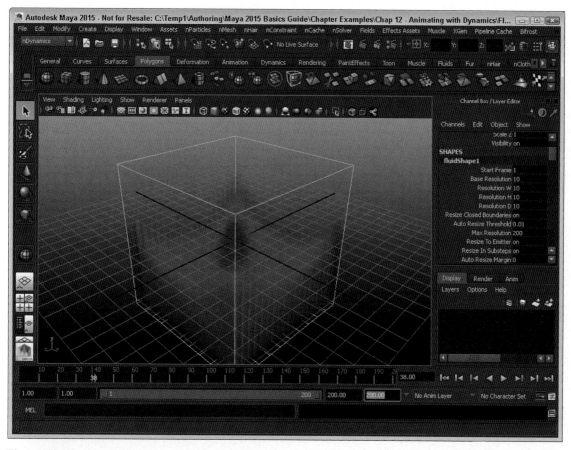

Figure 12-48
A 3D container being filled with fluid

Changing Fluid Properties

The type of fluid or gas that is created from a fluid emitter depends on the fluid's properties. The properties available for fluids are located in the Attribute Editor and include Density, Viscosity, Friction, Buoyancy, Dissipation, Turbulence, Temperature, Fuel, Color, Opacity, and so on. Once a property has changed, you can see the updated results immediately by dragging the Time Slider. You can also change the general shape of the fluid by scaling and sizing the container.

Creating Oceans and Ponds

The Fluid Effects menu includes two specialized water objects for creating oceans and ponds. The ocean object is created using the Fluid Effects, Ocean, Create Ocean menu command, and similar commands for a pond object. You can add a preview pane to an ocean object to see its effect in a local area. The Create Wake menu command adds waves, turbulence, and/or ripples to the ocean and pond objects. The menus can also add floating objects, buoys, and boats to the scene. Figure 12-49 shows an ocean object with a preview pane and a buoy object.

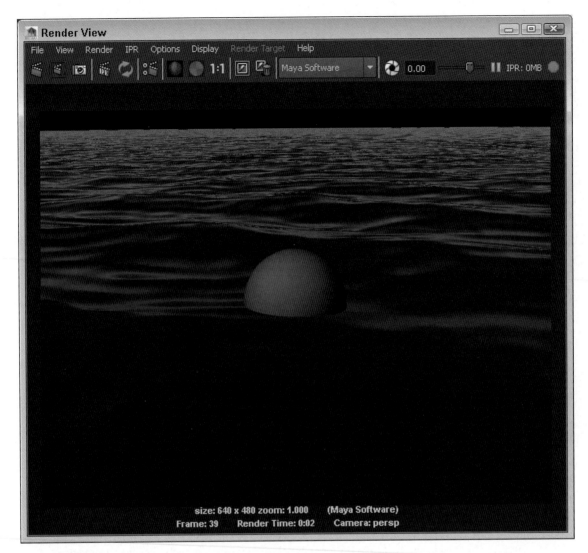

Figure 12-49
Ocean object with buoy

Lesson 12.7-Tutorial 1: Drape a Tablecloth

1. Select the File, Open Scene menu command, locate and open the Table.mb file.

2. Select the Create, Polygon Primitives, Plane menu command to create a polygon plane object.

3. Move and scale the plane object so it is centered above the table. Be sure to position the plane object so it doesn't intersect with the table.

4. In the Channel Box, click on the polyPlane1 node and change the Subdivisions Width and Height values to 50 each.

   Increasing the resolution of the plane object enables the cloth simulation to better approximate its motion accurately.

5. Select the Cloth menu set from the drop-down list and, with the plane object selected, choose the Cloth, Create Cloth Object menu command.

   The cloth object is tessellated and divided into triangles.

6. Select the table top object and choose the Cloth, Create Collision Object menu command.

Only the table top object was selected in order to speed up the cloth calculations. The more polygons involved in the calculations, the slower it takes to compute a solution.

7. In the Animation Controls, click the Step Forward One Frame button several times.

Each step will take some time to compute, but the plane object slowly descends and drapes over the table.

8. With the plane object selected, open the Attribute Editor and select the cpDefaultProperty node. Change the U and V Bend Resistance values to 1.0 and the U and V Bend Rate values to 2.0.

The default cloth material is like a thick rubber, but changing these values makes the cloth act more like fabric.

9. Drag the Time Slider back to Frame 1 and select the Simulation, Delete Cache menu command. Then slowly drag the Time Slider back up to Frame 24 allowing for time to compute each frame.

Because the default simulation is still saved in the cache, you need to delete the cache and rewind the frames before the updated simulation is displayed. Figure 12-50 shows the resulting tablecloth draped over a table.

10. Select File, Save Scene As and save the file as **Table with tablecloth.mb**.

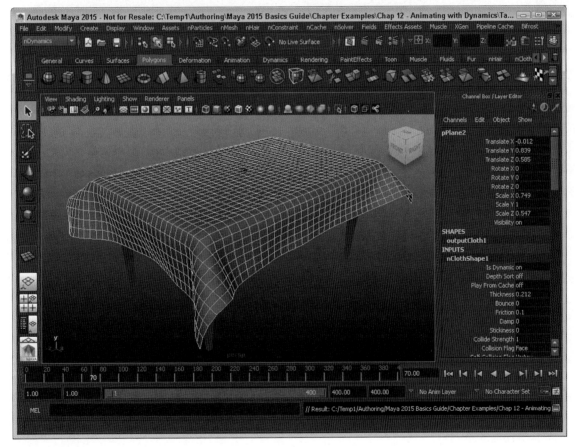

Figure 12-50
Table with tablecloth

Lesson 12.7-Tutorial 2: Fill a Container

1. Select the Dynamics menu set from the drop-down list.

2. Select the Fluid Effects, Create 3D Container with Emitter menu command.

A cubic container with an emitter is added to the scene.

3.   Open the Attribute Editor and select the fluidEmitter1 node. Change the Density/Voxel/Sec value to 2,000, and then enable the Emit Fluid Color option and set the Fluid Color to a dark red.

When the Emit Fluid Color option is selected, a dialog box appears asking if you want to set the color of the dynamic grid. Press the Set to Dynamic button.

4.   In the Attribute Editor, select the fluidShape1 node. In the Dynamic Simulation section, change the Gravity value to -9.8, and the Viscosity to 0.25.

Making the Gravity value negative reverses the direction of gravity and the increased viscosity causes the fluid to move around less.

5.   Drag the Time Slider to see the fluid move within the container.

The fluid moves downward under the effect of gravity and then fills the container, as shown in Figure 12-51.

6.   Select File, Save Scene As and save the file as **Fluid container.mb**.

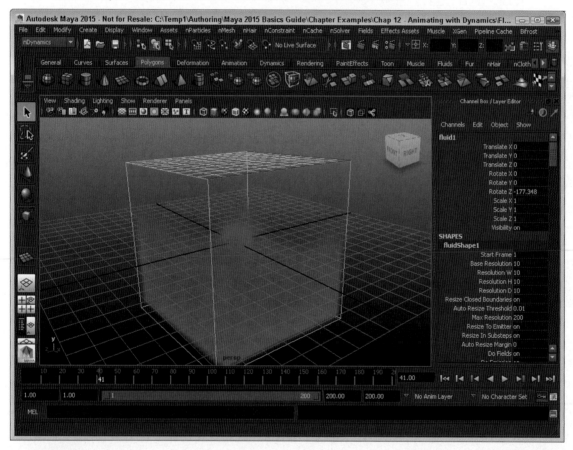

Figure 12-51
Fluid filling a container

Lesson 12.7-Tutorial 3: Create a Pond with Ripples

1.   Select the Dynamics menu set from the drop-down list.

2.   Select the Fluid Effects, Pond, Create Pond menu command.

A pond object is added to the scene.

3. Select the Fluid Effects, Pond, Create Wake menu command.

   A spherical icon is added to the center of the pond object.

4. Drag the Time Slider to Frame 48.

   Ripples appear in the pond, as shown in Figure 12-52.

5. Select File, Save Scene As and save the file as **Pond with ripples.mb**.

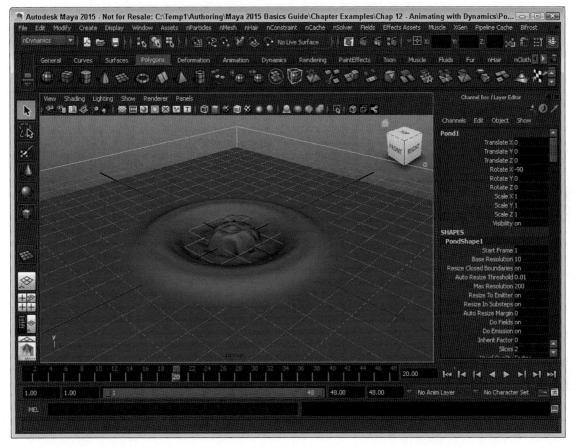

Figure 12-52
Pond with ripples

Chapter Summary

This chapter covers the basics of animating with dynamics. Creating and manipulating particles was discussed, including the various particle types, and particle attributes. You can use objects as particles with the Instancing feature. An emitter is a source that the particles start from. Several emitter types are available and objects can also act as particle emitters. Once a particle system is added to the scene, its motion is controlled using fields and goals. You can make particles collide with each other and with objects in the scene. Using constraints, you can link objects that are moving dynamically to one another or to constrained nails, pins, hinges, and barriers. The Effects features create special effects such as fire, lightning, and particle flow. Included in Maya Unlimited are features for working with dynamic cloth and fluid effects. Cloth objects are draped over collision objects under the effect of gravity. Fluid objects are created using an emitter within a container. Ocean and pond objects are specialized fluid objects that you can create in Maya.

What You Have Learned

In this chapter, you learned

* How to create a set of particles.

* How to set the particle count.

* How to set the particle lifespan and render type.

* How to create particle instances.

* How to cycle through different particle instances.

* How to create an emitter.

* How to change the emitter type.

* How to use an object as an emitter.

* How to add a field to the scene and connect an object to it.

* How to change field attributes.

* How to create a goal.

* How to enable particle collisions.

* How to respond to a collision event.

* How to create a rigid body object.

* How to create a soft body object.

* How to constrain motion with constraints.

* How to use nail, pin, hinge, barrier, and spring constraints.

* How to create fire and smoke.

* How to create fireworks and lightning.

* How to shatter objects.

* How to create and define cloth.

* How to specify a cloth collision object.

* How to create fluid containers and emitters.

* How to change fluid properties.

* How to create ocean and pond objects.

Key Terms From This Chapter

* **Dynamics.** A type of animation where the keyframes are computed using physics calculations after assigning physical properties to the scene objects.

<h1>Chapter 13</h1>

<h1>Rendering a Scene</h1>

IN THIS CHAPTER

13.1 Configure the render process.

13.2 Use special rendering features.

13.3 Use the Render View window.

13.4 Create a final render.

13.5 Render with Maya Vector and Mental Ray.

After you've modeled and animated your scene, you're ready for the rendering process. **Rendering** is where the software computes all of the colors, highlights, shadows, and motions of all the objects in the scene to produce an image or a movie file.

You can render your scenes using several methods, including software, hardware, vector, and Mental Ray. The Render, Render Using menu command allows you to choose which render method to use.

Before rendering, you'll need to configure the renderer. You can do this in the **Render Global Settings dialog box,** which you can open using the Window, Rendering Editors, Render Globals menu command. The Render Global Settings dialog box includes settings for the path and name of the render file. You can also set the destination file format and the image resolution.

The Render Global Settings dialog box also includes a tabbed panel with settings for the rendering method that is selected. For the software rendering solution, you can enable special rendering features such as **raytracing, motion blur,** and environment **fog**.

You can preview your renders using the Render View window, which opens automatically when you use the Render, Render Current View menu command. The Render View window also includes an interactive mode known as **Interactive Photorealistic Rendering** (IPR). Using this mode, you can get automatic scene updates as the lighting and shading attributes are changed.

The Render, Batch Render menu command renders the selected view panel using the settings found in the Render Global Settings dialog box.

The **Maya Vector** rendering method strips all scene objects of their details and renders scenes using solid black lines and filled objects reminiscent of a cartoon. For images destined for the Web, this is a good choice. It can export images and animations to the SWF format.

The **Mental Ray** renderer includes many additional lighting-based features, such as caustics, global illumination, and a final render, which enables scenes to be rendered with much more detail. The Mental Ray renderer also supports many proprietary materials, textures, and lights that you can use within your scene.

Lesson 13.1: Configure the Render Process

Before rendering a scene, you should check the rendering settings found in the Render Global Settings dialog box, shown in Figure 13-1. You can open this dialog box using the Window, Rendering Editors, Render Globals menu command. The dialog box includes two tabbed panels—Common and another tab named after the selected renderer.

Tip

You can also open the Render Global Settings dialog box by clicking on the Display Render Globals button in the Status Line.

Figure 13-1
The Render Settings dialog box

Choosing a Renderer

You can render scenes using Maya Software, which uses the computer's CPU, using Maya Hardware, which uses the computer's video card, or by using a specialized plug-in renderer, such as Maya Vector or Mental Ray. The advantage of hardware rendering is that it typically is much faster than rendering with a software solution, but this is dependent on the power of your installed video card. You can switch between the hardware and software options using the Render, Render Using menu command or by selecting the renderer in the Render Using drop-down list at the top of the Render Global Settings dialog box. In the Preferences dialog box, you can set which renderer should be used by default.

Saving Render Presets

You can save all your changes to the Render Global Settings dialog box as a preset that can be easily reloaded. To save a preset, use the Presets, Save Settings as Preset menu command in the Render Settings dialog box. You can then reload your saved presets using the Presets, Load Presets menu command.

Changing a File Name

At the top of the Render Global Settings dialog box, the current path and file name for the current project are listed. This defines where the rendered image is saved and what its name is. You can change the project path using the File, Project, Set menu command. The file name is the same name as the saved file unless you enter a new name in the File Name Prefix field.

Changing File Format

Maya can save rendered images to several different formats, including Maya IFF, Wavefront (RLA), Softimage (PIC), Softimage Depth (ZPIC), Alias, SGI, (RGB) TIFF, JPEG, Targa (TGA), Windows Bitmap (BMP), Dassault, Portable Pixmap (PPM), PostScript (PS), Encapsulated PostScript (EPS), Quantel, and HDR. You can select each of these formats in the Render Global Settings dialog box. You can also select which channels—including RGB, Alpha, and Depth—are saved with the image file. If the format doesn't support the various channels, the channels are saved as a separate file along with the RGB image file.

Changing Camera View and Resolution

The Camera drop-down list lets you select which camera view is used to render the scene. The Image Size section, shown in Figure 13-2, includes a number of settings that define the resolution of the rendered image. You can select from a number of presets or specify custom dimensions.

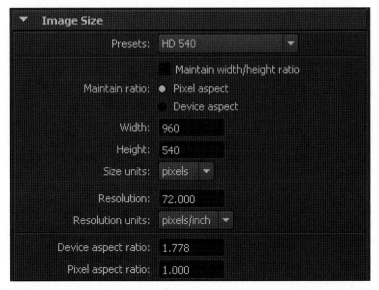

Figure 13-2
Image Size section

Using render layers

At the top of the Layer Editor (positioned below the Channel Box) are options for dividing the scene into Display layers and Render layers. Render layers allow you to specify different render settings for each layer. This approach lets you apply special render effects like motion blur to a single render layer that only includes those objects that render the render effect like birds flying through the scene. Each separate render layer can then be composited together to create the final image.

Lesson 13.1-Tutorial 1: Set Render Settings

1. Select the Window, Rendering Editor, Render Globals menu command.

    The Render Global Settings dialog box opens.

2. In the Render Using drop-down list, select Maya Software.

    A tab labeled Maya Software appears in the Render Global Settings dialog box.

3. Select the Maya IFF image format.

4. Choose the Perspective Camera in the Camera drop-down list.

5. In the Image Size section, choose the Targa NTSC Resolution Preset.

    The Width and Height values are updated.

6. Click the Close button to close the Render Global Settings dialog box.

Lesson 13.1-Tutorial 2: Change the Rendering Path

1. Select the Window, Rendering Editor, Render Globals menu command.

2. Select the File, Project, Set menu command.

    A Browse to Folder dialog box opens.

3. Locate the folder where you want to save the rendered scene to and click the OK button.

    The path in the Render Global Settings dialog box is updated to this new path.

Lesson 13.2: Use Special Rendering Features

On the Maya Software tab of the Render Global Settings dialog box are several sections that you can use to set the quality and special rendering features available in Maya, as shown in Figure 13-3. The Quality settings are for the overall quality of the render and the some of the special rendering features include Raytracing, and Motion Blur.

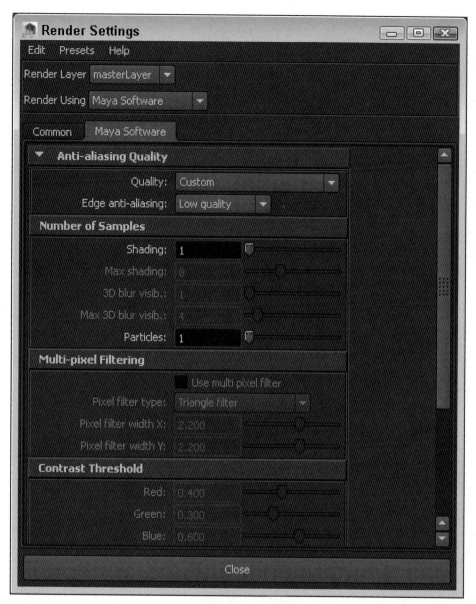

Figure 13-3
Maya software rendering settings

Adjusting Render Quality

At the top of the Maya Software tab in the Render Global Settings dialog box you can select one of several presets for the image quality and edge anti-aliasing. The Quality options include Custom, Preview, Intermediate, Production, Contrast Sensitive, and 3D Motion Blur. The Edge Anti-aliasing options include Low, Medium, High, and Highest. Higher-quality and anti-alias settings require more time to render. Figure 13-4 shows a simple scene rendered at the Preview Quality setting and Figure 13-5 shows the same scene rendered using the Production Quality setting. Notice how the edges appear jagged in the preview rendering because the anti-aliasing is set so low.

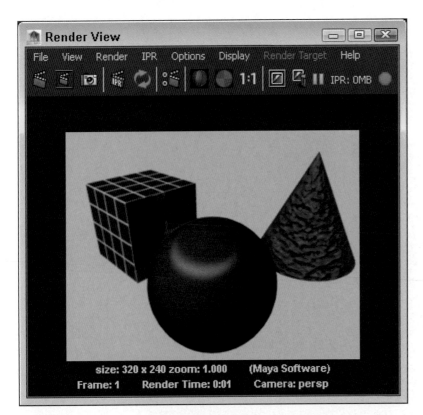

Figure 13-4
Scene rendered using the Preview Quality setting

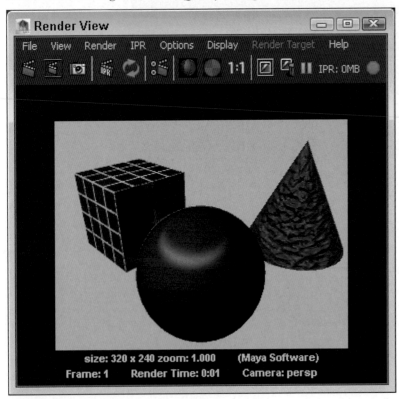

Figure 13-5
Scene rendered using the Production Quality setting

Enabling Raytracing

You can enable the Raytracing option in the Raytracing Quality section of the Render Global Settings dialog box, shown in Figure 13-6. Once raytracing is enabled, you can set the number of times a light ray is reflected, refracted, and able to cause a shadow. If you've enabled raytraced shadows for any of your lights, you'll need to enable raytracing here to see the shadows.

Figure 13-6
Raytracing settings

Enabling Motion Blur

Motion blur renders objects that move quickly through an animated scene blurred. This gives the illusion that the objects are moving fast. You can compute motion blur in 3D or in 2D (which is much quicker) and you can set the blur length and sharpness. Figure 13-7 shows the Motion Blur section of the Render Global Settings dialog box.

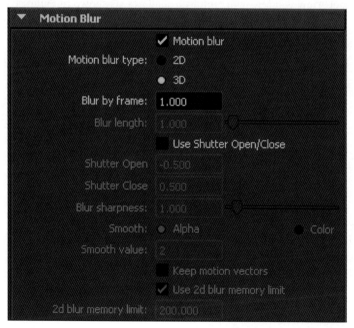

Figure 13-7
Motion Blur settings

Adding Environment Fog

Within the Render Options section of the Render Global Settings dialog box is a field where you can enable Environment Fog. Clicking on the Create Render Node button adds the Environment Fog node to the scene. Once added, you can change its attributes—including its color, saturation distance, and height—in the Attribute Editor.

Lesson 13.2-Tutorial 1: Change the Render Quality

1. Select the Window, Rendering Editor, Render Globals menu command.

2. Enable the Maya Software option in the Render Using drop-down list at the top of the dialog box.

3. Click on the Maya Software tab.

    Change the Quality setting to Production Quality.

4. The Edge Anti-aliasing setting is automatically changed to the Highest Quality setting.

Lesson 13.2-Tutorial 2: Enable Raytracing

1. Select the File, Open Scene menu command, locate and open the Glass on table.mb file.

2. Select the Point light in front of the glass object and open the Attribute Editor.

3. In the Shadows section, enable the Use Ray Trace Shadows option.

4. Select the Window, Rendering Editor, Render Globals menu command.

5. Enable the Maya Software option in the Render Using drop-down list at the top of the dialog box.

6. Click on the Maya Software tab.

7. Open the Raytracing Quality section and enable the Raytracing option.

8. Right-click on the Perspective view panel and select the Render, Render Current Frame menu command.

    The scene is rendered in the Render View window with raytraced shadows, as shown in Figure 13-8.

9. Select File, Save Scene As, and save the file as **Raytraced glass.mb**.

Figure 13-8
Raytraced glass

Lesson 13.2-Tutorial 3: Enable Motion Blur

1. Select the File, Open Scene menu command, locate and open the Simple animated rocket.mb file.

2. Drag the Frame Slider to Frame 10.

3. Select the Window, Rendering Editor, Render Globals menu command.

4. Enable the Maya Software option in the Render Using drop-down list at the top of the dialog box.

5. Click on the Maya Software tab.

6. In the Anti-aliasing Quality section, select the 3D Motion Blur Production option in the Quality drop-down list.

7. Open the Motion Blur section and enable the Motion Blur and the 3D options. Set the Blur by Frame to 1.0.

8. Right-click on the Perspective view panel to select it and select the Render, Render Current Frame menu command.

    The scene is rendered in the Render View window. The rocket is blurred as it zooms past the camera, as shown in Figure 13-9.

9. Select File, Save Scene As and save the file as **Motion blur rocket.mb**.

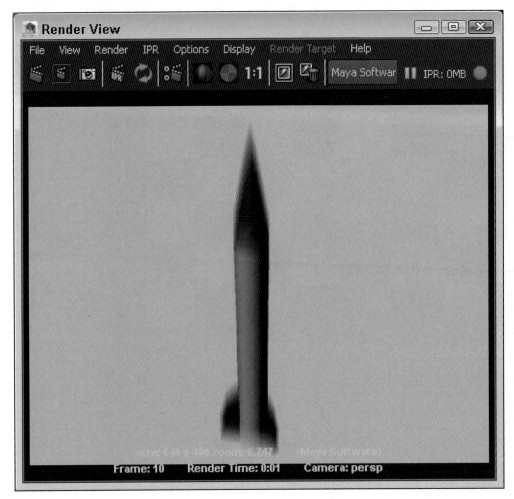

Figure 13-9
Motion blurred rocket

Lesson 13.2-Tutorial 4: Add Environment Fog

1. Select the File, Open Scene menu command, locate and open the Hot air balloon.mb file.

2. Select the Window, Rendering Editor, Render Globals menu command.

3. Enable the Maya Software option in the Render Using drop-down list at the top of the dialog box.

4. Click on the Maya Software tab.

5. Open the Render Options section and click the Create Render Node button next to the Environment Fog field.

   An Environment Fog node is automatically added to the scene and its attributes are displayed in the Attribute Editor.

6. Right-click on the Perspective view panel and select the Render, Render Current Frame menu command.

   The scene is rendered in the Render View window with environment fog added to the scene, as shown in Figure 13-10.

7. Select File, Save Scene As and save the file as **Balloon in fog.mb**.

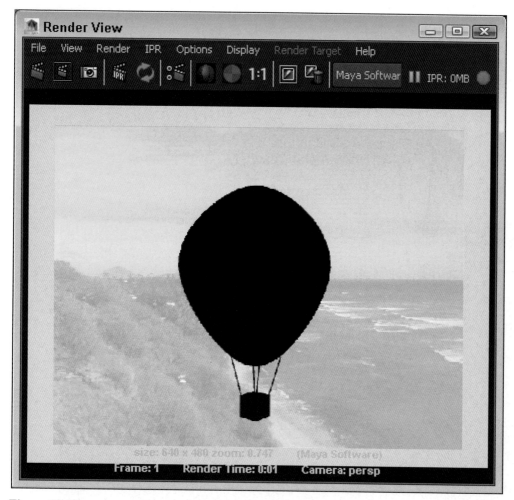

Figure 13-10
Balloon in the fog

Lesson 13.3: Use the Render View Window

When the Render, Render Current Frame menu command is used, the Render Frame window is opened automatically, but you can open this window at any time with the Window, Rendering Editors, Render View menu command.

Opening the Render View

Selecting the Render, Render Current Frame menu command or the Render, Redo Previous Render menu command causes the Render View window, shown in Figure 13-11, to open and render the active view panel. The Render View window includes a menu and toolbar.

Note

If no view panel is active, a simple warning dialog box will ask you to select a view panel to render.

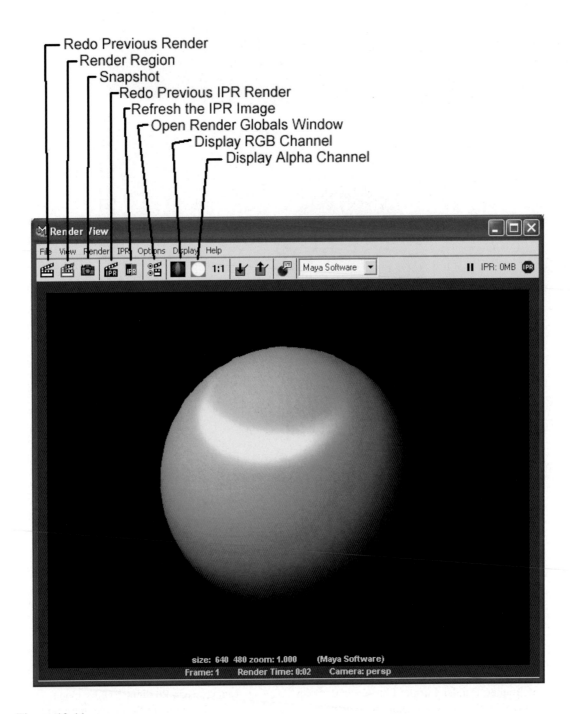

Redo Previous Render
Render Region
Snapshot
Redo Previous IPR Render
Refresh the IPR Image
Open Render Globals Window
Display RGB Channel
Display Alpha Channel

Figure 13-11
Render View window

Rendering a Region

With the Render View window open, you can drag within the window to define a region to be rendered. This region is outlined in red, as shown in Figure 13-12. Selecting the Render, Render Region menu command in the Render View window or clicking the Render Region button in the Render View window re-renders just the defined region. You can reset the region to the entire view using the View, Reset Region Marquee menu command.

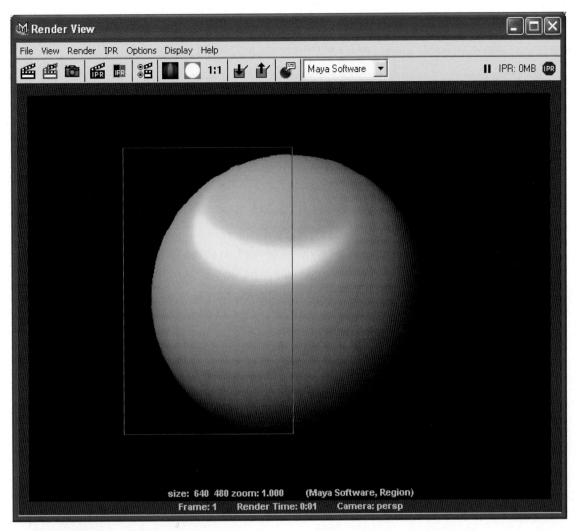

Figure 13-12
The Render region

Using Interactive Photorealistic Rendering (IPR)

The Render View window can render the current scene in an interactive mode called *Interactive Photorealistic Rendering* (IPR). In this mode, you can change object materials, textures, and scene lights, and the Render View window is updated. You can initialize this mode using the IPR, Redo Previous IPR Render menu command. Once in IPR mode, you can select a region that can be tuned (or updated). With a region selected, the IPR view automatically updates the region every time a light or shading attribute is changed. You can also update the entire image using the IPR, Refresh IPR Image menu command.

Note

> The IPR render mode keeps render data in local memory, and the amount used is displayed at the left end of the toolbar.

Saving Rendered Images

You can save any image rendered to the Render View window using the File, Save Image window menu command. This command opens a file dialog box in which you can name the file and select the image format to use. You can also save and re-open IRP files.

Lesson 13.3-Tutorial 1: Render a Region

1. Create a NURBS sphere with the Create, NURBS Primitives, Sphere menu command.

2. Select the Lighting/Shading, Assign New Material, Anisotropic menu command.

3. Click on the Color swatch in the Attribute Editor and select a bright red color.

4. Right-click on the Perspective view panel and select the Render, Render Current Frame menu command.

    The scene is rendered in the Render View window.

5. Drag with the mouse inside the Render View window to define a tuning region.

6. Click again on the Color swatch in the Attribute Editor and change the color to yellow. Then click the Render Region button again.

    As the Color attribute is changed, the region is updated, as shown in Figure 13-13.

7. Select File, Save Scene As and save the file as **Render region.mb**.

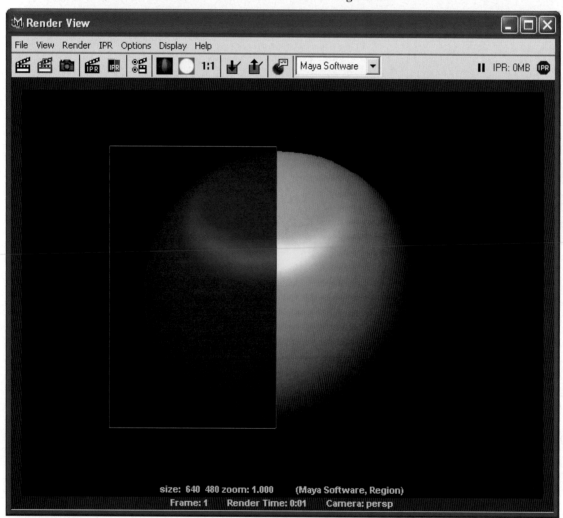

Figure 13-13
A Render region

Lesson 13.3-Tutorial 2: Use IPR Rendering

1. Select the File, Open Scene menu command to open the Geometric flower.mb file.

2. Right-click on the Perspective view panel and select the Render, IPR Render Current Frame menu command.

   The scene is rendered in the Render View window in IPR mode.

3. Drag with the mouse inside the Render View window to define a tuning region.

4. Select the object in the view panel, and then in the Attribute Editor, select the blinn1 node. In the Special Effects section, set the Glow Intensity to 0.5.

   As the Glow Intensity attribute is changed, the tuning region is updated, as shown in Figure 13-13.

5. Select File, Save Scene As and save the file as **IPR Render.mb**.

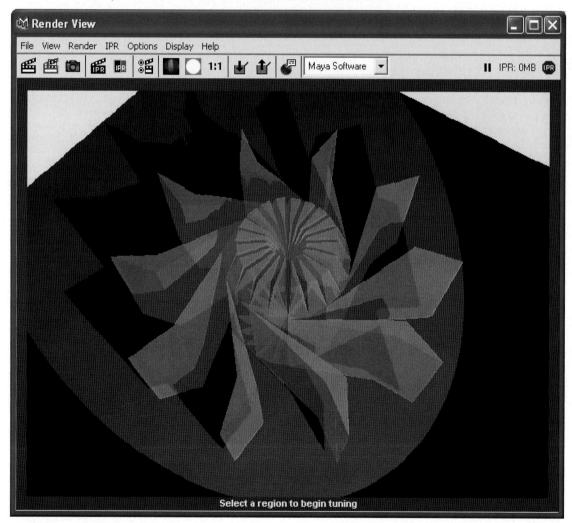

Figure 13-14
An IPR render

Lesson 13.4: Create a Final Render

The final step for producing output is to render a final version of the file. This file can then be composited with other images to create the final work. You typically do the compositing in another package.

Rendering a Single Frame

To render a single frame (which is the default), make sure that a single frame format is selected in the Render Global Settings dialog box, and then select Render, Render Current Frame and the resulting frame is rendered with the given settings to the Render View window.

Rendering an Animation Sequence

To render a sequence of frames, just select any of the available formats in the Render Settings dialog box that isn't a single frame format. This renders each frame of the animation as a separate file designated by a frame number. Then select Render, Render Current Frame and the resulting frame is rendered with the given settings to the Render View window.

Using Batch Rendering

The Render, Batch Render menu command renders the current scene using the defined settings. This command saves the file to the hard disk so that you can continue working in Maya on the scene. You can view the progress of the batch rendering process in the Help Line at the bottom of the interface.

Lesson 13.4-Tutorial 1: Render an Animation

1. Select the File, Open Scene menu command, locate and open the Simple animated rocket.mb file.

2. Select the Window, Rendering Editors, Render Globals menu command.

3. Enable the Maya Software option in the Render Using drop-down list at the top of the dialog box.

4. Select the File, Project, Set menu command. Choose the folder in which you want to save the rendered files and click the OK button.

5. Type the name **rocket** in the File Name Prefix field.

6. Select the name.#.ext option in the Frame/Animation Ext field.

7. Set the End Frame to 25.

   Selecting the name.#.ext option causes each frame of the animation to be rendered and saved with the prefix name followed by the frame number and the file extension. Figure 13-15 shows the Render Global Settings dialog box.

Tip

> If you want to save the file using a video format such as AVI, you don't need to specify a numbering format.

8. In the Image Size section, choose the 320*240 Preset.

9. Select the Maya Software tab.

10. In the Anti-aliasing Quality section, select the 3D Motion Blur Production option in the Quality drop-down list.

11. Open the Motion Blur section and enable the Motion Blur and the 3D options. Set the Blur by Frame to 1.0.

12. Right-click on the Perspective view and choose the Render, Render Current Frame menu command.

    The scene is rendered automatically and the rendered files saved to the designated path.

13. Select File, Save Scene As and save the file as **Rendered rocket.mb**.

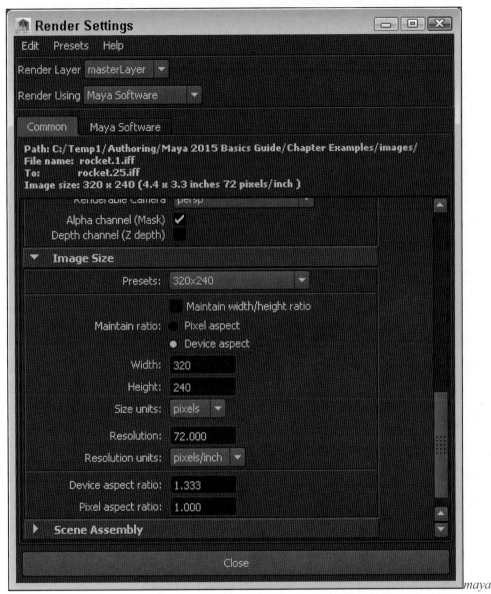

maya

Figure 13-15
Rendering an animation

Lesson 13.5: Render with Maya Vector and Mental Ray

In addition to the Maya Software and Maya Hardware rendering methods, Maya also includes two other rendering methods—Maya Vector and Mental Ray. You can use the Maya Vector renderer to reduce a scene to simple vector-based lines like a cartoon. Mental Ray is an advanced rendering engine that includes many additional settings, creating some amazing output. You can select each of these rendering methods by using the Render, Render Using menu.

Using Maya Vector

The Maya Vector rendering method lets you render and export scenes to Macromedia's Flash (SWF) format for use on the Web. The vector settings in the Render Global Settings dialog box include controls for determining how the edges and fills look. For fill objects, you can choose to use one, two, four, or full colors and choose whether shadows and highlights are included. For edges, you can set the edge weight, style, and color. Figure 13-16 shows the Maya Vector settings, and Figure 13-17 shows several objects rendered using the Maya Vector rendering method.

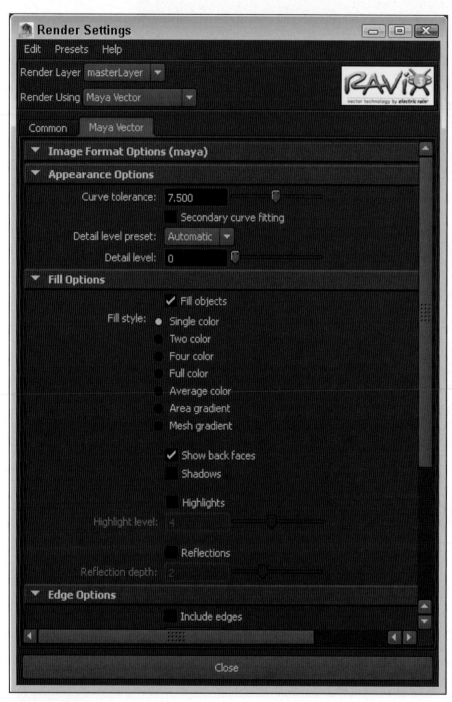

Figure 13-16
Maya Vector settings

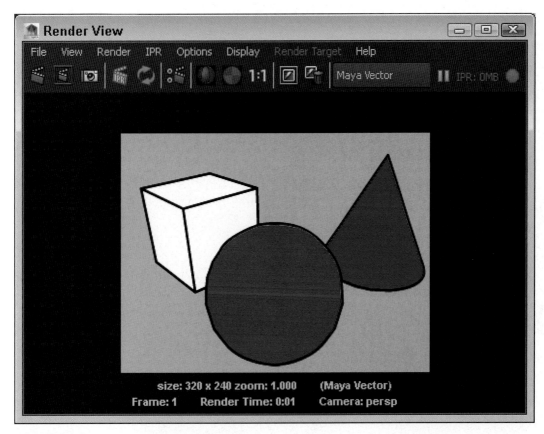

Figure 13-17
A Maya Vector rendered scene

Using Mental Ray

The Mental Ray rendering method offers additional rendering features such as Advanced Raytracing, Caustics and Global Illumination, Final Gather, and Image Based Lighting. These feature different ways to compute how light moves around the scene between the objects. With many of these features enabled, rendering with Mental Ray can take a considerable amount of time even for the simplest scenes, but the results are stunning. Figure 13-18 shows the categories of settings available for the Mental Ray renderer, and Figure 13-19 shows a simple scene rendered with Mental Ray.

Figure 13-18
Mental Ray settings

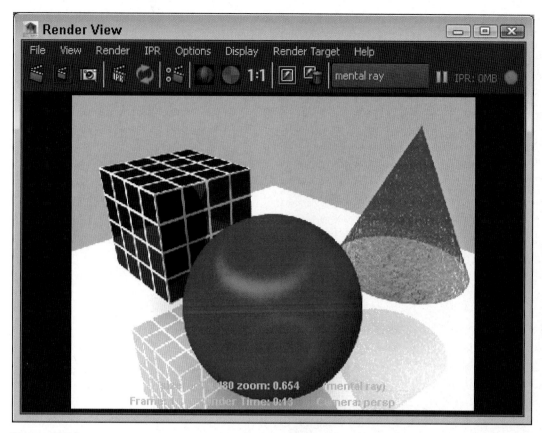

Figure 13-19
A Mental Ray rendered scene

Using Mental Ray Materials

To get even more out of the Mental Ray renderer, you can use specific materials, textures, and lights designed to work with Mental Ray. These materials are listed in the Lighting/Shading, Assign New Material menu; you can also select them from the Create Render Node dialog box, shown in Figure 13-20.

Figure 13-20
Mental Ray materials

Lesson 13.5-Tutorial 1: Render Using Vectors

1. Select the File, Open Scene menu command, and then locate and open the Rose in crystal ball.mb file.

2. Select the Window, Rendering Editors, Render Globals menu command.

3. Enable the Maya Vector option in the Render Using drop-down list at the top of the dialog box.

4. Select the Maya Vector tab. In the Fill Options section, enable the Fill Objects, Full Color, Shadows and Highlights options and in the Edge Options section. Enable the Include Edges option and set the Edge Width to 6.0.

5. Right click on the Perspective view to select it and choose the Render, Render Current Frame menu command.

    The scene is rendered in the Render View window using the Maya Vector renderer, as shown in Figure 13-21.

6. Select File, Save Scene As and save the file as **Vector rose.mb**.

Figure 13-21
Vector rendered crystal ball on a table

Lesson 13.5-Tutorial 2: Render with Mental Ray

1. Select the File, Open Scene menu command, and then locate and open the Rose in crystal ball.mb file.

2. Select the Window, Rendering Editors, Render Globals menu command.

3. Enable the Mental Ray option in the Render Using drop-down list at the top of the dialog box.

4. Select the Mental Ray tab. In the Raytracing section, enable the Ray Tracing option and in the Caustics and Global Illumination section, enable the Caustics and Global Illumination options. In the Final Gather section, enable the Final Gather option.

5. Right-click on the Perspective view to select it and choose the Render, Render Current Frame menu command.

   The scene is rendered in the Render View window using the Mental Ray renderer, as shown in Figure 13-22.

6. Select File, Save Scene As and save the file as **Mental Ray rose.mb**.

Figure 13-22
Mental Ray rendered crystal ball on a table

Chapter Summary

This chapter covers the rendering process. The Render Global Settings dialog box includes all the controls for configuring the renderer as well as several special render features including raytracing and motion blur. The Render View window lets you render to a window without having to save the image to a file. You can interactively render the Render View window using the IPR feature for quicker updates. You can render images at different settings, including preview, draft, and production qualities. You can specify that the render engine render using the Vector or Mental Ray renderer.

What You Have Learned

In this chapter, you learned

* How to configure a scene for rendering.

* How to choose a renderer and a render preset.

* How to change the render image file name and format.

* How to change a camera view and render resolution.

* How to adjust the render quality.

* How to enable raytracing, motion blur, and fog effects.

*   How to use the Render View window.

*   How to render a specific region.

*   How to use IPR rendering.

*   How to save rendered images.

*   How to render a single frame, an animation, or batch render.

*   How to render using Maya Vector and Mental Ray.

Key Terms From This Chapter

*   **Rendering.** The process of computing all the lighting, object, and material effects for a scene into a final image.

*   **Render Global Settings dialog box.** A dialog box of settings for configuring the rendering process.

*   **Render preset.** A saved configuration of render settings that you can recall at any time.

*   **Raytracing.** A rendering method that accurately traces the path of light rays traveling through the scene.

*   **Motion blur.** A rendering effect that blurs objects in relation to their speed in the scene.

*   **Fog.** A rendering effect that simulates fog being added to the scene.

*   **Render region.** An option to render only a selected region in the Render View window.

*   **Interactive Photorealistic Rendering.** A rendering mode that can display changes to the scene's materials, textures, and lights without having to re-render the entire scene.

*   **Maya Vector.** A renderer option that renders the scene as an illustration with lines and fills.

*   **Mental Ray.** A renderer option that provides accurate, high-detailed images.

Chapter 14

Using MEL Scripting

IN THIS CHAPTER

14.1 Use the command line.

14.2 Use the Script Editor.

MEL stands for *Maya Expression Language*. It is the scripting language that lets you create scripts that can do anything that you can do using the interface. The effects covered in Chapter 13 are great examples of what is possible with MEL Scripting.

MEL is a robust language that you can use to program actions and events in Maya, but you don't need to be a programmer to take advantage of MEL.

You can enter MEL commands directly into the **command line** found at the bottom of the interface. Once the command is entered, you can press the Enter key to execute it.

For a complete listing of the available MEL commands, select the Help, MEL Command Reference menu command.

For larger scripts, you can use the **Script Editor,** which includes two expandable panes into which you can enter script commands and see the results. You can also use the Script Editor to view the script commands for interface commands. Scripts within the Script Editor can be saved, loaded, and moved to the Shelf as a button for quick access.

Lesson 14.1: Use the Command Line

You can enter MEL Script commands into the command line.

Using MEL in the Command Line

The command line includes two parts, shown in Figure 14-1. The left part is where you can enter MEL commands and the resulting answer appears in the grayed out part on the right. If the command line isn't visible, you can make it appear using the Display, UI Elements, Command Line menu command.

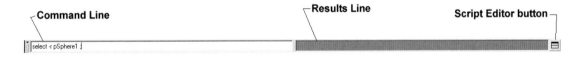

Figure 14-1
The command line

Repeating Command Line Commands

If the cursor is positioned within the command line, you can recall and execute commands that were previously entered into the command line using the Up and Down arrows. Pressing the Enter key executes the listed command.

Using the MEL Scripting Commands

MEL Scripting won't help you if you don't know any of the MEL commands. The following table provides a brief look at some of the more useful MEL commands. Table 14-1 only scratches the surface of the available commands, but it gives you some commands to try.

Each command line must have a semicolon (;) at the end of its line. This identifies the end of the command.

Table 14-1 MEL Commands

MEL Command	Description
help;	Lists helpful information on how to use a command, for example, help move.
rand(100);	Picks a random number between 0 and 100.
print "hello";	Prints the string listed in quotes.
sphere; nurbsCube; cylinder; cone; torus; circle; nurbsSquare;	Creates the listed NURBS primitive object.
polySphere; polyCube; polyCylinder; polyCone; polyTorus; polyPlane;	Creates the listed polygon primitive object.
move 5 0 0; rotate 90 0 0; scale 2 0 0;	Transforms the selected object the specified amount.
sphere -name "sp1" -radius 50;	Attributes have a dash (-) in front of them and their value after. This command creates a NURBS sphere with the name sp1 and a radius of 50.
polyEvaluate -f;	Counts the number of polygons in the selected object.
ls -sl;	Returns the name of the currently selected object.
select name;	Selects the object named name.
render; batchRender;	Renders the current view or begins the batch rendering process using the Render Global Settings.
convertUnit -fromUnit "in" -toUnit "cm" "11.5";	Returns the converted amount of 11.5 inches into centimeters.
curve -p 0 0 0 -p 1 1 1 -p 2 1 2 -p 8 5 3;	Creates a curve using the designated points.
delete;	Deletes the selected object.
duplicate;	Creates a copy of the selected object.
emitter;	Creates an Emitter object.
hide sp1; hide -all; showHidden -all;	Hides the specified object or, with -all, hides all objects. Shows all hidden objects.
play; playblast;	Starts playing the animation. Starts Playblast.
exit;	Exits the application.
undo; redo;	Undoes or redoes the last or next commands.

`refresh;`	Forces the view panel to be redrawn.
`spotlight;`	Creates a Spot light object.
`textCurves -t "hello";`	Creates text curves using the specified string.
`file -f -new;`	Opens a new scene.
`file -save;`	Saves the current scene.
`SaveSceneAs;`	Opens the Save As dialog box.

Lesson 14.1-Tutorial 1: Enter MEL Commands in the Command Line

1. Click in the command line at the bottom of the interface and type **cylinder;** and then press Enter.

    A new polygon cylinder object appears in the view panel.

2. Click again on the command line and type **move 0 0 5;**.

3. Click on the command line and press the Up arrow key twice.

4. Press Enter again.

    Another cylinder object is created and displayed in the view panel, as shown in Figure 14-2.

5. Select File, Save Scene As and save the file as **Simple cylinders.mb**.

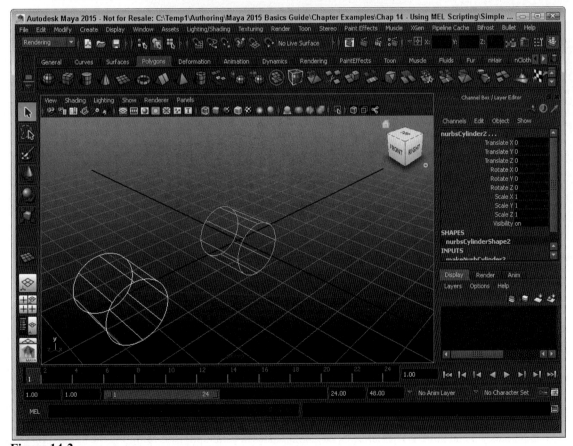

Figure 14-2
Cylinders created using the command line

Lesson 14.2: Use the Script Editor

You can create MEL Scripts in the Script Editor, shown in Figure 14-3. Clicking on the Script Editor button in the lower-right corner of the interface opens the Script Editor, or you can use the Window, General Editors, Script Editor menu command. The Script Editor, like the command line, includes two panes. The lower pane is where you can type script commands and the upper pane displays the results.

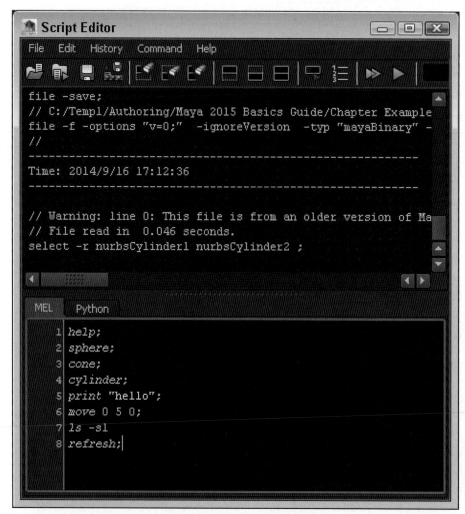

Figure 14-3
The Script Editor

Executing Script Commands

Select a command in the lower pane and press Ctrl/Command+Enter to execute the commands, or select the Script, Execute menu command in the Script Editor.

Viewing Interface Commands

The upper pane of the Script Editor displays the script command for every interface action. This is a great way to learn how to use new commands. To view the details of every interface action, you can enable the Script, Echo All Commands menu option. The Script menu also includes several options for limiting the amount of command details displayed in the upper pane. These options include Suppress Command Results, Suppress Info, Warning and Error Messages. To clear all the commands listed in the upper, lower, or both panes, choose the Edit, Clear History, Clear Input, or Clear All dialog menu commands.

Reusing Interface Commands

Any command that is listed in the upper pane of the Script Editor can be selected and moved to the lower pane using the Edit, Cut, Copy, and Paste menu commands. Once you move them to the lower pane, you can edit and execute the commands again. Figure 14-4 shows a series of commands that have been copied to the lower pane, where they have been edited.

Tip

You also can move selected script commands in the upper pane to the lower pane by dragging and dropping them.

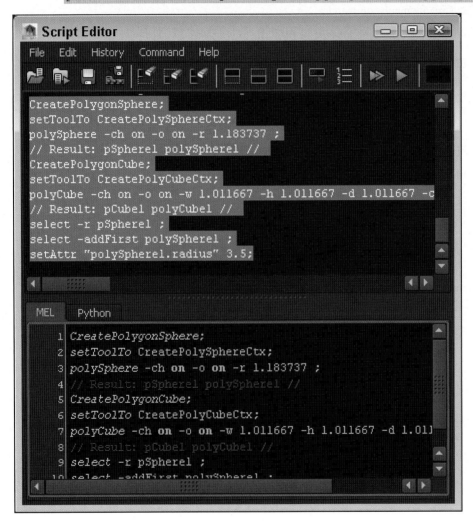

Figure 14-4
Commands copied to the lower pane

Saving Scripts

You can save commands that are listed in either pane as a text file for future loading and editing. To save the commands, select them in the Script Editor and choose the File, Save Selected menu command. This command opens a file dialog box where you can name the file. The File, Open Script menu command reopens a saved script file.

Adding Scripts to the Shelf

If you select script commands in the Script Editor and drag them with the middle mouse button to the Shelf, a button is created that allows you to execute the command by clicking it. Another way to do this is with the File, Save Selected to Shelf menu command.

Lesson 14.2-Tutorial 1: Use the Script Editor

1. Select the Window, General Editors, Script Editor menu command.

   The Script Editor opens.

2. In the lower pane, type **sphere –radius 2;**.

3. Select the Script, Execute menu command.

4. With the sphere object selected, type **move 0 –1 0;** in the lower pane.

5. Select the Move command and choose the Script, Execute menu command (or press the Ctrl/Command+Enter hotkey).

   A sphere with a radius of 2 is created and moved downward in the negative Y-axis.

6. Select File, Save Scene As and save the file as **Simple script.mb**.

Lesson 14.2-Tutorial 2: View Interface Commands and Save a Script

1. Select the Window, General Editors, Script Editor menu command.

2. Select the Create, Polygon Primitives, Cube menu command.

3. Click on the Select by Component Type button in the Status Line and drag over the top four vertices.

4. Select the Edit Mesh, Merge Components menu command from the Polygons menu set.

   The top vertices are merged to form a pyramid object and all the commands to create this object are displayed in the top pane of the Script Editor, as shown in Figure 14-5.

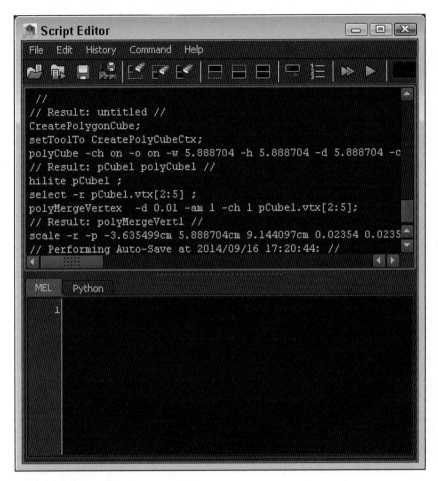

Figure 14-5
Interface commands

5. Drag over the commands in the upper pane of the Script Editor to select them and choose the File, Save Selected menu command.

6. In the dialog box that appears, save the file as **Pyramid.mel**.

7. Select the commands again and drag with the middle mouse button to the Shelf.

    A new button, named MEL, appears on the Shelf, as shown in Figure 14-6.

8. Select File, Save Scene As and save the file as **Pyramid.mb**.

new MEL script button

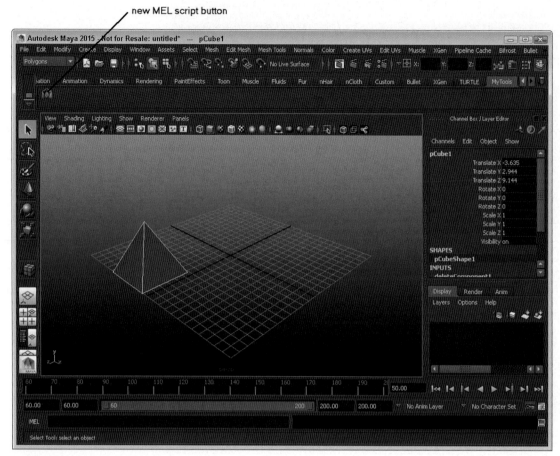

Figure 14-6
Pyramid

Lesson 14.2-Tutorial 3: Execute a Custom Script

1. Type **polySphere;** into the command line and press Enter.

2. Select the Window, General Editors, Script Editor menu command. Select the Edit, Clear All menu command in the Script Editor.

   The Script Editor opens and all existing text is removed.

3. Select the sphere and click the Select by Component Type button in the Status Line. Drag over the sphere to select all vertices. Select the Edit Polygons, Extrude Vertex menu command.

   The vertices of the sphere are extruded outward.

4. Select the commands in the top pane of the Script Editor. Select the File, Save Selected menu command. Save the file as **Extrude vertices.mel**.

5. Select all the commands in the upper pane of the Script Editor. Drag and drop the selected commands to lower pane. Select the Script, Execute menu command.

   The script commands are executed and another sphere with extruded vertices is created, as shown in Figure 14-7.

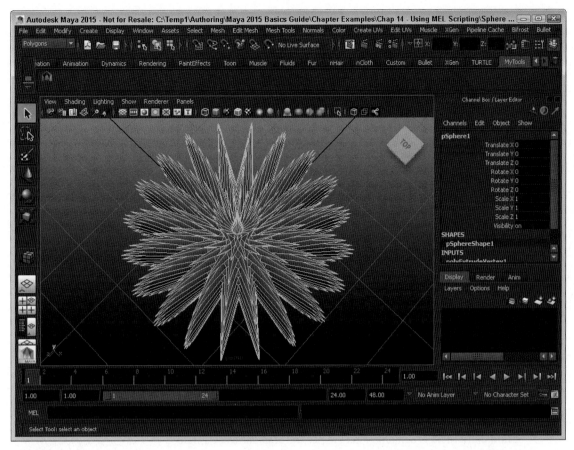

Figure 14-7
Sphere with extruded vertices

Chapter Summary

This chapter introduces MEL Scripting. You can enter and execute script commands using the command line and also using the Script Editor. Using the Script Editor lets you create and record new scripts and also load and save scripts.

What You Have Learned

In this chapter, you learned

* How to enter a MEL Script command into the command line.

* How to repeat commands entered into the command line.

* How to use several MEL Script commands.

* How to use the Script Editor.

* How to view interface commands.

* How to save scripts.

* How to add scripts to the Shelf.

Key Terms From This Chapter

* **MEL.** (Maya Expression Language.) A scripting language used to create scripts.

* **Command line.** An interface field where you execute script commands.

* **Script Editor.** A editor interface where you compile, save, and execute multi-line scripts.

* **Particles.** A collection of small objects that act together as a single unit.

* **Lifespan.** The number of frames that a particle exists in the scene.

* **Instance.** An object that is used in place of a particle.

* **Emitter.** An icon of objects that is the source of the particles.

* **Field.** An icon in the scene that represents a physical force, such as gravity or drag.

* **Goal.** An object in the scene that a particle system is attracted towards.

* **Event.** An action that occurs in the scene that spawns more particles, such as a collision.

* **Rigid body object.** A solid object that doesn't deform when it collides with other objects, such as a brick.

* **Soft body object.** An object that deforms when it collides with other objects, such as a pillow.

* **Constraint.** An icon that binds objects to a physical force that limits their motion, such as a hinge.

* **Cloth.** A specialized object type that simulates the dynamic interactions of cloth.

* **Cloth collision object.** An object that a cloth object drapes over.

* **Fluid container.** A container that defines the boundaries of a fluid.

* **Voxel.** A single cell of a fluid; used to compute fluid dynamics.

* **Fluid emitter.** An icon that marks the source of the fluid.

Glossary

* **Aligning.** The process of moving objects so that certain components have the same position.

* **Alpha channel.** An image that shows the transparency values of the scene as a grayscale image.

* **Angle of View.** A camera's angle value used to set the width of the scene viewed through the camera. Sets the width of the view area.

* **Animation controls.** A set of buttons that are used to control animation frames.

* **Anisotropic.** A material noted for its elliptical specular highlights.

* **Appending.** The process of attaching a polygon to an existing polygon.

* **Attributes.** Values that determine the properties of the node.

* **Auto Key.** The mode that automatically creates keys whenever an object is moved or a parameter is changed.

* **Auto Paint.** A painting mode that automatically applies strokes to the selected object.

* **Backface Culling.** A display option that makes object elements located on the backside invisible.

* **Bevel.** An operation that replaces an edge with a polygon face.

* **Beveling.** The process of smoothing a surface by adding a face to the surface edges.

* **Blinn.** A material that creates soft circular highlights and is good for metallic surfaces.

* **Bone.** An object that is connected between two joints and defines the rigid areas of a character.

* **Booleans.** A set of operations for combining two polygon objects together using a union, difference, or intersection.

* **Border.** A series of edges that line a polygon hole.

* **Brush.** An interface element used to Paint Effects into a scene.

* **Bump map.** A texture that is used to set the relief of a material where dark areas are raised and lighter areas are indented.

* **Canvas.** A 2D interface where you can paint and save objects.

* **Chamfer.** An operation that replaces the selected vertices with polygon faces.

* **Channel Box.** A panel of editable parameters that relate to the current selection.

* **Cleanup.** An operation that removes potential trouble parts of a polygon model, such as unattached vertices.

* **Cloth collision object.** An object that a cloth object drapes over.

* **Cloth.** A specialized object type that simulates the dynamic interactions of cloth.

* **Command line.** An interface field where you can execute script commands.

* **Components.** The subobjects that make up an entire object. Can include faces, vertices, CVs, and so on.

* **Connection Editor.** An interface for defining the connections between various nodes.

* **Constraint.** An icon that binds objects to a physical force that limits their motion, such as a hinge.

* **Construction history.** A list of commands executed to build a scene.

* **Convert.** A series of commands that lets you change one modeling type such as NURBS to another

modeling type such as a subdivision surface.

* **Crease.** A setting that causes selected edges to remain hard without smoothing.

* **Create Bar.** A selection list in the Hypershade where you can choose from default materials, textures, and nodes.

* **Curve degree.** The amount of curve applied to a line.

* **Curve Editing tool.** A tool used to edit the curvature of a curve using handles attached to the curve.

* **CV curve.** A curve created by placing CV points.

* **CV.** Control Vertex. A curve component that defines the curvature of the curve.

* **Default grid.** An invisible array of points that mark the origin of the scene.

* **Default lights.** A set of lights that are available by default as part of a new scene.

* **Default pose.** The skin's original position when it was first bound to the skeleton.

* **Depth map shadow.** A shadowing method created by saving the shadows into a bitmap that is projected onto the scene.

* **Depth of Field.** A camera effect where objects farther away from the focus point are gradually more blurry.

* **Dolly.** The act of zooming the camera to change the view's focus width.

* **Dope sheet.** An interface used to display and edit the timing of an animation.

* **Dynamics.** A type of animation where the keyframes are computed using physics calculations after assigning physical properties to the scene objects.

* **Edge loop.** A series of edges that run end to end across the surface of a polygon object.

* **Edge ring.** A series of parallel edges that run across the surface of a polygon object.

* **Emitter.** An icon of objects that is the source of the particles.

* **EP curve.** A curve created by placing points that the curve passes through.

* **Event.** An action that occurs in the scene that's used to spawn more particles such as a collision.

* **Extruding.** An operation that moves the selected component perpendicular from its current position.

* **Field.** An icon in the scene that represents a physical force such as gravity or drag.

* **Filleting.** The process of smoothing the corner between two adjacent faces.

* **Fluid container.** A container that defines the boundaries of a fluid.

* **Fluid emitter.** An icon that marks the source of the fluid.

* **Focal Length.** A camera setting used to determine where the camera's focus is located.

* **Fog.** A rendering effect that simulates fog being added to the scene.

* **Forward Kinematics.** Physics that allows the position of child objects to be calculated when the parent object is moved.

* **Framing.** The process of zooming and panning the camera to focus on the selected object.

* **Ghosting.** A setting that makes multiple copies of the animated objects appear at regular intervals along a motion path.

* **Goal.** An object in the scene that a particle system is attracted towards.

* **Graph Editor.** An interface that displays all animation actions as graphed curves, allowing editing

and modification.

* **Grouping.** The process of collecting multiple objects together into a named group.

* **Heads-Up Display.** A menu command for adding informative text to the view panel.

* **Help Line.** A text field that presents the next action that is expected.

* **Hotbox.** A comprehensive set of menu options accessible by pressing the spacebar.

* **Hotkey.** A keyboard shortcut that executes a command when pressed.

* **Hull.** A set of straight lines that connects a curve's CV points.

* **Hypergraph.** An interface that shows all scene objects as nodes in a hierarchical display.

* **Hypershade.** A interface where materials and shaders are created.

* **IK Handle.** An IK solution that is used for parts such as arms and legs.

* **IK Spline.** An IK solution that is used for parts such as tails.

* **Image plane.** A background plane where you can load a background texture or image.

* **Infinity conditions.** A setting that enables an animated sequence to repeat indefinitely.

* **Influence object.** An object that controls the local deformation of a character skin.

* **Instance.** An object that is used in place of a particle.

* **Interactive Photorealistic Rendering.** A rendering mode that can display changes to the scene's materials, textures, and lights without having to re-render the entire scene.

* **Inverse Kinematics.** A physics definition that allows objects at the end of a skeleton hierarchy to control the motion and position of the entire skeleton.

* **Isoparametric curve.** Representative lines that show the object's surface. Called *isoparms* for short.

* **Joint.** An object connected to a bone used to rotate and move skeleton bones.

* **Key object.** The last object that is selected. The key object is the base object for certain commands.

* **Keyframe.** An animation setting that records the state of an object for a given frame.

* **Lambert.** A material with no highlights; useful for cloth and non-reflective surfaces.

* **Layer.** A selection of objects grouped together in a set that can be easily selected.

* **Lens flare.** A lighting effect that simulates the effect of pointing a camera at a light source.

* **Lifespan.** The number of frames that a particle exists in the scene.

* **Light decay.** A light property that causes light intensity to gradually diminish as it gets farther from the light source.

* **Light intensity.** A value that denotes the power of a light source.

* **Linear curve.** A curve with a degree of 1, resulting in straight lines.

* **Lofting.** The process of creating a surface by connecting several cross sections.

* **Looping.** A setting that causes an animation to repeatedly play.

* **Mapping.** The method used to wrap a texture around an object.

* **Marking menu.** A dynamic set of menus accessible by right-clicking on an object.

* **Material.** A set of surface properties that are assigned to an object to simulate various object materials.

* **Maya Vector.** A renderer option that renders the scene as an illustration with lines and fills.

* **MEL.** Stands for Maya Expression Language. A scripting language used to create scripts.

* **Mental ray.** A renderer option that provides accurate, high-detailed images.

* **Menu set.** A dynamic set of menu options selected from a drop-down list at the top left of the interface.

* **Motion blur.** A rendering effect that blurs objects in relation to their speed in the scene.

* **Motion path.** A created curve that defines the animation path that an object follows.

* **Motion trail.** A curve that shows the path of the animated object.

* **Near and Far Clip planes.** Near and Far camera planes that define the points where objects are not visible.

* **Node.** A single set of material attributes that can be connected to other nodes to create a shader.

* **Normal.** A vector extending perpendicular from the surface of a polygon used to determine the polygon's inner and outer faces.

* **NURBS patch.** The surface area that lies in between isoparms.

* **NURBS.** A 3D surface created from curves that define its area. An acronym that stands for Non-Uniform Rational B-Spline.

* **Offset curve.** A duplicated curve that is moved parallel to the selected curve.

* **Option dialog box.** A dialog box with additional options; open it using the icon found to the right of specific menu options.

* **Outliner.** An interface that displays all scene objects as simple nodes.

* **Paint Effects.** An innovative Maya feature that lets you paint objects in the scene using brushes.

* **Particles.** A collection of small objects that act together as a single unit.

* **Phong.** A material with a hard circular highlight; good for glass surfaces.

* **Pivot point.** The point about which the object or objects are rotated.

* **Playblast.** A feature that plays the current animation in a separate media player.

* **Poking.** An operation that adds a vertex to the center of the selected face and attaches edges to the new vertex.

* **Polygon Proxy mode.** A mode that allows a polygon operation to be applied to the selected Subdivision surface.

* **Polygon.** A co-planar surface created from three or more linear edges.

* **Pop-up help.** A small text title that appears when the cursor is held over the top of an icon.

* **Quick Layout buttons.** A set of buttons for changing the interface layout.

* **Ray trace shadows.** A shadowing method that computes shadows by following light rays as they move around the scene.

* **Raytracing.** A rendering method that accurately traces the path of light rays traveling through the scene.

* **Reduce.** An operation that reduces the total number of polygons in a model.

* **Refining.** The process of increasing the level number and detail for the selected components.

* **Render Globals Settings.** A dialog box of settings for configuring the rendering process.

* **Render preset.** A saved configuration of render settings that you can recall at any time.

* **Render region.** An option to render only a selected region in the Render View window.

* **Rendering.** The process of computing all the lighting, object, and material effects for a scene into a final image.

* **Resolution.** A measure of the detail (or number of elements) used to display scene objects.

* **Revolving.** The process of creating a surface by rotating a curve about an axis.

* **Rigging.** The process of adding and configuring a skeleton to a character that is used to control its motion.

* **Rigid body object.** A solid object that doesn't deform when it collides with other objects such as a brick.

* **Root joint.** The top joint in the skeleton hierarchy.

* **Safe area.** A set of camera markings that denote where title and action areas are definitely visible.

* **Script Editor.** A editor interface where you can compile, save, and execute multi-line scripts.

* **Sculpt Geometry tool.** A tool used to push and pull on an object's surface.

* **Seamless texture.** An image that allows strokes drawn on one edge of the canvas to be wrapped to the opposite edge.

* **Selection mask.** A filter that limits the types of objects that can be selected.

* **Selection set.** A selection of objects that are named for quick recall.

* **Shader.** A complex set of connected material nodes that define a specific material.

* **Shading.** A display method used to show scene objects as solid objects.

* **Shelf.** A customizable set of icon buttons that are organized into separate groups.

* **Skeleton.** A hierarchical set of bones and joints used to define the underlying structure of a character.

* **Skin weight.** The amount of control each vertex has when a adjacent bone is moved.

* **Skin.** The model that is placed over a skeleton that is bound to the skeleton and deformed by it.

* **Smooth proxy.** A smoothed copy of an original polygon object.

* **Smooth skin.** A skin object that deforms as its bound skeleton is moved.

* **Snapping.** The process of automatically moving an object to precisely align with a specific component.

* **Soft body object.** An object that deforms when it collides with other objects, such as a pillow.

* **Soft Modification tool.** A tool used to edit local surface areas of the current object.

* **Status Line.** A set of toolbar icons located at the top of the interface.

* **Stitching.** The process of attached adjacent patches together so they move without creating holes.

* **Stroke.** The resulting lines produced by dragging a brush in the scene.

* **Subdividing.** An operation for splitting all polygon faces into two or more faces.

* **Subdivision surface.** A hybrid modeling type that combines the features of NURBS and Polygon objects.

* **Surface Editing tool.** A tool that uses a manipulator to edit the surface curvature.

* **Tangents.** Handles that control the curvature of a curve near each key point.

* **Tear-off menu.** A panel of menu options that is removed to float freely from the interface.

* **Texture.** A bitmap file that is wrapped around an object.

* **Time Slider.** An interface element that displays all the frames and keys for the current animation.

* **Toolbox.** A set of selection and transformation icons located to the left of the interface.

* **Topology.** The shape and curvature of the surface.

* **Torus.** A circular primitive object with a circular cross section, shaped like a doughnut.

* **Track.** The act of panning the camera to change the view's focal point.

* **Trimming.** The process of cutting holes into a NURBS surface.

* **Tumble.** The act of rotating a camera to change the view's orientation.

* **Universal Manipulator.** A manipulator that is used to move, rotate and scale objects all at once.

* **ViewCube.** A manipulator icon in the upper-right corner of the view panel for quickly changing the current view.

* **View panel.** The central scene window where objects are displayed.

* **Visor.** A dialog box that holds presets that can be quickly selected such as Paint Effects.

* **Voxel.** A single cell of a fluid; used to compute fluid dynamics.

* **Wedge.** A model structure created by rotating a face about an edge and connecting it to the original face's position.

* **Wireframe.** A display method that shows scene objects using contour lines.

Index